Aristophanes' *Clouds*

T0355519

MICHIGAN CLASSICAL COMMENTARIES

S. Douglas Olson
Aristophanes' *Clouds*: A Commentary

Andrew R. Dyck
A Commentary on Cicero, *De Divinatione II*

Carl Arne Anderson and T. Keith Dix
A Commentary on Aristophanes' *Knights*

Patrick Paul Hogan
A Student Commentary on Pausanius Book 1

Celia E. Schultz
A Commentary on Cicero, *De Divinatione I*

Erin K. Moodie
Plautus' *Poenulus*: A Student Commentary

Donka D. Markus
Reading Medieval Latin with the Legend of Barlaam and Josaphat

Patrick Paul Hogan
A Student Commentary on Pausanius Book 2

Charles Platter
A Student Commentary on Plato's *Euthyphro*

Aristophanes' *Clouds*

A Commentary

S. Douglas Olson

University of Michigan Press
Ann Arbor

Copyright 2021 by S. Douglas Olson

For questions or permissions, please contact um.press.perms@umich.edu

Published in the United States of America by
the University of Michigan Press
Printed and bound by CPI Group (UK) Ltd, Croydon, CR0 4YY

First published March 2021

A CIP catalog record for this book is available from the British Library.

ISBN 978-0-472-07477-8 (hardcover : alk. paper)
ISBN 978-0-472-05477-0 (paper : alk. paper)

For Rachel
seni çok seviyorum

Contents

Preface

No substantial scholarly edition of Aristophanes' *Clouds* has been published since K. J. Dover's over 50 years ago. Dover's *Clouds* was a landmark in English-language scholarship on ancient Greek poetry, and on comedy in particular, and the present volume does not aim to replace it. Instead, I have deliberately aimed the bulk of my comments at an intermediate audience: readers who know the basic forms, vocabulary and structures of classical Greek, but who may be unfamiliar with some of its complexities, with colloquial words and constructions, and with the cultural and literary environment in which Aristophanes' play was composed and performed. More advanced readers may find that I sometimes belabor points that seem obvious to them, including how Greek words are formed and how Greek syntax works. I hope that they too will nonetheless find useful observations here, especially in regard to matters of staging, usage and overall dramatic structure. I have done no manuscript work—a task a full new edition of the play will eventually require. But the text is my own, and more advanced readers may find it interesting to consider it beside those of Dover and Wilson.

After consultation with the press and the series editor, I have made a series of content and formatting decisions regarding the commentary portion of this text intended to render it as useful and transparent as possible for my primary audience. First, bold print is reserved for words that appear in precisely that form in the text itself; in the second note on 10, for example, σισύρα is not in bold because the word appears in the text in the form σισύραις. Second, I have broken up individual lexical items in the notes into their constituent parts, so that ἀπέραντον ("endless") in 3, for example, appears as ἀ-πέραντον as a shorthand way of making it apparent that the word comes from privative *alpha* + περαίνω. Because the vocabulary of ancient Greek is so large, attempting to memorize every item is not a useful way to approach the language, and an argument implicit throughout the commentary is that it is a better strategy to learn by seeing how words are formed and thus what they must mean even without consulting a dictionary. Third, and connected with this, I have kept the glossing of individual words to a minimum, and have concentrated instead on explaining syntax, usage and to a lesser extent forms. My assumption is that 21st-century "born-digital" students have constant, ready access to online lexica and form-analysis tools such as those available on the Perseus and TLG sites, and that the limited space available to me is better used for explaining issues that are not easily dealt with by a click of a mouse. Fourth, and perhaps more controversially, I have chosen not to offer references to standard grammars such as Smyth. This reflects a practical conviction, born out of many years of teaching, that—whatever their instructors may believe or desire—students neither want nor use such references and are in any case perfectly capable of consulting an index in a standard grammar should the mood strike them. Fifth and finally, I have occasionally omitted complete identifications of verb forms in particular where no confusion seemed possible; in such cases, the easiest and most obvious sense is the one I intend.

In the notes, "<" means "is derived from" or occasionally "is cognate with"; "~" means "is approximately equivalent to"; "cf." means "compare"; and "e.g." means "for example". A line-number reference followed by "n." refers the reader to the note on that line or set of lines for further information. "LSJ *s.v.*" refers to the entry in the large Liddell-Scott-Jones Greek lexicon for the word in question. For the reader's convenience, the titles of Aristophanes' other ten plays are given in English translation rather than in the standard abbreviated form (thus, for example, "*Wasps*" rather than "*V.*"). The names of other ancient authors and their words are similarly given in full. Comic fragments are cited from the now-standard Kassel-Austin edition.

The numbering of the lyric sections of Aristophanic comedies has become confused over the years, and a pedantic insistence on the original Brunck numbers (which on modern divisions of the text yields numerous half-lines, combined lines, and the like) serves the interest of no one. I have therefore retained Dover's numbering wherever possible.

Thanks are due Alexander Sens and especially Benjamin W. Millis for careful comments on earlier drafts of the introduction, text and commentary. I would also like to extend my gratitude to two anonymous referees, who helped shape the project in its early form. In addition, it is a pleasure to acknowledge the contributions of Richard Culbertson and Stephen Self, who worked through the first half of the play with me at the University of Minnesota in the fall of 2019, caught several significant errors, and led me to rethink, restructure or expand a number of individual notes. Much of the work on this project was completed at Bilkent University in Ankara (Turkey). I am grateful to Mustafa Nakeeb and Adnan Akay for making my time here possible. Like all my recent work, this book is dedicated to my lovely wife Rachel.

Introduction

Aristophanes' *Clouds*—first staged in 423 BCE, but preserved for us only in a revised version dating five years or so later—is among the most brilliantly funny of the poet's eleven surviving comedies. It is also a fundamental, if controversial source for the life and thought of the Athenian philosopher Socrates son of Sophroniskos of the deme Alopeke (*PA* 13101; *PAA* 856500; 469–400/399 BCE), one of the most important figures in the Western intellectual tradition. The play nonetheless remains a puzzle. Like most of Aristophanes' comedies, and especially those of the late 420s BCE (also *Acharnians*, *Knights*, *Wasps* and *Peace*), its central character is an old countryman with a clever but improbable idea, in this case that a Socratic education in unscrupulous rhetoric might be a means to wriggle out of a series of ruinous lawsuits. The play has all the standard features of a conventional Aristophanic drama: the initially puzzling introductory scene that sets the action up; a door-keeper scene, followed by a visit to a second, even more eccentric character; the entrance of the eponymous chorus, singing a song (the *parodos*); a metrically complex central section (the *parabasis*), apparently standard in late 5th-century Athenian comedies, in which the chorus speak directly to the audience and offer advice and warnings; a pair of similarly metrically complex *agônes* (debates) between two characters; a series of additional scenes, separated by more choral songs, including action in the second half of the play in which a series of "blocking figures" attempt to interfere with the hero's scheme; a shorter second *parabasis*; and a wild finale, at the end of which the protagonist leads the chorus out of the Theater. But Strepsiades—the "hero" of *Clouds*—is a more unsavory figure than most other Aristophanic characters of the same sort, and although his plans briefly work out for him, they ultimately backfire, and the chorus deliver a moralizing lecture about the ugly choices he has made. Perhaps even odder, the other surviving comedies mostly end with a great celebration commemorating the hero's triumph. *Clouds*, however, concludes with a shattered family, anger, arson and the threat of a lynching. And the unambiguous villain of the piece is Socrates, whom gods and men agree is a threat to civic decency who must at the very least be chased out of town.

I. The Poet and His Play

The original version of *Clouds* was produced at the City Dionysia festival in 423 BCE, when Aristophanes was probably in his early twenties. His career had begun at least four years earlier, in 427 BCE, with the production of *Daitalês* ("*Banqueters*"; see 528–36nn.), which took second place (festival unknown). *Babylônioi* ("*Babylonians*") was staged the next year and most likely took the prize at the City Dionysia. Both plays are preserved only in fragments, but *Daitalês* was apparently the story of an old father with two sons, one conventionally good and the other conventionally bad (and thus reminiscent of the Socratically educated Pheidippides in *Clouds*). *Babylônioi*, on the other hand, was a political comedy that could be read as aggressively critical of the Athenian people, their officials and the administration of the empire. The latter play seems to have become a cause célèbre when Cleon—the leading democratic politician of the day—hauled Aristophanes before the Council and charged him with speaking ill of the city in the presence of foreigners (cf. *Acharnians* 377–82, 502–3). The attack failed, although it may have been a close call, and Aristophanes was back on the dramatic program in 425 BCE, this time at the Lenaia festival with *Acharnians* (preserved), which took another first. *Knights*—a vicious attack on Cleon, for whom Aristophanes had clearly developed a deep personal loathing; also preserved—took first again at the Lenaia in 424 BCE.

Aristophanes was thus brilliantly successful on the Athenian stage as a very young man. A series of fragmentary inscriptions that preserve what must be copies of official dramatic records for the period adds a further dimension to the story, making it apparent that before 427 BCE no new poet had taken first at either the City Dionysia or the Lenaia for at least a decade (*IG* II^2 2325C and E Millis-Olson). Aristophanes was thus a breath of dramatic fresh air, probably because he pioneered a strikingly new style of comedy—hence perhaps Cleon's outraged reaction to *Babylônioi*, which seemed to him to violate a number of doubtless unwritten rules about what could and could not be done and said onstage. The same was true of Aristophanes' almost exact contemporary Eupolis, who took the prize just before him at the Lenaia and just after him at the City Dionysia, and whose *Noumêniai* ("*New Moons*"; lost already in antiquity) was third behind *Acharnians* at the Lenaia in 425 BCE. Far and away the greatest poet of the previous generation, by contrast, was Cratinus, who was now an old man. Cratinus placed second behind *Acharnians* in 425 BCE, in the same competition where Eupolis was third, and Aristophanes mocked him in *Knights* the next year, calling him an old drunk who ought to be allowed to retire and rest on his laurels rather than embarrassing himself any further in public (*Knights* 526–36). Cratinus had a play entitled *Satyroi* ("*Satyrs*") in the same festival, and was again ranked second behind Aristophanes.

Information preserved in the second ancient hypothesis (a brief scholarly introduction) to *Clouds*, doubtless drawing again on official city records, reports that two of the other entries at the City Dionysia in 423 BCE—it is generally assumed that there were five per festival—were Cratinus' *Pytinê* ("*Wine-flask*") and Ameipsias' *Konnos*; that Cratinus took the prize; and that Aristophanes was "unexpectedly rejected", implying a third-place finish or lower. This was thus a disaster, especially after the catty remarks Aristophanes had directed against Cratinus at the Lenaia a year earlier, and in *Wasps* in 422 BCE the poet complains at length about the audience's shabby treatment of him and his unprecedentedly brilliant offering the previous year (*Wasps* 1015–59). According to the second hypothesis to *Clouds*, Aristophanes also decided to rewrite his failed play, presumably in the hope of staging the revised version at another festival, at least at the deme-level, where local restagings of tragedies and comedies that premiered at the City Dionysia or the Lenaia may well already have been common. The original *Clouds* has been lost—of Aristophanes' approximately forty plays, only eleven are preserved, which nonetheless gives him an advantage over Cratinus, Eupolis and all their predecessors and contemporaries, whose work is known to us only through fragments—and what we have is the revised version. Unsurprisingly, *Clouds II* as well contains a long section extolling its own virtues and criticizing how it (i.e. the original version) had been received (518–62, esp. 521–5).

Most of what is known of the original *Clouds* and of the nature of the rewrite comes from the first hypothesis to the preserved play, which reports:

τοῦτο ταὐτόν ἐστι τῷ προτέρῳ. διεσκεύασται δὲ ἐπὶ μέρους ὡς ἂν δὴ ἀναδιδάξαι μὲν αὐτὸ τοῦ ποιητοῦ προθυμηθέντος, οὐκέτι δὲ τοῦτο δι' ἥν ποτε αἰτίαν ποιήσαντος. καθόλου μὲν οὖν σχεδὸν παρ' ἅπαν μέρος γεγενημένη ⟨ἡ⟩ διόρθωσις . . . τὰ μὲν γὰρ περιῄρηται, τὰ δὲ παραπέπλεκται καὶ ἐν τῇ τάξει καὶ ἐν τῇ τῶν προσώπων διαλλαγῇ μετεσχημάτισται, ἃ δὲ ὁλοσχερῆ τῆς διασκευῆς τοιαῦτα ὄντα τετύχηκεν· αὐτίκα ἡ παράβασις τοῦ χοροῦ ἤμειπται, καὶ ὅπου ὁ δίκαιος λόγος πρὸς τὸν ἄδικον λαλεῖ, καὶ τελευταῖον ὅπου καίεται ἡ διατριβὴ Σωκράτους

This [play] is the same as the previous one. It has been revised at specific points, as if the poet was anxious to restage it but then gave up the plan for some reason or other. As for the play as a whole, then, the correction, which has occurred in almost every part . . . because some elements have been removed, while others have been worked in and have been given a new form in the arrangement and alternation of speaking parts, and certain elements are entirely such [i.e. new] from the revision, for example the parabasis of the chorus has been switched out, and where the Just Argument speaks to the Unjust Argument, and the end, where Socrates' residence is set on fire.

The remarks in the hypothesis are by no means as clear or detailed as they might be: there is at least one gap in the text, and other portions are obscure. There can nonetheless be little doubt that whoever was ultimately responsible for this information was familiar with both versions of *Clouds* and knew in particular that the parabasis (510–626), the confrontation of the two Arguments (889–1104) and the finale (1476–1509) were different in the revised version than in the original. Some of this information is confirmed, and a bit more information added—suggesting that the first hypothesis is not merely being recycled in these notes—by two ancient comments (*scholia*) on the revised *Clouds* preserved in the margins of some early manuscripts of the play, which report:

(1) On 520 οὐχ ἡ αὐτὴ δέ ἐστιν οὐδὲ τοῦ αὐτοῦ μέτρου τῇ ἐν ταῖς πρώταις Νεφέλαις ("[the parabasis] is not the same nor in the same meter as in the first *Clouds*").

(2) On 543 ἴσως ἑαυτῷ, ἐπεὶ πεποίηκεν ἐν τῷ τέλει τούτου τοῦ δράματος καιομένην τὴν διατριβὴν Σωκράτους καί τινας τῶν φιλοσόφων λέγοντας ἰοὺ ἰού. ἐν δὲ ταῖς πρώταις Νεφέλαις τοῦτο οὐ πεποίηκεν ("Perhaps it is himself [that the poet is criticizing], since at the end of this play he has represented Socrates' residence being burned and some of the philosophers crying *iou iou*. He has not included this action in the first *Clouds*").

A handful of other bits of text attributed by ancient sources to *Clouds* but not in the text we have, and thus presumably drawn from the original, are preserved in ancient sources of one sort or another (Aristophanes fragments 392–401 Kassel-Austin; presented and translated in Appendix I). Unfortunately, they do little more than confirm that there were originally two versions of the text, one of which is now lost. It is nonetheless apparent that the *Clouds I*—brilliant though the poet claims it was—was defective in his own retrospective judgment and underwent substantial revision.

These questions are complicated by the fact—noted already in the second hypothesis—that this revision appears to have been incomplete. The evidence for this conclusion is in part a matter of staging practicalities. At 888–9 (n.) and for the scene that follows, five actors—taking the parts of Socrates, Strepsiades, Pheidippides, the Stronger Argument and the Weaker Argument—appear to be required, despite the fact that dramatic poets in this period had only three at their disposal. Ancient scholars had already hypothesized that a choral song dropped out of the text between 888 and 889, which would allow time for whoever played Socrates to change costume and return as one of the Arguments. But this still leaves us needing four actors, none of them a bit player, and it might just as easily be the case that the revised *Clouds* is something more like a reading text, in which difficulties of this sort would not be obvious or important, than a stage script intended for performance.

Other difficulties involve the play's content. At 549–59, the chorus, speaking for Aristophanes, refers to his *Knights* (424 BCE) and then complains that Eupolis turned that play "inside out"—i.e. stole the basic plot, while making superficial changes—to attack another Athenian politician, Hyperbolus, and that other comic poets subsequently piled onto Hyperbolus, putting the same, now-trite action onstage again and again. The play by Eupolis in question is *Marikas*, staged at the Lenaia in 421 BCE, and the reference to other poets repeating the theme in subsequent years puts the date of these lines in 419 BCE or so at the earliest. This section of the text must thus belong to the revised *Clouds* rather than the original. Since Hyperbolus seems to have been ostracized (i.e. forced to leave Athens for ten years) in 416 BCE, the second version of the play must also date before that. At 584–94, on the other hand, the chorus complains about the election of Cleon as general and proposes that he be thrown into the stocks. But Cleon died in summer of 422 BCE, so these lines must be from the first version of the play and would have been irrelevant when the second version was drafted. The implication is accordingly that—just as the second hypothesis suggests—the text of *Clouds* we have is not a finished product, and that Aristophanes gave up the revision before it was complete, or at least before he had worked it up into a condition where it was fit to be performed. How it survived is a mystery. But a number of Aristophanes' sons were also comic poets, and it is not difficult to imagine that they retained their father's papers, which were eventually sold, for example, to a collector working for one of the Hellenizing Ptolemaic kings in Egypt, who wanted the plays for the collection in the Library in Alexandria.

II. *Socrates in* Clouds

At Plato *Apology* 18b–19b, in the opening section of a defense speech supposedly delivered in 399 BCE, Socrates describes his old accusers—as opposed to the men who have hauled him into court at the moment—as having falsely asserted ὡς ἔστιν τις Σωκράτης σοφὸς ἀνήρ, τά τε μετέωρα φροντιστὴς καὶ τὰ ὑπὸ γῆς πάντα ἀνεζητηκὼς καὶ τὸν ἥττω λόγον κρείττω ποιῶν ("that there is a certain Socrates, a wise man, a ponderer of what is in the air, and one who has investigated everything beneath the earth, and who makes the weaker argument the stronger"). One of these individuals, he says expressly, is a comic poet, and he reiterates what is said about him: Σωκράτης ἀδικεῖ καὶ περιεργάζεται ζητῶν τά τε ὑπὸ γῆς καὶ οὐράνια καὶ τὸν ἥττω λόγον κρείττω ποιῶν καὶ ἄλλους ταὐτὰ ταῦτα διδάσκων ("Socrates is a criminal and a busybody, investigating what is beneath the earth and in the heavens, and making the weaker argument stronger, and teaching these same matters to other people"). Indeed, he notes expressly: ταῦτα . . . ἑωρᾶτε καὶ αὐτοὶ ἐν τῇ Ἀριστοφάνους κωμῳδίᾳ, Σωκράτη τινὰ ἐκεῖ περιφερόμενον, φάσκοντά τε ἀεροβατεῖν καὶ ἄλλην πολλὴν φλυαρίαν φλυαροῦντα, ὧν ἐγὼ οὐδὲν οὔτε μέγα οὔτε μικρὸν πέρι ἐπαΐω ("You yourselves saw these things in Aristophanes' comedy: a certain Socrates being carried about there, announcing that he was walking on air and talking a great deal of other nonsense, about which I know nothing either great or small"). These are the most dangerous charges against him, Socrates insists: not the easily refutable denunciations put forward by Anytus and the other contemporary accusers, but the prejudices the jury has absorbed over the years from enemies of other sorts, and especially from Aristophanes in what can only be his *Clouds*.

The *Apology* dates to perhaps a decade or so after Socrates' execution, and there is no reason to think that it represents an entirely faithful account of the defense speech the jury heard, if only because an *Apology* by Xenophon is also preserved that is very different from Plato's. Nor is it obvious why a group of average Athenians who had the opportunity to see and listen to Socrates in the marketplace every day would have had their view of him shaped decisively by a single Aristophanic comedy, and in particular by one that was a failure in the Theater and that in its revised (surviving) version may never have been staged. Instead, the impression created by the *Apology* is that Plato is writing for an audience with limited knowledge of Socrates, who had been executed a number of years before, and that knew him instead largely through the literary medium of *Clouds*, which was by then among the most important contemporary evidence for the character and intentions of the famous philosopher and condemned enemy of the state. Put another way, although it is easy to admire the idealized "Socrates" presented by Plato in the *Apology* and other dialogues, this does not require us to assume that Plato offers an accurate account of who his master really was. For that, our only substantial contemporary evidence is *Clouds*, which paints a different picture.

Aristophanes' Socrates teaches for money; is deeply invested in what we today would call scientific inquiry into the natural world; denies the existence, or at least the power, of the traditional gods and of the values they represent; offers instruction in rhetoric, and in particular a form of rhetoric that uses the "weaker argument" (i.e. a case that is obviously perversely wrong) to demolish the "stronger argument" (i.e. what is patently right); teaches wealthy, disaffected young men in particular; and turns them against their fathers, converting them into sources of amoral social and political destruction. This Socrates may be to some extent a composite figure (as K. J. Dover, the editor of the most important modern critical text and commentary on *Clouds*, argues), more of a caricature—a generic "sophist" and "free thinker"—than a portrait of a real person. But Aristophanes chose to name that caricature "Socrates", and he must have felt that the image was true enough to appeal to the average member of the audience in the Theater, for whom the real Socrates was a familiar local crank rather than a legendary figure from the past. That Aristophanes did not know Socrates well in 423 BCE is possible, despite the relatively small size of Athens in this period (several hundred thousand residents, with a working intellectual society of a few thousand?), and Plato's attempt in the *Symposium*—set in 416 BCE, but written thirty or forty years later—to present the two men as casual, friendly social acquaintances. But Aristophanes certainly knew Socrates much better than Plato did at that time, given that Plato was born around when *Clouds* was staged and was still a relatively young man in 399 BCE, when his master was executed. None of this means that *Clouds* is right about the threat Socrates supposedly posed to Athenian society or the response that threat required. At the very least, however, the play is a powerful witness to what an intelligent comic poet might believe his audience would find a compelling depiction of a polarizing contemporary social and intellectual figure. For other passages from comedy that mention Socrates and his associate Chairephon (always in a skeptical, and in some cases an outright hostile fashion), see Appendix II.

The question of Aristophanes' portrait of Socrates and his assessment of the likely attitude of his audience toward him is also wrapped up with the problem of the original version of the play and its revision (for which, see Section I). Something caused the original version of the comedy to fail disastrously, and we know *inter alia* that the final scene, in which the Thinkery is burned down and its inhabitants chased off stage, belongs to the revised text alone. As *Clouds II* could scarcely be more hostile to Socrates and what he represents, it is worth asking whether *Clouds I* may have been less overtly so, and whether its failure led Aristophanes to dial the hostility up in his revision. If so, the poet looks even worse than he might have otherwise, in that he has deliberately pandered to what he must have known were ugly, stupid prejudices driven by a blandly incoherent, anti-intellectual moralizing he could assume dominated in his audience. Perhaps Socrates himself was different in the late 420s and early 410s than he was by the end of the century, so that Aristophanes caught him at one point in his personal, social and philosophical trajectory, Plato at another. Both men might thus, in their own ways, be right. In any case, *Clouds* raises serious questions, intended or not, about the place of free intellectual inquiry in a nominally democratic society dominated by nonintellectuals.

III. Staging

Due to construction work in the 4th century BCE, almost nothing from Aristophanes' time survives of the stage area in the Theater of Dionysus in Athens. Most of what we know—or think we know—about such matters is thus a deduction from the text of the comedies, on the one hand, and from the staging of contemporary tragedy, on the other. The Theater was open to the sky and illuminated only by natural light; there was no curtain. The stage appears to have been raised a few feet, although not far enough to prevent actors from occasionally moving down from or up onto it, as in *Clouds* when the Stronger Argument deserts to the audience (1102–4) and Strepsiades and Xanthias chase Socrates and the other residents of the Thinkery out of the Theater at the end of the play. Between the stage and the first row of seats was an open area called the *orchestra* (literally "dancing area") that belonged primarily to the chorus. This area was normally entered through two side entrances known as *eisodoi* (literally "roads in"), through which the chorus both entered and exited.

At the back of the stage was a facade—often referred to by the Latin term *scaenae frons*—with at least one door and in some plays as many as three. Most often this facade represents a house, a row of houses (as in *Clouds*, where there seem to be two) or a palace. Painted stage flats may have served to add visual detail. There was a roof one story up, on which characters sometimes appear and onto which Strepsiades and one of his slaves briefly climb at the end of this version of Aristophanes' play. When characters enter or exit the stage, they generally do so through one of the doors in the facade or by making use of the left or right wing.

We know of two major pieces of stage machinery available in this period, although there may have been others (cf. 292n. on the "thunder machine"). The first was the *ekkyklêma*, a trolley that could be rolled out from the central door in the facade and that was used to offer a nominal glimpse inside the house or palace. The *ekkyklêma* is perhaps employed in *Clouds* when Strepsiades is granted his first glimpse of life inside the Thinkery, as a means of bringing various scientific instruments out for his and the audience's inspection (200–19 with 183n.). The second major piece of stage machinery available to Aristophanes was the *mêchanê* (theatrical crane), a long, counterweighted beam with a platform of some sort on the stage end that allowed gods and the like to fly onstage. This is how Socrates first appears in the play at 218, "walking on air and thinking about the sun" (225).

Props were probably rudimentary, although occasional passing references to objects that have clearly been onstage unmentioned for hundreds of lines (e.g. the *dinos* at 1473) raise the possibility that there was more to this aspect of the comedies than we can see from the record of the words spoken onstage—but the words alone—preserved in our texts.

Both tragic and comic poets in this period appear to have been allowed the use of three main actors, conventionally referred to as the protagonist, deuteragonist and tritagonist, who divided the parts in the play between them. In his other comedies, Aristophanes occasionally uses a fourth actor—perhaps a nonprofessional—for some minor speaking parts. As noted above, among the indications that the *Clouds* we have is not a final, polished version of Aristophanes' rewrite of his failed play of 423 BCE is the fact that one crucial scene (889–1112 with 888–9n.) appears to require five actors, none of them bit players. With the exception of this scene, the roles in the play can be divided among the three standard actors as follows:

- Protagonist: Strepsiades (1–509, 634–1112, 1131–1213, 1221–1302, 1321–1509)
- Deuteragonist: Pheidippides (1–125, 814–1112, 1167–1213, 1325–1475), Socrates' doorkeeper slave (133–221), the Second Creditor (1259a–1302), one of the residents of the Thinkery at the very end of the play (e.g. 1493–1509)
- Tritagonist: Strepsiades' slave (18–59), Socrates (218–509, 625–803, 866–87, 1502–9?), the First Creditor (1214–58).

A bit player presumably takes the part of one of the residents of the Thinkery at the end of the play (1493–1509). Two mute slaves, one called Xanthias, also take part in the final scene (note 1485–90), and others may come onstage to carry props on and off from time to time; the students in the Thinkery at 184–99 are similarly played by mutes.

Some information about costuming can be extracted from the text (e.g. 14 on Pheidippides' long hair, 54 on the threadbare character of Strepsiades' robe) or by reasonable conjecture. If the Weaker Argument is richly dressed and the Stronger Argument is in rags (920), for example, and if the Stronger Argument's human counterpart Strepsiades is likewise badly dressed (54, cf. 72), it is tempting to conclude that the Weaker Argument's human counterpart, Pheidippides, is dressed as his mother would have liked (69–70), in a splendid and expensive robe. All actors—but not the chorus—wore masks, which could be altered slightly (i.e. replaced with something different) to reflect new circumstances (for example, the now-pale, Socratically educated Pheidippides at 1171b). Adult male characters also wore long, deliberately ridiculous leather phalli (cf. 538–9 with 538n.). The chorus of Clouds are apparently dressed as women (344), but nothing can be said about their costume beyond this.

IV. Meter

A. SPOKEN METERS

In the following description, – represents a long syllable; ⏑ a short syllable; × an anceps syllable, which can be either long or short; and oo a pair of anceps syllables, one of which must be long.

1. Iambic. The basic meter of Aristophanic comedy (as of contemporary tragedy) is iambic trimeter, an ideal form of which is ×–∪– ×–∪– ×–∪– (i.e. three iambic metra). Most Aristophanic iambic trimeter lines have a caesura in one of two positions: ×–∪– ×|–∪– ×–∪– or ×–∪– ×–∪|– ×–∪–. In most positions in the line, two shorts (∪∪) can be substituted for either a long or a single short. Thus 67 scans ––∪∪– –|–∪∪ ––∪–. Iambs are also occasionally organized as dimeters (×–∪– ×–∪–), as at 1386–90, where the final line appears in an abbreviated ("catalectic") form as ––∪– ∪––; or as catalectic tetrameters (×–∪– ×–∪– | ×–∪– ∪––), as at 1034–84, 1397–1444. ("Catalectic" means "lacking a syllable at the end"; cf. anapaestic tetrameter catalectic and trochaic tetrameter catalectic below.) Cf. the tetrameter in the form ––∪– ––∪– –∪∪∪–– (ia ia ith) at 1113–14. Bacchiacs (∪–– ∪––), an abbreviated form of iamb, appear at 708 in what appears to be a paratragic lament.

2. Anapaestic tetrameter catalectic (⏖⏔⏖⏔ ⏖⏔⏖⏔ | ⏖⏔⏖⏔ ∪∪––) appears at 263–74, 291–7, 314–438, 476–7, 959–1009, and 1510–11, anapaestic monometer (⏖⏔⏖⏔) and dimeter (⏖⏔⏖⏔ ⏖⏔⏖⏔) at 439–56 (monometer at 451, 454), 510–11 (510 monometer), 889–948, and 1010–23 (1023 catalectic; monometer at 1011, 1016). The ⏖ and ⏔ indicate that a long syllable or a double short may be used interchangeably at this point in the line.

3. Trochaic tetrameter catalectic (–∪–× –∪–× | –∪–× –∪–) is used in the epirrhema and antepirrhema of the first parabasis (575–94 with n., 607–26) and in the second parabasis (1115–30 with n.).

4. Eupolideans (oo–× –∪∪– oo–× –∪–) appear in the parabasis proper in the first parabasis at 518–62 (n.). See above on the metrical symbol oo.

B. SUNG METERS

The songs in *Clouds*—performed by the chorus and/or the characters, to musical accompaniment provided by a pipe—are mostly dactylic or iambic. For complete analyses of the songs, see Appendix III.

V. Bibliography

The standard critical edition of *Clouds* is K. J. Dover, *Aristophanes. Clouds* (Oxford 1968), with a now dated but still generally valuable and insightful commentary and introduction. There is also a more recent student edition of the play, with facing English translation and limited notes: Alan S. Sommerstein, *Aristophanes' Clouds* (Warminster 1982). The text was edited (along with the other ten surviving complete comedies) in 2007 by Nigel Wilson for the Oxford Classical Text series. Unfortunately, Wilson failed to carry out most of the basic manuscript work necessary for such an edition, and includes a large number of dubious conjectures in his version of the play. The OCT text—which provides the basis for the TLG electronic edition—should accordingly be used only with extreme caution, with close attention to the critical apparatus (which is far more limited than it ought to be) and always in conjunction with Dover.

Perhaps the most insightful recent secondary study of *Clouds* is Martha Nussbaum, "Aristophanes and Socrates on Learning Practical Wisdom", *Yale Classical Studies* 26 (1980) 43–97. Nussbaum's intellectual horizons stretch far beyond the ancient world, and her article is a brilliant example of an engaged reading that sheds light on a complex classical text while also showing how it can made to illuminate modern social, political and moral concerns. Some suggestions for further readings (restricted to recent items in English) follow.

A. ON CLOUDS IN PARTICULAR

On the two versions of the play:
Thomas K. Hubbard, "Parabatic Self-Criticism and the Two Versions of Aristophanes' Clouds", *Classical Antiquity* 5 (1986) 182–97.
S. Douglas Olson, "*Clouds* 537–44 and the Original Version of the Play," *Philologus* 138 (1994) 32–7.

On the end of the play:
E. Christian Kopff, "Nubes 1493ff: Was Socrates Murdered?", *Greek, Roman and Byzantine Studies* 18 (1977) 113–22.
F. D. Harvey, "Nubes 1493ff: Was Socrates Murdered?", *Greek, Roman and Byzantine Studies* 22 (1981) 339–43.
Malcolm Davies, "'Popular Justice' and the End of Aristophanes' *Clouds*", *Hermes* 118 (1980) 237–42.

On *Clouds* and Cratinus' *Pytine* (which defeated Aristophanes' play at the festival):
Zachary P. Biles, "Intertextual Biography in the Rivalry of Cratinus and Aristophanes", *AJP* 123 (2002) 169–204.

On Chairephon:
Christopher Moore, "Chaerephon the Socratic", *Phoenix* 67 (2013) 284–300.

B. ON THE ARISTOPHANIC CORPUS AND THE COMIC GENRE GENERALLY

There are two standard, now somewhat dated handbooks on Aristophanes and his plays:

K. J. Dover, *Aristophanic Comedy* (Berkeley, 1972).

D. M. MacDowell, *Aristophanes and Athens* (Oxford, 1995).

On Aristophanes' two greatest rivals:

I. C. Storey, *Eupolis, Poet of Old Comedy* (Oxford, 2003).

Emmanuela Bakola, *Cratinus and the Art of Comedy* (Oxford, 2010).

S. Douglas Olson (ed.), *Eupolis. Translation and Commentary* (3 vols.: Fragmenta Comica 8.1–3, Heidelberg, 2014, 2016, 2017).

For more wide-ranging essays on ancient (especially Athenian) comedy, see the pieces collected in:

David Harvey and John Wilkins (eds.), *The Rivals of Aristophanes* (London, 2000).

Gregory W. Dobrov (ed.), *Brill's Companion to the Study of Greek Comedy* (Leiden, 2010).

Michael Fontaine and Adele C. Scafuro (eds.), *The Oxford Handbook of Greek and Roman Comedy* (Oxford, 2014).

Select fragments of comedy (translated with notes):

S. Douglas Olson (ed.), *Broken Laughter: Select Fragments of Greek Comedy* (Oxford, 2007).

Jeffrey Rusten (ed.), *The Birth of Comedy* (Baltimore, 2011).

Jeffrey Henderson (ed.), *Aristophanes. Fragments* (Loeb Classical Library 502; Cambridge MA, 2008).

I. C. Storey (ed.), *Fragments of Old Comedy* (3 vols.: Loeb Classical Library 513, 514, 515; Cambridge, MA, 2011).

For the extensive if problematic inscriptional evidence for the dramatic competitions in Athens:

Benjamin W. Millis and S. Douglas Olson (eds.), *Inscriptional Records for the Dramatic Festivals in Athens: IG II² 2318–2325 and Related Texts* (Brill Studies in Greek and Roman Epigraphy; Leiden, 2012).

For dramatic performances and festivals in the Greek world generally:

O. Taplin, *Comic Angels and Other Approaches to Greek Drama through Vase-Painting* (Oxford, 1993).

Eric Csapo, *Actors and Icons of the Ancient Theater* (Chichester, 2010).

Eric Csapo and Peter Wilson, *A Social and Economic History of the Theatre to 300 BC. Vol. II. Theatre Beyond Athens: Documents for a Social and Economic History of the Theatre to 300 BC* (Cambridge, 2019).

On the history of the parabasis and the comic chorus:
G. M. Sifakis, *Parabasis and Animal Choruses* (London, 1971).
Kenneth S. Rothwell, *Nature, Culture, and the Origins of Greek Comedy* (Cambridge, 2007).

C. MORE SPECIALIZED STUDIES ON VARIOUS ASPECTS OF
ARISTOPHANES' ART:

On Aristophanes as a poet:
Michael Silk, "Aristophanes as a Lyric Poet", *Yale Classical Studies* 26 (1980) 99–151.

On Aristophanes' language:
Andreas Willi, *The Languages of Aristophanes: Aspects of Linguistic Variation in Classical Attic Greek* (Oxford, 2003).

On meter:
L. P. E. Parker, *The Songs of Aristophanes* (Oxford, 1997).

On obscenity:
Jeffrey Henderson, *The Maculate Muse: Obscene Language in Attic Comedy*[2] (New York, 1991) (not always reliable in matters of detail).
James Robson, *Humour, Obscenity and Aristophanes* (Tübingen, 2006).

On costuming:
Laura M. Stone, *Costume in Aristophanic Comedy* (Salem, 1984).

On Aristophanes and the *agôn*:
Z. P. Biles, *Aristophanes and the Poetics of Competition* (Cambridge, 2011).

Text

ΣΤΡΕΨΙΑΔΗΣ
ἰοὺ ἰού.
ὦ Ζεῦ βασιλεῦ, τὸ χρῆμα τῶν νυκτῶν ὅσον·
ἀπέραντον. οὐδέποθ' ἡμέρα γενήσεται;
καὶ μὴν πάλαι γ' ἀλεκτρυόνος ἤκουσ' ἐγώ·
οἱ δ' οἰκέται ῥέγκουσιν· ἀλλ' οὐκ ἂν πρὸ τοῦ.   5
ἀπόλοιο δῆτ', ὦ πόλεμε, πολλῶν οὕνεκα,
ὅτ' οὐδὲ κολάσ' ἔξεστί μοι τοὺς οἰκέτας.
ἀλλ' οὐδ' ὁ χρηστὸς οὑτοσὶ νεανίας
ἐγείρεται τῆς νυκτός, ἀλλὰ πέρδεται
ἐν πέντε σισύραις ἐγκεκορδυλημένος.   10
ἀλλ' εἰ δοκεῖ, ῥέγκωμεν ἐγκεκαλυμμένοι.
ἀλλ' οὐ δύναμαι δείλαιος εὕδειν δακνόμενος
ὑπὸ τῆς δαπάνης καὶ τῆς φάτνης καὶ τῶν χρεῶν
διὰ τουτονὶ τὸν υἱόν. ὁ δὲ κόμην ἔχων
ἱππάζεταί τε καὶ ξυνωρικεύεται   15
ὀνειροπολεῖ θ' ἵππους. ἐγὼ δ' ἀπόλλυμαι
ὁρῶν ἄγουσαν τὴν σελήνην εἰκάδας·
οἱ γὰρ τόκοι χωροῦσιν. ἅπτε, παῖ, λύχνον
κἄκφερε τὸ γραμματεῖον, ἵν' ἀναγνῶ λαβὼν
ὁπόσοις ὀφείλω, καὶ λογίσωμαι τοὺς τόκους.   20
φέρ' ἴδω, τί ὀφείλω; δώδεκα μνᾶς Πασίᾳ.
τοῦ δώδεκα μνᾶς Πασίᾳ; τί ἐχρησάμην;
ὅτ' ἐπριάμην τὸν κοππατίαν. οἴμοι τάλας,
εἴθ' ἐξεκόπην πρότερον τὸν ὀφθαλμὸν λίθῳ.

ΦΕΙΔΙΠΠΙΔΗΣ
Φίλων, ἀδικεῖς· ἔλαυνε τὸν σαυτοῦ δρόμον.   25
(Στ.) τοῦτ' ἐστὶ τουτὶ τὸ κακὸν ὅ μ' ἀπολώλεκεν·
ὀνειροπολεῖ γὰρ καὶ καθεύδων ἱππικήν.
(Φε.) πόσους δρόμους ἐλᾷ τὰ πολεμιστήρια;
(Στ.) ἐμὲ μὲν σὺ πολλοὺς τὸν πατέρ' ἐλαύνεις δρόμους.
ἀτὰρ τί χρέος ἔβα με μετὰ τὸν Πασίαν;   30
τρεῖς μναῖ διφρίσκου καὶ τροχοῖν Ἀμεινίᾳ.
(Φε.) ἄπαγε τὸν ἵππον ἐξαλίσας οἴκαδε.
(Στ.) ἀλλ', ὦ μέλ', ἐξήλικας ἐμέ γ' ἐκ τῶν ἐμῶν,

ὅτε καὶ δίκας ὤφληκα χἄτεροι τόκου
ἐνεχυράσεσθαί φασιν.
        (Φε.) ἐτεόν, ὦ πάτερ—   35
τί δυσκολαίνεις καὶ στρέφει τὴν νύχθ' ὅλην;
(Στ.) δάκνει μέ τις δήμαρχος ἐκ τῶν στρωμάτων.
(Φε.) ἔασον, ὦ δαιμόνιε, καταδαρθεῖν τί με.
(Στ.) σὺ δ' οὖν κάθευδε· τὰ δὲ χρέα ταῦτ' ἴσθ' ὅτι
εἰς τὴν κεφαλὴν ἅπαντα τὴν σὴν τρέψεται.   40
φεῦ.   41a
εἴθ' ὤφελ' ἡ προμνήστρι' ἀπολέσθαι κακῶς,   41b
ἥτις με γῆμ' ἐπῆρε τὴν σὴν μητέρα·
ἐμοὶ γὰρ ἦν ἄγροικος ἥδιστος βίος
εὐρωτιῶν, ἀκόρητος, εἰκῇ κείμενος,
βρύων μελίτταις καὶ προβάτοις καὶ στεμφύλοις.   45
ἔπειτ' ἔγημα Μεγακλέους τοῦ Μεγακλέους
ἀδελφιδῆν ἄγροικος ὢν ἐξ ἄστεως,
σεμνήν, τρυφῶσαν, ἐγκεκοισυρωμένην.
ταύτην ὅτ' ἐγάμουν, συγκατεκλινόμην ἐγὼ
ὄζων τρυγός, τρασιᾶς, ἐρίων, περιουσίας,   50
ἡ δ' αὖ μύρου, κρόκου, καταγλωττισμάτων,
δαπάνης, λαφυγμοῦ, Κωλιάδος, Γενετυλλίδος.
οὐ μὴν ἐρῶ γ' ὡς ἀργὸς ἦν, ἀλλ' ἐσπάθα.
ἐγὼ δ' ἂν αὐτῇ θοἰμάτιον δεικνὺς τοδὶ
πρόφασιν ἔφασκον "ὦ γύναι, λίαν σπαθᾷς."   55

ΟΙΚΕΤΗΣ
ἔλαιον ἡμῖν οὐκ ἔνεστ' ἐν τῷ λύχνῳ.
(Στ.) οἴμοι. τί γάρ μοι τὸν πότην ἧπτες λύχνον;
δεῦρ' ἐλθ', ἵνα κλάῃς.
        (Οἰ.) διὰ τί δῆτα κλαύσομαι;
(Στ.) ὅτι τῶν παχειῶν ἐνετίθεις θρυαλλίδων.
μετὰ ταῦθ', ὅπως νῷν ἐγένεθ' υἱὸς οὑτοσί,   60
ἐμοί τε δὴ καὶ τῇ γυναικὶ τἀγαθῇ,
περὶ τοὐνόματος δὴ 'ντεῦθεν ἐλοιδορούμεθα·
ἡ μὲν γὰρ "ἵππον" προσετίθει πρὸς τοὔνομα,
Ξάνθιππον ἢ Χαίριππον ἢ Καλλιππίδην,
ἐγὼ δὲ τοῦ πάππου 'τιθέμην Φειδωνίδην.   65
τέως μὲν οὖν ἐκρινόμεθ'· εἶτα τῷ χρόνῳ
κοινῇ ξυνέβημεν, κἀθέμεθα Φειδιππίδην.
τοῦτον τὸν υἱὸν λαμβάνουσ' ἐκορίζετο·
"ὅταν σὺ μέγας ὢν ἅρμ' ἐλαύνῃς πρὸς πόλιν

ὥσπερ Μεγακλέης, ξυστίδ᾽ ἔχων—᾿· ἐγὼ δ᾽ ἔφην   70
"ὅταν μὲν οὖν τὰς αἶγας ἐκ τοῦ φελλέως
ὥσπερ ὁ πατήρ σου, διφθέραν ἐνημμένος—᾿.
ἀλλ᾽ οὐκ ἐπείθετο τοῖς ἐμοῖς οὐδὲν λόγοις,
ἀλλ᾽ ἵππερόν μοι κατέχεεν τῶν χρημάτων.
νῦν οὖν ὅλην τὴν νύκτα φροντίζων ὁδοῦ   75
μίαν ηὗρον ἀτραπὸν δαιμονίως ὑπερφυᾶ,
ἣν ἢν ἀναπείσω τουτονί, σωθήσομαι.
ἀλλ᾽ ἐξεγεῖραι πρῶτον αὐτὸν βούλομαι.
πῶς δῆτ᾽ ἂν ἥδιστ᾽ αὐτὸν ἐπεγείραιμι; πῶς;
Φειδιππίδη, Φειδιππίδιον.
              (Φε.) τί, ὦ πάτερ;   80
(Στ.) κύσον με καὶ τὴν χεῖρα δὸς τὴν δεξιάν.
(Φε.) ἰδού. τί ἐστιν;
        (Στ.) εἰπέ μοι, φιλεῖς ἐμέ;
(Φε.) νὴ τὸν Ποσειδῶ τουτονὶ τὸν ἵππιον.
(Στ.) μὴ ᾽μοιγε τοῦτον μηδαμῶς τὸν ἵππιον·
οὗτος γὰρ ὁ θεὸς αἴτιός μοι τῶν κακῶν.   85
ἀλλ᾽ εἴπερ ἐκ τῆς καρδίας μ᾽ ὄντως φιλεῖς,
ὦ παῖ, πιθοῦ.
       (Φε.) τί οὖν πίθωμαι δῆτά σοι;
(Στ.) ἔκστρεψον ὡς τάχιστα τοὺς σαυτοῦ τρόπους
καὶ μάνθαν᾽ ἐλθὼν ἂν ἐγὼ παραινέσω.
(Φε.) λέγε δή, τί κελεύεις;
          (Στ.) καί τι πείσει;
               (Φε.) πείσομαι,   90
νὴ τὸν Διόνυσον.
        (Στ.) δεῦρό νυν ἀπόβλεπε.
ὁρᾷς τὸ θύριον τοῦτο καὶ τῷκίδιον;
(Φε.) ὁρῶ. τί οὖν τοῦτ᾽ ἐστὶν ἐτεόν, ὦ πάτερ;
(Στ.) ψυχῶν σοφῶν τοῦτ᾽ ἐστὶ φροντιστήριον.
ἐνταῦθ᾽ ἐνοικοῦσ᾽ ἄνδρες οἳ τὸν οὐρανὸν   95
λέγοντες ἀναπείθουσιν ὡς ἔστιν πνιγεύς,
κἄστιν περὶ ἡμᾶς οὗτος, ἡμεῖς δ᾽ ἄνθρακες.
οὗτοι διδάσκουσ᾽, ἀργύριον ἤν τις διδῷ,
λέγοντα νικᾶν καὶ δίκαια κἄδικα.
(Φε.) εἰσὶν δὲ τίνες;
          (Στ.) οὐκ οἶδ᾽ ἀκριβῶς τοὔνομα·   100
μεριμνοφροντισταί, καλοί τε κἀγαθοί.
(Φε.) αἰβοῖ, πονηροί γ᾽. οἶδα· τοὺς ἀλαζόνας,
τοὺς ὠχριῶντας, τοὺς ἀνυποδήτους λέγεις,

ὧν ὁ κακοδαίμων Σωκράτης καὶ Χαιρεφῶν.
(Στ.) ἦ ἤ, σιώπα· μηδὲν εἴπῃς νήπιον,   105
ἀλλ᾽ εἴ τι κήδει τῶν πατρῴων ἀλφίτων,
τούτων γενοῦ μοι σχασάμενος τὴν ἱππικήν.
(Φε.) οὐκ ἂν μὰ τὸν Διόνυσον εἰ δοίης γέ μοι
τοὺς φασιανοὺς οὓς τρέφει Λεωγόρας.
(Στ.) ἴθ᾽, ἀντιβολῶ σ᾽, ὦ φίλτατ᾽ ἀνθρώπων ἐμοί,   110
ἐλθὼν διδάσκου.
        (Φε.) καὶ τί σοι μαθήσομαι;
(Στ.) εἶναι παρ᾽ αὐτοῖς φασιν ἄμφω τὼ λόγω,
τὸν κρείττον᾽, ὅστις ἐστί, καὶ τὸν ἥττονα.
τούτοιν τὸν ἕτερον τοῖν λόγοιν, τὸν ἥττονα,
νικᾶν λέγοντά φασι τἀδικώτερα.   115
ἢν οὖν μάθῃς μοι τὸν ἄδικον τοῦτον λόγον,
ἃ νῦν ὀφείλω διὰ σέ, τούτων τῶν χρεῶν
οὐκ ἂν ἀποδοίην οὐδ᾽ ἂν ὀβολὸν οὐδενί.
(Φε.) οὐκ ἂν πιθοίμην· οὐ γὰρ ἂν τλαίην ἰδεῖν
τοὺς ἱππέας τὸ χρῶμα διακεκναισμένος.   120
(Στ.) οὐκ ἄρα μὰ τὴν Δήμητρα τῶν γ᾽ ἐμῶν ἔδει
οὔτ᾽ αὐτὸς οὔθ᾽ ὁ ζύγιος οὔθ᾽ ὁ σαμφόρας,
ἀλλ᾽ ἐξελῶ σ᾽ ἐς κόρακας ἐκ τῆς οἰκίας.
(Φε.) ἀλλ᾽ οὐ περιόψεταί μ᾽ ὁ θεῖος Μεγακλέης
ἄνιππον. ἀλλ᾽ εἴσειμι, σοῦ δ᾽ οὐ φροντιῶ.   125
(Στ.) ἀλλ᾽ οὐδ᾽ ἐγὼ μέντοι πεσών γε κείσομαι,
ἀλλ᾽ εὐξάμενος τοῖσιν θεοῖς διδάξομαι
αὐτὸς βαδίζων εἰς τὸ φροντιστήριον.
πῶς οὖν γέρων ὢν κἀπιλήσμων καὶ βραδὺς
λόγων ἀκριβῶν σκινδαλάμους μαθήσομαι;   130
ἰτητέον. τί ταῦτ᾽ ἔχων στραγγεύομαι
ἀλλ᾽ οὐχὶ κόπτω τὴν θύραν; παῖ, παιδίον.

ΟΙΚΕΤΗΣ ΣΩΚΡΑΤΟΥΣ
βάλλ᾽ ἐς κόρακας. τίς ἐσθ᾽ ὁ κόψας τὴν θύραν;
(Στ.) Φείδωνος υἱὸς Στρεψιάδης Κικυννόθεν.
(Οἰ.) ἀμαθής γε νὴ Δί᾽, ὅστις οὑτωσὶ σφόδρα   135
ἀπεριμερίμνως τὴν θύραν λελάκτικας
καὶ φροντίδ᾽ ἐξήμβλωκας ἐξηυρημένην.
(Στ.) σύγγνωθί μοι· τηλοῦ γὰρ οἰκῶ τῶν ἀγρῶν.
ἀλλ᾽ εἰπέ μοι τὸ πρᾶγμα τοὐξημβλωμένον.
(Οἰ.) ἀλλ᾽ οὐ θέμις πλὴν τοῖς μαθηταῖσιν λέγειν.   140
(Στ.) λέγε νυν ἐμοὶ θαρρῶν· ἐγὼ γὰρ οὑτοσὶ

ἥκω μαθητὴς εἰς τὸ φροντιστήριον.
(Οἰ.) λέξω· νομίσαι δὲ ταῦτα χρὴ μυστήρια.
ἀνήρετ᾿ ἄρτι Χαιρεφῶντα Σωκράτης
ψύλλαν ὁπόσους ἄλλοιτο τοὺς αὑτῆς πόδας·   145
δακοῦσα γὰρ τοῦ Χαιρεφῶντος τὴν ὀφρῦν
ἐπὶ τὴν κεφαλὴν τὴν Σωκράτους ἀφήλατο.
(Στ.) πῶς δῆτα διεμέτρησε;
          (Οἰ.) δεξιώτατα.
κηρὸν διατήξας, εἶτα τὴν ψύλλαν λαβὼν
ἐνέβαψεν εἰς τὸν κηρὸν αὐτῆς τὼ πόδε,   150
κᾆτα ψυχείσῃ περιέφυσαν Περσικαί.
ταύτας ὑπολύσας ἀνεμέτρει τὸ χωρίον.
(Στ.) ὦ Ζεῦ βασιλεῦ, τῆς λεπτότητος τῶν φρενῶν.
(Οἰ.) τί δῆτ᾿ ἄν, ἕτερον εἰ πύθοιο Σωκράτους
φρόντισμα;
          (Στ.) ποῖον; ἀντιβολῶ, κάτειπέ μοι.   155
(Οἰ.) ἀνήρετ᾿ αὐτὸν Χαιρεφῶν ὁ Σφήττιος
ὁπότερα τὴν γνώμην ἔχοι τὰς ἐμπίδας
κατὰ τὸ στόμ᾿ ᾄδειν ἢ κατὰ τοὐρροπύγιον.
(Στ.) τί δῆτ᾿ ἐκεῖνος εἶπε περὶ τῆς ἐμπίδος;
(Οἰ.) ἔφασκεν εἶναι τοὔντερον τῆς ἐμπίδος   160
στενόν, διὰ λεπτοῦ δ᾿ ὄντος αὐτοῦ τὴν πνοὴν
βίᾳ βαδίζειν εὐθὺ τοὐρροπυγίου·
ἔπειτα κοῖλον πρὸς στενῷ προσκείμενον
τὸν πρωκτὸν ἠχεῖν ὑπὸ βίας τοῦ πνεύματος.
(Στ.) σάλπιγξ ὁ πρωκτός ἐστιν ἄρα τῶν ἐμπίδων.   165
ὦ τρισμακάριος τοῦ διεντερεύματος.
ἦ ῥᾳδίως φεύγων ἂν ἀποφύγοι δίκην,
ὅστις δίοιδε τοὔντερον τῆς ἐμπίδος.
(Οἰ.) πρῴην δέ γε γνώμην μεγάλην ἀφῃρέθη
ὑπ᾿ ἀσκαλαβώτου.
          (Στ.) τίνα τρόπον; κάτειπέ μοι.   170
(Οἰ.) ζητοῦντος αὐτοῦ τῆς σελήνης τὰς ὁδοὺς
καὶ τὰς περιφοράς, εἶτ᾿ ἄνω κεχηνότος
ἀπὸ τῆς ὀροφῆς νύκτωρ γαλεώτης κατέχεσεν.
(Στ.) ἥσθην γαλεώτῃ καταχέσαντι Σωκράτους.
(Οἰ.) ἐχθὲς δέ γ᾿ ἡμῖν δεῖπνον οὐκ ἦν ἑσπέρας.   175
(Στ.) εἶέν. τί οὖν πρὸς τἄλφιτ᾿ ἐπαλαμήσατο;
(Οἰ.) κατὰ τῆς τραπέζης καταπάσας λεπτὴν τέφραν,
κάμψας ὀβελίσκον, εἶτα διαβήτην λαβὼν
ἐκ τῆς παλαίστρας θοἰμάτιον ὑφείλετο.

(Στ.) τί δῆτ' ἐκεῖνον τὸν Θαλῆν θαυμάζομεν;   180
ἄνοιγ' ἄνοιγ' ἀνύσας τὸ φροντιστήριον
καὶ δεῖξον ὡς τάχιστά μοι τὸν Σωκράτη·
μαθητιῶ γάρ. ἀλλ' ἄνοιγε τὴν θύραν.
ὦ Ἡράκλεις, ταυτὶ ποδαπὰ τὰ θηρία;
(Οἰ.) τί ἐθαύμασας; τῷ σοι δοκοῦσιν εἰκέναι;   185
(Στ.) τοῖς ἐκ Πύλου ληφθεῖσι, τοῖς Λακωνικοῖς.
ἀτὰρ τί ποτ' εἰς τὴν γῆν βλέπουσιν οὑτοιί;
(Οἰ.) ζητοῦσιν οὗτοι τὰ κατὰ γῆς.
                         (Στ.) βολβοὺς ἄρα
ζητοῦσι. μή νυν τοῦτό γ' ἔτι φροντίζετε·
ἐγὼ γὰρ οἶδ' ἵν' εἰσὶ μεγάλοι καὶ καλοί.   190
τί γὰρ οἵδε δρῶσιν οἱ σφόδρ' ἐγκεκυφότες;
(Οἰ.) οὗτοι δ' ἐρεβοδιφῶσιν ὑπὸ τὸν Τάρταρον.
(Στ.) τί δῆθ' ὁ πρωκτὸς εἰς τὸν οὐρανὸν βλέπει;
(Οἰ.) αὐτὸς καθ' αὑτὸν ἀστρονομεῖν διδάσκεται.
ἀλλ' εἴσιθ', ἵνα μὴ 'κεῖνος ὑμῖν ἐπιτύχῃ.   195
(Στ.) μήπω γε, μήπω γ'· ἀλλ' ἐπιμεινάντων, ἵνα
αὐτοῖσι κοινώσω τι πραγμάτιον ἐμόν.
(Οἰ.) ἀλλ' οὐχ οἷόν τ' αὐτοῖσι πρὸς τὸν ἀέρα
ἔξω διατρίβειν πολὺν ἄγαν ἐστὶν χρόνον.
(Στ.) πρὸς τῶν θεῶν, τί γὰρ τάδ' ἐστίν; εἰπέ μοι.   200
(Οἰ.) ἀστρονομία μὲν αὕτη.
                         (Στ.) τουτὶ δὲ τί;
(Οἰ.) γεωμετρία.
                         (Στ.) τοῦτ' οὖν τί ἐστι χρήσιμον;
(Οἰ.) γῆν ἀναμετρεῖσθαι.
                         (Στ.) πότερα τὴν κληρουχικήν;
(Οἰ.) οὔκ, ἀλλὰ τὴν σύμπασαν.
                         (Στ.) ἀστεῖον λέγεις·
τὸ γὰρ σόφισμα δημοτικὸν καὶ χρήσιμον.   205
(Οἰ.) αὕτη δέ σοι γῆς περίοδος πάσης. ὁρᾷς;
αἵδε μὲν Ἀθῆναι.
                         (Στ.) τί σὺ λέγεις; οὐ πείθομαι,
ἐπεὶ δικαστὰς οὐχ ὁρῶ καθημένους.
(Οἰ.) ὡς τοῦτ' ἀληθῶς Ἀττικὴ τὸ χωρίον.
(Στ.) καὶ ποῦ Κικυννῆς εἰσιν, οὑμοὶ δημόται;   210
(Οἰ.) ἐνταῦθ' ἔνεισιν. ἡ δέ γ' Εὔβοι', ὡς ὁρᾷς,
ἡδὶ παρατέταται μακρὰ πόρρω πάνυ.
(Στ.) οἶδ'· ὑπὸ γὰρ ἡμῶν παρετάθη καὶ Περικλέους.
ἀλλ' ἡ Λακεδαίμων ποῦ 'στιν;

(Οἰ.) ὅπου 'στίν; αὑτηί.

(Στ.) ὡς ἐγγὺς ἡμῶν. τοῦτο μεταφροντίζετε,   215
ταύτην ἀφ' ἡμῶν ἀπαγαγεῖν πόρρω πάνυ.

(Οἰ.) ἀλλ' οὐχ οἷόν τε.

        (Στ.) νὴ Δί', οἰμώξεσθ' ἄρα.

φέρε· τίς γὰρ οὗτος οὑπὶ τῆς κρεμάθρας ἀνήρ;

(Οἰ.) αὐτός.

    (Στ.) τίς αὐτός;

        (Οἰ.) Σωκράτης.

           (Στ.) ὦ Σωκράτης.

ἴθ' οὗτος, ἀναβόησον αὐτόν μοι μέγα.   220

(Οἰ.) αὐτὸς μὲν οὖν σὺ κάλεσον· οὐ γάρ μοι σχολή.

(Στ.) ὦ Σώκρατες,

ὦ Σωκρατίδιον.

ΣΩΚΡΑΤΗΣ

        τί με καλεῖς, ὦ 'φήμερε;

(Στ.) πρῶτον μὲν ὅτι δρᾷς, ἀντιβολῶ, κάτειπέ μοι.

(Σω.) ἀεροβατῶ καὶ περιφρονῶ τὸν ἥλιον.   225

(Στ.) ἔπειτ' ἀπὸ ταρροῦ τοὺς θεοὺς ὑπερφρονεῖς

ἀλλ' οὐκ ἀπὸ τῆς γῆς, εἴπερ;

           (Σω.) οὐ γὰρ ἄν ποτε

ἐξηῦρον ὀρθῶς τὰ μετέωρα πράγματα,

εἰ μὴ κρεμάσας τὸ νόημα καὶ τὴν φροντίδα

λεπτὴν καταμείξας εἰς τὸν ὅμοιον ἀέρα.   230

εἰ δ' ὢν χαμαὶ τἄνω κάτωθεν ἐσκόπουν,

οὐκ ἄν ποθ' ηὗρον· οὐ γὰρ ἀλλ' ἡ γῆ βίᾳ

ἕλκει πρὸς αὑτὴν τὴν ἰκμάδα τῆς φροντίδος.

πάσχει δὲ ταὐτὸ τοῦτο καὶ τὰ κάρδαμα.

(Στ.) πῶς φής;   235

ἡ φροντὶς ἕλκει τὴν ἰκμάδ' εἰς τὰ κάρδαμα;

ἴθι νυν κατάβηθ', ὦ Σωκρατίδιον, ὡς ἐμέ,

ἵνα με διδάξῃς ὦνπερ οὕνεκ' ἐλήλυθα.

(Σω.) ἦλθες δὲ κατὰ τί;

        (Στ.) βουλόμενος μαθεῖν λέγειν·

ὑπὸ γὰρ τόκων χρήστων τε δυσκολωτάτων   240

ἄγομαι, φέρομαι, τὰ χρήματ' ἐνεχυράζομαι.

(Σω.) πόθεν δ' ὑπόχρεως σαυτὸν ἔλαθες γενόμενος;

(Στ.) νόσος μ' ἐπέτριψεν ἱππική, δεινὴ φαγεῖν.

ἀλλά με δίδαξον τὸν ἕτερον τοῖν σοῖν λόγοιν,

τὸν μηδὲν ἀποδιδόντα· μισθὸν δ' ὅντιν' ἂν   245

πράττῃ μ᾽, ὀμοῦμαί σοι καταθήσειν τοὺς θεούς.
(Σω.) ποίους θεοὺς ὀμεῖ σύ; πρῶτον γὰρ θεοὶ
ἡμῖν νόμισμ᾽ οὐκ ἔστι.
                    (Στ.) τῷ γὰρ ὄμνυτε;
σιδαρέοισιν, ὥσπερ ἐν Βυζαντίῳ;
(Σω.) βούλει τὰ θεῖα πράγματ᾽ εἰδέναι σαφῶς   250
ἅττ᾽ ἐστὶν ὀρθῶς;
                    (Στ.) νὴ Δί᾽, εἴπερ ἔστι γε.
(Σω.) καὶ συγγενέσθαι ταῖς Νεφέλαισιν εἰς λόγους,
ταῖς ἡμετέραισι δαίμοσιν;
                    (Στ.) μάλιστά γε.
(Σω.) κάθιζε τοίνυν ἐπὶ τὸν ἱερὸν σκίμποδα.
(Στ.) ἰδού, κάθημαι.
                    (Σω.) τουτονὶ τοίνυν λαβὲ   255
τὸν στέφανον.
                    (Στ.) ἐπὶ τί στέφανον; οἴμοι, Σώκρατες,
ὥσπερ με τὸν Ἀθάμανθ᾽ ὅπως μὴ θύσετε.
(Σω.) οὔκ, ἀλλὰ πάντας ταῦτα τοὺς τελουμένους
ἡμεῖς ποοῦμεν.
                    (Στ.) εἶτα δὴ τί κερδανῶ;
(Σω.) λέγειν γενήσει τρῖμμα, κρόταλον, παιπάλη.   260
ἀλλ᾽ ἔχ᾽ ἀτρεμεί.
                    (Στ.) μὰ τὸν Δί᾽ οὐ ψεύσει γέ με·
καταπαττόμενος γὰρ παιπάλη γενήσομαι.
(Σω.) εὐφημεῖν χρὴ τὸν πρεσβύτην καὶ τῆς εὐχῆς ἐπακούειν.
ὦ δέσποτ᾽ ἄναξ ἀμέτρητ᾽ Ἀήρ, ὃς ἔχεις τὴν γῆν μετέωρον,
λαμπρός τ᾽ Αἰθὴρ σεμναί τε θεαὶ Νεφέλαι βροντησικέραυνοι,   265
ἄρθητε, φάνητ᾽, ὦ δέσποιναι, τῷ φροντιστῇ μετέωροι.
(Στ.) μήπω, μήπω γε, πρὶν ἂν τουτὶ πτύξωμαι, μὴ καταβρεχθῶ.
τὸ δὲ μηδὲ κυνῆν οἴκοθεν ἐλθεῖν ἐμὲ τὸν κακοδαίμον᾽ ἔχοντα.
(Σω.) ἔλθετε δῆτ᾽, ὦ πολυτίμητοι Νεφέλαι, τῷδ᾽ εἰς ἐπίδειξιν·
εἴτ᾽ ἐπ᾽ Ὀλύμπου κορυφαῖς ἱεραῖς χιονοβλήτοισι κάθησθε   270
εἴτ᾽ Ὠκεανοῦ πατρὸς ἐν κήποις ἱερὸν χορὸν ἵστατε νύμφαις
εἴτ᾽ ἄρα Νείλου προχοαῖς ὑδάτων χρυσέαις ἀρύτεσθε πρόχοισιν
ἢ Μαιῶτιν λίμνην ἔχετ᾽ ἢ σκόπελον νιφόεντα Μίμαντος,
ὑπακούσατε δεξάμεναι θυσίαν καὶ τοῖς ἱεροῖσι χαρεῖσαι.

ΧΟΡΟΣ
ἀέναοι Νεφέλαι,   στρ.   275
ἀρθῶμεν φανεραὶ δροσερὰν φύσιν εὐάγητον   276-7
πατρὸς ἀπ᾽ Ὠκεανοῦ βαρυαχέος

ὑψηλῶν ὀρέων κορυφὰς ἔπι
δενδροκόμους, ἵνα   280
τηλεφανεῖς σκοπιὰς ἀφορώμεθα
καρποὺς τ᾽ ἀρδομέναν ἱερὰν χθόνα
καὶ ποταμῶν ζαθέων κελαδήματα
καὶ πόντον κελάδοντα βαρύβρομον·
ὄμμα γὰρ αἰθέρος ἀκάματον σελαγεῖται   285-6
μαρμαρέαισιν αὐγαῖς.
ἀλλ᾽ ἀποσεισάμεναι νέφος ὄμβριον
ἀθανάτας ἰδέας ἐπιδώμεθα
τηλεσκόπῳ ὄμματι γαῖαν.   290

(Σω.) ὦ μέγα σεμναὶ Νεφέλαι, φανερῶς ἠκούσατέ μου καλέσαντος.
ἤσθου φωνῆς ἅμα καὶ βροντῆς μυκησαμένης θεόσεπτον;
(Στ.) καὶ σέβομαί γ᾽, ὦ πολυτίμητοι, καὶ βούλομαι ἀνταποπαρδεῖν
πρὸς τὰς βροντάς· οὕτως αὐτὰς τετραμαίνω καὶ πεφόβημαι·
κεἰ θέμις ἐστίν, νυνί γ᾽ ἤδη, κεἰ μὴ θέμις ἐστί, χεσείω.   295
(Σω.) οὐ μὴ σκώψει μηδὲ ποήσεις ἅπερ οἱ τρυγοδαίμονες οὗτοι,
ἀλλ᾽ εὐφήμει· μέγα γάρ τι θεῶν κινεῖται σμῆνος ἀοιδαῖς.

(Χο.) παρθένοι ὀμβροφόροι,   ἀντ.
ἔλθωμεν λιπαρὰν χθόνα Παλλάδος εὔανδρον γᾶν   299-300
Κέκροπος ὀψόμεναι πολυήρατον,
    οὗ σέβας ἀρρήτων ἱερῶν, ἵνα
    μυστοδόκος δόμος
    ἐν τελεταῖς ἁγίαις ἀναδείκνυται
    οὐρανίοις τε θεοῖς δωρήματα   305
    ναοί θ᾽ ὑψερεφεῖς καὶ ἀγάλματα
    καὶ πρόσοδοι μακάρων ἱερώταται
    εὐστέφανοί τε θεῶν θυσίαι θαλίαι τε   308-9
παντοδαπαῖσιν ὥραις   310
ἦρί τ᾽ ἐπερχομένῳ Βρομία χάρις
εὐκελάδων τε χορῶν ἐρεθίσματα
καὶ μοῦσα βαρύβρομος αὐλῶν.

(Στ.) πρὸς τοῦ Διός, ἀντιβολῶ σε, φράσον· τίνες εἴσ᾽, ὦ Σώκρατες, αὗται
αἱ φθεγξάμεναι τοῦτο τὸ σεμνόν; μῶν ἡρῷναί τινές εἰσιν;   315
(Σω.) ἥκιστ᾽, ἀλλ᾽ οὐράνιαι Νεφέλαι, μεγάλαι θεαὶ ἀνδράσιν ἀργοῖς,
αἵπερ γνώμην καὶ διάλεξιν καὶ νοῦν ἡμῖν παρέχουσιν
καὶ τερατείαν καὶ περίλεξιν καὶ κροῦσιν καὶ κατάληψιν.
(Στ.) ταῦτ᾽ ἄρ᾽ ἀκούσασ᾽ αὐτῶν τὸ φθέγμ᾽ ἡ ψυχή μου πεπότηται

καὶ λεπτολογεῖν ἤδη ζητεῖ καὶ περὶ καπνοῦ στενολεσχεῖν   320
καὶ γνωμιδίῳ γνώμην νύξασ' ἑτέρῳ λόγῳ ἀντιλογῆσαι·
ὥστ', εἴ πως ἔστιν, ἰδεῖν αὐτὰς ἤδη φανερῶς ἐπιθυμῶ.
(Σω.) βλέπε νυν δευρὶ πρὸς τὴν Πάρνηθ'· ἤδη γὰρ ὁρῶ κατιούσας
ἡσυχῇ αὐτάς.
        (Στ.) φέρε, ποῦ; δεῖξον.
                (Σω.) χωροῦσ' αὗται πάνυ πολλαὶ
διὰ τῶν κοίλων καὶ τῶν δασέων, αὗται πλάγιαι.
                        (Στ.) τί τὸ χρῆμα;   325
ὡς οὐ καθορῶ.
        (Σω.) παρὰ τὴν εἴσοδον.
                (Στ.) ἤδη νυνὶ μόλις οὕτως.
(Σω.) νῦν γέ τοι ἤδη καθορᾷς αὐτάς, εἰ μὴ λημᾷς κολοκύνταις.
(Στ.) νὴ Δί' ἔγωγ'· ὦ πολυτίμητοι· πάντα γὰρ ἤδη κατέχουσιν.
(Σω.) ταύτας μέντοι σὺ θεὰς οὔσας οὐκ ᾔδεις οὐδ' ἐνόμιζες;
(Στ.) μὰ Δί', ἀλλ' ὁμίχλην καὶ δρόσον αὐτὰς ἡγούμην καὶ καπνὸν εἶναι.   330
(Σω.) οὐ γὰρ μὰ Δί' οἶσθ' ὁτιὴ πλείστους αὗται βόσκουσι σοφιστάς,
Θουριομάντεις, ἰατροτέχνας, σφραγιδονυχαργοκομήτας·
κυκλίων τε χορῶν ᾀσματοκάμπτας, ἄνδρας μετεωροφένακας,
οὐδὲν δρῶντας βόσκουσ' ἀργούς, ὅτι ταύτας μουσοποοῦσιν.
(Στ.) ταῦτ' ἄρ' ἐποίουν "ὑγρᾶν νεφελᾶν στρεπταίγλαν δάιον ὁρμάν"   335
"πλοκάμους θ' ἑκατογκεφάλα Τυφῶ" "πρημαινούσας τε θυέλλας",
εἶτ' "ἀερίας διεράς" "γαμψούς τε οἰωνοὺς ἀερονηχεῖς"
"ὄμβρους θ' ὑδάτων δροσερᾶν νεφελᾶν"· εἶτ' ἀντ' αὐτῶν κατέπινον
κεστρᾶν τεμάχη μεγαλᾶν ἀγαθᾶν κρέα τ' ὀρνίθεια κιχηλᾶν.
(Σω.) διὰ μέντοι τάσδ'. οὐχὶ δικαίως;
                (Στ.) λέξον δή μοι, τί παθοῦσαι,   340
εἴπερ νεφέλαι γ' εἰσὶν ἀληθῶς, θνηταῖς εἴξασι γυναιξίν;
οὐ γὰρ ἐκεῖναί γ' εἰσὶ τοιαῦται.
                (Σω.) φέρε, ποῖαι γάρ τινές εἰσιν;
(Στ.) οὐκ οἶδα σαφῶς· εἴξασιν δ' οὖν ἐρίοισιν πεπταμένοισιν,
κοὐχὶ γυναιξίν, μὰ Δί', οὐδ' ὁτιοῦν· αὗται δὲ ῥῖνας ἔχουσιν.
(Σω.) ἀπόκριναί νυν ἅττ' ἂν ἔρωμαι.
                (Στ.) λέγε νυν ταχέως ὅτι βούλει.   345
(Σω.) ἤδη ποτ' ἀναβλέψας εἶδες νεφέλην κενταύρῳ ὁμοίαν
ἢ παρδάλει ἢ λύκῳ ἢ ταύρῳ;
                (Στ.) νὴ Δί' ἔγωγ'. εἶτα τί τοῦτο;
(Σω.) γίγνονται πάνθ' ὅτι βούλονται· κᾆτ' ἢν μὲν ἴδωσι κομήτην
ἄγριόν τινα τῶν λασίων τούτων, οἷόνπερ τὸν Ξενοφάντου,
σκώπτουσαι τὴν μανίαν αὐτοῦ κενταύροις ᾔκασαν αὐτάς.   350
(Στ.) τί γὰρ ἢν ἅρπαγα τῶν δημοσίων κατίδωσι Σίμωνα, τί δρῶσιν;

(Σω.) ἀποφαίνουσαι τὴν φύσιν αὐτοῦ λύκοι ἐξαίφνης ἐγένοντο.
(Στ.) ταῦτ᾽ ἄρα, ταῦτα Κλεώνυμον αὗται τὸν ῥίψασπιν χθὲς ἰδοῦσαι,
ὅτι δειλότατον τοῦτον ἑώρων, ἔλαφοι διὰ τοῦτ᾽ ἐγένοντο.
(Σω.) καὶ νῦν γ᾽ ὅτι Κλεισθένη εἶδον, ὁρᾷς, διὰ τοῦτ᾽ ἐγένοντο γυναῖκες.   355
(Στ.) χαίρετε τοίνυν, ὦ δέσποιναι· καὶ νῦν, εἴπερ τινὶ κἄλλῳ,
οὐρανομήκη ῥήξατε κἀμοὶ φωνήν, ὦ παμβασίλειαι.
(Χο.) χαῖρ᾽, ὦ πρεσβῦτα παλαιογενές, θηρατὰ λόγων φιλομούσων·
σύ τε, λεπτοτάτων λήρων ἱερεῦ, φράζε πρὸς ἡμᾶς ὅ τι χρῄζεις·
οὐ γὰρ ἂν ἄλλῳ γ᾽ ὑπακούσαιμεν τῶν νῦν μετεωροσοφιστῶν   360
πλὴν εἰ Προδίκῳ, τῷ μὲν σοφίας καὶ γνώμης οὕνεκα, σοὶ δὲ
ὅτι βρενθύει τ᾽ ἐν ταῖσιν ὁδοῖς καὶ τὠφθαλμὼ παραβάλλεις
κἀνυπόδητος κακὰ πόλλ᾽ ἀνέχει κἀφ᾽ ἡμῖν σεμνοπροσωπεῖς.
(Στ.) ὦ Γῆ, τοῦ φθέγματος, ὡς ἱερὸν καὶ σεμνὸν καὶ τερατῶδες.
(Σω.) αὗται γάρ τοι μόναι εἰσὶ θεαί, τἄλλα δὲ πάντ᾽ ἐστὶ φλύαρος.   365
(Στ.) ὁ Ζεὺς δ᾽ ὑμῖν, φέρε, πρὸς τῆς Γῆς, οὑλύμπιος οὐ θεός ἐστιν;
(Σω.) ποῖος Ζεύς; οὐ μὴ ληρήσεις· οὐδ᾽ ἔστι Ζεύς.
                    (Στ.) τί λέγεις σύ;
ἀλλὰ τίς ὕει; τουτὶ γὰρ ἔμοιγ᾽ ἀπόφηναι πρῶτον ἁπάντων.
(Σω.) αὗται δήπου· μεγάλοις δέ σ᾽ ἐγὼ σημείοις αὐτὸ διδάξω.
φέρε, ποῦ γὰρ πώποτ᾽ ἄνευ νεφελῶν ὕοντ᾽ ἤδη τεθέασαι;   370
καίτοι χρῆν αἰθρίας ὕειν αὐτόν, ταύτας δ᾽ ἀποδημεῖν.
(Στ.) νὴ τὸν Ἀπόλλω, τοῦτό γέ τοι τῷ νυνὶ λόγῳ εὖ προσέφυσας·
καίτοι πρότερον τὸν Δί᾽ ἀληθῶς ᾤμην διὰ κοσκίνου οὐρεῖν.
ἀλλ᾽ ὅστις ὁ βροντῶν ἐστι φράσον, τοῦθ᾽ ὅ με ποιεῖ τετραμαίνειν.
(Σω.) αὗται βροντῶσι κυλινδόμεναι.
                    (Στ.) τῷ τρόπῳ, ὦ πάντα σὺ τολμῶν;   375
(Σω.) ὅταν ἐμπλησθῶσ᾽ ὕδατος πολλοῦ κἀναγκασθῶσι φέρεσθαι
κατακριμνάμεναι πλήρεις ὄμβρου δι᾽ ἀνάγκην, εἶτα βαρεῖαι
εἰς ἀλλήλας ἐμπίπτουσαι ῥήγνυνται καὶ παταγοῦσιν.
(Στ.) ὁ δ᾽ ἀναγκάζων ἐστὶ τίς αὐτάς—οὐχ ὁ Ζεύς;—ὥστε φέρεσθαι;
(Σω.) ἥκιστ᾽, ἀλλ᾽ αἰθέριος δῖνος.
                    (Στ.) Δῖνος; τουτί μ᾽ ἐλελήθει,   380
ὁ Ζεὺς οὐκ ὤν, ἀλλ᾽ ἀντ᾽ αὐτοῦ Δῖνος νυνὶ βασιλεύων.
ἀτὰρ οὐδέν πω περὶ τοῦ πατάγου καὶ τῆς βροντῆς μ᾽ ἐδίδαξας.
(Σω.) οὐκ ἤκουσάς μου τὰς νεφέλας ὕδατος μεστὰς ὅτι φημὶ
ἐμπιπτούσας εἰς ἀλλήλας παταγεῖν διὰ τὴν πυκνότητα;
(Στ.) φέρε, τουτὶ τῷ χρὴ πιστεύειν;
                    (Σω.) ἀπὸ σαυτοῦ ᾽γώ σε διδάξω.   385
ἤδη ζωμοῦ Παναθηναίοις ἐμπλησθεὶς εἶτ᾽ ἐταράχθης
τὴν γαστέρα, καὶ κλόνος ἐξαίφνης αὐτὴν διεκορκορύγησεν;
(Στ.) νὴ τὸν Ἀπόλλω, καὶ δεινὰ ποεῖ γ᾽ εὐθύς μοι καὶ τετάρακται,

χὥσπερ βροντὴ τὸ ζωμίδιον παταγεῖ καὶ δεινὰ κέκραγεν,
ἀτρέμας πρῶτον "παππὰξ παππάξ", κᾆπειτ' ἐπάγει "παπαπαππάξ"   390
χὥταν χέζω, κομιδῇ βροντᾷ "παπαπαππάξ", ὥσπερ ἐκεῖναι.
(Σω.) σκέψαι τοίνυν ἀπὸ γαστριδίου τυννουτουὶ οἷα πέπορδας·
τὸν δ' ἀέρα τόνδ' ὄντ' ἀπέραντον πῶς οὐκ εἰκὸς μέγα βροντᾶν;
(Στ.) ταῦτ' ἄρα καὶ τὤνόματ' ἀλλήλοιν, βροντὴ καὶ πορδή, ὁμοίω.
ἀλλ' ὁ κεραυνὸς πόθεν αὖ φέρεται λάμπων πυρί, τοῦτο δίδαξον,   395
καὶ καταφρύγει βάλλων ἡμᾶς, τοὺς δὲ ζῶντας περιφλεύει;
τοῦτον γὰρ δὴ φανερῶς ὁ Ζεὺς ἵησ' ἐπὶ τοὺς ἐπιόρκους.
(Σω.) καὶ πῶς, ὦ μῶρε σὺ καὶ Κρονίων ὄζων καὶ βεκκεσέληνε,
εἴπερ βάλλει τοὺς ἐπιόρκους, δῆτ' οὐχὶ Σίμων' ἐνέπρησεν
οὐδὲ Κλεώνυμον οὐδὲ Θέωρον; καίτοι σφόδρα γ' εἴσ' ἐπίορκοι·   400
ἀλλὰ τὸν αὑτοῦ γε νεὼν βάλλει καὶ Σούνιον, ἄκρον Ἀθηνέων,
καὶ τὰς δρῦς τὰς μεγάλας· τί μαθών; οὐ γὰρ δὴ δρῦς γ' ἐπιορκεῖ.
(Στ.) οὐκ οἶδ'· ἀτὰρ εὖ σὺ λέγειν φαίνει. τί γάρ ἐστιν δῆθ' ὁ κεραυνός;
(Σω.) ὅταν εἰς ταύτας ἄνεμος ξηρὸς μετεωρισθεὶς κατακλῃσθῇ,
ἔνδοθεν αὐτὰς ὥσπερ κύστιν φυσᾷ, κᾄπειθ' ὑπ' ἀνάγκης   405
ῥήξας αὐτὰς ἔξω φέρεται σοβαρὸς διὰ τὴν πυκνότητα
ὑπὸ τοῦ ῥοίβδου καὶ τῆς ῥύμης αὐτὸς ἑαυτὸν κατακαίων.
(Στ.) νὴ Δί' ἐγὼ γοῦν ἀτεχνῶς ἔπαθον τουτὶ ποτε Διασίοισιν
ὀπτῶν γαστέρα τοῖς συγγενέσιν· κᾆτ' οὐκ ἔσχων ἀμελήσας,
ἡ δ' ἄρ' ἐφυσᾶτ', εἶτ' ἐξαίφνης διαλακήσασα πρὸς αὐτὼ   410
τὠφθαλμώ μου προσετίλησεν καὶ κατέκαυσεν τὸ πρόσωπον.
(Χο.) ὦ τῆς μεγάλης ἐπιθυμήσας σοφίας ἄνθρωπε παρ' ἡμῶν,
ὡς εὐδαίμων ἐν Ἀθηναίοις καὶ τοῖς Ἕλλησι γενήσει
εἰ μνήμων εἶ καὶ φροντιστὴς καὶ τὸ ταλαίπωρον ἔνεστιν
ἐν τῇ ψυχῇ καὶ μὴ κάμνεις μήθ' ἑστὼς μήτε βαδίζων,   415
μήτε ῥιγῶν ἄχθει λίαν μήτ' ἀριστᾶν ἐπιθυμεῖς
οἴνου τ' ἀπέχει καὶ γυμνασίων καὶ τῶν ἄλλων ἀνοήτων
καὶ βέλτιστον τοῦτο νομίζεις, ὅπερ εἰκὸς δεξιὸν ἄνδρα,
νικᾶν πράττων καὶ βουλεύων καὶ τῇ γλώττῃ πολεμίζων.
(Στ.) ἀλλ' οὕνεκά γε ψυχῆς στερρᾶς δυσκολοκοίτου τε μερίμνης   420
καὶ φειδωλοῦ καὶ τρυσιβίου γαστρὸς καὶ θυμβρεπιδείπνου,
ἀμέλει, θαρρῶν οὕνεκα τούτων ἐπιχαλκεύειν παρέχοιμ' ἄν.
(Σω.) ἄλλο τι δῆτ' οὐ νομιεῖς ἤδη θεὸν οὐδένα πλὴν ἅπερ ἡμεῖς,
τὸ Χάος τουτὶ καὶ τὰς Νεφέλας καὶ τὴν Γλῶτταν, τρία ταυτί;
(Στ.) οὐδ' ἂν διαλεχθείην γ' ἀτεχνῶς τοῖς ἄλλοις οὐδ' ἂν ἀπαντῶν,   425
οὐδ' ἂν θύσαιμ', οὐδ' ἂν σπείσαιμ', οὐδ' ἐπιθείην λιβανωτόν.
(Χο.) λέγε νυν ἡμῖν ὅτι σοι δρῶμεν θαρρῶν· ὡς οὐκ ἀτυχήσεις
ἡμᾶς τιμῶν καὶ θαυμάζων καὶ ζητῶν δεξιὸς εἶναι.
(Στ.) ὦ δέσποιναι, δέομαι τοίνυν ὑμῶν τουτὶ πάνυ μικρόν,

τῶν Ἑλλήνων εἶναί με λέγειν ἑκατὸν σταδίοισιν ἄριστον.　　　　430

(Χο.) ἀλλ᾽ ἔσται σοι τοῦτο παρ᾽ ἡμῶν· ὥστε τὸ λοιπόν γ᾽ ἀπὸ τουδὶ
ἐν τῷ δήμῳ γνώμας οὐδεὶς νικήσει πλείονας ἢ σύ.

(Στ.) μὴ ᾽μοιγε λέγειν γνώμας μεγάλας· οὐ γὰρ τούτων ἐπιθυμῶ,
ἀλλ᾽ ὅσ᾽ ἐμαυτῷ στρεψοδικῆσαι καὶ τοὺς χρήστας διολισθεῖν.

(Χο.) τεύξει τοίνυν ὧν ἱμείρεις· οὐ γὰρ μεγάλων ἐπιθυμεῖς.　　　435
ἀλλὰ σεαυτὸν θαρρῶν παράδος τοῖς ἡμετέροις προπόλοισιν.

(Στ.) δράσω ταῦθ᾽ ὑμῖν πιστεύσας· ἡ γὰρ ἀνάγκη με πιέζει
διὰ τοὺς ἵππους τοὺς κοππατίας καὶ τὸν γάμον ὅς μ᾽ ἐπέτριψεν.
νῦν οὖν ἀτεχνῶς ὅ τι βούλονται
τουτὶ τό γ᾽ ἐμὸν σῶμ᾽ αὐτοῖσιν　　　　440
παρέχω, τύπτειν, πεινῆν, διψῆν,
αὐχμεῖν, ῥιγῶν, ἀσκὸν δείρειν,
εἴπερ τὰ χρέα διαφευξοῦμαι
τοῖς τ᾽ ἀνθρώποις εἶναι δόξω
θρασύς, εὔγλωττος, τολμηρός, ἴτης,　　　　445
βδελυρός, ψευδῶν συγκολλητής,
εὑρησιεπής, περίτριμμα δικῶν,
κύρβις, κρόταλον, κίναδος, τρύμη,
μάσθλης, εἴρων, γλοιός, ἀλαζών,
κέντρων, μιαρός, στρόφις, ἀργαλέος,　　　　450
ματιολοιχός.
ταῦτ᾽ εἴ με καλοῦσ᾽ ἀπαντῶντες,
δρώντων ἀτεχνῶς ὅτι χρῄζουσιν·
κεἰ βούλονται,
νὴ τὴν Δήμητρ᾽ ἔκ μου χορδὴν　　　　455
τοῖς φροντισταῖς παραθέντων.

(Χο.) λῆμα μὲν πάρεστι τῷδέ γ᾽
　　οὐκ ἄτολμον, ἀλλ᾽ ἕτοιμον.
ἴσθι δ᾽ ὡς
　　ταῦτα μαθὼν παρ᾽ ἐμοῦ κλέος οὐρανόμηκες　　　　460-1
ἐν βροτοῖσιν ἕξεις.
(Στ.) τί πείσομαι;
　　　　(Χο.) τὸν πάντα χρόνον μετ᾽ ἐμοῦ
ζηλωτότατον βίον ἀν-
　　θρώπων διάξεις.　　　　465
(Στ.) ἆρά γε τοῦτ᾽ ἄρ᾽ ἐγώ ποτ᾽
ὄψομαι;
　　　　(Χο.) ὥστε γέ σου
πολλοὺς ἐπὶ ταῖσι θύραις

ἀεὶ καθῆσθαι
βουλομένους ἀνακοινοῦ-   470
    σθαί τε καὶ εἰς λόγον ἐλθεῖν
πράγματα κἀντιγραφὰς
    πολλῶν ταλάντων,
ἄξια σῇ φρενὶ συμ-
    βουλευσομένους μετὰ σοῦ.   475

ἀλλ' ἐγχείρει τὸν πρεσβύτην ὅτιπερ μέλλεις προδιδάσκειν
καὶ διακίνει τὸν νοῦν αὐτοῦ καὶ τῆς γνώμης ἀποπειρῶ.

(Σω.) ἄγε δή, κάτειπέ μοι σὺ τὸν σαυτοῦ τρόπον,
ἵν' αὐτὸν εἰδὼς ὅστις ἐστὶ μηχανὰς
ἤδη 'πὶ τούτοις πρός σε καινὰς προσφέρω.   480
(Στ.) τί δέ; τειχομαχεῖν μοι διανοεῖ, πρὸς τῶν θεῶν;
(Σω.) οὔκ, ἀλλὰ βραχέα σου πυθέσθαι βούλομαι,
εἰ μνημονικὸς εἶ.
                (Στ.) δύο τρόπω, νὴ τὸν Δία·
ἢν μέν γ' ὀφείληταί τί μοι, μνήμων πάνυ,
ἐὰν δ' ὀφείλω, σχέτλιος, ἐπιλήσμων πάνυ.   485
(Σω.) ἔνεστι δῆτά σοι λέγειν ἐν τῇ φύσει;
(Στ.) λέγειν μὲν οὐκ ἔνεστ', ἀποστερεῖν δ' ἔνι.
(Σω.) πῶς οὖν δυνήσει μανθάνειν;
                        (Στ.) ἀμέλει, καλῶς.
(Σω.) ἄγε νυν, ὅπως, ὅταν τι προβάλωμαι σοφὸν
περὶ τῶν μετεώρων, εὐθέως ὑφαρπάσει.   490
(Στ.) τί δαί; κυνηδὸν τὴν σοφίαν σιτήσομαι;
(Σω.) ἄνθρωπος ἀμαθὴς οὑτοσὶ καὶ βάρβαρος.
δέδοικά σ', ὦ πρεσβῦτα, μὴ πληγῶν δέει.
φέρ' ἴδω, τί δρᾷς, ἤν τίς σε τύπτῃ;
                        (Στ.) τύπτομαι,
ἔπειτ' ἐπισχὼν ὀλίγον ἐπιμαρτύρομαι·   495
εἶτ' αὖθις ἀκαρῆ διαλιπὼν δικάζομαι.
(Σω.) ἴθι νυν, κατάθου θοἰμάτιον.
                        (Στ.) ἠδίκηκά τι;
(Σω.) οὔκ, ἀλλὰ γυμνοὺς εἰσιέναι νομίζεται.
(Στ.) ἀλλ' οὐχὶ φωράσων ἔγωγ' εἰσέρχομαι.
(Σω.) κατάθου. τί ληρεῖς;
                        (Στ.) εἰπὲ δή νύν μοι τοδί·   500
ἢν ἐπιμελὴς ὦ καὶ προθύμως μανθάνω,
τῷ τῶν μαθητῶν ἐμφερὴς γενήσομαι;

(Σω.) οὐδὲν διοίσεις Χαιρεφῶντος τὴν φύσιν.

(Στ.) οἴμοι κακοδαίμων, ἡμιθνὴς γενήσομαι.

(Σω.) οὐ μὴ λαλήσεις, ἀλλ᾿ ἀκολουθήσεις ἐμοὶ   505
ἀνύσας τι δευρὶ θᾶττον.

               (Στ.) εἰς τὼ χεῖρέ νυν
δός μοι μελιτοῦτταν πρότερον, ὡς δέδοικ᾿ ἐγὼ
εἴσω καταβαίνων ὥσπερ εἰς Τροφωνίου.

(Σω.) χώρει. τί κυπτάζεις ἔχων περὶ τὴν θύραν;

(Χο.) ἀλλ᾿ ἴθι χαίρων   510
τῆς ἀνδρείας οὕνεκα ταύτης.
εὐτυχία γένοιτο τἀν-
    θρώπῳ, ὅτι προήκων
εἰς βαθὺ τῆς ἡλικίας
νεωτέροις τὴν φύσιν αὑ-   515
    τοῦ πράγμασιν χρωτίζεται
καὶ σοφίαν ἐπασκεῖ.

ὦ θεώμενοι, κατερῶ πρὸς ὑμᾶς ἐλευθέρως
τἀληθῆ, νὴ τὸν Διόνυσον τὸν ἐκθρέψαντά με.
οὕτω νικήσαιμί τ᾿ ἐγὼ καὶ νομιζοίμην σοφός,   520
ὡς ὑμᾶς ἡγούμενος εἶναι θεατὰς δεξιοὺς
καὶ ταύτην σοφώτατ᾿ ἔχειν τῶν ἐμῶν κωμῳδιῶν
πρώτους ἠξίωσ᾿ ἀναγεῦσ᾿ ὑμᾶς, ἣ παρέσχε μοι
ἔργον πλεῖστον· εἶτ᾿ ἀνεχώρουν ὑπ᾿ ἀνδρῶν φορτικῶν
ἡττηθεὶς οὐκ ἄξιος ὤν· ταῦτ᾿ οὖν ὑμῖν μέμφομαι   525
τοῖς σοφοῖς, ὧν οὕνεκ᾿ ἐγὼ ταῦτ᾿ ἐπραγματευόμην.
ἀλλ᾿ οὐδ᾿ ὣς ὑμῶν ποθ᾿ ἑκὼν προδώσω τοὺς δεξιούς·
ἐξ ὅτου γὰρ ἐνθάδ᾿ ὑπ᾿ ἀνδρῶν, οὓς ἡδὺ καὶ λέγειν,
ὁ σώφρων τε χὠ καταπύγων ἄριστ᾿ ἠκουσάτην,
κἀγώ, παρθένος γὰρ ἔτ᾿ ἦν κοὐκ ἐξῆν πώ μοι τεκεῖν,   530
ἐξέθηκα, παῖς δ᾿ ἑτέρα τις λαβοῦσ᾿ ἀνείλετο,
ὑμεῖς δ᾿ ἐξεθρέψατε γενναίως κἀπαιδεύσατε·
ἐκ τούτου μοι πιστὰ παρ᾿ ὑμῶν γνώμης ἔσθ᾿ ὅρκια.
νῦν οὖν Ἠλέκτραν κατ᾿ ἐκείνην ἥδ᾿ ἡ κωμῳδία
ζητοῦσ᾿ ἦλθ᾿, ἤν που ᾿πιτύχῃ θεαταῖς οὕτω σοφοῖς·   535
γνώσεται γάρ, ἤπερ ἴδῃ, τἀδελφοῦ τὸν βόστρυχον.
ὡς δὲ σώφρων ἐστὶ φύσει σκέψασθ᾿· ἥτις πρῶτα μὲν
οὐδὲν ἦλθε ῥαψαμένη σκύτινον καθειμένον,
ἐρυθρὸν ἐξ ἄκρου, παχύ, τοῖς παιδίοις ἵν᾿ ᾖ γέλως·
οὐδ᾿ ἔσκωψεν τοὺς φαλακρούς, οὐδὲ κόρδαχ᾿ εἵλκυσεν,   540

οὐδὲ πρεσβύτης ὁ λέγων τἄπη τῇ βακτηρίᾳ
τύπτει τὸν παρόντ' ἀφανίζων πονηρὰ σκώμματα,
οὐδ' εἰσῇξε δᾷδας ἔχουσ', οὐδ' "ἰοὺ ἰού" βοᾷ,
ἀλλ' αὑτῇ καὶ τοῖς ἔπεσιν πιστεύουσ' ἐλήλυθεν.
κἀγὼ μὲν τοιοῦτος ἀνὴρ ὢν ποιητὴς οὐ κομῶ,   545
οὐδ' ὑμᾶς ζητῶ 'ξαπατᾶν δὶς καὶ τρὶς ταῦτ' εἰσάγων,
ἀλλ' αἰεὶ καινὰς ἰδέας εἰσφέρων σοφίζομαι
οὐδὲν ἀλλήλαισιν ὁμοίας καὶ πάσας δεξιάς·
ὃς μέγιστον ὄντα Κλέων' ἔπαισ' εἰς τὴν γαστέρα
κοὐκ ἐτόλμησ' αὖθις ἐπεμπηδῆσ' αὐτῷ κειμένῳ.   550
οὗτοι δ', ὡς ἅπαξ παρέδωκεν λαβὴν Ὑπέρβολος,
τοῦτον δείλαιον κολετρῶσ' ἀεὶ καὶ τὴν μητέρα.
Εὔπολις μὲν τὸν Μαρικᾶν πρώτιστον παρείλκυσεν
ἐκστρέψας τοὺς ἡμετέρους Ἱππέας κακὸς κακῶς,
προσθεὶς αὐτῷ γραῦν μεθύσην τοῦ κόρδακος οὕνεχ', ἣν   555
Φρύνιχος πάλαι πεπόηχ', ἣν τὸ κῆτος ἤσθιεν.
εἶθ' Ἕρμιππος αὖθις ἐποίησεν εἰς Ὑπέρβολον,
ἄλλοι τ' ἤδη πάντες ἐρείδουσιν εἰς Ὑπέρβολον,
τὰς εἰκοὺς τῶν ἐγχέλεων τὰς ἐμὰς μιμούμενοι.
ὅστις οὖν τούτοισι γελᾷ, τοῖς ἐμοῖς μὴ χαιρέτω·   560
ἢν δ' ἐμοὶ καὶ τοῖσιν ἐμοῖς εὐφραίνησθ' εὑρήμασιν,
εἰς τὰς ὥρας τὰς ἑτέρας εὖ φρονεῖν δοκήσετε.

ὑψιμέδοντα μὲν θεῶν   στρ.
Ζῆνα τύραννον εἰς χορὸν
πρῶτα μέγαν κικλήσκω·   565
τόν τε μεγασθενῆ τριαί-
     νης ταμίαν, γῆς τε καὶ ἁλμυρᾶς θαλάσ-
     σης ἄγριον μοχλευτήν·
καὶ μεγαλώνυμον ἡμέτερον πατέρ',
     Αἰθέρα σεμνότατον, βιοθρέμμονα πάντων·   570
τόν θ' ἱππονώμαν, ὃς ὑπερ-
     λάμπροις ἀκτῖσιν κατέχει
γῆς πέδον, μέγας ἐν θεοῖς
ἐν θνητοῖσί τε δαίμων.

ὦ σοφώτατοι θεαταί, δεῦρο τὸν νοῦν προσέχετε·   575
ἠδικημέναι γὰρ ὑμῖν μεμφόμεσθ' ἐναντίον·
πλεῖστα γὰρ θεῶν ἁπάντων ὠφελούσαις τὴν πόλιν,
δαιμόνων ἡμῖν μόναις οὐ θύετ' οὐδὲ σπένδετε,
αἵτινες τηροῦμεν ὑμᾶς· ἢν γὰρ ᾖ τις ἔξοδος

μηδενὶ ξὺν νῷ, τότ' ἢ βροντῶμεν ἢ ψακάζομεν.   580
εἶτα τὸν θεοῖσιν ἐχθρὸν βυρσοδέψην Παφλαγόνα
ἡνίχ' ἡρεῖσθε στρατηγόν, τὰς ὀφρῦς ξυνήγομεν
κἀποοῦμεν δεινά, βροντὴ δ' ἐρράγη δι' ἀστραπῆς,
ἡ σελήνη δ' ἐξέλειπε τὰς ὁδούς, ὁ δ' ἥλιος
τὴν θρυαλλίδ' εἰς ἑαυτὸν εὐθέως ξυνελκύσας   585
οὐ φανεῖν ἔφασκεν ὑμῖν, εἰ στρατηγήσοι Κλέων.
ἀλλ' ὅμως εἵλεσθε τοῦτον· φασὶ γὰρ δυσβουλίαν
τῇδε τῇ πόλει προσεῖναι, ταῦτα μέντοι τοὺς θεούς,
ἅττ' ἂν ὑμεῖς ἐξαμάρτητ', ἐπὶ τὸ βέλτιον τρέπειν.
ὡς δὲ καὶ τοῦτο ξυνοίσει ῥᾳδίως διδάξομεν·   590
ἢν Κλέωνα τὸν λάρον δώρων ἑλόντες καὶ κλοπῆς
εἶτα φιμώσητε τούτου τῷ ξύλῳ τὸν αὐχένα,
αὖθις εἰς τἀρχαῖον ὑμῖν, εἴ τι κἀξημάρτετε,
ἐπὶ τὸ βέλτιον τὸ πρᾶγμα τῇ πόλει ξυνοίσεται.

ἀμφί μοι αὖτε, Φοῖβ' ἄναξ   ἀντ.   595
Δήλιε, Κυνθίαν ἔχων
ὑψικέρατα πέτραν·
ἥ τ' Ἐφέσου μάκαιρα πάγχρυσον ἔχεις
    οἶκον, ἐν ᾧ κόραι σε Λυ-
    δῶν μεγάλως σέβουσιν·   600
ἥ τ' ἐπιχώριος ἡμετέρα θεὸς
    αἰγίδος ἡνίοχος, πολιοῦχος Ἀθάνα·
Παρνασσίαν θ' ὃς κατέχων
    πέτραν σὺν πεύκαις σελαγεῖ
Βάκχαις Δελφίσιν ἐμπρέπων,   605
κωμαστὴς Διόνυσος.

ἡνίχ' ἡμεῖς δεῦρ' ἀφορμᾶσθαι παρεσκευάσμεθα,
ἡ σελήνη ξυντυχοῦσ' ἡμῖν ἐπέστειλεν φράσαι
πρῶτα μὲν χαίρειν Ἀθηναίοισι καὶ τοῖς ξυμμάχοις·
εἶτα θυμαίνειν ἔφασκε· δεινὰ γὰρ πεπονθέναι   610
ὠφελοῦσ' ὑμᾶς ἅπαντας οὐ λόγοις ἀλλ' ἐμφανῶς,
πρῶτα μὲν τοῦ μηνὸς εἰς δᾷδ' οὐκ ἔλαττον ἢ δραχμήν,
ὥστε καὶ λέγειν ἅπαντας ἐξιόντας ἑσπέρας
"μὴ πρίῃ, παῖ, δᾷδ'· ἐπειδὴ φῶς Σεληναίης καλόν."
ἄλλα τ' εὖ δρᾶν φησιν, ὑμᾶς δ' οὐκ ἄγειν τὰς ἡμέρας   615
οὐδὲν ὀρθῶς, ἀλλ' ἄνω τε καὶ κάτω κυδοιδοπᾶν·
ὥστ' ἀπειλεῖν φησιν αὐτῇ τοὺς θεοὺς ἑκάστοτε
ἡνίκ' ἂν ψευσθῶσι δείπνου κἀπίωσιν οἴκαδε

τῆς ἑορτῆς μὴ τυχόντες κατὰ λόγον τῶν ἡμερῶν.
κᾆθ' ὅταν θύειν δέῃ, στρεβλοῦτε καὶ δικάζετε·   620
πολλάκις δ' ἡμῶν ἀγόντων τῶν θεῶν ἀπαστίαν,
ἡνίκ' ἂν πενθῶμεν ἢ τὸν Μέμνον' ἢ Σαρπηδόνα,
σπένδεθ' ὑμεῖς καὶ γελᾶτ'· ἀνθ' ὧν λαχὼν Ὑπέρβολος
τῆτες ἱερομνημονεῖν κᾄπειθ' ὑφ' ἡμῶν τῶν θεῶν
τὸν στέφανον ἀφῃρέθη· μᾶλλον γὰρ οὕτως εἴσεται   625
κατὰ σελήνην ὡς ἄγειν χρὴ τοῦ βίου τὰς ἡμέρας.

(Σω.) μὰ τὴν Ἀναπνοήν, μὰ τὸ Χάος, μὰ τὸν Ἀέρα,
οὐκ εἶδον οὕτως ἄνδρ' ἄγροικον οὐδαμοῦ
οὐδ' ἄπορον οὐδὲ σκαιὸν οὐδ' ἐπιλήσμονα,
ὅστις σκαλαθυρμάτι' ἄττα μικρὰ μανθάνων   630
ταῦτ' ἐπιλέλησται πρὶν μαθεῖν. ὅμως γε μὴν
αὐτὸν καλῶ θύραζε δευρὶ πρὸς τὸ φῶς.
ποῦ Στρεψιάδης; ἔξει τὸν ἀσκάντην λαβών;
(Στ.) ἀλλ' οὐκ ἐῶσί μ' ἐξενεγκεῖν οἱ κόρεις.
(Σω.) ἀνύσας τι κατάθου καὶ πρόσεχε τὸν νοῦν.
                              (Στ.) ἰδού.   635
(Σω.) ἄγε δή, τί βούλει πρῶτα νυνὶ μανθάνειν
ὧν οὐκ ἐδιδάχθης πώποτ' οὐδέν; εἰπέ μοι.
πότερον περὶ μέτρων ἢ περὶ ἐπῶν ἢ ῥυθμῶν;
(Στ.) περὶ τῶν μέτρων ἔγωγ'· ἔναγχος γάρ ποτε
ὑπ' ἀλφιταμοιβοῦ παρεκόπην διχοινίκῳ.   640
(Σω.) οὐ τοῦτ' ἐρωτῶ σ', ἀλλ' ὅτι κάλλιστον μέτρον
ἡγεῖ, πότερον τὸ τρίμετρον ἢ τὸ τετράμετρον.
(Στ.) ἐγὼ μὲν οὐδὲν πρότερον ἡμιέκτεω.
(Σω.) οὐδὲν λέγεις, ὤνθρωπε.
                         (Στ.) περίδου νυν ἐμοί,
εἰ μὴ τετράμετρόν ἐστιν ἡμιέκτεως.   645
(Σω.) ἐς κόρακας· ὡς ἄγροικος εἶ καὶ δυσμαθής.
ταχύ γ' ἂν δύναιο μανθάνειν περὶ ῥυθμῶν.
(Στ.) τί δέ μ' ὠφελήσουσ' οἱ ῥυθμοὶ πρὸς τἄλφιτα;
(Σω.) πρῶτον μὲν εἶναι κομψὸν ἐν συνουσίᾳ
ἐπαΐειν θ' ὁποῖός ἐστι τῶν ῥυθμῶν   650
κατ' ἐνόπλιον, χὠποῖος αὖ κατὰ δάκτυλον.
(Στ.) κατὰ δάκτυλον; νὴ τὸν Δί', ἀλλ' οἶδ'.
                         (Σω.) εἰπὲ δή.   652
(Στ.) πρὸ τοῦ μέν, ἔτ' ἐμοῦ παιδὸς ὄντος, οὑτοσί.   654
(Σω.) ἀγρεῖος εἶ καὶ σκαιός.
                         (Στ.) οὐ γάρ, ὦ ζυρέ,   655

τούτων ἐπιθυμῶ μανθάνειν οὐδέν.

(Σω.) τί δαί;

(Στ.) ἐκεῖν' ἐκεῖνο, τὸν ἀδικώτατον λόγον.

(Σω.) ἀλλ' ἕτερα δεῖ σε πρότερα τούτου μανθάνειν,
τῶν τετραπόδων ἅττ' ἐστὶν ὀρθῶς ἄρρενα.

(Στ.) ἀλλ' οἶδ' ἔγωγε τἄρρεν', εἰ μὴ μαίνομαι·   660
κριός, τράγος, ταῦρος, κύων, ἀλεκτρυών.

(Σω.) ὁρᾷς ἃ πάσχεις; τήν τε θήλειαν καλεῖς
ἀλεκτρυόνα κατὰ ταὐτὸ καὶ τὸν ἄρρενα.

(Στ.) πῶς δή, φέρ';

(Σω.) ὅπως; ἀλεκτρυὼν κἀλεκτρυών.

(Στ.) νὴ τὸν Ποσειδῶ. νῦν δὲ πῶς με χρὴ καλεῖν;   665

(Σω.) ἀλεκτρύαιναν, τὸν δ' ἕτερον ἀλέκτορα.

(Στ.) ἀλεκτρύαιναν; εὖ γε, νὴ τὸν Ἀέρα·
ὥστ' ἀντὶ τούτου τοῦ διδάγματος μόνου
διαλφιτώσω σου κύκλῳ τὴν κάρδοπον.

(Σω.) ἰδοὺ μάλ' αὖθις, τοῦθ' ἕτερον· τὴν κάρδοπον   670
ἄρρενα καλεῖς θήλειαν οὖσαν.

(Στ.) τῷ τρόπῳ;
ἄρρενα καλῶ 'γὼ κάρδοπον;

(Σω.) μάλιστά γε,
ὥσπερ γε καὶ Κλεώνυμον.

(Στ.) πῶς δή; φράσον.

(Σω.) ταὐτὸν δύναταί σοι κάρδοπος Κλεωνύμῳ.

(Στ.) ἀλλ', ὦγάθ', οὐδ' ἦν κάρδοπος Κλεωνύμῳ,   675
ἀλλ' ἐν θυείᾳ στρογγύλῃ γ' ἀνεμάττετο.
ἀτὰρ τὸ λοιπὸν πῶς με χρὴ καλεῖν;

(Σω.) ὅπως;
τὴν καρδόπην, ὥσπερ καλεῖς τὴν Σωστράτην.

(Στ.) τὴν καρδόπην θήλειαν;

(Σω.) ὀρθῶς γὰρ λέγεις.

(Στ.) ἐκεῖνο † δ' ἦν ἂν †· "καρδόπη Κλεωνύμη".   680

(Σω.) ἔτι δέ γε περὶ τῶν ὀνομάτων μαθεῖν σε δεῖ,
ἅττ' ἄρρεν' ἐστίν, ἅττα δ' αὐτῶν θήλεα.

(Στ.) ἀλλ' οἶδ' ἔγωγ' ἃ θήλε' ἐστίν.

(Σω.) εἰπὲ δή.

(Στ.) Λύσιλλα, Φίλιννα, Κλειταγόρα, Δημητρία.

(Σω.) ἄρρενα δὲ ποῖα τῶν ὀνομάτων;

(Στ.) μυρία.   685
Φιλόξενος, Μελησίας, Ἀμεινίας.

(Σω.) ἀλλ', ὦ πόνηρε, ταῦτά γ' ἔστ' οὐκ ἄρρενα.

(Στ.) οὐκ ἄρρεν' ὑμῖν ἐστιν;

        (Σω.) οὐδαμῶς γ'· ἐπεὶ

πῶς ἂν καλέσειας ἐντυχὼν Ἀμεινίᾳ;

(Στ.) ὅπως ἄν; ὡδί· "δεῦρο δεῦρ', Ἀμεινία".   690

(Σω.) ὁρᾷς; γυναῖκα τὴν Ἀμεινίαν καλεῖς.

(Στ.) οὔκουν δικαίως, ἥτις οὐ στρατεύεται;

ἀτὰρ τί ταῦθ' ἃ πάντες ἴσμεν μανθάνω;

(Σω.) οὐδέν, μὰ Δί'· ἀλλὰ κατακλινεὶς δευρί—

                 (Στ.) τί δρῶ;

(Σω.) ἐκφρόντισόν τι τῶν σεαυτοῦ πραγμάτων.   695

(Στ.) μὴ δῆθ', ἱκετεύω, 'νταῦθά γ'· ἀλλ' εἴπερ γε χρή,

χαμαί μ' ἔασον αὐτὰ ταῦτ' ἐκφροντίσαι.

(Σω.) οὐκ ἔστι παρὰ ταῦτ' ἄλλα.

             (Στ.) κακοδαίμων ἐγώ·

οἵαν δίκην τοῖς κόρεσι δώσω τήμερον.

(Χο.) φρόντιζε δὴ καὶ διάθρει   στρ.   700

    πάντα τρόπον τε σαυτὸν

στρόβει πυκνώσας. ταχὺς δ', ὅταν εἰς ἄπορον   702–3

    πέσῃς, ἐπ' ἄλλο πήδα

νόημα φρενός· ὕπνος δ' ἀπέ-   705

    στω γλυκύθυμος ὀμμάτων.

(Στ.) ἀτταταῖ ἀτταταῖ.

(Χο.) τί πάσχεις; τί κάμνεις;

(Στ.) ἀπόλλυμαι δείλαιος. ἐκ τοῦ σκίμποδος

δάκνουσί μ' ἐξέρποντες οἱ Κορίνθιοι   710

καὶ τὰς πλευρὰς δαρδάπτουσιν

καὶ τὴν ψυχὴν ἐκπίνουσιν

καὶ τοὺς ὄρχεις ἐξέλκουσιν

καὶ τὸν πρωκτὸν διορύττουσιν

καί μ' ἀπολοῦσιν.   715

(Χο.) μή νυν βαρέως ἄλγει λίαν.

(Στ.) καὶ πῶς; ὅτε μου

φροῦδα τὰ χρήματα, φρούδη χροιά,

φρούδη ψυχή, φρούδη δ' ἐμβάς·

καὶ πρὸς τούτοις ἔτι τοῖσι κακοῖς   720

φρουρᾶς ᾄδων

ὀλίγου φροῦδος γεγένημαι.

(Σω.) οὗτος, τί ποεῖς; οὐχὶ φροντίζεις;

               (Στ.) ἐγώ;

νὴ τὸν Ποσειδῶ.
       (Σω.) καὶ τί δῆτ' ἐφρόντισας;
(Στ.) ὑπὸ τῶν κόρεων εἴ μού τι περιλειφθήσεται.   725
(Σω.) ἀπολεῖ κάκιστ'.
       (Στ.) ἀλλ', ὦ 'γάθ', ἀπόλωλ' ἀρτίως.
(Χο.) οὐ μαλθακιστέ', ἀλλὰ περικαλυπτέα·
ἐξευρετέος γὰρ νοῦς ἀποστερητικὸς
κἀπαιόλημ'.
       (Στ.) οἴμοι, τίς ἂν δῆτ' ἐπιβάλοι
ἐξ ἀρνακίδων γνώμην ἀποστερητρίδα;   730
(Σω.) φέρε νυν ἀθρήσω πρῶτον, ὅ τι δρᾷ, τουτονί.
οὗτος, καθεύδεις;
       (Στ.) μὰ τὸν Ἀπόλλω 'γὼ μὲν οὔ.
(Σω.) ἔχεις τι;
       (Στ.) μὰ Δί' οὐ δῆτ' ἔγωγ'.
              (Σω.) οὐδὲν πάνυ;
(Στ.) οὐδέν γε πλὴν εἰ τὸ πέος ἐν τῇ δεξιᾷ.
(Σω.) οὐκ ἐγκαλυψάμενος ταχέως τι φροντιεῖς;   735
(Στ.) περὶ τοῦ; σὺ γάρ μοι τοῦτο φράσον, ὦ Σώκρατες.
(Σω.) αὐτὸς ὅ τι βούλει πρῶτος ἐξευρὼν λέγε.
(Στ.) ἀκήκοας μυριάκις ἁγὼ βούλομαι,
περὶ τῶν τόκων, ὅπως ἂν ἀποδῶ μηδενί.
(Σω.) ἴθι νυν, καλύπτου καὶ σχάσας τὴν φροντίδα   740
λεπτὴν κατὰ μικρὸν περιφρόνει τὰ πράγματα
ὀρθῶς διαιρῶν καὶ σκοπῶν.
               (Στ.) οἴμοι τάλας.
(Σω.) ἔχ' ἀτρέμα· κἂν ἀπορῇς τι τῶν νοημάτων,
ἀφεὶς ἄπελθε, κᾆτα τῇ γνώμῃ πάλιν
κίνησον αὖθις αὐτὸ καὶ ζυγώθρισον.   745
(Στ.) ὦ Σωκρατίδιον φίλτατον—
              (Σω.) τί, ὦ γέρον;
(Στ.) ἔχω τόκου γνώμην ἀποστερητικήν.
(Σω.) ἐπίδειξον αὐτήν.
       (Στ.) εἰπὲ δή νύν μοι—
              (Σω.) τὸ τί;
(Στ.) γυναῖκα φαρμακίδ' εἰ πριάμενος Θετταλὴν
καθέλοιμι νύκτωρ τὴν σελήνην, εἶτα δὴ   750
αὐτὴν καθείρξαιμ' εἰς λοφεῖον στρογγύλον
ὥσπερ κάτροπτον, κᾆτα τηροίην ἔχων—
(Σω.) τί δῆτα τοῦτ' ἂν ὠφελήσειέν σ';
              (Στ.) ὅ τι;

εἰ μηκέτ᾽ ἀνατέλλοι σελήνη μηδαμοῦ,
οὐκ ἂν ἀποδοίην τοὺς τόκους.
            (Σω.) ὁτιὴ τί δή;   755
(Στ.) ὁτιὴ κατὰ μῆνα τἀργύριον δανείζεται.
(Σω.) εὖ γ᾽. ἀλλ᾽ ἕτερον αὖ σοι προβαλῶ τι δεξιόν.
εἴ σοι γράφοιτο πεντετάλαντός τις δίκη,
ὅπως ἂν αὐτὴν ἀφανίσειας, εἰπέ μοι.
(Στ.) ὅπως; ὅπως; οὐκ οἶδ᾽· ἀτὰρ ζητητέον.   760
(Σω.) μή νυν περὶ σαυτὸν εἶλλε τὴν γνώμην ἀεί,
ἀλλ᾽ ἀποχάλα τὴν φροντίδ᾽ εἰς τὸν ἀέρα
λινόδετον ὥσπερ μηλολόνθην τοῦ ποδός.
(Στ.) ηὕρηκ᾽ ἀφάνισιν τῆς δίκης σοφωτάτην,
ὥστ᾽ αὐτὸν ὁμολογεῖν σέ μοι.
            (Σω.) ποίαν τινά;   765
(Στ.) ἤδη παρὰ τοῖσι φαρμακοπώλαις τὴν λίθον
ταύτην ἑόρακας, τὴν καλήν, τὴν διαφανῆ,
ἀφ᾽ ἧς τὸ πῦρ ἅπτουσι;
            (Σω.) τὴν ὕαλον λέγεις;
(Στ.) ἔγωγε. φέρε, τί δῆτ᾽ ἄν, εἰ ταύτην λαβών,
ὁπότε γράφοιτο τὴν δίκην ὁ γραμματεύς,   770
ἀπωτέρω στὰς ὧδε πρὸς τὸν ἥλιον
τὰ γράμματ᾽ ἐκτήξαιμι τῆς ἐμῆς δίκης;
(Σω.) σοφῶς γε, νὴ τὰς Χάριτας.
               (Στ.) οἴμ᾽, ὡς ἥδομαι
ὅτι πεντετάλαντος διαγέγραπταί μοι δίκη.
(Σω.) ἄγε δή, ταχέως τουτὶ ξυνάρπασον—
                    (Στ.) τὸ τί;   775
(Σω.) ὅπως ἀποστρέψαις ἂν ἀντιδικῶν δίκην
μέλλων ὀφλήσειν μὴ παρόντων μαρτύρων.
(Στ.) φαυλότατα καὶ ῥᾷστ᾽.
            (Σω.) εἰπὲ δή.
                (Στ.) καὶ δὴ λέγω·
εἰ πρόσθεν ἔτι μιᾶς ἐνεστώσης δίκης,
πρὶν τὴν ἐμὴν καλεῖσθ᾽, ἀπαγξαίμην τρέχων.   780
(Σω.) οὐδὲν λέγεις.
          (Στ.) νὴ τοὺς θεοὺς ἔγωγ᾽, ἐπεὶ
οὐδεὶς κατ᾽ ἐμοῦ τεθνεῶτος εἰσάξει δίκην.
(Σω.) ὑθλεῖς. ἄπερρ᾽· οὐκ ἂν διδαξαίμην σ᾽ ἔτι.
(Στ.) ὁτιὴ τί; ναί, πρὸς τῶν θεῶν, ὦ Σώκρατες.
(Σω.) ἀλλ᾽ εὐθὺς ἐπιλήθει σύ γ᾽ ἅττ᾽ ἂν καὶ μάθης·   785
ἐπεὶ τί νυνὶ πρῶτον ἐδιδάχθης; λέγε.

(Στ.) φέρ' ἴδω, τί μέντοι πρῶτον ἦν; τί πρῶτον ἦν;
τίς ἦν ἐν ᾗ ματτόμεθα μέντοι τἄλφιτα;
οἴμοι, τίς ἦν;
    (Σω.) οὐκ ἐς κόρακας ἀποφθερεῖ,
ἐπιλησμότατον καὶ σκαιότατον γερόντιον;   790
(Στ.) οἴμοι. τί οὖν δῆθ' ὁ κακοδαίμων πείσομαι;
ἀπὸ γὰρ ὀλοῦμαι μὴ μαθὼν γλωττοστροφεῖν.
ἀλλ', ὦ Νεφέλαι, χρηστόν τι συμβουλεύσατε.
(Χο.) ἡμεῖς μέν, ὦ πρεσβῦτα, συμβουλεύομεν,
εἴ σοί τις υἱός ἐστιν ἐκτεθραμμένος,   795
πέμπειν ἐκεῖνον ἀντὶ σαυτοῦ μανθάνειν.
(Στ.) ἀλλ' ἔστ' ἔμοιγ' υἱὸς καλός τε κἀγαθός.
ἀλλ' οὐκ ἐθέλει γὰρ μανθάνειν, τί ἐγὼ πάθω;
(Χο.) σὺ δ' ἐπιτρέπεις;
           (Στ.) εὐσωματεῖ γὰρ καὶ σφριγᾷ,
κἄστ' ἐκ γυναικῶν εὐπτέρων καὶ Κοισύρας.   800
ἀτὰρ μέτειμί γ' αὐτόν· ἢν δὲ μὴ 'θέλῃ,
οὐκ ἔσθ' ὅπως οὐκ ἐξελῶ 'κ τῆς οἰκίας.
ἀλλ' ἐπανάμεινόν μ' ὀλίγον εἰσελθὼν χρόνον.
(Χο.) ἆρ' αἰσθάνει πλεῖστα δι' ἡ-   ἀντ.
    μᾶς ἀγάθ' αὐτίχ' ἕξων   805
μόνας θεῶν; ὡς ἕτοιμος ὅδ' ἐστὶν ἅπαν-
τα δρᾶν ὅσ' ἂν κελεύῃς.
σὺ δ' ἀνδρὸς ἐκπεπληγμένου
    καὶ φανερῶς ἐπηρμένου
γνοὺς ἀπολάψεις ὅτι πλεῖστον δύνασαι   810–11
ταχέως· φιλεῖ γάρ πως τὰ τοι-
    αῦθ' ἑτέρᾳ τρέπεσθαι.

(Στ.) οὔτοι μὰ τὴν Ὁμίχλην ἔτ' ἐνταυθοῖ μενεῖς·
ἀλλ' ἔσθι' ἐλθὼν τοὺς Μεγακλέους κίονας.   815
(Φε.) ὦ δαιμόνιε, τί χρῆμα πάσχεις, ὦ πάτερ;
οὐκ εὖ φρονεῖς, μὰ τὸν Δία τὸν Ὀλύμπιον.
(Στ.) ἰδού γ' ἰδοὺ Δί' Ὀλύμπιον· τῆς μωρίας,
τὸ Δία νομίζειν ὄντα τηλικουτονί.
(Φε.) τί δὲ τοῦτ' ἐγέλασας ἐτεόν;
                (Στ.) ἐνθυμούμενος   820
ὅτι παιδάριον εἶ καὶ φρονεῖς ἀρχαϊκά.
ὅμως γε μὴν πρόσελθ', ἵν' εἰδῇς πλείονα
καί σοι φράσω τι πρᾶγμ', ὃ μαθὼν ἀνὴρ ἔσει.
ὅπως δὲ τοῦτο μὴ διδάξεις μηδένα.

(Φε.) ἰδού· τί ἐστιν;
    (Στ.) ὤμοσας νυνὶ Δία.   825
(Φε.) ἔγωγ᾽.
    (Στ.) ὁρᾷς οὖν ὡς ἀγαθὸν τὸ μανθάνειν;
οὐκ ἔστιν, ὦ Φειδιππίδη, Ζεύς.
    (Φε.) ἀλλὰ τίς;
(Στ.) Δῖνος βασιλεύει τὸν Δί᾽ ἐξεληλακώς.
(Φε.) αἰβοῖ· τί ληρεῖς;
    (Στ.) ἴσθι τοῦθ᾽ οὕτως ἔχον.
(Φε.) τίς φησι ταῦτα;
    (Στ.) Σωκράτης ὁ Μήλιος   830
καὶ Χαιρεφῶν, ὃς οἶδε τὰ ψυλλῶν ἴχνη.
(Φε.) σὺ δ᾽ εἰς τοσοῦτον τῶν μανιῶν ἐλήλυθας
ὥστ᾽ ἀνδράσιν πείθει χολῶσιν;
    (Στ.) εὐστόμει
καὶ μηδὲν εἴπῃς φλαῦρον ἄνδρας δεξιοὺς
καὶ νοῦν ἔχοντας, ὧν ὑπὸ τῆς φειδωλίας   835
ἀπεκείρατ᾽ οὐδεὶς πώποτ᾽, οὐδ᾽ ἠλείψατο,
οὐδ᾽ εἰς βαλανεῖον ἦλθε λουσόμενος· σὺ δὲ
ὥσπερ τεθνεῶτος καταλόει μου τὸν βίον.
ἀλλ᾽ ὡς τάχιστ᾽ ἐλθὼν ὑπὲρ ἐμοῦ μάνθανε.
(Φε.) τί δ᾽ ἂν παρ᾽ ἐκείνων καὶ μάθοι χρηστόν τις ἄν;   840
(Στ.) ἄληθες; ὅσαπέρ ἐστιν ἀνθρώποις σοφά·
γνώσει δὲ σαυτὸν ὡς ἀμαθὴς εἶ καὶ παχύς.
ἀλλ᾽ ἐπανάμεινόν μ᾽ ὀλίγον ἐνταυθοῖ χρόνον.
(Φε.) οἴμοι· τί δράσω παραφρονοῦντος τοῦ πατρός;
πότερον παρανοίας αὐτὸν εἰσαγαγὼν ἕλω   845
ἢ τοῖς σοροπηγοῖς τὴν μανίαν αὐτοῦ φράσω;
(Στ.) φέρ᾽ ἴδω, σὺ τοῦτον τίνα νομίζεις; εἰπέ μοι.
(Φε.) ἀλεκτρυόνα.
    (Στ.) καλῶς γε. ταυτηνὶ δὲ τί;
(Φε.) ἀλεκτρυόν᾽.
    (Στ.) ἄμφω ταὐτό; καταγέλαστος εἶ.
μή νυν τὸ λοιπόν, ἀλλὰ τήνδε μὲν καλεῖν   850
ἀλεκτρύαιναν, τουτονὶ δ᾽ ἀλέκτορα.
(Φε.) ἀλεκτρύαιναν; ταῦτ᾽ ἔμαθες τὰ δεξιὰ
εἴσω παρελθὼν ἄρτι παρὰ τοὺς γηγενεῖς;
(Στ.) χἀτερά γε πόλλ᾽· ἀλλ᾽ ὅ τι μάθοιμ᾽ ἑκάστοτε,
ἐπελανθανόμην ἂν εὐθὺς ὑπὸ πλήθους ἐτῶν.   855
(Φε.) διὰ ταῦτα δὴ καὶ θοἰμάτιον ἀπώλεσας;
(Στ.) ἀλλ᾽ οὐκ ἀπολώλεκ᾽, ἀλλὰ καταπεφρόντικα.

(Φε.) τὰς δ' ἐμβάδας ποῖ τέτροφας, ὦνόητε σύ;
(Στ.) ὥσπερ Περικλέης, εἰς τὸ δέον ἀπώλεσα.
ἀλλ' ἴθι βάδιζ', ἴωμεν· εἶτα τῷ πατρὶ   860
πιθόμενος ἐξάμαρτε· κἀγώ τοί ποτε,
οἶδ', ἐξέτει σοι τραυλίσαντι πιθόμενος·
ὃν πρῶτον ὀβολὸν ἔλαβον ἡλιαστικόν,
τούτου 'πριάμην σοι Διασίοις ἁμαξίδα.
(Φε.) ἦ μὴν σὺ τούτοις τῷ χρόνῳ ποτ' ἀχθέσει.   865
(Στ.) εὖ γ', ὅτι ἐπείσθης. δεῦρο δεῦρ', ὦ Σώκρατες,
ἔξελθ'· ἄγω γάρ σοι τὸν υἱὸν τουτονὶ
ἄκοντ' ἀναπείσας.
                    (Σω.) νηπύτιος γάρ ἐστ' ἔτι
καὶ τῶν κρεμαστῶν οὐ τρίβων τῶν ἐνθάδε.
(Φε.) αὐτὸς τρίβων εἴης ἄν, εἰ κρέμαιό γε.   870
(Στ.) οὐκ ἐς κόρακας; καταρᾷ σὺ τῷ διδασκάλῳ;
(Σω.) ἰδοὺ "κρέμαι"'· ὡς ἠλίθιον ἐφθέγξατο
καὶ τοῖσι χείλεσιν διερρυηκόσιν.
πῶς ἂν μάθοι ποθ' οὗτος ἀπόφευξιν δίκης
ἢ κλῆσιν ἢ χαύνωσιν ἀναπειστηρίαν;   875
καίτοι ταλάντου τοῦτ' ἔμαθεν Ὑπέρβολος.
(Στ.) ἀμέλει, δίδασκε. θυμόσοφός ἐστιν φύσει·
εὐθύς γέ τοι παιδάριον ὂν τυννουτονὶ
ἔπλαττεν ἔνδον οἰκίας ναῦς τ' ἔγλυφεν
ἁμαξίδας τε συκίνας ἠργάζετο,   880
κἀκ τῶν σιδίων βατράχους ἐποίει, πῶς δοκεῖς;
ὅπως δ' ἐκείνω τὼ λόγω μαθήσεται,
τὸν κρείττον', ὅστις ἐστί, καὶ τὸν ἥττονα,
ὃς τἄδικα λέγων ἀνατρέπει τὸν κρείττονα·
ἐὰν δὲ μή, τὸν γοῦν ἄδικον πάσῃ τέχνῃ.   885
(Σω.) αὐτὸς μαθήσεται παρ' αὐτοῖν τοῖν λόγοιν.
ἐγὼ δ' ἀπέσομαι.
                (Στ.) τοῦτό νυν μέμνησ', ὅπως
πρὸς πάντα τὰ δίκαι' ἀντιλέγειν δυνήσεται.

ΚΡΕΙΤΤΩΝ ΛΟΓΟΣ
χώρει δευρί, δεῖξον σαυτὸν
τοῖσι θεαταῖς, καίπερ θρασὺς ὤν.   890

ΗΤΤΩΝ ΛΟΓΟΣ
ἴθ' ὅποι χρῄζεις· πολὺ γὰρ μᾶλλόν σ'
ἐν τοῖς πολλοῖσι λέγων ἀπολῶ.

(Κρ.) ἀπολεῖς σύ; τίς ὤν;
                (Ητ.) λόγος.
                      (Κρ.) ἥττων γ' ὤν.
(Ητ.) ἀλλά σε νικῶ τὸν ἐμοῦ κρείττω
φάσκοντ' εἶναι.
         (Κρ.) τί σοφὸν ποῶν;   895
(Ητ.) γνώμας καινὰς ἐξευρίσκων.
(Κρ.) ταῦτα γὰρ ἀνθεῖ διὰ τουτουσὶ
τοὺς ἀνοήτους.
(Ητ.) οὔκ, ἀλλὰ σοφούς.
            (Κρ.) ἀπολῶ σε κακῶς.
(Ητ.) εἰπέ, τί ποιῶν;
          (Κρ.) τὰ δίκαια λέγων.   900
(Ητ.) ἀλλ' ἀνατρέψω γ' αὔτ' ἀντιλέγων·
οὐδὲ γὰρ εἶναι πάνυ φημὶ Δίκην.
(Κρ.) οὐκ εἶναι φής;
         (Ητ.) φέρε γάρ, ποῦ 'στιν;
(Κρ.) παρὰ τοῖσι θεοῖς.   904a
(Ητ.) πῶς δῆτα Δίκης οὔσης ὁ Ζεὺς   904b
οὐκ ἀπόλωλεν τὸν πατέρ' αὑτοῦ   905
δήσας;
      (Κρ.) αἰβοῖ, τουτὶ καὶ δὴ
χωρεῖ τὸ κακόν· δότε μοι λεκάνην.
(Ητ.) τυφογέρων εἶ κἀνάρμοστος.
(Κρ.) καταπύγων εἶ κἀναίσχυντος.
(Ητ.) ῥόδα μ' εἴρηκας.
        (Κρ.) καὶ βωμολόχος.   910
(Ητ.) κρίνεσι στεφανοῖς.
          (Κρ.) καὶ πατραλοίας.
(Ητ.) χρυσῷ πάττων μ' οὐ γιγνώσκεις.
(Κρ.) οὐ δῆτα πρὸ τοῦ γ', ἀλλὰ μολύβδῳ.
(Ητ.) νῦν δέ γε κόσμος τοῦτ' ἐστὶν ἐμοί.
(Κρ.) θρασὺς εἶ πολλοῦ.
           (Ητ.) σὺ δέ γ' ἀρχαῖος.   915
(Κρ.) διὰ σὲ δὲ φοιτᾶν
οὐδεὶς ἐθέλει τῶν μειρακίων·
καὶ γνωσθήσει ποτ' Ἀθηναίοις
οἷα διδάσκεις τοὺς ἀνοήτους.
(Ητ.) αὐχμεῖς αἰσχρῶς.
         (Κρ.) σὺ δέ γ' εὖ πράττεις.   920
καίτοι πρότερόν γ' ἐπτώχευες,

Τήλεφος εἶναι Μυσὸς φάσκων,
ἐκ πηριδίου
γνώμας τρώγων Πανδελετείους.
(Ητ.) ὤμοι σοφίας—
　　　　(Κρ.) οἴμοι μανίας—　　　　　　925
(Ητ.) ἧς ἐμνήσθης—
　　　　(Κρ.) τῆς σῆς πόλεώς θ᾽
ἥτις σε τρέφει
λυμαινόμενον τοῖς μειρακίοις.
(Ητ.) οὐχὶ διδάξεις τοῦτον Κρόνος ὤν.
(Κρ.) εἴπερ γ᾽ αὐτὸν σωθῆναι χρὴ　　　930
καὶ μὴ λαλιὰν μόνον ἀσκῆσαι.
(Ητ.) δεῦρ᾽ ἴθι, τοῦτον δ᾽ ἔα μαίνεσθαι.
(Κρ.) κλαύσει, τὴν χεῖρ᾽ ἢν ἐπιβάλλῃς.
(Χο.) παύσασθε μάχης καὶ λοιδορίας.
ἀλλ᾽ ἐπίδειξαι　　　　　　　　　935
σύ τε τοὺς προτέρους ἅττ᾽ ἐδίδασκες,
σύ τε τὴν καινὴν　　　　　　　937a
παίδευσιν, ὅπως ἂν ἀκούσας σφῷν　　937b
ἀντιλεγόντοιν κρίνας φοιτᾷ.
(Κρ.) δρᾶν ταῦτ᾽ ἐθέλω.
　　　　(Ητ.) κἄγωγ᾽ ἐθέλω.
(Χο.) φέρε δή, πότερος λέξει πρότερος;　　940
(Ητ.) τούτῳ δώσω·
κᾆτ᾽ ἐκ τούτων ὧν ἂν λέξῃ
ῥηματίοισιν καινοῖς αὐτὸν
καὶ διανοίαις κατατοξεύσω,
τὸ τελευταῖον δ᾽, ἢν ἀναγρύζῃ,　　　945
τὸ πρόσωπον ἅπαν καὶ τὠφθαλμὼ
κεντούμενος ὥσπερ ὑπ᾽ ἀνθρηνῶν
ὑπὸ τῶν γνωμῶν ἀπολεῖται.

(Χο.) νῦν δείξετον τὼ πισύνω　　　στρ.
τοῖς περιδεξίοισιν　　　　　　950
λόγοισι καὶ φροντίσι καὶ
　　γνωμοτύποις μερίμναις
† ὁπότερος αὐτοῖν λέγων
　　ἀμείνων φανήσεται· † νῦν γὰρ ἅπας
ἐνθάδε κίνδυνος ἀνεῖται σοφίας,　　955
ἧς πέρι τοῖς ἐμοῖς φίλοις
　　ἐστὶν ἀγὼν μέγιστος.

ἀλλ', ὦ πολλοῖς τοὺς πρεσβυτέρους ἤθεσι χρηστοῖς στεφανώσας,
ῥῆξον φωνὴν ᾗτινι χαίρεις, καὶ τὴν σαυτοῦ φύσιν εἰπέ.   960
(Κρ.) λέξω τοίνυν τὴν ἀρχαίαν παιδείαν ὡς διέκειτο
ὅτ' ἐγὼ τὰ δίκαια λέγων ἤνθουν καὶ σωφροσύνη 'νενόμιστο.
πρῶτον μὲν ἔδει παιδὸς φωνὴν γρύξαντος μηδέν' ἀκοῦσαι·
εἶτα βαδίζειν ἐν ταῖσιν ὁδοῖς εὐτάκτως εἰς κιθαριστοῦ
τοὺς κωμήτας γυμνοὺς ἁθρόους, κεἰ κριμνώδη κατανείφοι.   965
εἶτ' αὖ προμαθεῖν ᾆσμ' ἐδίδασκεν, τὼ μηρὼ μὴ ξυνέχοντας,
ἢ "Παλλάδα περσέπολιν δεινάν" ἢ "τηλέπορόν τι βόαμα",
ἐντειναμένους τὴν ἁρμονίαν ἣν οἱ πατέρες παρέδωκαν.
εἰ δέ τις αὐτῶν βωμολοχεύσαιτ' ἢ κάμψειέν τινα καμπήν,   969
οἵας οἱ νῦν, τὰς κατὰ Φρῦνιν ταύτας τὰς δυσκολοκάμπτους,   971
ἐπετρίβετο τυπτόμενος πολλὰς ὡς τὰς Μούσας ἀφανίζων.
ἐν παιδοτρίβου δὲ καθίζοντας τὸν μηρὸν ἔδει προβαλέσθαι
τοὺς παῖδας, ὅπως τοῖς ἔξωθεν μηδὲν δείξειαν ἀπηνές·
εἶτ' αὖ πάλιν αὖθις ἀνισταμένους συμψῆσαι, καὶ προνοεῖσθαι   975
εἴδωλον τοῖσιν ἐρασταῖσιν τῆς ἥβης μὴ καταλείπειν.
ἠλείψατο δ' ἂν τοὐμφαλοῦ οὐδεὶς παῖς ὑπένερθεν τότ' ἄν, ὥστε
τοῖς αἰδοίοισι δρόσος καὶ χνοῦς, ὥσπερ μήλοισιν, ἐπήνθει·
οὐδ' ἂν μαλακὴν φυρασάμενος τὴν φωνήν πρὸς τὸν ἐραστὴν
αὐτὸς ἑαυτὸν προαγωγεύων τοῖν ὀφθαλμοῖν ἐβάδιζεν,   980
οὐδ' ἂν ἑλέσθαι δειπνοῦντ' ἐξῆν κεφάλαιον τῆς ῥαφανῖδος,
οὐδ' ἂν ἄνηθον τῶν πρεσβυτέρων ἁρπάζειν οὐδὲ σέλινον,
οὐδ' ὀψοφαγεῖν, οὐδὲ κιχλίζειν, οὐδ' ἴσχειν τὼ πόδ' ἐναλλάξ.
(Ητ.) ἀρχαῖά γε καὶ Διπολιώδη καὶ τεττίγων ἀνάμεστα
καὶ Κηκείδου καὶ Βουφονίων.
                               (Κρ.) ἀλλ' οὖν ταῦτ' ἐστὶν ἐκεῖνα   985
ἐξ ὧν ἄνδρας Μαραθωνομάχας ἡμὴ παίδευσις ἔθρεψεν.
σὺ δὲ τοὺς νῦν εὐθὺς ἐν ἱματίοισι διδάσκεις ἐντετυλίχθαι·
ὥστε μ' ἀπάγχεσθ' ὅταν, ὀρχεῖσθαι Παναθηναίοις δέον αὐτούς,
τὴν ἀσπίδα τῆς κωλῆς προέχων ἀμελῇ τις Τριτογενείας.
πρὸς ταῦτ', ὦ μειράκιον, θαρρῶν ἐμὲ τὸν κρείττω λόγον αἱροῦ·   990
κἀπιστήσει μισεῖν ἀγορὰν καὶ βαλανείων ἀπέχεσθαι,
καὶ τοῖς αἰσχροῖς αἰσχύνεσθαι, κἂν σκώπτῃ τίς σε, φλέγεσθαι,
καὶ τῶν θάκων τοῖς πρεσβυτέροις ὑπανίστασθαι προσιοῦσιν
καὶ μὴ περὶ τοὺς σαυτοῦ γονέας σκαιουργεῖν ἄλλο τε μηδὲν
αἰσχρὸν ποιεῖν, ὅ τι τῆς Αἰδοῦς μέλλει τἀγάλμ' ἀναπλήσειν,   995
μηδ' εἰς ὀρχηστρίδος εἰσάττειν, ἵνα μὴ πρὸς ταῦτα κεχηνὼς
μήλῳ βληθεὶς ὑπὸ πορνιδίου τῆς εὐκλείας ἀποθραυσθῇς,
μηδ' ἀντειπεῖν τῷ πατρὶ μηδέν, μηδ' Ἰαπετὸν καλέσαντα
μνησικακῆσαι τὴν ἡλικίαν ἐξ ἧς ἐνεοττοτροφήθης.

(Ητ.) εἰ ταῦτ᾽, ὦ μειράκιον, πείσει τούτῳ, νὴ τὸν Διόνυσον   1000
τοῖς Ἱπποκράτους υἱέσιν εἴξεις καί σε καλοῦσι βλιτομάμμαν.
(Κρ.) ἀλλ᾽ οὖν λιπαρός γε καὶ εὐανθὴς ἐν γυμνασίοις διατρίψεις,
οὐ στωμύλλων κατὰ τὴν ἀγορὰν τριβολεκτράπελ᾽, οἷάπερ οἱ νῦν,
οὐδ᾽ ἑλκόμενος περὶ πραγματίου γλισχραντιλογεξεπιτρίπτου·
ἀλλ᾽ εἰς Ἀκαδήμειαν κατιὼν ὑπὸ ταῖς μορίαις ἀποθρέξει   1005
στεφανωσάμενος καλάμῳ λεπτῷ μετὰ σώφρονος ἡλικιώτου,
σμίλακος ὄζων καὶ ἀπραγμοσύνης καὶ λεύκης φυλλοβολούσης
ἦρός θ᾽ ὥρᾳ χαίρων, ὁπόταν πλάτανος πτελέᾳ ψιθυρίζῃ.
ἢν ταῦτα ποῇς ἁγὼ φράζω,
καὶ πρὸς τούτοις προσέχῃς τὸν νοῦν,   1010
ἕξεις αἰεὶ
στῆθος λιπαρόν, χροιὰν λαμπράν,
ὤμους μεγάλους, γλῶτταν βαιάν,
πυγὴν μεγάλην, πόσθην μικράν.
ἢν δ᾽ ἅπερ οἱ νῦν ἐπιτηδεύῃς,   1015
πρῶτα μὲν ἕξεις
χροιὰν ὠχράν, ὤμους μικρούς,
στῆθος λεπτόν, γλῶτταν μεγάλην,
πυγὴν μικράν, ψήφισμα μακρόν·
καί σ᾽ ἀναπείσει τὸ μὲν αἰσχρὸν ἅπαν   1020
καλὸν ἡγεῖσθαι, τὸ καλὸν δ᾽ αἰσχρόν·
καὶ πρὸς τούτοις τῆς Ἀντιμάχου
καταπυγοσύνης ἀναπλήσει.

(Χο.) ὦ καλλίπυργον σοφίαν   ἀντ.
κλεινοτάτην ἐπασκῶν,   1025
ὡς ἡδύ σου τοῖσι λόγοις
          σῶφρον ἔπεστιν ἄνθος.
εὐδαίμονές γ᾽ ἦσαν ἄρ᾽ οἱ
          ζῶντες τότ᾽ ἐπὶ τῶν προτέρων·
πρὸς τάδε σ᾽, ὦ κομψοπρεπῆ μοῦσαν ἔχων,   1030–1
δεῖ σε λέγειν τι καινόν, ὡς
          ηὐδοκίμηκεν ἀνήρ.

δεινῶν δέ σοι βουλευμάτων ἔοικε δεῖν πρὸς αὐτόν,
εἴπερ τὸν ἄνδρ᾽ ὑπερβαλεῖ καὶ μὴ γέλωτ᾽ ὀφλήσεις.   1035

(Ητ.) καὶ μὴν πάλαι ᾽γὼ ᾽πνιγόμην τὰ σπλάγχνα κἀπεθύμουν
ἅπαντα ταῦτ᾽ ἐναντίαις γνώμαισι συνταράξαι·
ἐγὼ γὰρ Ἥττων μὲν Λόγος δι᾽ αὐτὸ τοῦτ᾽ ἐκλήθην

ἐν τοῖσι φροντισταῖσιν, ὅτι πρώτιστος ἐπενόησα
τοῖσιν νόμοις καὶ ταῖς δίκαις τἀναντί᾽ ἀντιλέξαι.   1040
καὶ τοῦτο πλεῖν ἢ μυρίων ἔστ᾽ ἄξιον στατήρων,
αἱρούμενον τοὺς ἥττονας λόγους ἔπειτα νικᾶν.
σκέψαι δὲ τὴν παίδευσιν ᾗ πέποιθεν, ὡς ἐλέγξω,
ὅστις σε θερμῷ φησὶ λοῦσθαι πρῶτον οὐκ ἐάσειν.
καίτοι τίνα γνώμην ἔχων ψέγεις τὰ θερμὰ λουτρά;   1045
(Κρ.) ὁτιὴ κάκιστόν ἐστι καὶ δειλὸν ποεῖ τὸν ἄνδρα.
(Ητ.) ἐπίσχες· εὐθὺς γάρ σε μέσον ἔχω λαβὴν ἄφυκτον.
καί μοι φράσον· τῶν τοῦ Διὸς παίδων τίν᾽ ἄνδρ᾽ ἄριστον
ψυχὴν νομίζεις, εἰπέ, καὶ πλείστους πόνους πονῆσαι;
(Κρ.) ἐγὼ μὲν οὐδέν᾽ Ἡρακλέους βελτίον᾽ ἄνδρα κρίνω.   1050
(Ητ.) ποῦ ψυχρὰ δῆτα πώποτ᾽ εἶδες Ἡράκλεια λουτρά;
καίτοι τίς ἀνδρειότερος ἦν;
                            (Κρ.) ταῦτ᾽ ἐστὶ ταῦτ᾽ ἐκεῖνα,
ἃ τῶν νεανίσκων ἀεὶ δι᾽ ἡμέρας λαλούντων
πλῆρες τὸ βαλανεῖον ποεῖ, κενὰς δὲ τὰς παλαίστρας.
(Ητ.) εἶτ᾽ ἐν ἀγορᾷ τὴν διατριβὴν ψέγεις· ἐγὼ δ᾽ ἐπαινῶ.   1055
εἰ γὰρ πονηρὸν ἦν, Ὅμηρος οὐδέποτ᾽ ἂν ἐποίει
τὸν Νέστορ᾽ ἀγορητὴν ἄν, οὐδὲ τοὺς σοφοὺς ἅπαντας.
ἄνειμι δῆτ᾽ ἐντεῦθεν εἰς τὴν γλῶτταν, ἣν ὁδὶ μὲν
οὔ φησι χρῆναι τοὺς νέους ἀσκεῖν, ἐγὼ δέ φημι·
καὶ σωφρονεῖν αὖ φησι χρῆναι· δύο κακὼ μεγίστω.   1060
ἐπεὶ σὺ διὰ τὸ σωφρονεῖν τῷ πώποτ᾽ εἶδες ἤδη
ἀγαθόν τι γενόμενον; φράσον, καί μ᾽ ἐξέλεγξον εἰπών.
(Κρ.) πολλοῖς· ὁ γοῦν Πηλεὺς ἔλαβε διὰ τοῦτο τὴν μάχαιραν.
(Ητ.) μάχαιραν; ἀστεῖόν γε κέρδος ἔλαβεν ὁ κακοδαίμων.
Ὑπέρβολος δ᾽ οὐκ τῶν λύχνων πλεῖν ἢ τάλαντα πολλὰ   1065
εἴληφε διὰ πονηρίαν, ἀλλ᾽ οὐ μὰ Δί᾽ οὐ μάχαιραν.
(Κρ.) καὶ τὴν Θέτιν γ᾽ ἔγημε διὰ τὸ σωφρονεῖν ὁ Πηλεύς.
(Ητ.) κᾆτ᾽ ἀπολιποῦσά γ᾽ αὐτὸν ᾤχετ᾽· οὐ γὰρ ἦν ὑβριστής,
οὐδ᾽ ἡδὺς ἐν τοῖς στρώμασιν τὴν νύκτα παννυχίζειν·
γυνὴ δὲ σιναμωρουμένη χαίρει. σὺ δ᾽ εἶ Κρόνιππος.   1070
σκέψαι γάρ, ὦ μειράκιον, ἐν τῷ σωφρονεῖν ἅπαντα
ἄνεστιν ἡδονῶν θ᾽ ὅσων μέλλεις ἀποστερεῖσθαι,
παίδων, γυναικῶν, κοττάβων, ὄψων, πότων, καχασμῶν.
καίτοι τί σοι ζῆν ἄξιον, τούτων ἐὰν στερηθῇς;
εἶέν. πάρειμ᾽ ἐντεῦθεν εἰς τὰς τῆς φύσεως ἀνάγκας.   1075
ἥμαρτες, ἠράσθης, ἐμοίχευσάς τι, κᾆτ᾽ ἐλήφθης·
ἀπόλωλας, ἀδύνατος γὰρ εἶ λέγειν. ἐμοὶ δ᾽ ὁμιλῶν
χρῶ τῇ φύσει, σκίρτα, γέλα, νόμιζε μηδὲν αἰσχρόν·

μοιχὸς γὰρ ἦν τύχῃς ἁλούς, τάδ' ἀντερεῖς πρὸς αὐτόν,
ὡς οὐδὲν ἠδίκηκας. εἶτ' εἰς τὸν Δί' ἐπανενεγκεῖν,   1080
κἀκεῖνος ὡς ἥττων ἔρωτός ἐστι καὶ γυναικῶν·
καίτοι σὺ θνητὸς ὢν θεοῦ πῶς μεῖζον ἂν δύναιο;
(Κρ.) τί δ', ἢν ῥαφανιδωθῇ πιθόμενός σοι τέφρᾳ τε τιλθῇ;
ἕξει τινὰ γνώμην λέγειν τὸ μὴ εὐρύπρωκτος εἶναι;
(Ητ.) ἢν δ' εὐρύπρωκτος ᾖ, τί πείσεται κακόν;   1085
(Κρ.) τί μὲν οὖν ἂν ἔτι μεῖζον πάθοι τούτου ποτέ;
(Ητ.) τί δῆτ' ἐρεῖς, ἢν τοῦτο νικηθῇς ἐμοῦ;
(Κρ.) σιγήσομαι. τί δ' ἄλλο;
                    (Ητ.) φέρε δή μοι φράσον·
συνηγοροῦσιν ἐκ τίνων;
(Κρ.) ἐξ εὐρυπρώκτων.
                    (Ητ.) πείθομαι.   1090
τί δαί; τραγῳδοῦσ' ἐκ τίνων;
(Κρ.) ἐξ εὐρυπρώκτων.
                    (Ητ.) εὖ λέγεις.
δημηγοροῦσι δ' ἐκ τίνων;
(Κρ.) ἐξ εὐρυπρώκτων.
                    (Ητ.) ἆρα δῆτ'
ἔγνωκας ὡς οὐδὲν λέγεις;   1095
καὶ τῶν θεατῶν ὁπότεροι πλείους σκόπει.
(Κρ.) καὶ δὴ σκοπῶ.
                    (Ητ.) τί δῆθ' ὁρᾷς;
(Κρ.) πολὺ πλείονας, νὴ τοὺς θεούς,
τοὺς εὐρυπρώκτους· τουτονὶ
    γοῦν οἶδ' ἐγὼ κἀκεινονὶ
καὶ τὸν κομήτην τουτονί.   1100
(Ητ.) τί δῆτ' ἐρεῖς;
(Κρ.) ἡττήμεθ'. ὦ βινούμενοι,
πρὸς τῶν θεῶν δέξασθέ μου θοἰμάτιον, ὡς
    ἐξαυτομολῶ πρὸς ὑμᾶς.

(Ητ.) τί δῆτα; πότερα τοῦτον ἀπάγεσθαι λαβὼν   1105
βούλει τὸν υἱόν, ἢ διδάσκω σοι λέγειν;
(Στ.) δίδασκε καὶ κόλαζε, καὶ μέμνησ' ὅπως
εὖ μοι στομώσεις αὐτὸν ἐπὶ μὲν θάτερα
οἷον δικιδίοις, τὴν δ' ἑτέραν αὐτοῦ γνάθον
στόμωσον οἵαν εἰς τὰ μείζω πράγματα.   1110
(Ητ.) ἀμέλει, κομιεῖ τοῦτον σοφιστὴν δεξιόν.
(Φε.) ὠχρὸν μὲν οὖν οἶμαί γε καὶ κακοδαίμονα.

(Χο.) χωρεῖτέ νυν. οἶμαι δὲ σοὶ
  ταῦτα μεταμελήσειν.

τοὺς κριτὰς ἃ κερδανοῦσιν, ἤν τι τόνδε τὸν χορὸν   1115
ὠφελῶσ᾽ ἐκ τῶν δικαίων, βουλόμεσθ᾽ ἡμεῖς φράσαι·
πρῶτα μὲν γάρ, ἢν νεᾶν βούλησθ᾽ ἐν ὥρᾳ τοὺς ἀγρούς,
ὕσομεν πρώτοισιν ὑμῖν, τοῖσι δ᾽ ἄλλοις ὕστερον.
εἶτα τὰς καρπὸν τεκούσας ἀμπέλους φυλάξομεν,
ὥστε μήτ᾽ αὐχμὸν πιέζειν μήτ᾽ ἄγαν ἐπομβρίαν.   1120
ἢν δ᾽ ἀτιμάσῃ τις ἡμᾶς θνητὸς ὢν οὔσας θεάς,
προσεχέτω τὸν νοῦν, πρὸς ἡμῶν οἷα πείσεται κακὰ
λαμβάνων οὔτ᾽ οἶνον οὔτ᾽ ἄλλ᾽ οὐδὲν ἐκ τοῦ χωρίου·
ἡνίκ᾽ ἂν γὰρ αἵ τ᾽ ἐλαῖαι βλαστάνωσ᾽ αἵ τ᾽ ἄμπελοι,
ἀποκεκόψονται· τοιαύταις σφενδόναις παιήσομεν.   1125
ἢν δὲ πλινθεύοντ᾽ ἴδωμεν, ὕσομεν καὶ τοῦ τέγους
τὸν κέραμον αὐτοῦ χαλάζαις στρογγύλαις συντρίψομεν.
κἂν γαμῇ ποτ᾽ αὐτὸς ἢ τῶν ξυγγενῶν ἢ τῶν φίλων,
ὕσομεν τὴν νύκτα πᾶσαν, ὥστ᾽ ἴσως βουλήσεται
κἂν ἐν Αἰγύπτῳ τυχεῖν ὢν μᾶλλον ἢ κρῖναι κακῶς.   1130

(Στ.) πέμπτη, τετράς, τρίτη, μετὰ ταύτην δευτέρα,
εἶθ᾽, ἣν ἐγὼ μάλιστα πασῶν ἡμερῶν
δέδοικα καὶ πέφρικα καὶ βδελύττομαι,
εὐθὺς μετὰ ταύτην ἔσθ᾽ ἔνη τε καὶ νέα·
πᾶς γάρ τις ὀμνύς, οἷς ὀφείλων τυγχάνω,   1135
θείς μοι πρυτανεῖ᾽ ἀπολεῖν μέ φησι κἀξολεῖν·
ἐμοῦ τε μέτρια καὶ δίκαι᾽ αἰτουμένου,
"ὦ δαιμόνιε, τὸ μέν τι νυνὶ μὴ λάβῃς,
τὸ δ᾽ ἀναβαλοῦ μοι, τὸ δ᾽ ἄφες", οὔ φασίν ποτε
οὕτως ἀπολήψεσθ᾽, ἀλλὰ λοιδοροῦσί με,   1140
ὡς ἄδικός εἰμι, καὶ δικάσεσθαί φασί μοι.
νῦν οὖν δικαζέσθων· ὀλίγον γάρ μοι μέλει,
εἴπερ μεμάθηκεν εὖ λέγειν Φειδιππίδης.
τάχα δ᾽ εἴσομαι κόψας τὸ φροντιστήριον.
παῖ, ἠμί, παῖ παῖ.
          (Ητ.) Στρεψιάδην ἀσπάζομαι.   1145
(Στ.) κἄγωγέ σ᾽. ἀλλὰ τουτονὶ πρῶτον λαβέ·
χρὴ γὰρ ἐπιθαυμάζειν τι τὸν διδάσκαλον.
καί μοι τὸν υἱὸν εἰ μεμάθηκε τὸν λόγον
ἐκεῖνον, εἴφ᾽, ὃν ἀρτίως εἰσήγαγες.
(Ητ.) μεμάθηκεν—

(Στ.) εὖ γ', ὦ παμβασίλει' Ἀπαιόλη.   1150
(Ητ.) ὥστ' ἀποφύγοις ἂν ἥντιν' ἂν βούλῃ δίκην.
(Στ.) κεἰ μάρτυρες παρῆσαν ὅτ' ἐδανειζόμην;
(Ητ.) πολλῷ γε μᾶλλον, κἂν παρῶσι χίλιοι.

(Στ.) βοάσομαι τἄρα τὰν ὑπέρτονον
βοάν. ἰώ, κλάετ', ὦβολοστάται   1155
αὐτοί τε καὶ τἀρχαῖα χοἰ τόκοι τόκων·
οὐδὲν γὰρ ἄν με φλαῦρον ἐργάσαισθ' ἔτι,
οἷος ἐμοὶ τρέφεται
τοῖσδ' ἐνὶ δώμασι παῖς,
ἀμφήκει γλώττῃ λάμπων,   1160
πρόβολος ἐμός, σωτὴρ δόμοις, ἐχθροῖς βλάβη,
λυσανίας πατρῴων μεγάλων κακῶν·
ὃν κάλεσον τρέχων ἔνδοθεν ὡς ἐμέ.   1163–4
ὦ τέκνον, ὦ παῖ, ἔξελθ' οἴκων,   1165
ἄιε σοῦ πατρός.
(Ητ.) ὅδ' ἐκεῖνος ἀνήρ.
(Στ.) ὦ φίλος, ὦ φίλος.
(Ητ.) ἄπιθι λαβών.
(Στ.) ἰὼ ἰώ, τέκνον.   1170

ἰοὺ ἰού·   1171a
ὡς ἥδομαί σου πρῶτα τὴν χροιὰν ἰδών.   1171b
νῦν μέν γ' ἰδεῖν εἶ πρῶτον ἐξαρνητικὸς
κἀντιλογικός, καὶ τοῦτο τοὐπιχώριον
ἀτεχνῶς ἐπανθεῖ, τὸ "τί λέγεις σύ;" καὶ δοκεῖν
ἀδικοῦντ' ἀδικεῖσθαι καὶ κακουργοῦντ', οἶδ' ὅτι·   1175
ἐπὶ τοῦ προσώπου τ' ἐστὶν Ἀττικὸν βλέπος.
νῦν οὖν ὅπως σώσεις μ', ἐπεὶ κἀπώλεσας.
(Φε.) φοβεῖ δὲ δὴ τί;
            (Στ.) τὴν ἕνην τε καὶ νέαν.
(Φε.) ἕνη γάρ ἐστι καὶ νέα τις ἡμέρα;
(Στ.) εἰς ἥν γε θήσειν τὰ πρυτανεῖά φασί μοι.   1180
(Φε.) ἀπολοῦσ' ἄρ' αὔθ' οἱ θέντες· οὐ γάρ ἐσθ' ὅπως
μί' ἡμέρα γένοιτ' ἂν ἡμέραι δύο.
(Στ.) οὐκ ἂν γένοιτο;
            (Φε.) πῶς γάρ; εἰ μή πέρ γ' ἅμα
αὐτὴ γένοιτ' ἂν γραῦς τε καὶ νέα γυνή.
(Στ.) καὶ μὴν νενόμισταί γ'.
            (Φε.) οὐ γάρ, οἶμαι, τὸν νόμον   1185

ἴσασιν ὀρθῶς, ὅ τι νοεῖ.
           (Στ.) νοεῖ δὲ τί;
(Φε.) ὁ Σόλων ὁ παλαιὸς ἦν φιλόδημος τὴν φύσιν.
(Στ.) τουτὶ μὲν οὐδέν πω πρὸς ἔνην τε καὶ νέαν.
(Φε.) ἐκεῖνος οὖν τὴν κλῆσιν εἰς δύ᾽ ἡμέρας
ἔθηκεν, εἴς γε τὴν ἔνην τε καὶ νέαν,   1190
ἵν᾽ αἱ θέσεις γίγνοιντο τῇ νουμηνίᾳ.
(Στ.) ἵνα δὴ τί τὴν ἔνην προσέθηκεν;
                             (Φε.) ἵν᾽, ὦ μέλε,
παρόντες οἱ φεύγοντες ἡμέρᾳ μιᾷ
πρότερον ἀπαλλάττοινθ᾽ ἑκόντες, εἰ δὲ μή,
ἕωθεν ὑπανῷντο τῇ νουμηνίᾳ.   1195
(Στ.) πῶς οὐ δέχονται δῆτα τῇ νουμηνίᾳ
ἀρχαὶ τὰ πρυτανεῖ᾽, ἀλλ᾽ ἕνῃ τε καὶ νέᾳ;
(Φε.) ὅπερ οἱ προτένθαι γὰρ δοκοῦσί μοι παθεῖν·
ὅπως τάχιστα τὰ πρυτανεῖ᾽ ὑφελοίατο,
διὰ τοῦτο προυτένθευσαν ἡμέρᾳ μιᾷ.   1200
(Στ.) εὖ γ᾽. ὦ κακοδαίμονες, τί κάθησθ᾽ ἀβέλτεροι,
ἡμέτερα κέρδη τῶν σοφῶν, ὄντες λίθοι,
ἀριθμός, πρόβατ᾽ ἄλλως, ἀμφορῆς νενημένοι;
ὥστ᾽ εἰς ἐμαυτὸν καὶ τὸν υἱὸν τουτονὶ
ἐπ᾽ εὐτυχίαισιν ᾀστέον μοὐγκώμιον.   1205
"μάκαρ, ὦ Στρεψίαδες,
αὐτός τ᾽ ἔφυς, ὡς σοφός,
χοῖον τὸν υἱὸν τρέφεις"
φήσουσι δή μ᾽ οἱ φίλοι χοἰ δημόται
ζηλοῦντες ἡνίκ᾽ ἂν σὺ νι-   1210
    κᾷς λέγων τὰς δίκας.
ἀλλ᾽ εἰσάγων σε βούλομαι
πρῶτον ἑστιᾶσαι.

ΧΡΗΣΤΗΣ Α΄

εἶτ᾽ ἄνδρα τῶν αὑτοῦ τι χρὴ προϊέναι;
οὐδέποτέ γ᾽, ἀλλὰ κρεῖττον εὐθὺς ἦν τότε   1215
ἀπερυθριᾶσαι μᾶλλον ἢ σχεῖν πράγματα,
ὅτε τῶν ἐμαυτοῦ γ᾽ ἕνεκα νυνὶ χρημάτων
ἕλκω σε κλητεύσοντα, καὶ γενήσομαι
ἐχθρὸς ἔτι πρὸς τούτοισιν ἀνδρὶ δημότῃ.
ἀτὰρ οὐδέποτέ γε τὴν πατρίδα καταισχυνῶ   1220
ζῶν, ἀλλὰ καλοῦμαι Στρεψιάδην—
                     (Στ.) τίς οὑτοσί;

(Χρ.) εἰς τὴν ἕνην τε καὶ νέαν.
(Στ.) μαρτύρομαι
ὅτι εἰς δύ᾽ εἶπεν ἡμέρας. τοῦ χρήματος;
(Χρ.) τῶν δώδεκα μνῶν, ἃς ἔλαβες ὠνούμενος
τὸν ψαρὸν ἵππον.
(Στ.) ἵππον; οὐκ ἀκούετε;   1225
ὃν πάντες ὑμεῖς ἴστε μισοῦνθ᾽ ἱππικήν.
(Χρ.) καὶ νὴ Δί᾽ ἀποδώσειν γ᾽ ἐπώμνυς τοὺς θεούς.
(Στ.) μὰ τὸν Δί᾽· οὐ γάρ πω τότ᾽ ἐξηπίστατο
Φειδιππίδης μοι τὸν ἀκατάβλητον λόγον.
(Χρ.) νῦν δὲ διὰ τοῦτ᾽ ἔξαρνος εἶναι διανοεῖ;   1230
(Στ.) τί γὰρ ἄλλ᾽ ἂν ἀπολαύσαιμι τοῦ μαθήματος;
(Χρ.) καὶ ταῦτ᾽ ἐθελήσεις ἀπομόσαι μοι τοὺς θεούς,
ἵν᾽ ἂν κελεύσω ᾽γώ σε;
(Στ.) τοὺς ποίους θεούς;
(Χρ.) τὸν Δία, τὸν Ἑρμῆν, τὸν Ποσειδῶ.
(Στ.) νὴ Δία·
κἂν προσκαταθείην γ᾽ ὥστ᾽ ὀμόσαι τριώβολον.   1235
(Χρ.) ἀπόλοιο τοίνυν ἕνεκ᾽ ἀναιδείας ἔτι.
(Στ.) ἁλσὶν διασμηχθεὶς ὄναιτ᾽ ἂν οὑτοσί.
(Χρ.) οἴμ᾽, ὡς καταγελᾷς.
(Στ.) ἓξ χοᾶς χωρήσεται.
(Χρ.) οὔτοι μὰ τὸν Δία τὸν μέγαν καὶ τοὺς θεοὺς
ἐμοῦ καταπροίξει.
(Στ.) θαυμασίως ἥσθην θεοῖς,   1240
καὶ Ζεὺς γέλοιος ὀμνύμενος τοῖς εἰδόσιν.
(Χρ.) ἦ μὴν σὺ τούτων τῷ χρόνῳ δώσεις δίκην.
ἀλλ᾽ εἴτ᾽ ἀποδώσεις μοι τὰ χρήματ᾽ εἴτε μή,
ἀπόπεμψον ἀποκρινάμενος.
(Στ.) ἔχε νυν ἥσυχος·
ἐγὼ γὰρ αὐτίκ᾽ ἀποκρινοῦμαί σοι σαφῶς.   1245
(Χρ.) τί σοι δοκεῖ δράσειν; ἀποδώσειν σοι δοκεῖ;
(Στ.) ποῦ ᾽σθ᾽ οὗτος ἀπαιτῶν με τἀργύριον; λέγε,
τουτὶ τί ἐστι;
(Χρ.) τοῦθ᾽ ὅ τι ἐστί; κάρδοπος.
(Στ.) ἔπειτ᾽ ἀπαιτεῖς τἀργύριον τοιοῦτος ὤν;
οὐκ ἂν ἀποδοίην οὐδ᾽ ἂν ὀβολὸν οὐδενὶ   1250
ὅστις καλέσειε κάρδοπον τὴν καρδόπην.
(Χρ.) οὐκ ἄρ᾽ ἀποδώσεις;
(Στ.) οὐχ ὅσον γ᾽ ἔμ᾽ εἰδέναι.
οὔκουν ἀνύσας τι θᾶττον ἀπολιταργιεῖς

ἀπὸ τῆς θύρας;
     (Χρ.) ἄπειμι· καὶ τοῦτ᾽ ἴσθ᾽, ὅτι
θήσω πρυτανεῖ᾽, ἢ μηκέτι ζῴην ἐγώ.   1255
(Στ.) προσαποβαλεῖς ἄρ᾽ αὐτὰ πρὸς ταῖς δώδεκα.
καίτοι σε τοῦτό γ᾽ οὐχὶ βούλομαι παθεῖν
ὁτιὴ ᾽κάλεσας εὐηθικῶς τὴν κάρδοπον.

ΧΡΗΣΤΗΣ Β΄
ἰώ μοί μοι.   1259a
(Στ.) ἔα.   1259b
τίς οὑτοσί ποτ᾽ ἔσθ᾽ ὁ θρηνῶν; οὔ τι που   1260
τῶν Καρκίνου τις δαιμόνων ἐφθέγξατο;
(Χρ.) τί δ᾽, ὅστις εἰμί, τοῦτο βούλεσθ᾽ εἰδέναι;
ἀνὴρ κακοδαίμων.
           (Στ.) κατὰ σεαυτόν νυν τρέπου.
(Χρ.) ὦ σκληρὲ δαῖμον, ὦ τύχαι θραυσάντυγες
ἵππων ἐμῶν, ὦ Παλλάς, ὥς μ᾽ ἀπώλεσας.   1265
(Στ.) τί δαί σε Τλημπόλεμός ποτ᾽ εἴργασται κακόν;
(Χρ.) μὴ σκῶπτέ μ᾽, ὦ τᾶν, ἀλλά μοι τὰ χρήματα
τὸν υἱὸν ἀποδοῦναι κέλευσον ἅλαβεν,
ἄλλως τε μέντοι καὶ κακῶς πεπραγότι.
(Στ.) τὰ ποῖα ταῦτα χρήμαθ᾽;
              (Χρ.) ἁδανείσατο.   1270
(Στ.) κακῶς ἄρ᾽ ὄντως εἶχες, ὥς γ᾽ ἐμοὶ δοκεῖς.
(Χρ.) ἵππους γ᾽ ἐλαύνων ἐξέπεσον, νὴ τοὺς θεούς.
(Στ.) τί δῆτα ληρεῖς ὥσπερ ἀπ᾽ ὄνου καταπεσών;
(Χρ.) ληρῶ, τὰ χρήματ᾽ ἀπολαβεῖν εἰ βούλομαι;
(Στ.) οὐκ ἔσθ᾽ ὅπως σύ γ᾽ αὐτὸς ὑγιανεῖς.
                    (Χρ.) τί δαί;   1275
(Στ.) τὸν ἐγκέφαλον ὥσπερ σεσεῖσθαί μοι δοκεῖς.
(Χρ.) σὺ δὲ νὴ τὸν Ἑρμῆν προσκεκλήσεσθαί γ᾽ ἐμοί,
εἰ μἀποδώσεις τἀργύριον.
           (Στ.) κάτειπέ νυν,
πότερα νομίζεις καινὸν αἰεὶ τὸν Δία
ὕειν ὕδωρ ἑκάστοτ᾽, ἢ τὸν ἥλιον   1280
ἕλκειν κάτωθεν ταὐτὸ τοῦθ᾽ ὕδωρ πάλιν;
(Χρ.) οὐκ οἶδ᾽ ἔγωγ᾽ ὁπότερον, οὐδέ μοι μέλει.
(Στ.) πῶς οὖν ἀπολαβεῖν τἀργύριον δίκαιος εἶ,
εἰ μηδὲν οἶσθα τῶν μετεώρων πραγμάτων;
(Χρ.) ἀλλ᾽ εἰ † σπανίζεις τἀργυρίου μοι τὸν τόκον   1285
ἀπόδοτε †.

Clouds   53

(Στ.) τοῦτο δ᾽ ἔσθ᾽, ὁ τόκος, τί θηρίον;
(Χρ.) τί δ᾽ ἄλλο γ᾽ ἢ κατὰ μῆνα καὶ καθ᾽ ἡμέραν
πλέον πλέον τἀργύριον αἰεὶ γίγνεται
ὑπορρέοντος τοῦ χρόνου;
                    (Στ.) καλῶς λέγεις.
τί δῆτα; τὴν θάλαττάν ἐσθ᾽ ὅτι πλείονα   1290
νυνὶ νομίζεις ἢ πρὸ τοῦ;
        (Χρ.) μὰ Δί᾽, ἀλλ᾽ ἴσην·
οὐ γὰρ δίκαιον πλείον᾽ εἶναι.
                    (Στ.) κᾆτα πῶς
αὕτη μέν, ὦ κακόδαιμον, οὐδὲν γίγνεται
ἐπιρρεόντων τῶν ποταμῶν πλείων, σὺ δὲ
ζητεῖς ποῆσαι τἀργύριον πλέον τὸ σόν;   1295
οὐκ ἀποδιώξει σαυτὸν ἀπὸ τῆς οἰκίας;
φέρε μοι τὸ κέντρον.
            (Χρ.) ταῦτ᾽ ἐγὼ μαρτύρομαι.
(Στ.) ὕπαγε. τί μέλλεις; οὐκ ἐλᾷς, ὦ σαμφόρα;
(Χρ.) ταῦτ᾽ οὐχ ὕβρις δῆτ᾽ ἐστίν;
                    (Στ.) ἄξεις; ἐπιαλῶ
κεντῶν ὑπὸ τὸν πρωκτόν σε τὸν σειραφόρον.   1300
φεύγεις; ἔμελλόν σ᾽ ἄρα κινήσειν ἐγὼ
αὐτοῖς τροχοῖς τοῖς σοῖσι καὶ ξυνωρίσιν.

(Χο.) οἷον τὸ πραγμάτων ἐρᾶν φλαύρων· ὁ γὰρ   στρ.
    γέρων ὅδ᾽ ἐρασθεὶς
ἀποστερῆσαι βούλεται   1305
τὰ χρήμαθ᾽ ἁδανείσατο.
κοὐκ ἔσθ᾽ ὅπως οὐ τήμερον
    λήψεταί τι πρᾶγμ᾽ ὃ τοῦ-
    τον ποιήσει τὸν σοφι-
    στήν, † ὧν πανουργεῖν ἤρξατ᾽, ἐξ-   1310a
    αίφνης † τι κακὸν λαβεῖν †·   1310b

οἶμαι γὰρ αὐτὸν αὐτίχ᾽ εὑρήσειν ὅπερ   ἀντ.
    πάλαι ποτ᾽ ἐζήτει,
εἶναι τὸν υἱὸν δεινόν οἱ
γνώμας ἐναντίας λέγειν
τοῖσιν δικαίοις, ὥστε νι-   1315
    κᾶν ἅπαντας οἷσπερ ἂν
    ξυγγένηται, κἂν λέγῃ
    παμπόνηρ᾽. ἴσως δ᾽ ἴσως βουλήσεται
κἄφωνον αὐτὸν εἶναι.   1320

(Στ.) ἰοὺ ἰού.
ὦ γείτονες καὶ ξυγγενεῖς καὶ δημόται,
ἀμυνάθετέ μοι τυπτομένῳ πάσῃ τέχνῃ.
οἴμοι κακοδαίμων τῆς κεφαλῆς καὶ τῆς γνάθου.
ὦ μιαρέ, τύπτεις τὸν πατέρα;
                    (Φε.) φήμ᾽, ὦ πάτερ.   1325
(Στ.) ὁρᾶθ᾽ ὁμολογοῦνθ᾽ ὅτι με τύπτει;
                    (Φε.) καὶ μάλα.
(Στ.) ὦ μιαρὲ καὶ πατραλοῖα καὶ τοιχωρύχε.
(Φε.) αὖθίς με ταὐτὰ ταῦτα καὶ πλείω λέγε.
ἆρ᾽ οἶσθ᾽ ὅτι χαίρω πόλλ᾽ ἀκούων καὶ κακά;
(Στ.) ὦ λακκόπρωκτε.
                    (Φε.) πάττε πολλοῖς τοῖς ῥόδοις.   1330
(Στ.) τὸν πατέρα τύπτεις;
                    (Φε.) κἀποφανῶ γε νὴ Δία
ὡς ἐν δίκῃ σ᾽ ἔτυπτον.
                    (Στ.) ὦ μιαρώτατε,
καὶ πῶς γένοιτ᾽ ἂν πατέρα τύπτειν ἐν δίκῃ;
(Φε.) ἔγωγ᾽ ἀποδείξω καί σε νικήσω λέγων.
(Στ.) τουτὶ σὺ νικήσεις;
                    (Φε.) πολύ γε καὶ ῥᾳδίως.   1335
ἑλοῦ δ᾽ ὁπότερον τοῖν λόγοιν βούλει λέγειν.
(Στ.) ποίοιν λόγοιν;
                    (Φε.) τὸν κρείττον᾽ ἢ τὸν ἥττονα.
(Στ.) ἐδιδαξάμην μέντοι σε νὴ Δί᾽, ὦ μέλε,
τοῖσιν δικαίοις ἀντιλέγειν, εἰ ταῦτά γε
μέλλεις ἀναπείσειν, ὡς δίκαιον καὶ καλὸν   1340
τὸν πατέρα τύπτεσθ᾽ ἐστὶν ὑπὸ τῶν υἱέων.
(Φε.) ἀλλ᾽ οἴομαι μέντοι σ᾽ ἀναπείσειν, ὥστε γε
οὐδ᾽ αὐτὸς ἀκροασάμενος οὐδὲν ἀντερεῖς.
(Στ.) καὶ μὴν ὅ τι καὶ λέξεις ἀκοῦσαι βούλομαι.

(Χο.) σὸν ἔργον, ὦ πρεσβῦτα, φροντίζειν ὅπῃ   στρ.   1345
τὸν ἄνδρα κρατήσεις·
ὡς οὗτος, εἰ μή τῳ 'πεποίθειν, οὐκ ἂν ἦν
οὕτως ἀκόλαστος,
ἀλλ᾽ ἔσθ᾽ ὅτῳ θρασύνεται· δῆλόν ⟨γέ τοι⟩
τὸ λῆμα τἀνθρώπου.   1350

ἀλλ᾽ ἐξ ὅτου τὸ πρῶτον ἤρξαθ᾽ ἡ μάχη γενέσθαι
ἤδη λέγειν χρὴ πρὸς χορόν· πάντως δὲ τοῦτο δράσεις.

(Στ.) καὶ μὴν ὅθεν γε πρῶτον ἠρξάμεσθα λοιδορεῖσθαι
ἐγὼ φράσω· 'πειδὴ γὰρ εἱστιώμεθ', ὥσπερ ἴστε,
πρῶτον μὲν αὐτὸν τὴν λύραν λαβόντ' ἐγὼ 'κέλευσα   1355
ᾆσαι Σιμωνίδου μέλος, τὸν Κριόν, ὡς ἐπέχθη·
ὁ δ' εὐθέως ἀρχαῖον εἶν' ἔφασκε τὸ κιθαρίζειν
ᾄδειν τε πίνονθ' ὡσπερεὶ κάχρυς γυναῖκ' ἀλοῦσαν.
(Φε.) οὐ γὰρ τότ' εὐθὺς χρῆν σ' ἀράττεσθαί τε καὶ πατεῖσθαι,
ᾄδειν κελεύονθ', ὡσπερεὶ τέττιγας ἑστιῶντα;   1360
(Στ.) τοιαῦτα μέντοι καὶ τότ' ἔλεγεν ἔνδον, οἷάπερ νῦν,
καὶ τὸν Σιμωνίδην ἔφασκ' εἶναι κακὸν ποιητήν.
κἀγὼ μόλις μέν, ἀλλ' ὅμως ἠνεσχόμην τὸ πρῶτον·
ἔπειτα δ' ἐκέλευσ' αὐτὸν ἀλλὰ μυρρίνην λαβόντα
τῶν Αἰσχύλου λέξαι τί μοι· κᾆθ' οὗτος εὐθὺς εἶπεν·   1365
"ἐγὼ γὰρ Αἰσχύλον νομίζω πρῶτον ἐν ποιηταῖς—
ψόφου πλέων, ἀξύστατον, στόμφακα, κρημνοποιόν;"
κἀνταῦθα πῶς οἴεσθέ μου τὴν καρδίαν ὀρεχθεῖν;
ὅμως δὲ τὸν θυμὸν δακὼν ἔφην· "σὺ δ' ἀλλὰ τούτων
λέξον τι τῶν νεωτέρων, ἅττ' ἐστὶ τὰ σοφὰ ταῦτα."   1370
ὁ δ' εὐθὺς ᾖσ' Εὐριπίδου ῥῆσίν τιν', ὡς ἐκίνει
ἀδελφός, ὦλεξίκακε, τὴν ὁμομητρίαν ἀδελφήν.
κἀγὼ οὐκέτ' ἐξηνεσχόμην, ἀλλ' εὐθέως ἀράττω
πολλοῖς κακοῖς καἰσχροῖσι· κᾆτ' ἐντεῦθεν, οἷον εἰκός,
ἔπος πρὸς ἔπος ἠρειδόμεσθ'· εἶθ' οὗτος ἐπαναπηδᾷ,   1375
κἄπειτ' ἔφλα με κἀσπόδει κἄπνιγε κἀπέθλιβεν.
(Φε.) οὔκουν δικαίως, ὅστις οὐκ Εὐριπίδην ἐπαινεῖς
σοφώτατον;
           (Στ.) σοφώτατόν γ' ἐκεῖνον, ὦ—τί σ' εἴπω;
ἀλλ' αὖθις αὖ τυπτήσομαι.
                      (Φε.) νὴ τὸν Δί', ἐν δίκῃ γ' ἄν.
(Στ.) καὶ πῶς δικαίως; ὅστις, ὦναίσχυντέ, σ' ἐξέθρεψα   1380
αἰσθανόμενός σου πάντα τραυλίζοντος, ὅ τι νοοίης.
εἰ μέν γε βρῦν εἴποις, ἐγὼ γνοὺς ἂν πιεῖν ἐπέσχον·
μαμμᾶν δ' ἂν αἰτήσαντος ἧκόν σοι φέρων ἂν ἄρτον·
κακκᾶν δ' ἂν οὐκ ἔφθης φράσας, κἀγὼ λαβὼν θύραζε
ἐξέφερον ἂν καὶ προὐσχόμην σε. σὺ δέ με νῦν ἀπάγχων   1385
βοῶντα καὶ κεκραγόθ' ὅτι
χεζητιῴην, οὐκ ἔτλης
ἔξω 'ξενεγκεῖν, ὦ μιαρέ,
θύραζέ μ', ἀλλὰ πνιγόμενος
αὐτοῦ 'πόησα κακκᾶν.   1390

(Χο.) οἶμαί γε τῶν νεωτέρων τὰς καρδίας   ἀντ.
πηδᾶν ὅ τι λέξει·
εἰ γὰρ τοιαῦτά γ' οὗτος ἐξειργασμένος
λαλῶν ἀναπείσει,
τὸ δέρμα τῶν γεραιτέρων λάβοιμεν ἂν   1395
ἀλλ' οὐδ' ἐρεβίνθου.

σὸν ἔργον, ὦ καινῶν ἐπῶν κινητὰ καὶ μοχλευτά,
πειθώ τινα ζητεῖν, ὅπως δόξεις λέγειν δίκαια.
(Φε.) ὡς ἡδὺ καινοῖς πράγμασιν καὶ δεξιοῖς ὁμιλεῖν
καὶ τῶν καθεστώτων νόμων ὑπερφρονεῖν δύνασθαι·   1400
ἐγὼ γὰρ ὅτε μὲν ἱππικῇ τὸν νοῦν μόνῃ προσεῖχον,
οὐδ' ἂν τρί' εἰπεῖν ῥήμαθ' οἷός τ' ἦν πρὶν ἐξαμαρτεῖν·
νυνὶ δ' ἐπειδή μ' οὑτοσὶ τούτων ἔπαυσεν αὐτός,
γνώμαις δὲ λεπταῖς καὶ λόγοις ξύνειμι καὶ μερίμναις,
οἶμαι διδάξειν ὡς δίκαιον τὸν πατέρα κολάζειν.   1405
(Στ.) ἵππευε τοίνυν νὴ Δί'· ὡς ἔμοιγε κρεῖττόν ἐστιν
ἵππων τρέφειν τέθριππον ἢ τυπτόμενον ἐπιτριβῆναι.
(Φε.) ἐκεῖσε δ' ὅθεν ἀπέσχισάς με τοῦ λόγου μέτειμι,
καὶ πρῶτ' ἐρήσομαί σε τουτί· παῖδά μ' ὄντ' ἔτυπτες;
(Στ.) ἔγωγέ σ', εὐνοῶν τε καὶ κηδόμενος.
                              (Φε.) εἰπὲ δή μοι,   1410
οὐ κἀμὲ σοὶ δίκαιόν ἐστιν εὐνοεῖν ὁμοίως
τύπτειν τ', ἐπειδήπερ γε τοῦτ' ἔστ' εὐνοεῖν, τὸ τύπτειν;
πῶς γὰρ τὸ μὲν σὸν σῶμα χρὴ πληγῶν ἀθῷον εἶναι,
τοὐμὸν δὲ μή; καὶ μὴν ἔφυν ἐλεύθερός γε κἀγώ.
"κλάουσι παῖδες, πατέρα δ' οὐ κλάειν δοκεῖς;"   1415
φήσεις νομίζεσθαι σὺ παιδὸς τοῦτο τοὔργον εἶναι·
ἐγὼ δέ γ' ἀντείποιμ' ἂν ὡς δὶς παῖδες οἱ γέροντες·
εἰκός τε μᾶλλον τοὺς γέροντας ἢ νέους τι κλάειν
ὅσῳπερ ἐξαμαρτάνειν ἧττον δίκαιον αὐτούς.
(Στ.) ἀλλ' οὐδαμοῦ νομίζεται τὸν πατέρα τοῦτο πάσχειν.   1420
(Φε.) οὔκουν ἀνὴρ ὁ τὸν νόμον θεὶς τοῦτον ἦν τὸ πρῶτον,
ὥσπερ σὺ κἀγώ, καὶ λέγων ἔπειθε τοὺς παλαιούς;
ἧττόν τι δῆτ' ἔξεστι κἀμοὶ καινὸν αὖ τὸ λοιπὸν
θεῖναι νόμον τοῖς υἱέσιν, τοὺς πατέρας ἀντιτύπτειν;
ὅσας δὲ πληγὰς εἴχομεν πρὶν τὸν νόμον τεθῆναι,   1425
ἀφίεμεν, καὶ δίδομεν αὐτοῖς προῖκα συγκεκόφθαι.
σκέψαι δὲ τοὺς ἀλεκτρυόνας καὶ τἄλλα τὰ βοτὰ ταυτί,
ὡς τοὺς πατέρας ἀμύνεται· καίτοι τί διαφέρουσιν
ἡμῶν ἐκεῖνοι, πλήν γ' ὅτι ψηφίσματ' οὐ γράφουσιν;

(Στ.) τί δῆτ’, ἐπειδὴ τοὺς ἀλεκτρυόνας ἅπαντα μιμεῖ, 1430
οὐκ ἐσθίεις καὶ τὴν κόπρον κἀπὶ ξύλου καθεύδεις;
(Φε.) οὐ ταὐτόν, ὦ τᾶν, ἐστίν, οὐδ’ ἂν Σωκράτει δοκοίη.
(Στ.) πρὸς ταῦτα μὴ τύπτ’· εἰ δὲ μή, σαυτόν ποτ’ αἰτιάσει.
(Φε.) καὶ πῶς;
      (Στ.) ἐπεὶ σὲ μὲν δίκαιός εἰμ’ ἐγὼ κολάζειν,
σὺ δ’, ἢν γένηταί σοι, τὸν υἱόν.
                    (Φε.) ἢν δὲ μὴ γένηται, 1435
μάτην ἐμοὶ κεκλαύσεται, σὺ δ’ ἐγχανὼν τεθνήξεις.
(Στ.) ἐμοὶ μέν, ὦνδρες ἥλικες, δοκεῖ λέγειν δίκαια,
κἄμοιγε συγχωρεῖν δοκεῖ τούτοισι τἀπιεική·
κλάειν γὰρ ἡμᾶς εἰκός ἐστ’, ἢν μὴ δίκαια δρῶμεν.
(Φε.) σκέψαι δὲ χἀτέραν ἔτι γνώμην.
                    (Στ.) ἀπὸ γὰρ ὀλοῦμαι. 1440
(Φε.) καὶ μὴν ἴσως γ’ οὐκ ἀχθέσει παθὼν ἃ νῦν πέπονθας.
(Στ.) πῶς δή; δίδαξον γάρ· τί μ’ ἐκ τούτων ἐπωφελήσεις;
(Φε.) τὴν μητέρ’ ὥσπερ καὶ σὲ τυπτήσω.
                    (Στ.) τί φῄς; τί φῂς σύ;
τοῦθ’ ἕτερον αὖ μεῖζον κακόν.
            (Φε.) τί δ’ ἢν ἔχων τὸν ἥττω
λόγον σε νικήσω λέγων 1445
τὴν μητέρ’ ὡς τύπτειν χρεών;
(Στ.) τί δ’ ἄλλο γ’ ἤ, ταῦτ’ ἢν ποῇς,
οὐδέν σε κωλύσει σεαυτὸν ἐμβαλεῖν
εἰς τὸ βάραθρον μετὰ Σωκράτους 1449–50
καὶ τὸν λόγον τὸν ἥττω;
ταυτὶ δι’ ὑμᾶς, ὦ Νεφέλαι, πέπονθ’ ἐγὼ
ὑμῖν ἀναθεὶς ἅπαντα τἀμὰ πράγματα.
(Χο.) αὐτὸς μὲν οὖν σαυτῷ σὺ τούτων αἴτιος
στρέψας σεαυτὸν εἰς πονηρὰ πράγματα. 1455
(Στ.) τί δῆτα ταῦτ’ οὔ μοι τότ’ ἠγορεύετε,
ἀλλ’ ἄνδρ’ ἄγροικον καὶ γέροντ’ ἐπήρατε;
(Χο.) ἡμεῖς ποοῦμεν ταῦθ’ ἑκάστοθ’ ὅντιν’ ἂν
γνῶμεν πονηρῶν ὄντ’ ἐραστὴν πραγμάτων,
ἕως ἂν αὐτὸν ἐμβάλωμεν εἰς κακόν, 1460
ὅπως ἂν εἰδῇ τοὺς θεοὺς δεδοικέναι.
(Στ.) ὤμοι, πονηρά γ’, ὦ Νεφέλαι, δίκαια δέ·
οὐ γάρ με χρῆν τὰ χρήμαθ’ ἁδανεισάμην
ἀποστερεῖν. νῦν οὖν ὅπως, ὦ φίλτατε,
τὸν Χαιρεφῶντα τὸν μιαρὸν καὶ Σωκράτη 1465
ἀπολεῖς μετ’ ἐμοῦ ’λθών, οἳ σὲ κἄμ’ ἐξηπάτων.

(Φε.) ἀλλ' οὐκ ἂν ἀδικήσαιμι τοὺς διδασκάλους.
(Στ.) ναὶ ναί· καταιδέσθητι πατρῷον Δία.
(Φε.) ἰδού γε Δία πατρῷον· ὡς ἀρχαῖος εἶ·
Ζεὺς γάρ τις ἔστιν;
        (Στ.) ἔστιν.
                (Φε.) οὐκ ἔστ', οὔκ, ἐπεὶ   1470
Δῖνος βασιλεύει τὸν Δί' ἐξεληλακώς.
(Στ.) οὐκ ἐξελήλακ', ἀλλ' ἐγὼ τοῦτ' ᾠόμην
διὰ τουτονὶ τὸν δῖνον. ὤμοι δείλαιος,
ὅτε καὶ σὲ χυτρεοῦν ὄντα θεὸν ἡγησάμην.
(Φε.) ἐνταῦθα σαυτῷ παραφρόνει καὶ φληνάφα.   1475
(Στ.) οἴμοι παρανοίας. ὡς ἐμαινόμην ἄρα
ὅτ' ἐξέβαλον καὶ τοὺς θεοὺς διὰ Σωκράτη.
ἀλλ', ὦ φίλ' Ἑρμῆ, μηδαμῶς θύμαινέ μοι,
μηδέ μ' ἐπιτρίψῃς, ἀλλὰ συγγνώμην ἔχε
ἐμοῦ παρανοήσαντος ἀδολεσχίᾳ·   1480
καί μοι γενοῦ ξύμβουλος, εἴτ' αὐτοὺς γραφὴν
διωκάθω γραψάμενος, εἴθ' ὅ τι σοι δοκεῖ.
ὀρθῶς παραινεῖς οὐκ ἐῶν δικορραφεῖν,
ἀλλ' ὡς τάχιστ' ἐμπιμπράναι τὴν οἰκίαν
τῶν ἀδολεσχῶν. δεῦρο δεῦρ', ὦ Ξανθία,   1485
κλίμακα λαβὼν ἔξελθε καὶ σμινύην φέρων·
κἄπειτ' ἐπαναβὰς ἐπὶ τὸ φροντιστήριον
τὸ τέγος κατάσκαπτ', εἰ φιλεῖς τὸν δεσπότην,
ἕως ἂν αὐτοῖς ἐμβάλῃς τὴν οἰκίαν.
ἐμοὶ δὲ δᾷδ' ἐνεγκάτω τις ἡμμένην·   1490
κἀγώ τιν' αὐτῶν τήμερον δοῦναι δίκην
ἐμοὶ ποήσω, κεἰ σφόδρ' εἴσ' ἀλαζόνες.

ΜΑΘΗΤΗΣ Α΄
ἰοὺ ἰού.
(Στ.) σὸν ἔργον, ὦ δᾴς, ἱέναι πολλὴν φλόγα.
(Μα.) ἄνθρωπε, τί ποιεῖς;
            (Στ.) ὅ τι ποῶ; τί δ' ἄλλο γ' ἢ   1495
 διαλεπτολογοῦμαι ταῖς δοκοῖς τῆς οἰκίας;

ΜΑΘΗΤΗΣ Β΄
οἴμοι· τίς ἡμῶν πυρπολεῖ τὴν οἰκίαν;
(Στ.) ἐκεῖνος οὕπερ θοἰμάτιον εἰλήφατε.
(Μα.) ἀπολεῖς, ἀπολεῖς.
            (Στ.) τοῦτ' αὐτὸ γὰρ καὶ βούλομαι,

ἢν ἡ σμινύη μοι μὴ προδῷ τὰς ἐλπίδας,   1500
ἢ 'γὼ πρότερόν πως ἐκτραχηλισθῶ πεσών.
(Σω.) οὗτος, τί ποιεῖς ἐτεόν, οὑπὶ τοῦ τέγους;
(Στ.) ἀεροβατῶ καὶ περιφρονῶ τὸν ἥλιον.
(Σω.) οἴμοι τάλας, δείλαιος ἀποπνιγήσομαι.
(Μα.) ἐγὼ δὲ κακοδαίμων γε κατακαυθήσομαι.   1505
(Στ.) τί γὰρ μαθόντες τοὺς θεοὺς ὑβρίζετε
καὶ τῆς σελήνης ἐσκοπεῖσθε τὴν ἕδραν;
δίωκε, παῖε, βάλλε, πολλῶν οὕνεκα,
μάλιστα δ' εἰδὼς τοὺς θεοὺς ὡς ἠδίκουν.
(Χο.) ἡγεῖσθ' ἔξω· κεχόρευται γὰρ   1510
μετρίως τό γε τήμερον ἡμῖν.

Commentary

Two doors are visible in the stage front. Statues of Hermes (1478–85n.) and Poseidon (83 with n.) stand beside the two doors. A large drinking cup (δῖνος) is also visible somewhere onstage (cf. 1473 with n.); perhaps Hermes holds it. A pair of actors come on carrying a simple bed, on which they lie down and cover themselves up with sheepskins that serve as blankets (10, 730). This is a "canceled entrance", which by standard theatrical convention does not count as part of the action, but nonetheless informs the audience in the Theater that the opening action will be set within rather than outside a house, and that it is nighttime. Eventually the play is understood to begin; perhaps a signal of some sort is given, equivalent in effect to the modern dimming of the lights and raising of the curtain. One of the characters—soon identified as the son, and given a name at 67—sleeps calmly. The other—his father, left unidentified by name until 134—rolls restlessly about. Finally the older man sits up and begins to talk to himself, but also to the audience.

1–274 The prologue of an Aristophanic comedy—the portion of the play that precedes the arrival of the chorus, here at 275—typically introduces the audience to the main characters (in this case Strepsiades, Pheidippides and Socrates) and allows the hero to launch his or her wild and improbable plot (here the idea of using a Socratic education as a way to get out of paying debts). Iambic trimeter, like much of the text; see Introduction §IV.A.1.

1 ἰοὺ ἰού "Argh!"; an inarticulate cry, here suggesting grief and aggravation. Contrast 1170 (joy), 1321 (a desperate cry for attention), 1493 (terror), and see 543 with 537–48n.

2 τὸ χρῆμα τῶν νυκτῶν ὅσον literally "the thing of the nights, how big!", i.e. "how long the nights are!" This use of χρῆμα + gen. is a colloquialism, i.e. casual, everyday language of a sort regarded as insufficiently refined e.g. for tragedy, but very common in comedy.

3 ἀ-πέραντον "(it's) endless" or "(they're) endless" (< privative *alpha* + περαίνω, "bring to an end, finish", cognate with πέρας, "end, limit, bound"); also 393, in the sense "boundless, limitless".

4 καὶ μήν and **γ(ε)** both add emphasis to **πάλαι** in different ways: "*long* ago, in fact!"   **ἀλεκτρυόνος** "a rooster" (666n.); genitive with **ἤκουσ(α)**. Chickens were common domestic birds, and Strepsiades actually brings a pair onstage later in the play (847–51).

5 οἱ δ(ὲ) οἰκέται ῥέγκουσιν "my slaves are snoring". In fact, one is already up (18–19). Aristophanic characters routinely own slaves, most likely because average Athenians did as well; cf. 614, 1488n. It eventually emerges that Strepsiades is well to do (if financially stretched), and he has at least two (1485–90). Abusing slaves onstage is treated as unironic good fun; see 57–8.   **οὐκ ἄν** The verb is to be supplied from the first half of the verse, "they wouldn't (have been snoring)".   **πρὸ τοῦ** = πρὸ τούτου (τοῦ χρόνου), "before this time, previously" (also 654).

6–7 The war with the Peloponnesian League in this period made it much easier for Athenian slaves to desert to the other side with no fear of being returned. Strepsiades is accordingly supposed to be unwilling to punish his slaves (*sc.* for not being up at the crack of dawn), since they may run off if he does.   **ἀπ-όλοιο** "might you be ruined!" (2nd-person singular aorist optative middle < ἀπ-όλλυμι), i.e. "damn you!"; a colloquial curse, as again at 1236.   **πολλῶν οὕνεκα** "on account of many things, for many reasons"; as often, the preposition follows its case (e.g. 238 with n., 361, 511, 555).   This is a somewhat unusual use of **δῆτ(α)** (again in 269), positive statements normally being strengthened by δή instead. Cf. 79n. (on the particle used in questions, as more commonly).   **ὅτ(ε)** "when", i.e. "because now", as again in 34, 717, 1217, 1474. ὅτι, by contrast, is never elided.   **κολάσ(αι)** aorist active infinitive < κολάζω, "punish".

8 χρηστός is a very general term of commendation ("excellent"), but is used here sarcastically (~ "wonderful").   The *iota* on the end of **οὑτοσ-ί** is an Attic colloquialism that converts the demonstrative into a deictic ("the one *here*", normally accompanied by a gesture, in other cases merely adding an emphatic sense that the object or person in question is sufficiently well-known to be regarded as almost visible); cf. 14 and 77 τουτονί, 26 τουτί, etc.

9 τῆς νυκτός "at night, during the night" (genitive of time within which).   **πέρδεται** "he farts", as Aristophanic characters often do when happy or relaxed (e.g. *Knights* 115; *Ecclesiazusae* 464). From an old Indo-European root and cognate with the English (which as a Germanic language has shifted to an initial *f*).

10 πέντε is here probably a "round number" meaning simply "numerous". A σισύρα is a goatskin or sheepskin with the hair still on, here serving as a blanket; treated as proverbially cozy (μαλθακή) at *Birds* 122.   ἐγ-κεκορδυλημένος < ἐγ-κορδυλέω, literally "put on a headband" and thus ~ "wrap, swaddle". The verb is a *hapax legomenon* (a word attested only once in Greek); this does not mean that Aristophanes invented it, but only that it was not much needed in the type of literary material that survives for us.

11 ἀλλ(ὰ) εἰ δοκεῖ literally "but if this seems good", i.e. "well, all right then!"   ῥέγκωμεν hortatory present active subjunctive < ῥέγκω, "snore". Strepsiades lies back down, covers himself up in a sheepskin, and begins to toss and turn once more (action unnoted by our text, which merely tells us what was *said* onstage; cf. 91n.). Eventually he sits back up. Cf. 729–30n. on the repetition of this scene later in the play.

12 δείλαιος "miserable (me)".   δακνόμενος "since I'm being bitten", at first suggesting bedbugs or fleas, as at 634. But 13 makes it clear that Strepsiades is speaking metaphorically, as again in 37.

13 ὑπὸ τῆς δαπάνης καὶ τῆς φάτνης καὶ τῶν χρεῶν "by my expense(s) and my manger and my debts", i.e. by the debts he has incurred for money to keep his horses.

14 For deictic τουτον-ί, 8n.   κόμην ἔχων "wearing his hair (long)", in late 5th-century Athens a sign not of rebellion but of upper-class pretensions (cf. 332 with n., 348 with n., 545, 1100): Pheidippides aspires to looks like a fancy, rich young man. He accordingly needs horses (15), which in the ancient world—as in the modern one—were expensive to buy and keep.

15 ἱππάζεται "he drives horses".   ξυνωρικ-εύεται < συνωρίς ("racing-chariot"; cf. 1302) + the suffix -εύω/-εύομαι, used with verbs that describe a lifestyle or way of behaving (also e.g. 381 βασιλ-εύω, "be a king", 696 ἱκετ-εύω, "be a suppliant", 921 πτωχ-εύω, "be a beggar", 1406 ἱππ-εύω, "be a horseman").

16 ὀνειρο-πολεῖ (τε) ἵππους "and he dreams about horses", setting up Pheidippides' first words in 25, 28, 32. The idea is repeated in 27.   ἀπ-όλλυμαι literally "I'm being ruined", but used routinely to mean ~ "I'm in agony" (also 709).

17 ἄγουσαν τὴν σελήνην εἰκάδας "the moon bringing on the twenties". The Athenians used a lunar calendar (615n.), and "the twenties" are the end of the month; for a different way of counting used after the 20ᵗʰ, see 1131–4 with 1131n. The implication is that the action is taking place on the 19ᵗʰ or so; see 1131n. (time within the play moves forward a few days to cover Pheidippides' education inside the Thinkery).

18 οἱ . . . τόκοι "my interest payments", normally due on the first day of the month (cf. 756, 1132–4, 1178–80).   **χωροῦσιν** "are coming", i.e. "will soon be due". ἅπτω is "set on fire" (LSJ *s.v.* B; cf. 768, 1490) and thus in reference to a lamp "light" (also 57).   **παῖ** is vocative < παῖς, "slave" (also 132, 614, etc.). Free Aristophanic characters routinely issue orders of this sort, which are then rapidly completed by slaves, some of whom speak (as in this scene), while many do not (e.g. 1297, 1485–1509).

19 (ἔ)κ-φερε "bring out!", *sc.* from the house onto the stage.   **τὸ γραμματεῖον** "my account book", normally a folding wooden box with wax on the interior sides that could be written on, closed to keep the text safe, and later easily erased. Cf. 766–72, where Strepsiades imagines melting the letters out of an official court-document, which must be written in a similar style of book.   **ἀνα-γνῶ** aorist active subjunctive (appropriate in a purpose clause introduced by a primary-tense verb; cf. λογίσωμαι in 20) < ἀνα-γιγνώσκω, "read".

20 ὁ-πόσοις ὀφείλω This is an indirect question, and the direct πόσοις; in the imagined original direct question ("To how many people do I owe money?"; cf. 21) is replaced by a form with the prefix ὁ-. Because the question is introduced by a primary tense verb, the original indicative ὀφείλω is retained. Cf. 144–5 (where the question is introduced by a secondary tense verb, and an optative is used), 157–8n. on ὁ-πότερα. For πόσος/ὅσος and ποῖος/οἷος, 155n.   **λογίσωμαι τοὺς τόκους** "I might compute the interest I owe", which is the topic keeping him awake. At some point in these lines, a Slave enters from Strepsiades' house carrying the items requested and a lamp. He remains onstage, holding the lamp so that Strepsiades can read, until he is chased back into the house at 57–8.

21 φέρ(ε) ἴδω "alright, let me see!" (also 494, 787, 847); colloquial Attic.   **δώδεκα μνᾶς** "twelve minas", i.e. 1200 drachmas or 1/5 of a talent (= 6000 drachmas), as much as a skilled laborer could make in four years or so of full-time employment. This is the amount the otherwise anonymous First Creditor claims he is owed at 1224–5 (likewise for a horse; cf. 23), and that character is therefore identified as Pasias in most manuscripts. Whether Aristophanes expected his audience to be so retentive of seemingly throwaway details is unclear.

22 τοῦ; = τίνος; "for what?" (a genitive of price, but referring to the item purchased rather than the money paid for it, as again in 31).   **τί ἐχρησάμην;** "what use did I make of them?, how did I use them?" τί is the internal object of the verb (99n.).

23 ἐπριάμην "I bought" (< *πρίαμαι, which supplies the aorist of ὠνέομαι, "buy"; * indicates that the word is not actually attested in the form under which it is lemmatized in modern lexica).   **τὸν κοππα-τίαν** sc. ἵππον, as in 438 (plural). The letter *koppa* (equivalent to our *q*) was not used in the Athenian alphabet, but was still employed e.g. in Corinth. A κοππα-τία is a horse with a *koppa*-brand; cf. the mention of a horse with a *san*-brand in 122 (n.).   **οἴμοι τάλας** "alas, miserable me!" (also 742, 1504); an articulate cry of lament (see also 925 with n.) reminiscent not of everyday speech but of the language of tragedy, to which Aristophanic characters also appeal repeatedly, including for emotional effect, as here and in 30 (n.). Contrast 773 with n. (pleasure). τάλας is cognate with τλάω, "endure" (119n.).

24 εἴθ(ε) ἐξ-εκόπην ... τὸν ὀφθαλμόν "if only I had had my eye gouged out!" (< ἐκ-κόπτω); a weak pun—at least by modern standards—on κοππα-τίαν in 23. εἴθε indicates a wish, as again in 41b.

25 Pheidippides, who is dreaming of horses and horse-racing, as predicted (16), talks in his sleep, as again in 28, 32. Philon is an imaginary opponent in a race.   **ἀ-δικεῖς** here ~ "you're cheating".   **ἔλαυνε τὸν σαυτοῦ δρόμον** i.e. "stay in your own lane!"

27 ὀνειρο-πολεῖ γὰρ καὶ καθ-εύδων ἱππικήν literally "because he dreams about horsemanship even when he's asleep", the point being that Pheidippides *always* thinks about horses. τέχνην is to be supplied with ἱππικήν; the adjective is of a typical late 5th-century type that Aristophanes elsewhere sometimes mocks intellectual poseurs for using; cf. 203 κληρουχικήν, 205 δημοτικόν, 483 μνημονικός, 728 ἀποστερητικός, etc.

28 Addressed to an imaginary race-official.   **δρόμους** here "heats" (an internal accusative, as again in 29 with n.); contrast 25.   **τὰ πολεμιστήρια** ("the war-chariots", one of the categories of vehicle that were raced) is the subject of ἐλᾷ (here ~ "run").

29 ἐμὲ . . . τὸν πατέρ(α) is the external object of **ἐλαύνεις**, **πολλοὺς . . .
δρόμους** the internal object (99n.), with the position of ἐμέ at the very
beginning of the sentence lending it special emphasis; "you're driving *me*,
your father, a lot of heats!"

30 ἀτάρ (~ "but") marks a break in the thought or a sudden change of topic,
and is probably colloquial; cf. 187, 382, etc.   **χρέως ἔβη** rather than Doric
χρέος ἔβα is expected in Attic, and the words thus represent an elevated
poetic register; a *scholion* identifies them as a quotation from Euripides (fr.
1011). Cf. 278n. (on "Doric *alpha*"). Strepsiades uses **τί χρέος;** to mean "What
debt?" (cf. 13); in the Euripidean original, it probably meant simply "What?"

31 τρεῖς μναῖ = 300 drachmas or 1/20 of a talent; cf. 21n.   **δι-φρίσκου καὶ
τροχοῖν** "for a light chariot and two wheels" (genitives of price; see 22n.). δι-
φρίσκος (a *hapax* diminutive of δί-φρος, properly something that carries two
people) must be another specialty racing event, like the war-chariots in 28.
τροχοῖν is a dual (rare in Attic of this period, except for natural sets such as
eyes and hands; cf. English "pair", which is today commonly applied to cards,
pants, shoes and socks, but not much else except in archaic expressions such
as "a pair of horses").   A man named Ἀμεινίας—the proper spelling of the
name in Attica in the classical period, routinely converted to the common
later homophone Ἀμυνίας in the manuscripts, as in all witnesses except
V here—is attacked at 686–92 in a way normally reserved for socially and
politically important persons. This is perhaps an initial, glancing reference
to him as not just rich but less favorably a person who likes to lend money to
others at interest.

32 Addressed to an imaginary slave.   **ἐξ-αλίσας** "after you let him roll in
the dust" (< ἐξ-αλίνδω), something Xenophon's wealthy Ischomachus also has
a slave do with his horse after a ride before stabling it (*Oeconomicus* 11.18).

33 ὦ μέλ(ε) "my good sir, my friend"; a colloquial form of address often
expressing exasperation, as again in 1192, 1338.   **ἐξ-ήλικας ἐμέ γ(ε) ἐκ
τῶν ἐμῶν** "you've rolled (perfect < ἐξ-αλίνδω) *me* free of my (property)". γ(ε)
adds further emphasis to ἐμέ.

34 For **ὅτε**, 6–7n.   **καί** is adverbial, "in fact".   **ὤφληκα** perfect <
ὀφλισκάνω, "become a debtor" and thus with a form of δίκην (a sort of
accusative of respect) "lose a lawsuit and accordingly owe money" (also 777),
here for the principal and interest on some of his debts.   **(κ)α(ὶ ἕ)τεροι**
"and other (creditors)". κ and the rough breathing on the ε have combined to
produce χ, and χἄτεροι is therefore written rather than κἄτεροι or χἄτεροι.

34–5 τόκου / ἐνεχυράσεσθαί φασιν "they say they're going to take sureties (ἐνέχυρα) for the interest", i.e. some of his property will be seized by the court to guarantee that his creditors lose nothing if he fails to make his monthly payments. Cf. 241 τὰ χρήματ(α) ἐνεχυράζομαι ("I'm having my property taken as sureties"). Strepsiades describes his attempts to negotiate with such people at 1137–41: maddeningly, they insist on having their money, no matter what alternative suggestions he offers.

35 Pheidippides wakes up momentarily to complain about Strepsiades' apparent unwillingness to let him have a good night's sleep.   ἐτεός is "true, genuine", and neuter accusative **ἐτεόν** is here adverbial, adding emphasis to the question (~ an aggravated "*really*"), as again in 93, 820, 1502.

36 τὴν νύχ(τα) ὅλην is accusative of extent of time, "throughout the whole night, all night long"; cf. 75 ὅλην τὴν νύκτα, 463 τὸν πάντα χρόνον, 1129 τὴν νύκτα πᾶσαν.

37 Every Athenian citizen belonged to a "deme" (based on the original place of residence of his family; cf. 134), and the annual official in charge of the deme was the **δήμ-αρχος**. This passage suggests that a demarch's powers included the ability to enforce the seizure of property as ἐνέχυρα (34–5). But Strepsiades imagines the demarch as a bedbug or flea emerging from the sheepskins to "bite" him and keep him awake; cf. 12 δακνόμενος with n.   στρώματα (also 1069) is a -μα-noun (155n.) < στόρνυμι ("spread"), thus "bed, bedding".

38 δαιμόνιε "strange creature". An ostensibly friendly form of address, but often with a tone bordering on exasperation, as again in 816, 1138; seemingly treated as colloquial in the classical period. See 76n. on δαίμων.   τι is the internal object (99n.) of **κατα-δαρθεῖν**, "to get a bit of sleep".   Pheidippides lies back down in bed and drifts off again (cf. 78–9). Strepsiades nonetheless continues talking to—or at—him.

39 σὺ δ(έ) draws a sharp contrast with Strepsiades, who will be staying awake and worrying.   **ἴσθ(ι)** imperative < οἶδα, "be aware!"

40 εἰς τὴν κεφαλὴν ... τὴν σήν Troubles of all sorts are routinely said to settle on a person's head (e.g. *Acharnians* 833). Here the point of future **τρέψεται** is "when I die and you inherit the situation".

41a φεῦ "Yi!, Man!" Another inarticulate cry (cf. 1), here expressing grief.

41b εἴθ(ε) ὤφελ(ε) . . . ἀπ-ολέσθαι κακῶς "if only she had perished miserably!", i.e. "I hope she died a miserable death"; tragic style, amusingly out of keeping with the pedestrian matters about which Strepsiades goes on to complain.   **ἡ προ-μνήστρι(α)** "the matchmaker". Athenian society was nominally sex-segregated, and many marriages were probably arranged. Euripides (*Hippolytus* 589), Plato (*Theatetus* 149d–50a) and Xenophon (*Memorabilia* 2.6.36) all refer casually to matchmakers, making it clear that they were a common feature of everyday life.

42 ἥτις με γῆμ(αι) ἐπ-ῆρε "whoever she was who encouraged me to marry"; the verb is normally used in the active of men, and in the passive of women. ἐπ-ῆρε is aorist active indicative < ἐπ-αίρω; cf. 1457 ἐπήρατε. But scribes often neglected *iota*-subscript, and the proper reading might be imperfect ἐπ-ῆρε ("kept encouraging").

43 ἐμοὶ . . . ἦν ~ "I had". The most common function of a dative is to signal indirect interest in an action: a "very pleasant rustic lifestyle" existed (**ἦν ἄγροικος ἥδιστος βίος**), and Stepsiades was involved; cf. 56 with n., 107n., 175, 327n.

44–5 Catalogs of all sorts are a basic feature of comic language (50–2, 317–18, etc.), and part of their humor and appeal consists in their tendency to gather together unexpected and sometimes ill-matched items.   **εὐρωτιῶν** "being unbathed", i.e. "that involved no bathing". Taking an occasional bath was proper, normal behavior (cf. 836–7 with n., 991 with n.), and comedy comments unfavorably on people who stink (e.g. *Acharnians* 852–3). But Strepsiades was an unsophisticated countryman when he married, and the implication is that he now bathes, even if he might prefer not to.   **ἀ-κόρητος** "undisturbed by bedbugs" (κόρεις; cf. 634).   **εἰκῇ κείμενος** "lying around at random", i.e. "left to my own devices".   **βρύων μελίτταις καὶ προ-βάτοις καὶ στεμφύλοις** "full of honey-bees, and sheep and goats"—Greek πρό-βατα covers both—"and olive-cakes", all typical features of the Attic countryside. "Olive-cake" is the solid residue left after olives are crushed for oil; it appears to have been eaten, pulverized pits and all, or burned for fuel.

46–7 Μεγακλέους τοῦ Μεγακλέους / ἀδελφιδῆν "a niece of Megakles son of Megakles". Megakles was a name borne by a number of members of one of Athens' most powerful families, the Alkmeonidai, including a Megakles son of Megakles (*PA* 9597; *PAA* 636465) who was politically prominent in this period. Regardless of whether Aristophanes is referring to him in particular, therefore, the point is that the girl came from a wealthy, well-connected background. That Strepsiades was deliberately matched with her (41b–2) suggests that—despite the representation of him here as dirty, unsophisticated, and the like—we are to imagine him not as an average Athenian peasant, but as belonging to a relatively prosperous family (cf. 50 περιουσίας), even if he is now socially and economically in over his head (16–35).   **ἄγροικος ὤν** is concessive, "although I was a countryman", and is to be taken in strong contrast with **ἐξ ἄστεως**, which refers to the girl, "who was from the city".

48 σεμνήν "classy" (thus Dover).   **ἐγ-κεκοισυρωμένην** ~ "Koisyracized" (probably an Aristophanic coinage, and in any case an innovative, witty word). Koisyra is a real name and is associated with the Alkmeonid family (46–7n.) not only by the *scholia*, but by several ostraka from the early 5th century that refer to Megakles son of Hippokrates as "the son of Koisyra". This passage suggests that the name became a password referring to a demanding and expensive woman; cf. 800 (Strepsiades notes that Pheidippides is descended from Koisyra and is therefore disinclined to listen to his father).

49 συγ-κατ-εκλινόμην "I lay down with her", *sc.* in their marriage bed.

50 ὄζων "smelling of" + genitive (as routinely with such verbs; cf. 398, 761–3n., 1007).   **τρυγός, τρασιᾶς, ἐρίων, περι-ουσίας** "new wine, a fig-drying tray, wool, abundance/profit", with the final item in the list making the point that the young Strepsiades was relatively rich—for a "simple country-person".

51–2 μύρου, κρόκου, κατα-γλωττισμάτων, / δαπάνης, λαφυγμοῦ, Κωλιάδος, Γενετυλλίδος "perfumed oil, saffron, French kisses, expense, gluttony, Kôlias, Genetyllis". The last two items refer, respectively, to a local cult of Aphrodite and an obscure goddess linked at *Thesmophoriazusae* 130 to female sexuality (which, the contents of this portion of Strepsiades' list suggests, was a significant part of his bride's appeal).

53–5 οὐ μὴν ἐρῶ γ(ε) ὡς "I certainly won't say that . . ."; walking the criticism back for a moment, only to take it in another direction in what follows. ἐρῶ is the Attic future of εἴρω B.   **ἐσπάθα . . . λίαν σπαθᾷς** A σπάθη was a wooden blade used as a beater to force the threads placed on a loom closer together (= σπαθάω). Producing cloth for the household was among a woman's basic domestic duties, and Strepsiades initially seems to be saying that his extravagant wife at least did this. But the verb also had a colloquial sense ~ "squander", so that the punchline in 55, **λίαν σπαθᾷς**, means "you're spending far too much money".   The intensifying adverb **λίαν** (also 416, 716) generally has negative overtones in comedy, "way too much".   ἄν +

imperfect refers to repeated or habitual action; thus ἄν . . . / . . . ἔφασκον is "I always used to say".   **(τ)ὸ ἱμάτιον . . . τοδί** "this robe here", which must be threadbare, showing how little money Strepsiades has (and had).   **πρό-φασιν** "(as a) reason" (the second element is < φημί); in apposition to ἱμάτιον.

56 ἔλαιον ἡμῖν οὐκ ἔν-εστ(ι) ἐν τῷ λύχνῳ i.e. "Our lamp's out of oil", meaning no more light to do accounts by. For the dative, 43n., 57n.

57 οἴμοι is here an expression of angry exasperation ~ "Damn it!"; contrast 23.   **τί γάρ . . . λύχνον;** is compact and colloquial—i.e. an example of how people really spoke, rather than of conventionally complete, clear literary syntax—and γάρ marks the rest of the remark as an explanation of why Strepsiades said οἴμοι: "Because why did you . . . ?"   **μοι** merely expresses Strepsiades' investment in the issue, ~ "pray tell, please"; cf. 43n.   **τὸν πότην . . . λύχνον** "the drinking lamp", i.e. "the thirsty lamp", the one that consumes oil greedily; perhaps a commonplace expression (also at Plato Comicus fr. 206.2).   Why imperfect **ἦπτες** is used rather than aorist ἦψες (also metrically possible) is unclear; Dover suggests that it recalls the imperfective imperative ἅπτε in 18 (n.). Perhaps the point is instead that the Slave supposedly does this constantly.

58 ἵνα κλάῃς "so you can wail" (< κλαίω), i.e. "so I can hit you and make you wail". The future of the verb is generally deponent, thus **κλαύσομαι** in the Slave's response.   Post-positive **δῆτα** ("in fact") shows that the question involves a logical connection between two things, in this case between being hit and whatever the Slave has supposedly done. Colloquial; cf. 79, 87, 148, 154, 486, etc.

59 ὅτι "because".   **τῶν παχειῶν . . . θρυαλλίδων** "(one) of the thick wicks", meaning one that feeds more oil to the flame; cf. 57, 585 with n. The omission of the accusative (direct object of **ἐν-ετίθεις**) on which the genitive is dependent is another colloquial compression (cf. 57n.). As often, the root-verb takes one object (a wick), the pre-verb another (an implied τῷ λύχνῳ); cf. 74, 288–9.   Strepsiades takes a swing at the Slave—with his fist? or his stick? cf. 541–2n.—who runs back into the house. Whether the old man connects with his target is unclear (for us, but not for the original audience).

60 ὅπως "when" (LSJ *s.v.* A.I.7).   **νῷν** dative dual < νώ ("to the two of us, for the two of us").

61 serves to remind the audience of who is being discussed, after the interruption in 56–9.   **τῇ γυναικὶ τ(ῇ) ἀγαθῇ** is sarcastic, "my lovely wife".

62 (ἐ)ντεῦθεν "after this", i.e. after the birth of their son, and thus not merely repeating the sense of 60 μετὰ ταῦ(τα).   **ἐλοιδορούμεθα** "we began to quarrel"; but the verb suggests an exchange of verbal abuse rather than simple disagreement. Cf. 934, 1140.

63 ἵππον not "a horse" but "the element *hippos*", the point being that *hippos*-names imply wealth (14n.) and thus sound distinguished.   **προσ-ετίθει** conative imperfect < προσ-τίθημι, "she was trying to add".

64 Examples of the sort of name Strepsiades' wife would have liked: "The syntactical relation of 64 to 63 is not easily defined, but presents no problem of intelligibility" (Dover).

65 "whereas *I* was trying to name him Pheidonides, (the name) of his grandfather". It emerges at 134 that the grandfather's name was actually Pheidon, of which Pheidonides is a patronymic; so what Strepsiades means is really ~ "(after the name) of his grandfather". Naming a boy after an older male relative was common practice (cf. 46 "Megakles son of Megakles"). But the joke is that Pheidon is literally "Thrifty" or "Miserly" (cf. 421): Strepsiades' family was accustomed to saving money, whereas his wife liked to spend it.   θέσθαι ὄνομα is "to give a name" to a person; cf. 67 (ἐ)θέμεθα Φειδιππίδην, "we named him Pheidippides"; LSJ *s.v.* τίθημι A.IV.   **ἐγὼ δέ** is in pointed contrast to 63 ἡ μέν. That Strepsiades did not simply lay down the law on the matter either tells us something nominally damning about his relationship with his wife (he was not the dominant party, as a Greek man would have been expected to be) or suggests that some ancient marriages were more egalitarian than is generally assumed.

66 τέως μὲν οὖν . . . . · εἶτα τῷ χρόνῳ "for a while, therefore . . . ; but then eventually".

67 Φειδ-ιππίδην i.e. ~ Φειδωνίδην with the *hippos*-element jammed into the middle. This is not a real Athenian name and—to the extent that Greeks paid attention to what proper names "really meant", as opposed to their being conventional designations for people or places—must be intended to sound ridiculous (literally "Son of Thrifty Horse").

68 λαμβάνουσ(α) ἐκορίζετο Two contemporary actions: "she used to hold him in her arms and say to him fondly".

69–72 Both Strepsiades' hopes for his son and those of his wife are expressly incompletely, "what a sight you'll be!" or something similar being implied at the end.

69 πρὸς πόλιν is not "toward the city (out of the country)" but "up toward the Acropolis", as part of a ritual procession or the like, in a fashion worthy of the famous Uncle Megakles (for whom, see also 124–5). That the target of this play is Socrates and his school has not yet even been hinted at, and it is an intriguing possibility that all the various references to and remarks about the well-known Megakles (46–7n.) in the prologue serve to create the deliberately false impression that it is actually going to be directed against him.

70 ξυστίδ(α) ἔχων "wearing a *xystis*", which a *scholion* identifies as a purple- or saffron-dyed robe worn by horsemen in processions and by kings in tragedy, i.e. showy clothing adopted only by the rich and on special occasions. What Megakles is supposed to be celebrating is obscure to us today, but the original audience may well have recognized this as a reference to some notorious recent event.

71 Supply ἐλαύνῃς from the mother's parallel wish in 69, with the verb used here in a slightly different sense: "when you drive the goats (into the village/ farm)", like a simple peasant.   **μὲν οὖν** is "to the contrary" (as also in 221, 1112); there is no balancing δέ, because Strepsiades' revery breaks off before he can offer the balancing clause.   φελλεύς is poor, rocky land suited only for marginal purposes such as grazing goats, areas with richer soil or more water being reserved for fruit trees, vines, grain or vegetables.

72 διφθέραν ἐνημμένος "clothed in (perfect middle-passive participle < ἐνάπτω) a *diphthera*", a rough outer garment made of cowhide—and thus radically different from Uncle Megakles' *xystis* (70).

73–4 abruptly bring the narrative back to the present after the extended description of the background to the action at 41–55, 60–72. Cf. 75–6n.

73 οὐδέν is an internal accusative with **οὐκ ἐπείθετο**, "he rendered no obedience whatsoever", or (rendered adverbially) "he didn't heed at all"; cf. 99n., 106 τι κήδει with n.

74 ἵππερόν μοι κατ-έχεεν τῶν χρημάτων "he poured horse-fever down over my property, he drowned my property in horse-fever"; the root-verb takes the accusative, the pre-verb the genitive (cf. 59n.), while the dative signals interest or involvement (here to Strepsiades' disadvantage).   ἵππερος is a coinage intended to recall words such as ἴκτερος ("jaundice") and ὕδερος ("dropsy").

75–6 An unexpected twist that sets the direction of the action that follows: Strepsiades is not merely desperate about how to handle his debts, and thus unable to sleep (as e.g. 12–14, 34–7, 39–40, seemed to suggest), but has used the night to develop a plan.

75 ὅλην τὴν νύκτα 36n.; to be taken with the participle that follows.

75–6 ὁδοῦ / μίαν . . . ἀτραπόν literally "a single path of a road", i.e. "one narrow route to get me out (of this situation)".

76 δαίμων (cognate with English "demon") is a generic term for a deity whose presence or power can be sensed, even if he or she cannot necessarily be identified by name, or for one that does not fit neatly in the normal system of categorization (thus Socrates' term for the Clouds at 253). Someone who is δαιμόνιος (38 with n.) is seemingly under the power of a δαίμων, while someone persecuted or inspired by a bad one is κακο-δαίμων (104, 698), and someone inspired by new wine is a τρυγο-δαίμων (296 with n.). Adverbial **δαιμονίως** is thus ~ "devilishly".   ὑπερ-φυής is "beyond nature", i.e. "beyond the ordinary run of things, extraordinary". This is *inter alia* buildup—even more emphatic in 77—for what is to come, and the poet accordingly increases the suspense by sending his main character off in a different direction for a few verses (through 87).

77 ἀνα-πείσω aorist active subjunctive < ἀνα-πείθω. The verb here takes a double accusative, of (1) the person to be persuaded (**τουτονί**, i.e. Pheippides) and (2) the thing he is to be persuaded of (**ἥν**, referring back to the path in 76 and thus the plan it represents).   **σωθήσομαι** future passive < σῴζω ("save"; the *iota*-subscript is preserved only when the *zeta* is present).

78 ἐξεγεῖραι aorist active infinitive < ἐξεγείρω, "wake up".   **πρῶτον** is adverbial, "first".

79 The repetition of **πῶς;** adds a desperate tone: "How . . . ? *How*?" Cf. the repetition of e.g. ἄν-οιγ(ε) at 181, μήπω γε at 196 (cf. 267), ἐκεῖνο at 656.   **δῆτ(α)** (58n.) here marks the logical connection between Strepsiades' need to wake Pheidippides up and his desire to do so in the least offensive fashion possible.   **ἥδιστ(α)** (superlative neuter plural < ἡδύς) is adverbial, "most pleasantly", i.e. "in the nicest way I can". This is further proof—if any were needed—that Strepsiades is not in control of his son, but is instead controlled by him.

80 Φειδιππίδη is a vocative, **Φειδιππίδιον** a diminutive of the nominative form (used, as it often is, in place of a vocative). The tone of the latter is wheedling; "sweet little Pheidippides"; cf. 132 παιδίον (Strepsiades needs a slave to answer the door), 223 Σωκρατίδιον (Strepsiades needs Socrates to pay attention to him). Pheidippides responds by sitting up in bed.

81 κύσον με καὶ τὴν χεῖρα δὸς τὴν δεξιάν ("kiss me and give me your right hand!"; the verbs are aorist active imperatives, from κυνέω and δίδωμι, respectively) is probably an example of *hysteron-proteron* (literally "the later former", i.e. reversing the proper order of events); cf. 836–7, and contrast *Frogs* 754–5 "Give me your right hand and let me kiss you!" A kiss is a typical gesture of greeting, much as in various parts of Europe and the Middle East today.

82 The adverb **ἰδού** (~ "there you go!, voila!") is a colloquial way of signaling that one has performed an action another party has requested; cf. 255, 635, 825, etc.   **εἰπέ μοι** (literally "tell me!") is a typical means of adding urgency to a question, as again at 200, 637, 847.

83 νὴ τὸν Ποσειδῶ "Yes, by Poseidon!" Aristophanic oaths, particularly when sworn by major deities, tend to have a bland generic character and to be chosen mostly to fit the metrical space available in the line. But the second half of this one (**τὸν ἵππιον**, "god of horses") makes it significant: this is a god to whom Pheidippides feels a real kinship. Cf. 91n., 773n. Positive oaths, or oaths reinforcing a positive statement, take **νή**; negative oaths, or oaths reinforcing a negative statement, take μά (e.g. 108, 121).   Deictic **τουτονί** suggests the presence of a statue of Poseidon onstage (see 8n.), even if no other reference is made to it in the course of the play.

84 A verb—λέγε or the like—is omitted after **μή** (thus "don't (mention)!") in a way typical of the casual speech that comic dialogue aspires to imitate. Cf. 433 μὴ 'μοιγε ("Don't (talk) to me about . . . !"). Either **'μοιγε** (Wilson) or μοι γε (Dover) could be printed without altering the letters that have been passed down in the manuscripts, meaning that this is purely a matter of modern editorial decision-making. But (ἔ)μοιγε is emphatic—"Don't mention Poseidon to *me*!"—and is thus to be preferred as better matching Strepsiades' mood, as again in 433. Contrast 108, where unemphatic γέ μοι rather than emphatic γ' ἔμοι is clearly right on the same principle.   **μηδαμῶς** is a colloquial means of reinforcing **μή** ("not in any way, not at all"). Cf. οὐδαμῶς reinforcing οὐ (or an implied οὐ) at e.g. 688; *Wasps* 1126.

85 αἴτιός μοι τῶν κακῶν "responsible for troubles for me", i.e. "responsible for my troubles".

86 The suffix -περ intensifies εἰ; thus "if in fact".   The adverb ὄντως is < εἰμι (cf. participial forms such as ὄντος) and is thus "in reality, really".

87 πιθοῦ is a 2ⁿᵈ-person singular aorist middle imperative, while πίθωμαι is deliberative aorist middle subjunctive (describing an imagined action: "in regard to what could I obey you?").   For δῆτα, 58n.

88 ἔκ-στρεψον literally "turn inside out!" (thus the *scholia*), i.e. "reverse!" (also 554).   τοὺς σαυτοῦ τρόπους This use of the reflexive pronoun (literally "of yourself") rather than the possessive adjective (which in this case would have been σούς) to indicate possession seems to reflect an emerging trend in spoken Greek in this period, and is common in comedy; cf. 478, 960, 994, etc.   ὡς τάχιστα "as quickly as possible" (also 182, 839, 1484).

89 ἃ (ἅ)ν παρ-αινέσω The verb is aorist subjunctive, because this is as yet only imaginary action; ~ "the things I have it in mind to propose". Conditional, relative and temporal clauses with the subjunctive take ἄν (e.g. 404, 589, 1458–9).

90 With a verb, δή adds emphasis in a way English does by means of stress; "*tell* (me)!"   τι πείσει; literally "will you render some obedience?" or "will you obey somehow?" (an internal accusative; see 99n.), i.e. "will you do what I say?"

91 νὴ τὸν Διόνυσον is a relatively common oath in Aristophanes and is perhaps used here simply to avoid repeating the metrically equivalent νὴ τὸν Ποσειδῶ in 83, rather than as a way to suggest that Pheidippides likes drinking as well as racing horses; used again by Pheidippides again at 108; by the poet himself, speaking through the chorus, at 519 (n.); and by the Weaker Argument at 1000 (n.).   Despite LSJ *s.v.*, δεῦρο can mean both "here" and "there", provided a gesture or the context makes the sense clear. This is in any case a reasonable point in the action for Pheidippides to get out of bed; pull on some clothing—the sort of action that our texts, which merely record the words said onstage, routinely ignore (cf. 11n., 729–30n.)—; and follow Strepsiades over toward center stage.

92 τὸ θύριον (< θύρα, "door", with which it is cognate) and τ(ὸ οἰ)κίδιον (< οἶκος, "house") are wheedling diminutives used to pave the way for the request in 107, 111: if this is only a "little door" and a "little house", it is no great matter to ask Pheidippides to become a student there. The door and house in question, in any case, are one of the two in the stage front and are not physically small in any obvious way.

93 τοῦτ(ο) picks up τ(ὸ οἰ)κίδιον in 92, the door being ignored as merely a part of the larger structure.   **ἐτεόν** 35n.

94 φροντιστήριον is < φρόντις ("thought, reflection, meditation"), thus "Thinkery". The word is not attested before this and is not found again outside this play until the Roman period. It is thus probably a mocking Aristophanic coinage; cf. 266n. on φροντιστής.

95–6 τὸν οὐρανόν is the object of **λέγοντες,** but also supplies the subject for **ἔστιν.** The word is placed at the beginning of the clause because it is the key term for everything that follows ("as for the sky, when they discuss it . . ."). Supply ἡμᾶς or the like as the object of **ἀνα-πείθουσιν** ("they do their best to convince (us)"). Socrates and his school are associated already here at the very beginning of Aristophanes' play with speculation about what we today would call scientific rather than merely philosophic matters. This is very much at odds with Plato's portrait of Socrates in the *Apology*; cf. 98n., and see Introduction §II.   A **πνιγεύς** (< πνίγω, "suffocate, choke"; cf. 1504 ἀπο-πνιγήσομαι) is a hemispherical terracotta baking-shell roughly similar to a modern Weber grill, which was placed over burning charcoal (**(οἱ) ἄνθρακες**) to get it hot enough for baking. The idea is thus that the sky is a solid shell that rests above the—implicitly flat—earth on which we stand. The image is put in the mouth of the astronomer Meton at *Birds* 1000–1 and was earlier assigned to the pre-Socratic philosopher Hippon by the comic poet Cratinus (fr. 167). Regardless of who used it first, therefore, this is an established trope and not something Aristophanes made up.

98 ἀργύριον literally "silver", i.e. "money", with the metal itself coming from the local mines at Laurion and thus from slave-labor. This characterization as well (cf. 95–6n.) stands in stark contrast to what Plato's Socrates has to say about himself in the *Apology*: according to Aristophanes, he taught for money. Cf. 669, 876, 1146, and see Introduction §II.

99 λέγοντα governs **καὶ δίκαια κ(αὶ) ἄδικα,** "by saying both just things and unjust things", i.e. "whether one makes a honest argument or a dishonest argument". These are internal accusatives—the arguments are the product of the speech rather than pre-existing it—for which Greek tends to use a vivid verb (here λέγω) and a bland, often cognate noun (here ~ λόγους) or a pronoun such as τι (e.g. 22, 106) or οὐδέν (e.g. 73). English, by contrast, generally uses a bland verb (here "make") and puts the crucial information in the object ("an honest argument or a dishonest argument").   **νικᾶν** is "to win (one's arguments)", but Strepsiades means above all else "to win (one's cases in court)". The point is momentarily put off, and the old man returns to it again only at 112–18, after the mysterious thinkers have been identified.

100 οὐκ οἶδ(α) ἀκριβῶς τ(ὸ ὄ)νομα is an oddly evasive remark—Strepsiades *does* certainly know who he is talking about—and must again reflect the old man's desire to convince Pheidippides (cf. 80n., 92n.): the longer the ugly words "Socrates and Chairephon" (cf. 102–4) can be kept out of the conversation, the better.

101 Perhaps best divided thus, as two separate and arguably conflicting characterizations: **μεριμνο-φροντισταί** (attested nowhere else and almost certainly another mocking coinage; cf. 94n., 266n.) are ~ "careful thinkers", while **καλοί τε κἀγαθοί** is an old tag that means ~ "aristocrats" (cf. 797; normally without τε, required by the meter in both of these lines)—which Socrates and his people emphatically are not.

102 αἰβοῖ a colloquial expression of disgust; "yuck!, ick!" (also 829, 906).   **γ(ε)** adds emphasis to **πονηροί** in the same way that an exclamation mark might in an English text: "nasty people!" Cf. 1462 πονηρά γ(ε) ("nasty actions!").   **οἶδα** "I know (who you're talking about)".   **ἀλαζών** (also 449, 1492) is an abusive term for a self-promoting talker of nonsense and fakery, similar to English "bullshitter".

103 ὠχριῶντας is < ὠχριάω, "to be yellowish, pallid" (ὠχρός; cognate with English "ochre"), i.e. to lack a tan as a result of spending time indoors, which the Greeks regarded as a mark of being less than "a real man". Cf. Pheidippides' objections at 119–20, 1112 regarding the consequences of becoming one of Socrates' students; the Socratically educated Strepsiades' regrets at 718 (n.), and his joyous remark when he sees his newly educated son at 1171b; the blanched faces of the current students at 185–6; and the Stronger Argument's warning at 1017.   **ἀν-υπο-δήτους** literally "not (privative *alpha*) bound (< δέω) beneath (ὑπό)", i.e. "wearing no sandals (ὑπο-δήματα)". Socrates notoriously went barefoot in all seasons (363), something a person of Pheidippides' social status would never consider doing except as an ostentatious display of nominal simplicity.

104 ὧν "among whom (are)", i.e. "who include".   The definite article (here ὁ) is sometimes given with only the first member of a coordinated pair; cf. 622 τὸν Μέμνον' ἢ Σαρπηδόνα, 1418 τοὺς γέροντας ἢ νέους (where the manuscripts have added another, metrically impossible τούς), 1465 τὸν Χαιρεφῶντα τὸν μιαρὸν καὶ Σωκράτη.   **κακο-δαίμων** 76n.   **Χαιρεφῶν**

of the deme Sphettos (*PA* 15203; *PAA* 976969) was Socrates' long-time associate, and at one point supposedly visited Delphi to ask if anyone was wiser than his friend (Plato *Apology* 20e–1a). In *Clouds* he is intimately associated with the management of the Thinkery (cf. 144–58, 501–3, 830–1, 1465), but never appears onstage, unless he is one of the anonymous characters who flee the burning building at the very end (1493–1505n.).

105 ἤ ἤ is a colloquial way of getting someone's attention, here in order to register a protest; "hey hey!"   **μηδὲν εἴπῃς** A form of μή + 2nd-person subjunctive is routinely used to give a negative command, here "don't say anything!" (a "prohibitive subjunctive"); cf. 614, 834, 1138, 1479 (parallel to a present imperative in 1478).   νή-πιος is < ἔπος ("word") with the privative prefix νη-, and is thus literally "unable to talk" and so "infantile" (< Latin *infans*, which has the same root sense as the Greek word).

106 τι is an internal accusative (99n.) with **κήδει**: "if you feel any concern" or (rendered adverbially) "if you care at all", with a genitive of what the subject cares about.   ἄλφιτα are literally "barley groats" (i.e. hulled but unground barley), a basic household staple used in particular to make μᾶζα (unbaked barley-cake); cf. 640 (a barley-meal dealer), 669n. (a kneading-trough for making barley-cakes), 675–6n. (on the etymology of μᾶζα and *matzo*). The word is used metaphorically here to mean ~ "ability to put food on the table", as again in 176, 648, 669.

107 τούτων γενοῦ "become (deponent aorist middle imperative < γίγνομαι; also 1481) one of these people!"   **μοι** A dative meaning "for my sake" (cf. σοι in 111, μοι in 116), i.e. a so-called "dative of advantage", is often used with an imperative in a sense very close to English "please"; thus the *Odyssey* begins ἄνδρα μοι ἔννεπε, Μοῦσα, "please tell (us), Muse!" (not "tell me, Muse!"). Cf. 43n., 220, 595.   **σχασάμενος** < σχάζω, "let go" and thus here "abandon". For the way the participle coordinates with the main verb, 146–7n., 149–50n., and cf. ἐλθών in 111.   **τὴν ἱππικήν** "your horsemanship" (cf. 27 with n.).

108 οὐκ ἄν "I wouldn't (do that)".   **μὰ τὸν Διόνυσον** 91n.   **εἰ ... γέ** in a protasis following a negative "is perhaps colloquial in tone" (Denniston, *Greek Particles* 126; cf. *Acharnians* 966; *Wasps* 297–8; *Wealth* 924).   **δοίης** aorist optative < δίδωμι.   **γέ μοι** 84n.

109 φασιανούς "pheasants", apparently kept for show, like the famous peacocks that belonged to Pyrilampes son of Antiphon (*PA* 12493; *PAA* 795965), who exhibited them on the first day of the month (Antipho fr. 57;

adesp. com. fr. 702).   Leogoras of the deme Kydathenaion (*PA* 9075; *PAA* 605075) was notoriously wealthy, well-connected and extravagant; cf. *Wasps* 1269b/70a; Eupolis fr. 50; Plato Comicus fr. 114.2–3.

110 ἴθ(ι) 2nd-person singular imperative < εἶμι (*ibo*); used colloquially much like English "come on!", as again in 220, 237, etc.

111 διδάσκου present middle-passive imperative, "try to get yourself taught!, try to get yourself an education!"

112 The discussion returns to the point where it broke off after 99: what is the attraction of the Thinkery for Strepsiades?   **ἄμφω τὼ λόγω** is an accusative dual. Cf. the nominative dual ὁμοίω in 394 and the genitive dual τούτοιν . . . τοῖν λόγοιν in 114.

113 Dover takes parenthetic **ὅστις ἐστί** to mean "no matter what it is", i.e. "on any subject" or "in any given case", as again in 883. It might just as well mean "whatever that is" and be an effective bit of small-scale characterization: Strepsiades could not care less about the better/stronger argument (i.e. the one that *ought* to win), his interest being exclusively in the worse/weaker argument (called "the unjust/wrong argument" in 116), since he is in the wrong and he knows it. The personified Arguments themselves actually come onstage at 889–1112.

114 τούτοιν . . . τοῖν λόγοιν 112n.

115 νικᾶν λέγοντά φασι τ(ὰ) ἀ-δικώτερα cf. 99 with n.

116 μοι "to my advantage, for me" (107n.) and thus ~ "as I am asking".

118 ἄν has two standard positions, directly next to its verb and second in its clause; here in its first appearance it occupies both, as again at the beginning of 119. The particle is often repeated with **οὐδ(έ)** ("not even", introducing another clause), with no effect on the meaning.   **ἀπο-δοίην** (also 755) aorist active optative < ἀπο-δίδωμι, "give back", i.e. "pay back".   An ὀβολός = 1/6 of a drachma; nominally the smallest monetary unit, although in practice obols could be divided. But the word originally meant an iron "spit" (for roasting meat; ὀβελός in Attic in this period, cf. 178 ὀβελίσκον; see also 1285–6n.), these having once been used as a primitive form of currency; a handful of spits was a δράγμα/δραχμή (< δράσσομαι, "take hold of"; for the formation, 155n.).

119 In the second half of the verse, ἄν has been pushed out of second position by γάρ (also post-positive), but is in any case in its other standard position (cf. 118n. and e.g. 167), directly next to the verb τλαίην (optative < τλάω, "endure" and thus here ~ "put up with"; cf. 23 τάλας with n.).

120 τοὺς ἱππέας ("the knights", i.e. the wealthy young men who made up Athens' cavalry) are the direct object of 119 ἰδεῖν, while τὸ χρῶμα ("my color", i.e. "my skin-tone") is accusative of respect with δια-κεκναισμένος (perfect passive participle < δια-κναίω, literally "scrape away"). For the sense, 103n.

121 ἄρα "in that case" (also e.g. 165, 188). Post-positive (i.e. never the first word in its clause); contrast interrogative ἆρα (466 with n.), which comes first.   μὰ τὴν Δήμητρα (cf. the positive form at 455) is another common Aristophanic oath and thus cannot automatically be assumed to have been chosen because Demeter is the goddess of grain and so of household provisions (cf. 106n.).   ἔδει is 2nd-person singular future middle (deponent) < ἐσθίω, "eat"; with the genitive τῶν γ(ε) ἐμῶν "eat any of my (goods/food)". The verb agrees with its first subject (122 "you yourself"), but then picks up additional subjects after that.

122 ὁ ζύγιος "In a racing team of four horses . . . the two in the middle are ζύγιοι" (because they were attached directly to the ζυγόν, "yoke", and did the pulling), "the two on the outside σειρα-φόροι" (because they "bore" only a σεῖρα, "rope, rein") (Dover).   ὁ σαμ-φόρας "your horse with a *san*-brand"; cf. 23n., 1298. σάν is a rough—supposedly Dorian—equivalent of the letter the Athenians called *sigma*.

123 ἐξ-ελῶ future active < ἐξ-ελαύνω, "drive out".   ἐς κόρακας ("to the ravens!") is a colloquial curse that refers literally to dumping a body somewhere unburied, allowing scavenger birds to feed on it; cf. 133 with n., 646, 789, 871. Note ἐς (routine with this expression, and thus not merely a random scribal variation) in place of the standard Attic εἰς, confirming the fixed antique character of the expression.

124 περι-όψεται deponent is future middle < περι-οράω, "overlook, ignore".   θεῖος (cognate with e.g. Spanish *tio*) is an Attic word for "uncle" (not the adjective meaning "divine"). For Uncle Megakles, cf. 69–70.

125 Onstage settings can shift abruptly in Attic comedy, and εἴσ-ειμι ("I'm going into (the house)") makes it clear that somewhere in the last thirty lines or so we have ceased to be inside Strepsiades' house and are now in the street in front of the Thinkery.   **φροντιῶ** future < φροντίζω, "think about, pay attention to" (+ genitive). Pheidippides stalks off into his father's house.

126 "Well, *I* won't just lie there after I've fallen either!" (an image borrowed from wrestling, a favorite Greek sport; cf. 179, 551, 1047); i.e. if Pheidippides can take a firm stand, so can his father!   **μέν-τοι** (~ "however"; see 329n.) adds emphasis to the pronoun, which is only here because Strepsiades means "*I*" rather than "I", as again at e.g. 340.

127 εὐξάμενος τοῖσιν θεοῖς "after I make a prayer", for good luck—something accomplished simply by saying this. For the coordination of the participle with the main verb, 149–50n.   Future middle **διδάξομαι** might be either "I'll get myself taught" or "I'll get myself an education", there being no separate future passive form of the verb in Attic.

128 βαδίζω (also 162, 415, etc.) is a colloquial Attic equivalent of βαίνω. The action in question is properly contemporary with that of the main verb (127); English would say "I'll go and get myself taught/get myself an education".

129 anticipates Strepsiades' disastrous performance as a student at 627–790. **(ἐ)πι-λήσμων** "forgetful" (< ἐπι-λανθάνομαι, "let (something) escape one's notice, forget something", as in 631 with n.).   **βραδύς** is literally "slow", precisely as in colloquial English.

130 λόγων ἀκριβῶν σκινδαλάμους literally "slivers of precise arguments", i.e. precise little arguments of the sort Strepsiades anticipates needing in court.

131 ἰτη-τέον (< εἶμι, *ibo*) is a verbal adjective (always passive in sense) of a sort seemingly popularized by intellectuals in this period to indicate necessity: literally "(it is) needing to be gone", i.e. "I have to go". Cf. 727 οὐ μαλθακισ-τέ(α), ἀλλὰ περι-καλυπ-τέα, literally "it must not be softened, but it must be covered up", i.e. "you can't be weak, you have to cover yourself up again", 728 ἐξ-ευρε-τέος, "must be discovered", 760 ζητητέον, "must be sought", etc.   **ταῦτ(α)** is an internal accusative with **ἔχων στραγγεύομαι** ("go on loitering"); literally "go on loitering these (loiterings)", although English would use an adverb and say "loiter this way". This use of the participle of ἔχω is a colloquial way of saying "go on, continue, keep" doing something (thus also 509, 752), in this case hanging about Socrates' door without knocking; see LSJ s.v. B.IV.2.

132 ἀλλ(ὰ) οὐχὶ κόπτω literally "but I don't knock", i.e. "rather than knocking". Over the last few lines, Strepsiades has made his way up to the door of the Thinkery, which he now pounds on or kicks (cf. 136 with n.).   **παιδίον** 8on.

133 What follows is a typical Aristophanic scene: a visitor knocks at a door, wanting to speak with the master; a slave opens the door and tries to shoo the visitor away; the slave's behavior offers an initial glimpse into the character of the household; and eventually the master appears. Here it looks like the door-keeper steps outside and closes the door behind him, since Strepsiades must ask that it be opened again in 181–3. Dover and Wilson (following the *scholia*) identify the character who answers the door as a μαθητής ("student"), among other reasons because he is rude to Strepsiades and knows some of the secrets reserved for Socrates' pupils (cf. 140). But Agathon's door-keeper slave is equally rude to Inlaw in *Thesmophoriazusae*; the secrets belong to the household rather than to the school *per se*; the students are a separate group who come on at 184; and—most important—since 132 prepares us for the appearance of a slave and there is no indication to the contrary in the text, there is no reason to assume that this is *not* a slave.   **βάλλ(ε) ἐς κόρακας** literally "throw (yourself) to the ravens!", i.e. "go to hell!" See 123n.

134 Within Attica, an Athenian identified himself by three names: his own, his father's (in the genitive, thus "son of . . ."), and that of his deme (here with the suffix -θεν, "from . . .", as opposed to the more common use of an adjectival form, as in 156; for demes, see 37n.). Like most early Aristophanic heroes, Strepsiades has an invented name—literally "Son of Twister", i.e. ~ "Wriggle-son"—that tells the audience something important about him, here his desire to "twist" his way out of his situation; cf. 434n., 776. Early Aristophanic heroes are often assigned their name relatively late in the action—Strepsiades actually much earlier than most.   For Φείδων, 65n.   The location of Kikynna (mentioned again in 210) has not been identified with any certainty. But Strepsiades says expressly at 138 that he is from deep in the country and is thus not a sophisticated city person. Cf. 46–7n., 628.

135 ἀ-μαθής "uneducated" (< privative *alpha* + μανθάνω).   σφόδρα is an adverbial intensifier ("really, a lot"; cf. 191, 400, 1492), and **οὑτωσὶ σφόδρα** is literally "thus much", i.e. "so vigorously". It modifies λελάκτικας in the next line, but is probably to be taken separately from the adverb at the beginning there.

136 ἀ-περι-μερίμνως "without thinking about it", i.e. "thoughtlessly". **λελάκτικας** perfect < λακτίζω ("kick"); perhaps a bullying characterization of a much more modest knock.

137 ἐξ-ήμβλωκας perfect < ἐξ-αμβλόω, "cause to miscarry" (used here metaphorically).

138 σύγ-γνωθι 2nd-person singular aorist active imperative < συγ-γιγνώσκω, "share an understanding with" + dative, and thus "forgive" (since if one shares a sense of what happened in some situation with another person, one has gone a long way toward not holding him or her entirely responsible for what was done).   The genitive **τῶν ἀγρῶν** modifies the adverb **τηλοῦ**, "in a distant part of the fields, far out in the country". For Strepsiades' rustic background, cf. 43–50, 71–2.

140 οὐ θέμις ("it's not right, it's not permitted") has a sacred or moral flavor: this is not a practical prohibition, but something approaching what we would call a religious one. Cf. 143, 295.

141 θαρρῶν (< θαρσέω/Attic θαρρέω), "get up your courage (and + main verb)!", i.e. "don't worry—go ahead and . . . !"; also 422, 427, etc.

143 μύω is to shut one's eyes or mouth, and **μυστήρια** are not just "mysteries" in the prosaic modern English sense, but "sacred secrets" of the type shared for example during the rituals at Eleusis. Cf. 140, 303 with n.

144–71 The Slave's report is our first glimpse into life in the Thinkery, which—despite his respectful presentation of events and Strepsiades' apparent enthusiasm—turns out to be a dirty, hungry place devoted to trivial and ridiculous "research".

144 ἀν-ήρετ(ο) aorist middle (deponent) < ἀν-είρομαι, "ask someone (accusative) a question" (also 156).   **ἄρτι** (adverb) "just now, just a moment ago" (also 853). For Chairephon, 104n.

145 ψύλλαν ὁπόσους ἄλλοιτο τοὺς αὑτῆς πόδας "regarding a flea, how many of its own feet it could jump". This is an indirect report of a question, not a quotation of the question itself. The original πόσους; is accordingly converted into ὁ-πόσους (cf. 157–8 with n., 214, 1248, etc.), and since the question was posed in the past and the introductory verb is thus in a secondary tense (144 ἀν-ήρετ(ο)), the verb goes into the optative (replacing the original indicative ἄλλεται). Contrast e.g. 214, where the indicative is retained after an implied primary tense. For the fronting of the crucial word "flea" (prolepsis), 250–1n.

146–7 δακοῦσα aorist active participle < δάκνω. When an aorist participle is coordinated with an aorist main verb, the idea is often that the participial action is completed first; cf. 149–50n., 274n.   **ὀφρῦν** "brow, eyebrow" (a cognate); cf. 582.   **ἀφ-ήλατο** deponent aorist middle < ἀφ-άλλομαι, "jump off".

148 δια-μετρέω is "measure out" or "complete a measurement"; cf. 149n.   **δεξιώτατα** is adverbial, "very right-handedly", i.e., "very adroitly, very cleverly". Cf. 629 σκαιός ("left-handed" = "clumsy, stupid").

149 κηρὸν δια-τήξας "after melting (< δια-τήκω) some wax". The pre-verb intensifies the sense (~ "thoroughly, completely"; cf. 148 δι-εμέτρησε with n., 166 δι-εντερεύματος with n.).   The repeated use of **εἶτα** (cf. 151 κα(ὶ εἶ)τα) or ἔπειτα (e.g. 163) to add new sections to a story is a bit of naive narrative style typical of comedy and presumably of everyday speech.

149–50 λαβὼν / ἐν-έβαψεν 146–7n. English normally coordinates two finite verbs in a situation such as this and says "he took . . . and he dipped". Greek, by contrast, likes to use a combination of a participle and a finite verb and say ~ "under the circumstances of taking, he dipped". Cf. 107 γενοῦ . . . σχασάμενος τὴν ἱππικήν (in English "abandon horsemanship and become!"), 111 ἐλθὼν διδάσκου (in English "go and try to learn!"), 152 ὑπολύσας ἀνεμέτρει τὸ χωρίον (in English "he took them off and tried to measure the distance"), 288–90, etc.   **ἐν-έβαψεν** < ἐμ-βάπτω (cognate with "baptize").   **τὼ πόδε** accusative dual < πούς (assimilating the flea to a person by ignoring the fact that they actually have *six* feet).

151 ψυχείσῃ ("after it cooled"; aorist passive participle < ψύχω) ought properly to refer to the wax (masculine), but actually agrees with the flea (feminine).   **Περσικαί** "Persian (shoes)" of a type apparently fashionable for women in Athens in this period (*Lysistrata* 229–30; *Ecclesiazusae* 319).

153 τῆς λεπτότητος is an exclamatory genitive ("what refinement, what subtlety!"), a type of ablatival genitive that identifies the cause of something (here the speaker's reaction); common in comedy (also e.g. 364, 818, 925, 1476) and thus probably in everyday speech. For "subtlety of thought" as typical of Socrates and his students, also 229–30, 320, 359, 740–1, etc.

154 τί δῆτ(α) ἄν; "What would you (say), then?" The missing verb is obvious and can accordingly be omitted in casual, colloquial speech.

155 φρόντισ-μα is the product of an important noun-formation strategy that was particularly active in the late 5th century: verbal root + -μα = the product of the action in question, thus φρόντισμα < φροντίζω is a "thought, reflection"; cf. 205 σόφισ-μα ("bit of cleverness" < σοφίζω, "be σοφός"), 248 νόμισ-μα ("currency, coinage" < νομίζω, "use customarily"), etc. Contrast nouns in -σις (gerunds), which describe the action itself (e.g. 269 ἐπίδει-ξιν, 764 ἀφάνι-σιν, 874–5 ἀπόφευ-ξιν . . . / κλῆ-σιν . . . χαύνω-σιν with n., 937b παίδευ-σιν). φρόντισμα is attested only here before the Roman period and is thus perhaps supposed to sound amusingly eccentric ("thinkification").   οἷος and cognates describe quality; contrast ὅσος and cognates, which describe quantity (e.g. indirect ὁ-πόσοις in 20). With the initial π, which turns the word into an interrogative, **ποῖον;** is thus "what sort (of φρόντισμα)?" Cf. 342 τοιαῦται ("of this sort, like this") with n., 650–1.   **κάτ-ειπε** aorist active imperative < κατα-λέγω, "describe in detail" (cognate with English "catalog"); also 170 and 224 in the same position in the line, where the poet clearly found it useful.

156 ἀν-ήρετ(ο) αὐτόν 144n.   **ὁ Σφήττιος** is Chairephon's deme-name (cf. 134n.), "from Sphettos".

157–8 ὁ-πότερα τὴν γνώμην ἔχοι literally "whether he had the opinion that . . .", i.e. "whether he was of the opinion that . . ." Since this is an indirect report of a question, the original πότερα; (signaling that there will two alternatives, one of which must be chosen; see 203n.) is converted into **ὁ-πότερα;**, and since the question was posed in the past and is thus introduced by a secondary tense, the original 2nd-person indicative ἔχεις is moved into the 3rd-person optative. Cf. 145n. The second option is introduced by ἤ.   **τὰς ἐμπίδας** "gnats" (= the subject of the infinitive in 158).   **κατά** ("in accord with") is here ~ "through" or "with".   ἄδω is a contracted form of ἀείδω (also 721, 1358, 1360).   **τὸ (ὀ)ρρο-πύγ-ιον** "rump (of an animal)"; < ὀρρός ("tailbone") + πυγή ("buttocks") + a diminutive ending. This is not a dirty word. But it is a surprise, and it is therefore reserved for the end.

159 This line—like most of what Strepsiades has to say between here and 180—does not advance the discussion and is instead an example of a common Aristophanic device that serves to break up what would otherwise be a long descriptive speech, making it look more like ordinary conversation; cf. the brief, unnecessary responses at the end of 652, 694, etc.

160–2 τὸ (ἔ)ντερον "the gut" (as in English "gastro-entero-logy" = "stomach-gut-study"). λεπτός is normally "delicate, fine" (cf. 153 with n.); here "narrow". **βίᾳ** "with violence involved" (43n.), i.e. "violently" (also 232). **βαδίζειν** 128n. Adverbial **εὐθύ** or **εὐθύς** + genitive is "straight to, straight toward". **τοῦ (ὀ)ρρο-πυγ-ίου** 157–8n.

163 κοῖλον πρὸς στενῷ προσ-κείμενον "as something hollow attached to something narrow" (modifying τὸν πρωκτόν in 164, but saving that word for as long as possible); this is all a set-up for 165. **ὑπὸ βίας τοῦ πνεύματος** echoes 161–2 αὐτοῦ τὴν πνοὴν / βίᾳ and thus sums up the joke for anyone who may have found it hard to follow.

164 πρωκτός *is* a dirty—i.e. colloquial and impolite—word ("asshole"); contrast 157–8 n. on the less marked πυγή. Gleefully repeated by Strepsiades in 165 and then used again by him in 193, 714, 1300; cf. the abusive εὐρύ-πρωκτος (of a man who allows himself to be used sexually by other men) at 1084–1100.

165 σάλπιγξ "a trumpet" of the sort used for giving signals in war (not really a "musical instrument"). **ἄρα** marks this as a conclusion drawn from what has just been said (121n.).

166 τοῦ δι-εντερεύ-ματος "for his thorough (δια-; see 149n., 168) understanding of guts (ἔντερα)" or perhaps simply "his through-gutting" (since Socrates' explanation of the gnat's buzz is that wind moves through its guts). This is another example (cf. 153n.) of an ablatival genitive, i.e. of the genitive taking over functions that in Proto-Indo-European were carried out by the ablative (a case Greek lost, but Latin retained). In this case, it gives the cause for **τρισ-μακάριος**, "three times blessed", i.e. "extremely blessed, extremely lucky". For the eccentric word in -μα (almost certainly an Aristophanic coinage), 155n.

167 ἦ "certainly!" **φεύγων ἂν ἀπο-φύγοι δίκην** In Greek, a prosecutor "pursues" (διώκω), while a defendant "flees" (φεύγω; cf. 874 ἀπό-φευξις with n., 1151). Note the contrast between the imperfective participle ("when he was an defendant") and the aorist main verb ("he would escape", conceived of as a single action).

168 ὅσ-τις "anyone who"; furnishing an explicit subject for the verb in 167. **δί-οιδε** With the pre-verb (cf. 149n., 166n.), not just "is acquainted with" but "is thoroughly acquainted with".

169 πρῴην is "recently", but often specifically "the day before yesterday". "Yesterday" is ἐχθές (175) or χθές (353), as still in Modern Greek.   **δέ γε** marks these words as picking up the thread of the conversation after an interruption (as again in 175, 211, 681; contrast 914 with n.), which is to say that the Slave ignores Strepsiades' buffoonish interjection in 165–8.   **ἀφ-ῃρέθη** "he was deprived of" (aorist passive < ἀφ-αιρέω) + accusative, i.e. "he had X taken away from him".

170 ἀσκαλαβώτης ("reptile" or "lizard") is seemingly a general term for the creature described more specifically in 173 as a γαλεώτης ("gecko", i.e. a Mediterranean wall-lizard). The word is reserved for the end of the Slave's remark as a surprise.   **τίνα τρόπον;** is adverbial; "in what way?", i.e. "how?"   **κάτ-ειπε** 155n.

171–2 ζητοῦντος αὐτοῦ … κεχηνότος genitive absolute, providing the background for the main action described in 173; such constructions are called "absolute" because they are "absolved"—i.e. "freed from"—the rest of the sentence. This is another charge that Socrates vehemently rejects in Plato's *Apology* a generation later, but that Aristophanes brings against him again and again in *Clouds*: he practices astronomy and is thus implicitly an atheist. See 225–6 with n., 1506–7 with n.; Introduction §II.   **περι-φοράς** "rotations, orbits" (< περί, "around" + φέρω, in the passive "be carried").   **κεχηνότος** perfect active participle < χάσκω ("gape", i.e. "stand obliviously with one's mouth open"; cf. 996; Χάος, "Void", the original state of the Hesiodic universe and one of the gods Socrates swears by at 627).

173 νύκτωρ (adverb) "by night (νύξ)"; cf. 750.   **γαλεώτης** 170n.   **κατ-έχεσεν** (< κατα-χέζω, "shit down on"; another crude, colloquial word; cf. 295 χεσείω with n., 391, 1387 χεζητιῴην with n.) is reserved for the end of the line as the punchline; note Strepsiades' appreciative quotation in 174.

174 ἥσθην aorist passive < ἥδομαι, "feel pleasure". Aorists are often used of emotions and the like to signal that one is experiencing a state that began immediately before this ("I felt pleasure (and now I'm pleased)"); Dover suggests that Strepsiades actually laughs before he says this. Cf. 185 τί ἐθαύμασας; (literally "why did you feel wonder?" or "what were you astonished at?", i.e. "why are you so shocked?"), 1240 (ἥσθην again).

175 ἐχθὲς δέ γ(ε) 169n.   **ἡμῖν δεῖπνον οὐκ ἦν** For this use of the dative (= English "we didn't have any dinner"), 43n.   **ἑσπέρας** "in the evening" (genitive of time within which).

176 εἰέν is a colloquial Attic interjection, here ~ "well then—" (also 1075, where it means ~ "alright!"). **τ(ὰ) ἄλφιτ(α)** 106n. **ἐπαλαμήσατο** deponent aorist middle < παλαμάομαι, "handle, manage, deal with"; < παλάμη ("palm (of the hand)", which is a cognate).

177–8 What Socrates undertakes here at first appears to be a demonstration of a geometry problem, using ash (τέφρα) for a drawing surface and a bent spit (ὀβελίσκος; diminutive < ὀβελός, for which see 118n.). **κατα-πάσας** aorist active participle < κατα-πάσσω, "sprinkle down over". **κάμψας** aorist active participle < κάμπτω, "bend". **δια-βήτην** i.e. the compass (< δια-βαίνω, because it resembled a man standing with his legs spread) into which the spit had been transformed.

179 Literally "he stole (ὑφ-είλετο < ὑφ-αιρέω) the robe from the wrestling school (παλαίστρα, < παλαίω, "wrestle")", i.e. from whatever area there functioned as a locker room. Stealing clothing in this setting was a common crime—allegedly punishable with execution on the spot, if the thief was caught red-handed—and the general idea is clear: Socrates will sell the robe to get money for dinner. But the definite articles ("*the* robe . . . *the* wrestling school") are odd and seem to hint at an incident that was notorious in Aristophanes' time, but obscure to us.

180 ἐκεῖνος (properly "that one") with a personal name often means "the famous"; cf. 534. Thales of Miletus was an early 5th-century philosopher and natural scientist who enjoyed a popular reputation as a genius similar to Albert Einstein today.

181 ἄν-οιγ(ε) ἄν-οιγ(ε) The repetition of the order (again in a more extended form in 183) indicates urgency (79n.), as does the addition of colloquial **ἀνύσας** (aorist active participle < ἀνύω, "accomplish, effect"), which is used routinely in comedy to mean ~ "hurry up and . . . !" (cf. 506 with n., 635, 1253).

182 ὡς τάχιστα 88n.

183 μαθητιάω is a desiderative, i.e. a verb that expresses an urgent desire to do something, in this case to be a μαθητής. Cf. 295 χεσείω with n., 1387 χεζητιῴην (< χεζητιάω) with n.   Somewhere in the course of these verses, the Thinkery door is opened and the audience is nominally allowed to look inside—which perhaps means that two groups of odd-looking mute characters (representing Socrates' students) come onstage (184–99), and that a set of props representing different fields of study are shoved out on the theatrical trolley (cf. 200–17). See Introduction §III.

184 ὦ Ἡράκλεις is a standard, doubtless colloquial comic invocation—i.e. a call to a divine figure to join the speaker in witnessing something or to safeguard him against its likely consequences—in response to an unexpected or frightening sight; ~ a shocked "Good Lord!"   πο-δαπός is properly "from what place?" (note the initial interrogative *pi*) and thus by extension "what kind?"; cf. 310 παντο-δαπαῖσιν ὥραις ("in seasons of every sort", i.e. "in every season").   A θηρ-ίον (properly a diminutive of θήρ, although the word lacks a true diminutive sense) is a "wild creature, wild beast"; cf. 1286, 1427–9n.

185 is unnecessary to explain the situation in the Thinkery, and instead serves as a feed for the nasty joke that follows.   **τί ἐθαύμασας;** 174n.   **τῷ;** = τίνι;, as again in 248, 375, etc. Cf. τοῦ; = τίνος; at 736, 1223.   **εἰκέναι** is a metrically useful variant of ἐοικέναι (perfect active infinitive with present sense < ἔοικα, "look like, resemble").

186 At Pylos in 425 BCE, in a major turning point in the first part of the Peloponnesian War, the Athenians under the command of Cleon captured a large number of Spartan prisoners (see Thucydides 4.37), who had been kept locked up ever since. Socrates' students—who also never see the sun (103n.)—are thus just as pale as the Spartan captives, whose miserable condition is treated as a source of unapologetic good humor.   **ληφθεῖσι** aorist passive participle < λαμβάνω.

187 Strepsiades' attention turns to one particular subgroup of students; note deictic **οὑτοί**, making it clear that he points.   **ἀτάρ** 30n.   The addition of **ποτ(ε)** to the interrogative **τί;** converts the sense to ~ "why in the world?"; cf. 874 πῶς . . . ποθ';, 1086 τί . . . ποτέ;, 1260 τίς . . . ποτ';.

188 τὰ κατὰ γῆς "subterranean matters", i.e. what goes on in the Underworld. But Strepsiades doltishly takes the words more literally than that.   **βολβοί** are purse-tassel hyacinth "bulbs" (a cognate), a bitter, onion-like vegetable still gathered and eaten as a rustic delicacy in rural Italy today.

189–90 μή νυν τοῦτό γ' ἔτι φροντίζετε is addressed to the first group of students.   **τοῦτο** i.e. where such bulbs can be found; the addition of **γ(ε)** converts the meaning from "that" to "*that*"; cf. 196 with n.   **ἵν(α)** "where" (LSJ *s.v.* A.I); contrast the more common use of the word as a conjunction in e.g. 195, 196.   **μεγάλοι καὶ καλοί** As is often the case in such constructions, καί is not translated into English: "nice big ones" (not "nice and big ones").

191 γάρ here implies some previous remark that has been left unexpressed (e.g. "I'm puzzled"), as in colloquial English "So—why . . . ?", where "So" stands in for ~ "I don't get it". Cf. 200, where the clause could be taken as explaining the immediately preceding πρὸς τῶν θεῶν ("I say this because I'm puzzled"), 218, 248, 342 (~ "(I recognize you're baffled), because . . ."), etc.   **σφόδρ(α)** (135n.) is here to be taken with **ἐγ-κεκυφότες** (perfect active participle < ἐγ-κύπτω, literally "stoop over into", i.e. "turn one's nose to the ground").

192 ἐρεβο-διφῶσιν is an invented word < Ἔρεβος (a term for the Underworld) + διφάω ("search"), "they're doing Underworld research"—in this case **ὑπὸ τὸν Τάρταρον** ("below Tartaros", the deepest portion of the Underworld).

193 ὁ πρωκτός 164n.

194 κα(τὰ) αὑτόν "by itself, independently".

195 Addressed to the students.   **εἴσ-ι(τε)** 2nd-person plural imperative < εἴσ-ειμι.   **ἵνα μὴ 'κεῖνος ὑμῖν ἐπιτύχῃ** "so that he doesn't bump into you (outside)", spending time in the sun being forbidden to normal residents of the Thinkery (198–9). (ἐ)κεῖνος is Socrates.   **ὑμῖν** The manuscripts have ἡμῖν ("us"), a common error that reflects the fact that *eta* and *upsilon* eventually came to be pronounced alike; cf. 366, 688.

196 μήπω γε The addition of the particle makes the sense "not *yet*!"; cf. 189–90n. Doubled for emphasis.   **ἐπι-μεινάντων** is a 3rd-person plural "jussive" (< Latin *iubeo*, because the form issues an order) aorist active imperative < ἐπι-μένω: "let them wait!, let them stay!"

197 κοινώσω aorist active subjunctive (not future active indicative) in a purpose clause (which in primary sequence uses a subjunctive without ἄν).   **τι πραγμάτ-ιον ἐμόν** literally "a little thing that belongs to me": Strepsiades is referring to his penis, the students' exposed πρωκτοί (193–4) having given him lustful thoughts.

198 οὐχ οἷόν τ(ε) is to be taken with ἐστίν in the next line, "it's not possible" (also 217).   **πρὸς τὸν ἀέρα** "in the open air".

199 τρίβω is "rub", and δια-τρίβω is "wear out" in the sense "use up (time), pass (time)", as also in 1002 (cf. 1055 ἐν ἀγορᾷ τὴν διατριβήν, "spending time in the marketplace").   ἄγαν is another adverbial intensifier (cf. 53–5n., 135n.) and in the 5ᵗʰ century generally has a negative sense, as also in 1120 (where it functions adjectivally).   The students go back into the Thinkery, and Strepsiades turns his attention in a new direction (200–17).

200–3 These lines are the earliest evidence for Greek scientific instruments, although what they consist of—in the case of "geometry", probably compasses and the like (cf. 177–8 with nn.)—is unclear.

200 πρὸς τῶν θεῶν "by the gods!"; cf. 481, 784, 1103; πρὸς τοῦ Διός at 314; πρὸς τῆς Γῆς at 366.   For the use of **γάρ**, 191n.

201 ἀστρο-νομ-ία is an abstract noun < ἀστήρ ("star") + νέμω ("portion out, distribute", and so "manage, govern"; cf. νόμος, "law"), and thus properly ~ "setting rules for stars". For other abstracts ending in -ία, e.g. 202 γεω-μετρ-ία with n., 621 ἀ-παστ-ία with n., 1236 ἀν-αιδ-εία.

202 γεω-μετρ-ία is < γῆ ("land") + μετρέω ("measure"; cf. 148) + the abstract ending -ία (201n.); etymologized in 203 in a way that responds to Strepsiades' specific question while simultaneously setting up the joke in 204–5 that brings the exchange to an end. Geometry was most likely *not* studied for purely practical purposes in places like the Thinkery, even if it had real-world applications.   **τί** is accusative of respect with **χρήσιμον**, "useful for what?"

203 See 202n.   **ἀνα-μετρεῖσθαι** ("to measure out, to measure carefully") is deponent; **γῆν** is its object.   **πότερα** or πότερον—the choice depends on metrical circumstances and does not affect the meaning—implies two possible answers, only one of which Strepsiades articulates, thus ". . . (or some other kind)?"; cf. 157 with n., 638 with n., 642, 845–6, etc. English has no real equivalent, and the word is accordingly to be left untranslated (~ "cleruchic land, or what?").   **τὴν κληρουχικὴν (γῆν)** When the Athenians conquered a place and wanted to be sure it caused no trouble in the future, they sometimes distributed "shares" (κλῆροι) of the land to their own citizens, who became a sort of local garrison. For the -ικός ending on the adjective (the second element of which is ἔχω), 27n.

204 ἀστεῖον is < ἄστυ and thus means "typical of the city" and by extension "clever", or in other contexts "lovely, charming" (e.g. 1064, in a sarcastic characterization of a prize). Cf. Strepsiades on his own rural cloddishness at 138; English "urbane" < Latin *urbanus* ("from the *urbs*, from the city").

205 σόφισμα 155n.   **δημοτικόν** "oriented toward the δῆμος" (27n.). Strepsiades imagines that the idea is to divide the whole world up into private property for Athenian citizens.

206 Herodotus refers to περί-οδοι (literally "trips around, tours", and thus "maps") as existing already in the early 5th century. They were apparently still enough of a novelty in Aristophanes' time that someone like Strepsiades could be imagined to never have seen one, although the audience in the Theater could simultaneously find his clumsy literal misunderstandings funny. This would be simpler if the map were set up on an easel or something similar and thus visible to them, hence presumably the repeated demonstratives (212 ἡδί, 214 αὑτηί) and the joke in 212–13, which makes much easier sense if Euboea is actually visible.   **σοι** is "for your benefit" and thus ~ "I'll have you know!"

208 καθ-ημένους *sc.* "in court". A standard comic criticism of Athens is that its citizens are addicted to lawsuits (cf. 494–6 with 494 n., 1220–1 with n.) and paid jury-service (cf. 863 with n.), an idea central to Aristophanes' *Wasps* (staged the year after the original *Clouds*). See also 1427–9n. (on love of passing legislation).

209 ὡς "(rest assured) that . . . !" A colloquial ellipse; cf. 258 ("see to it that . . . !"), 326 ("you can be sure that . . . !"), etc.

210 The initial **καί** is surprised or indignant (~ English "So where's . . . ?"); cf. 717.   **Κικυννῆς** is nominative plural of Κικυννεύς ("resident of Kikynna"; cf. 134n.).   **ο(ἱ ἐ)μοὶ δημόται** "my fellow demesmen" (37n.), who were conventionally among a man's closest personal associates, along with his family and neighbors; cf. 1209, 1218–19, 1322.

211–13 Euboea, a long fertile island lying north and east of Attica, revolted from the Athenian Empire in 446 BCE and was emphatically put down by an expedition led by Pericles (as Strepsiades gloatingly observes); cf. 859n.   **παρα-τέταται** perfect middle participle < παρα-τείνω ("stretch out alongside"). Strepsiades understands the verb as a passive ("has been stretched out", not "is stretched out"), and thus responds with **παρ-ετάθη** (aorist, because he is thinking of an event in the past rather than of the current situation).   **μακρὰ πόρρω πάνυ** is literally "very long forward", i.e. ~ "all the way out"; cf. 216 πόρρω πάνυ ~ "way far away". πάνυ (cognate with πᾶς and thus ~ "altogether") is an adverbial intensifier; cf. 53–5n., 135n., 199n.

214 When the Slave repeats Strepsiades' question back to him, he converts ποῦ into the indirect ὅ-που (cf. 145n.). But since the main verb—the implied "you ask"—is in a primary tense (the present), the original tense and mood of (ἐ)στίν are retained.

215 ἐγγύς "close to" + genitive.   **μετα-φροντίζετε** ("think differently!") is a conjecture by Richard Bentley, the great—and famously difficult—18th-century British classical scholar (cf. 1401 and 1418 for more of his emendations). The manuscripts have the clumsy πάνυ φροντίζετε ("really think!"; cf. 211–13n.), and Bentley's suggestion is based on (1) the gloss μεταβουλεύεσθε in the *scholia* to R, the oldest manuscript of the play; (2) μέγα βουλεύεσθε ("think a big thought!") in the quotation of the line in the *Suda* (an enormous 10th-century Byzantine dictionary incorporating much older material), where ΜΕΓΑ seems to represent an error for ΜΕΤΑ dating back to a period when the text was still written in capital letters. LSJ omits the verb (attested nowhere else), since it had not yet been generally accepted into the text of Aristophanes when the dictionary was compiled in the late 19th century.

216 πόρρω πάνυ 211–13n.

217 οὐχ οἷόν τε supply ἐστί, as in 198–9.   Inarticulate sounds are frequently combined with the ending -ζω to produce a verb that means to make that sound. οἴμοι is what one says when one is in pain, despair or the like (e.g. 23, 57, 256), and **οἰμώξεσθ(ε)** is thus "you'll say οἴμοι", i.e. "you'll be sorry (if you deliberately transplant Athens' bitter enemy so close to Athens itself)".

218 Somewhere before this—or only now and abruptly?—Socrates appears dangling over the stage on the theatrical crane; see Introduction §III. In the meantime, prop-men return the scientific props used in 200–17 to wherever they came from.   **φέρε** "hey!, look!, come on!" (colloquial); often used to introduce a question, as also at e.g. 324, 342, 366.   **γάρ** 191n.   **ὁ (ἐ)πὶ τῆς κρεμάθρας ἀνήρ** literally "the man on the hook"; cf. 225–6n.

219 αὐτός Dover suggests that this was a normal way of saying "the master", like Latin *ipse*. But Strepsiades does not understand what the Slave means (thus his response **τίς αὐτός;** "Who αὐτός?"), so more likely what is intended is "It's *him*!" Socrates does not respond to Strepsiades' remark at the end of the line, and nominative ὦ Σωκράτης (~ "Oh! it's Socrates!") is therefore better than the manuscripts' vocative ὦ Σώκρατες ("Hey Socrates!"), as in 222. Cf. 328.

220 For colloquial ἴθ(ι) ("come on!"), 110n.   Addressing the person
with whom one is speaking as οὗτος (~ "you there!"; also 723, 732, 1502)
is brusque and colloquial, but not necessarily rude.   ἀνα-βόησον
(aorist active imperative, like κάλεσον in 221) is "call upon! call out to!" +
accusative.   For μοι ~ "please!", 107n.   μέγα is adverbial, "loudly".

221 μὲν οὖν 71n.   κάλεσον 220n. The Slave goes back inside the Thinkery.

222–3 ὦ Σώκρατες, / ὦ Σωκρατίδιον 80n.   (ἐ)φ-ήμερε is < ἐπί + ἡμέρα
and thus "that lasts (only) a day" (= English "ephemeral"). Socrates speaks as
if he were a god—for whom the theatrical crane is generally reserved.

224 πρῶτον μέν "first of all—". But no second point follows, as is often the
case (e.g. 643, 649).   ὅ-τι δρᾷς is an indirect question for direct τί δρᾷς;

225–6 ἀερο-βατῶ is < ἀήρ + a by-form of βαίνω, "walk on/in air"; quoted by
Plato at *Apology* 19c (the defendant notes that the jury has seen "Socrates" in
Aristophanes' play "saying that he is walking on air and talking much other
nonsense"). For Socrates as astronomer, 171–2n. In 226, Strepsiades twists this
into a charge of atheism by converting Socrates' περι-φρονῶ ("I think about,
I speculate regarding"; cf. 741) into ὑπερ-φρονεῖς ("you show contempt for";
also 1400).   A ταρρός is not a basket (as this scene is conventionally
imagined) but something more like "a wicker platform" (= the weight-bearing
portion of the crane on which Socrates is swung in over the stage; cf. 218 with
n.).

227 ἀλλ(ά) οὐκ "rather than".   εἴ-περ "if in fact (that's what you're doing)"
looks like a polite colloquial saying of saying ~ "unless I'm misunderstanding
the situation".

227–30 "Because I would have never have discovered . . . , except by
suspending . . . and mixing . . .".   **231–2** say something very similar, but
in a negative fashion, "Because if I were observing . . . , I would never have
discovered", with an absurd "scientific explanation" attached in **233** and
an even more absurd "scientific comparison" in **234**. Socrates is talking
pretentious nonsense.

227–8 γάρ "(Yes, I'm working from a ταρρός), because . . ." (191n.).   ἄν
renders οὐ . . . ποτε / ἐξηῦρον contrary to fact, "I would never have
discovered".   μετ-έωρα is < μετά ("in the middle") + ἀείρω ("raise up");
thus "midair, heavenly". Cf. 264 (where the earth is μετέωρος), 360 μετεωρο-

σοφιστῶν (people who spend their time thinking about such matters), and English "meteorology" (literally "study of μετέωρα").

229–30 λεπτήν is properly predicative of **τὴν φροντίδα** ("so that it is light"), but actually modifies **τὸ νόημα** as well. For Socrates' thought as λεπτός, 153n.   The ἀήρ is the moist, dense air that surrounds us and that we breathe; above it is the fiery αἰθήρ, to which human beings have no access. Cf. 264–5 (personified as two of Socrates' deities), 285 (the sun as the "eye of the αἰθήρ"), 371 (perfectly clear weather is αἴθριος), 569–70 (the personified Αἰθήρ as father of the Clouds), 627 (Ἀήρ as a god Socrates swears by), 667 (the same oath picked up by Strepsiades).

231 χαμαί adverb, "on earth".   **τ(ὰ) ἄνω** is the object of **ἐσκόπουν** (conative, "if I was trying . . .").

232 οὐ γὰρ ἀλλ(ά) literally "for it's not but . . .", i.e. "for the way it is, is that . . . , for the fact is, that . . ."   **βίᾳ** 160–2n.

233–4 τὴν ἰκμάδα τῆς φροντίδος "the moisture of thought".   **πάσχει δὲ ταὐτὸ τοῦτο καὶ τὰ κάρδαμα** "cress"—a spicy herb—"has the very same thing happen to it." Socrates is perhaps echoing arguments about the nature of air made earlier by Diogenes of Apollonia, but see 235–6n.

235–6 πῶς φῄς; literally "How do you say?", i.e. "Huh?" In 236, Strepsiades mangles Socrates' image in a way that even those members of the audience— the vast majority?—who did not recognize the allusion in 234 can see is mocking.

237 νυν without an accent is not temporal, and is instead like the "now" in English "come on now!" (similarly e.g. 323, 497).   **κατά-βηθ(ι)** aorist active imperative < καταβαίνω, "come down".   **ὡς** is often used in Attic as equivalent to common εἰς (also 1163/4), but only when the object is a person.

238 ὧν-περ οὕνεκ(α) is a colloquially compressed equivalent of ταῦτα ὧν οὕνεκ(α), "the things on account of which, for which", with -περ added as an intensifier (thus ~ "precisely the things"; cf. 405 ὥσ-περ, 418 ὅ-περ, etc.). οὕνεκα is a poetic form, used here *metri gratia* in place of the normal Attic ἕνεκα, as again in 420 (n.), 422, 511, 1508. For its position, 6n.   The stagehands in control of the *mêchanê* lower Socrates to the stage, perhaps requiring a break in the dialogue left unnoticed by our text.

239 κατὰ τί; "in pursuit of what?, with an eye to what?"

241 ἄγω καὶ φέρω is a standard phrase for "driving" off an enemy's flocks and "carrying" off whatever else one can seize from him. Here Strepsiades gives his complaint more specific content with **τὰ χρήματ(α) ἐνεχυράζομαι** (34–5n.).

242 πόθεν; literally "from what source?", i.e. "how?"   **ὑπό-χρεως** is a masculine nominative singular adjective, "subject to debt (χρέος)". With a long final syllable, one would expect ὑπο-χρέως, but ancient sources claim that this sort of accentuation is specifically Attic; seemingly a triumph of the separate tendency to put an accent on the first element of a compound when it modifies the second.

243 Since the audience is now well acquainted with Strepsiades' situation, he can describe it to Socrates in what would otherwise be an impossibly allusive way as a "voracious equine disease".   **ἐπι-τρίβω** is literally "rub upon" (cf. 199n., 260 τρῖμ-μα with n.) and thus figuratively "crush, ruin" (also 438, 972, etc.).   **δεινὴ φαγεῖν** literally "clever at eating" (an epexegetic, i.e. "explanatory" infinitive; cf. 260, 430, 1172, 1313–14).

246 Middle πράττομαι is "charge"; here it takes both an external (**μ(ε)**) and an internal (245 **μισθόν**) object.   **τοὺς θεούς** is the direct object of **ὀμοῦμαι**, **σοι** the indirect object: "I'll swear by the gods to you".   **κατα-θήσειν** future active infinitive < κατα-τίθημι, "pay".

247 ποίους; without the definitive article is not a simple question (contrast 1233), but is dismissive, like ποῖος; in 367 (n.) in a similar context.

248–9 νόμισ-μ(α) is properly "currency" (155n.), setting up the joke that follows, but Socrates means something like "We don't deal in gods". Cf. the use of νομίζω in the sense "consider someone a god" in 423.   **τῷ;** "by what?" (185n.).   The Greek city of Byzantium (modern Istanbul) used iron coins (cf. Plato Comicus fr. 103). But 249 is otherwise difficult to make complete sense of, which is to say that it must be mostly a joke: Socrates' people do not swear by gods, whom he describes with a word that normally means money (248); Strepsiades amusingly confounds the two ideas by responding ~ "What do you swear by, (if you don't swear by ordinary money)? Iron coins?"; and with the laugh-line out of the way, the poet moves on to the next stage in the argument (250–3).

250–1 βούλει τὰ θεῖα πράγματ' εἰδέναι σαφῶς / ἅττ' ἐστὶν ὀρθῶς; is a proleptic accusative construction, in which the subject of the dependent clause is pulled out and made the accusative object of the main verb; traditionally called a "lilies-of-the-field" construction after the Biblical "Consider the lilies of the field, how they grow", meaning "Consider how the lilies of the field grow". Cf. 145, 479, 493, 731, 842, 961, etc.   ἄττ(α) = ἅ-τινα (in an indirect question, the direct form of which would be τίνα;), as also in e.g. 345, 659. This is the colloquial Attic form of an Ionic form (ἅσσα), with Attic *tau* for *sigma*.   εἴπερ ἔστι γε "if it's *possible*".

252 συγ-γενέσθαι . . . εἰς λόγους i.e. "to engage in conversation with". But this is really a secondary result of the preliminary teaching referred to in 250–1: only after Strepsiades understands how divine affairs actually work can he develop a relationship with Socrates' gods.

253 The adverb μάλιστα is the superlative of μάλα, "very" (comparative μᾶλλον, "more", as in e.g. 625), and is used colloquially—often intensified by γε, as here and in 672—to mean ~ "absolutely!" Cf. 316 ἥκιστα with n.

254–62 This scene appears to represent a parody of an initiation into a private mystery cult (although not the Eleusinian Mysteries, a parody of which would have been too offensive to an Athenian audience to be imaginable even for a comic poet). Cf. 140, 143.

254 τοί-νυν (~ "in that case") pushes on to the next point, as again in 255, 356, etc. A colloquial Attic particle, in origin a dative of σύ/τύ + logical νυν (vs. temporal νῦν); cf. 327n., 329n. on μέν-τοι.   Α σκίμπους (also 709) is a light, low bed, presumably the same one Strepsiades and Pheidippides were lying on when the action began, now temporarily repurposed as a cult accessory.

255–6 ἰδού 82n.   τοί-νυν 254n.   ἐπὶ τί στέφανον; "For what purpose (should I take) a garland?" On a normal, day-to-day level, putting on a garland might well suggest participation in a sacrifice—although not being the victim, which is Strepsiades' ridiculous contribution to the situation.

257 ὥσπερ με τὸν Ἀθάμαντα The *scholia* identify this as a reference to Sophocles' lost *Athamas*, the hero of which was supposed to be sacrificed (for reasons unclear), but was rescued by Heracles.   με is the object of μὴ θύσετε (a prohibition). But Greek enclitics have a pronounced fondness for second position (or as close to that as possible), hence this one here well before its verb; cf. μοι in 533.   ὅπως "(See to it) that . . . !" + future; a colloquial ellipse, also in 489–90, 824, 1177, 1464 (and cf. 209 ὡς).

258–9 πάντας . . . τοὺς τελουμένους is the external object of **ποοῦμεν**, **ταῦτα** the internal object: "we do these things to all . . ."   **τελουμένους** < τελέω, here "initiate".   **πάντας ταῦτα** is a suggestion by the mid-18th-century German scholar Johann Jakob Reiske (primarily an Arabist) for the manuscripts' flat πάντα ταῦτα (all witnesses but EK, which have πάντα ταῦτα, supporting the idea that that was the original word order).   **ποοῦμεν** = ποιοῦμεν (conventionally written thus when the syllable is short, as also at e.g. 296, 895).   **κερδανῶ** future active < κερδαίνω, "profit" (here + internal accusative **τί**).

260 λέγειν is an epexegetic infinitive (243n.) with the nouns in the second half of the line; "an X at speaking, an X for speaking".   **τρῖμ-μα, κρόταλον, παιπάλη** literally "something smoothed, a castanet, fine flour", and thus figuratively ~ "subtle, fast with words, refined". Cf. περί-τριμμα δικῶν, / . . . κρόταλον in a list of abusive terms for legal opponents at 447–8. τρῖμ-μα is < τρίβω; cf. 243n.

261–2 Socrates sprinkles flour on Strepsiades, who plays the fool—as he routinely does—by fidgeting and making foolish remarks.   **ἀ-τρεμεί** is an adverb < privative *alpha* + τρέμω ("tremble, quake"), and **ἔχ(ε) ἀ-τρεμεί** is thus "hold still!"   **ψεύσει . . . με** "you won't deceive me" (deponent future middle < ψεύδομαι), i.e. "in the end you'll turn out to be telling the truth".   **κατα-παττόμενος . . . παιπάλη γενήσομαι** "I'll turn out to be flour by being sprinkled (with it)"; cf. the figurative use of the noun in 260.

263–74 Anapaestic tetrameter catalectic; see Introduction §IV.A.2. This is a (parody of a) prayer and includes a number of standard features: a call for silence and its counterpart, close attention, from the human participants (263); elaborate address of the deities (264–5); requests that the deities "appear" (266) and "come" (269); a list of locations where the deities might be located at the moment, as an attempt to ensure that they hear the appeal (270–3); and a request that the deities accept and approve of the actions (274), since this should guarantee a favorable response to whatever requests are eventually made. Much of the language is elevated in one way or another. Strepsiades' buffoonish interjection in 267–8—like many such interjections in Aristophanes, intended mostly for "the world at large", i.e. the audience in the Theater—is ignored.

263 εὐ-φημεῖν literally "to speak well" (cf. English "euphemism"); but this really means "to say nothing inappropriate" and thus in practice "to keep quiet". Cf. 297, where imperative εὐ-φήμει means "Hush!", 833 εὐ-στόμει with n.   ἐπ-ακούειν is to listen to remarks intended for another person, whereas ὑπ-ακούειν (274, 360) is to pay attention to something said to oneself.

264–5 Ἀήρ . . . Αἰθήρ 229–30n. Modern typographic conventions require a distinction between uppercase and lowercase letters, here making it clear that these are conceived of as personified figures. The Greek is more ambiguous, and the choice is sometimes an impossible one; cf. 380–1n., 584–6n., 608.   μετ-έωρον 227–8n., 266; two-termination, as is usual for compound adjectives.   βροντησι-κέραυνοι ("thunder-lightning-bolt-equipped") is an elevated "poetic" adjective (also two-termination) intended to sound simultaneously grand and ridiculous; cf. 270 χιονο-βλήτοισι, 335–8n. (on "dithyrambic language"), 971 δυσκολο-κάμπτους.

266 ἄρθητε and φάνητ(ε) are aorist passive imperatives < αἴρω, "raise up", and φαίνω, "reveal", respectively.   τῷ φροντιστῇ i.e. Strepsiades. The word (~ "thinker") is attested nowhere in the 5th century except in this play and may be another coinage; cf. 94n. on φροντιστήριον, 101 μεριμνοφροντισταί.

267 After a negative clause (here μήπω, "don't (do this)!"), πρίν means "until" and takes an indicative (of something that really happened in the past) or a subjunctive + ἄν (of anticipated action, as here). Contrast after an affirmative clause meaning "before" at 631, 780 (n.).   πτύξωμαι aorist middle subjunctive < πτύσσω, "fold", thus "fold myself up in, wrap myself up in".   τουτί is a reference to Strepsiades' ἱμάτιον (outer robe; cf. 53–5).   μὴ κατα-βρεχθῶ "so I don't get drenched" (aorist passive subjunctive < κατα-βρέχω in a negative purpose clause), i.e. because clouds bring rain.

268 τὸ δὲ . . . ἐλθεῖν ἐμέ is an exclamatory infinitive; "(To think) that I came!"; cf. 819.   κυνῆν "a cap" (accusative), of a kind apparently made originally from the skin of a dog (κύων, κυνός).

269 δῆτ(α) 6–7n.   τῷδ(ε) εἰς ἐπί-δειξιν literally "for putting on a display for this man"—Strepsiades—i.e. "to show yourselves to this man". On nouns in -σις, 155n.

270–3 Olympus (270) is the obvious place for deities to be lingering, while the other places mentioned are watery or snowy spots at the distant ends of the earth: the semimythical Ocean in the far west, described again as the Clouds' father in 278; the Nile Delta; Lake Maiotis = the Sea of Azov (located north of the Black Sea, between what is today Russia and the Ukraine); Mount Mimas (on what is today the Ionian coast of Turkey).

270 χιονο-βλήτοισι ("snow-struck", < χιών + βάλλω) is another high-style, two-termination adjective; cf. 264–5n.

271 Ὠκεανοῦ πατρὸς ἐν κήποις i.e. in the gardens of the Hesperides ("Goddesses of the West", here called νύμφαι), where golden apples grew.   **ἵστατε** is here "you arrange, you organize".

272 Νείλου προ-χοαῖς ὑδάτων "at the mouths of the waters of the Nile". The absence of a preposition is elevated poetic style; cf. 299–313.   **ἀρύτω** is the Attic form of the common ἀρύω ("draw water"); here with dative **χρυσέαις . . . πρό-χοισιν** indicating the vessel used in the drawing (a "dative of means").

273 ἔχετ(ε) is here "you inhabit"; cf. 596, 598 (both lyric, which routinely uses elevated language).   Α **σκόπελος** is a "lookout-place" (< σκοπέω) and thus a "peak"; cf. σκοπιά in 281. Poetic vocabulary.

274 ὑπ-ακούσατε 263n.   Aorist participles imagine actions as complete and are thus commonly used to describe something done before the main verb but not specifically producing the grounds for it (which is the job of the perfect); cf. 146–7n. With an aorist main verb, however, they can refer instead to something done simultaneously: the Clouds will receive (**δεξάμεναι**) the sacrifice, be pleased (**χαρεῖσαι**; aorist passive participle < χαίρω) by the rites, and listen to what is being said (**ὑπ-ακούσατε**), all at the same time, but with the latter action foregrounded.

275–90 ~ 298–313 A dactylic song, consisting of two balanced, metrically symmetrical parts (*strophe* and *antistrophe*); see Appendix III.1. Aristophanic choruses normally have an entrance song (the *parodos*), which they sing on their way down the side corridors into the open area in front of the stage (the *orchestra* or "dancing area"). In this case, however, Strepsiades at least only *hears* the Clouds and does not catch his first glimpse of them until 326. Whether this means that the song was performed offstage—Dover speculates that it could not be heard and that this was among the causes of the failure of the original—or is merely more evidence for Strepsiades' rustic cluelessness— is he idiotically scanning the sky all this time, never bothering to look in front of him?—is unclear. For the chorus' costume (not easily identified), cf. 340–1, 344 with n.

275–90 The Clouds emerge from Ocean to look on the world generally; contrast 298–313, where their focus narrows to Attica. The vocabulary is relentlessly poetic, with numerous decorative touches: the song is supposed to "sound beautiful" (or at least "mock-beautiful").

275 ἀέ-ναοι "ever-flowing", although Dover suggests that by the 5ᵗʰ century the word suggested little more than "eternal". A two-termination adjective.

276–7 Oddly numbered lines such as this—mostly in lyric sections— reflect differences between contemporary scholars' sense of how the text should be divided and that of the late-18ᵗʰ-century Alsatian scholar Richard Brunck, the numbering of whose edition of Aristophanes is retained (except, unfortunately, in Wilson's Oxford text and thus the TLG) because of the chaos that would otherwise result in the secondary literature.   **ἀρθῶμεν** hortatory aorist passive subjunctive < αἴρω, "raise up".   **φύσιν** 486–7n.   The *scholia* identify εὐ-άγητος (two terminations) as an unexpected—mock-high poetic?—form of εὐ-άγης III "bright" (also with a long *alpha*, unlike εὐάγης I, "pure, undefiled").

278 βαρυ-αχής ("deep-echoing", < βαρύς + ἠχέω) is a rare poetic word, and the elevated effect is heightened by the use of "Doric *alpha*" (common in tragic lyric, but not in comedy, where βαρυηχής would be expected), as also in 282 ἀρδομέναν, 289 ἀθανάτας, 300 γᾶν. Cf. 30 with n. (tragic quotation), 335–8 (dithyrambic language), 1154–5 with n. (tragic quotation). Note that inherited ē: does not ordinarily go to *alpha* in Doric, hence Aristophanes' -αχής here rather than hyper-Doric -αχάς.

279 Note the recessive accent on **ἔπι** (normally ἐπί), which indicates that the preposition is to be taken with the word that precedes it; a poeticism.

280 δενδρο-κόμους literally "tree-haired" (two terminations), i.e. "covered with trees in the way a head is covered with hair". A rare poetic word attested only once elsewhere in this period, at Euripides *Helen* 1107 (lyric).

281 τηλε-φανεῖς σκοπιάς literally "far-appearing look-out points", i.e. "peaks visible in the distance"; both words are rare and poetic.   ἀφ-οράω is "look off (from somewhere) at" + accusative; here middle seemingly with the sense "for our own pleasure/edification".

282 καρπούς is an accusative of respect with **ἀρδομέναν** ("watered as regards its crops"). Most manuscripts have an additional **τε** after ἀρδομέναν, as if "crops" were another direct object of 281 ἀφορώμεθα, along with **χθόνα**.   Note the "Doric *alpha*" (278n.) in the final syllable of **ἀρδομέναν**, ἀρδομένην being expected in Attic.   **ἱεράν** is ornamental: the chorus do not mean that the earth is "sacred" in any significant sense, but are merely describing it in an elevated manner. ζα-θέων in 283 is similar.

283 ποταμῶν ζα-θέων κελαδή-ματα "the roar of the very divine rivers". Both ζά-θεος (< the poetic prefix ζα- ~ "extremely" + θεός) and κελάδη-μα (< the poetic verb κελαδέω, "resound", + the noun-making suffix -μα (155n.); cf. κελάδοντα in 284) are rare poetic vocabulary, like εὐ-κελάδων in 312.

284 κελάδοντα 283n.   **βαρύ-βρομον** "deep-roaring" (< βαρύς + βρέμω) is more elevated vocabulary; used again in 313.

285–6 ὄμμα . . . αἰθέρος ἀ-κάματον "the tireless eye of the upper air" (229–30n.); a clichéd way of referring to the sun.   **γάρ** makes it clear that this is an explanation of something, apparently the fact that the Clouds can see so far.

287 μαρμαρέαισιν αὐγαῖς "with gleaming rays"; both words are poetic.

288–90 ἀπο-σεισάμεναι The pre-verb governs genitive **ἀ-θανάτας ἰδέας** (note the "Doric *alpha*", ἀθανάτης being expected in Attic; see 278 n.), while the root verb governs **νέφος ὄμβριον**.   **ἐπ-ιδώμεθα** deponent aorist middle subjunctive < ἐφ-οράω.   τηλε-σκόπος (< the adverb τῆλε "far" + σκοπέω; cf. English "telescope").   γαῖα is poetic; Attic prose uses γῆ.

291–7 Anapaestic tetrameter catalectic; cf. Introduction §IV.A.2.

291 Socrates acknowledges the arrival of the Clouds, whom he hears, but does not yet see.   **μέγα** is adverbial with **σεμναί** ("greatly deserving of reverence", i.e. "deserving great reverence").   **φανερῶς** goes with **ἠκούσατέ μου**: "you openly heard me", i.e. "you made it clear that you heard me by appearing".

292 Addressed to Strepsiades.   **ᾔσθου** deponent aorist middle < αἰσθάνομαι, + genitive.   **θεό-σεπτον** (< θεός + σέβομαι) is Dover's suggestion in place of the manuscripts' θεοσέπτου (altered by a careless scribe to match the case of the words that precede it) and—if right—is an internal accusative with **μυκησαμένης** ("producing a god-revering bellow"; < μῦ, the sound cows made in the ancient world, as well as our own, although with a slightly different spelling). The *scholia* suggest a reference to a theatrical "thunder-machine" (βροντεῖον) that perhaps introduced or accompanied the Clouds' song.

293–5 A typically coarse, clownish interjection by Strepsiades, with attempts at proper and respectful language (**σέβομαι** "I feel respect", picking up θεόσεπτον in 292, and εἰ θέμις ἐστίν; see 140n.) quickly punctured by crudities (ἀντ-απο-παρδεῖν, "to emit a fart in response" and χεσείω, "I need to take a shit"). Most of this is nominally directed to the Clouds themselves, but οὕτως αὐτὰς τετραμαίνω καὶ πεφόβημαι ("that's how . . . !") is an explanatory interjection intended for Socrates (or the world at large).   τετραμαίνω καὶ πεφόβημαι "I tremble at and am afraid of" + accusative.   ἤδη is ~ "at this very point in time", and can thus be used to intensify forms of νῦν (as here), but also independently to mean "now" (e.g. 320, 322, 323).   χεσείω is a desiderative (183n.) of χέζω (173n.); reserved for the end as a sort of punchline.

296 οὐ μή + future indicative is a prohibition, "Don't . . . !"; cf. 367, 505.   σκώψει deponent future middle < σκώπτω "joke, jeer" (often with an accusative of the person or thing mocked, as at 350, 540, etc.).   τρύξ is new, barely fermented wine ("must"), and Aristophanes uses the word elsewhere to produce an idiosyncratic term for comedy, τρυγ-ῳδία, modeled on τραγ-ῳδία "tragedy". οἱ τρυγο-δαίμονες οὗτοι are thus ~ "the notorious wine-inspired comic poets"; see 76n.

297 εὐ-φήμει 263n.   A σμῆνος (neuter) is properly a hive or swarm of bees, and by extension a crowd of anything (here appropriately one that floats through the air).

298–313 The second half of the Clouds' entrance song (cf. 275–90 ~ 298–313n.), addressed to one another and full of conventional praise of Athens' piety culminating in 311–13 in a reference to the dramatic festival at which the original play was staged. Most of these expensive gifts and services to the gods were paid for with tribute forcibly extracted from the Athens' subject-allies, i.e. with other people's money: whatever else one may wish to say of it, *Clouds*—like most Athenian literature—is an unapologetically imperial document.

298 ὀμβρο-φόροι (< ὄμβρος "rain-storm" + φέρω) is a rare poetic adjective (two terminations).

299–301 λιπαρὰν χθόνα is an accusative of direction dependent on ἔλθωμεν (the absence of a preposition is again an indication of elevated style; cf. 272n.), while εὔ-ανδρον γᾶν is the object of ὀψόμεναι (deponent future participle < ὁράω, indicating purpose; cf. 837 λουσόμενος, "in order to take a bath").   εὔ-ανδρον Adjectives in εὐ- are common in elevated poetry; cf. in this song alone 308–9 εὐ-στέφανοι, 312 εὐ-κέλαδων.   Παλλάδος i.e.

"of Athena". Κέκροψ was an early (mythical) king of Athens, and "land of Kekrops" and the like are a standard poetic periphrasis for "Athens/Attica". πολυ-ήρατος ("much-loved, much-desired"; < ἐράω) is poetic vocabulary.

302–4 refer to the Eleusinian Mysteries.   οὗ "where".   ἄ-ρρητος is < privative *alpha* + εἴρω, "say", and thus "not to be divulged".   **μυστο-δόκος** is a high-style formation < μύστης, "someone who keeps their mouth shut" (see 143n.), + δέχομαι.   **ἀνα-δείκνυται** ("are put on display") governs all the nouns that follow, where the sense evolves into ~ "are visible".

305 δωρή-ματα, a -μα noun (155n.) < δωρέω, probably refers to temple dedications.

306 ὑψ-ερεφής (< ὕψι "high" + ὄροφος "roof") is Homeric vocabulary.

307 πρόσ-οδοι literally "processions toward (a temple or something similar)".   One of the most basic functions of the genitive is to modify another noun (sometimes an adjective), often by indicating possession, as with **μακάρων** here and **θεῶν** in 308–9. But in e.g. "first of all" (368), "a value of many talents" (cf. 473), "a bucket of fish" and "a piece of bread", the second term would in Greek in every case similarly be a genitive that more specifically defines the first.

308–9 εὐ-στέφανοι literally "well-garlanded", i.e. "in which lovely garlands are worn".

310 παντο-δαπαῖσιν ὥραις 184n. The absense of ἐν is not a poeticism (contrast 272, 299–300 with n., 311 ἦρί τ᾽ ἐπερχομένῳ), but is normal with plural ὥραις.

311–13 An allusive description of the City Dionysia festival.   **ἦρί τ(ε) ἐπ-ερχομένῳ** "and (in) approaching spring (ἔαρ/ἦρ)", i.e. "at the beginning of spring".   **Βρομία χάρις** "the Bromian"—i.e. Dionysian—"grace", and thus "that in which Dionysus takes pleasure".   **εὐ-κελάδων τε χορῶν ἐρεθίσ-ματα** "and provocations (< ἐρεθίζω) of choruses that produce fine noise (283n., 299–301n.)", alluding to the competitive character of the festival.   **αὐλῶν μοῦσα βαρύ-βρομος** is an elaborate way of saying "the music produced by the deep-roaring (284n.) pipes", which were played in pairs by an αὐλητής and provided the musical accompaniment for all the sung parts in Athenian drama. The adjective (two terminations) properly belongs to the genitive, but in another elevated poetic gesture ("hypallage") it has been transferred to the nominative it modifies.

314–438 Anapaestic tetrameter catalectic; see Introduction §IV.A.2.

314 πρὸς τοῦ Διός 200n.   **φράσον** aorist active imperative < φράζω, "tell (me)!"

315 τοῦτο τὸ σεμνόν is the internal object of **αἱ φθεγξάμεναι**, ~ "who pronounced this awe-inspiring speech".   **μῶν** (= μὴ οὖν) expects a negative answer, "certainly not?"   **ἡρῷναι** "female heroes", because the Clouds are superhuman female figures, but not something one would normally refer to as "gods".   **τινές** ("some sort of") adds a bit of additional uncertainty to the question.

316–18 Aristophanic characters often make remarks inconsistent with their proper identity when this suits the playwright's purposes, as Socrates here describes the Clouds as patrons of lazy intellectuals (*sc.* like himself).   **ἥκιστα** (properly "least!") is here adverbial ("scarcely!"), as again at 380. Cf. 253 μάλιστα (literally "most!") with n.   **ἀργός** is < privative *alpha* + ἔργον, literally "not-working".   **γνώμην καὶ διά-λεξιν καὶ νοῦν . . . / καὶ τερατείαν καὶ περί-λεξιν καὶ κροῦσιν καὶ κατά-ληψιν** "opinion and arguing and intelligence . . . and the ability to inspire wonder and circumlocution and the power to make a point and to control a response". Some of these are probably technical rhetorical terms, while others may be deliberately absurd Aristophanic inventions modeled on them.

319 ταῦτ(α) ἄρ(α) "That's why . . . !" (colloquial), as also at 335, 353, etc.   **πεπότηται** deponent perfect middle < ποτάομαι ("fly"), a common image for excitement. Cf. English "my heart leapt".

320 λεπτο-λογεῖν "to talk subtly"; cf. 153n., 1496 δια-λεπτο-λογοῦμαι. The compound is otherwise attested only much later, in texts that are probably drawing it direct from *Clouds*, which had by that point become a classic.   **ἤδη** 293–5n.   **περὶ καπνοῦ στενο-λεσχεῖν** literally "to engage in narrow chatter (cf. 1480n.) about smoke", i.e. "about nothing".

321 "and to puncture (< νύσσω) an opinion with a nice little opinion and argue against it with a different argument".

322 εἴ πως ἔστιν "if it's in anyway (possible)"; polite.   **φανερῶς** goes with **ἰδεῖν αὐτάς**.

323 νυν 237n.   **δευρί** Note the *iota*, suggesting that this is accompanied by a gesture.   **πρὸς τὴν Πάρνηθ(α)** Mount Parnes is located about 20 miles north of the Acropolis, i.e. directly behind the audience and directly in front of the actors (whose view of it would have been blocked, however, by the Acropolis, which the Theater of Dionysus backs up against).

324 ἡσυχῇ is "quietly, gently" (an adverb < ἥσυχος); appropriate both to the way real clouds move and to the fact that the chorus are no longer singing. φέρε 218n. πάνυ (211–13n.) reinforces πολλαί ("very many").

325 διὰ τῶν κοίλων καὶ τῶν δασέων ("through the hollows and the brush-covered parts") is appropriate to clouds coming down a mountain (cf. 323), while αὗται πλάγιαι ("these to the side") refers to the actual position of the chorus in the Theater (cf. 326). τί τὸ χρῆμα; literally "What's the thing?", i.e. ~ "What's this?, What's going on?"

326 ὡς "(I say this) since . . ." (209n.). παρὰ τὴν εἴσοδον "(There they are,) along the entrance-way" (into the orchestra). μόλις ("barely"; also 1363) and οὕτως (i.e. "if I look in the direction you suggest") both modify an implied καθορῶ.

327 The particle τοι ("you can be sure") is in origin a dative of σύ/τύ and thus adds emphasis by specifying that the addressee has an indirect relationship to the action, which somehow matters to him or her (43n.). Cf. 254n., 365 (where τοι—having been drawn as far forward as possible—strengthens the word that follows), 372, 861, 878. εἰ μὴ λημᾷς κολοκύνταις literally "unless you're bleary-eyed with gourds" (an instrumental dative), i.e. "unless you have (gourd-like) styes in your eyes and thus can't see".

328 This remark is addressed to Socrates rather than the Clouds, and exclamatory nominative ὦ πολυτίμητοι rather than vocative ὦ πολυτίμητοι is therefore wanted. Cf. 219 with n.

329 μέν-τοι is in origin a combination of μέν and τοι (327n.; cf. 254n. on τοί-νυν) that serves to add emphasis. But by this period it often has an adversative sense approaching "but, however", as also in e.g. 126, 588. Contrast 340 with n., 787.

330 ὁμίχλην καὶ δρόσον . . . καὶ καπνόν "mist and vapor and smoke".

331 γάρ "(You thought that) because . . ." (191n.). ὁτιή (also e.g. 755–6, 784) is a colloquial Attic form of ὅτι. βόσκω (also 334) is the verb used for keeping domestic animals, as well as for providing support for dependent members of a household (children, slaves, women).   σοφιστής in this period appears to be a more or less neutral term ("someone devoted to σοφία" and thus ~ "intellectual" rather than a pejorative "sophist"), although the words in apposition to it in 332 are all implicitly critical.

332 Θουριο-μάντεις is a reference to the foundation of the Athenian colony of Thyrii in the mid-440s BCE, which apparently inspired prophecies by numerous seers (μάντεις), a group Aristophanes routinely treats as self-interested frauds (e.g. *Peace* 1052–1126).   **ἰατρο-τέχνας** "medical artificers" (a *hapax*).   **σφραγιδ-ονυχ-αργο-κομήτας** "seal-ring-fingernail-lazy-longhairs", i.e. wealthy people (cf. 14n.) who have possessions valuable enough to keep under seal and whose nails are unbroken because they do no hard physical labor.

333 κυκλίων τε χορῶν ᾀσματο-κάμπτας "song-benders of cyclic choruses", i.e. the poets who competed in the third great poetic event at the City Dionysia, the tribally organized dithyramb contests; cf. 335–8n. κάμπτω is a negative term in such contexts (969n.).   A φέναξ is a "cheat, impostor"— formations in -αξ are routinely hostile (cf. 351 ἅρπαξ, 1367 στόμφαξ; contrast onomatopoeic παππάξ at 390)—and a μετεωρο-φέναξ is one who interests himself in μετέωρα (227–8n.). The point becomes clear in 335–6.

334 οὐδὲν δρῶντας English generally uses a conjunction such as *when, since, although,* or *because* to specify the relationship between the main action (here **βόσκουσ(ι)**, "they support"; 331n.) and a subordinate action of this kind. Greek does not—"doing nothing" is merely a verbal adjective + object describing the poets who benefit from the Clouds' patronage—and translation requires divining the nature of the connection (here concessive, "although they do nothing") and inserting the appropriate term to bridge the syntactic gap between the two languages.   **μουσο-ποοῦσιν** "write poetry about"; cf. 335 ἐποίουν with n., 358–9n., 1030–1.

335 ταῦτ(α) ἄρ(α) 319n.   ποιέω is used here in the specific sense "produce (poetry)" (LSJ *s.v.* A.I.4); a ποιη-τής ("poet") is someone who engages in this activity, a ποίη-μα ("poem"; cf. 155n.) what he produces. Imperfect because Strepsiades is looking back on the habitual activity of these people that led to the support described in detail in 338–9 (where note again imperfect κατ-έπινον).

335–8 The words within quotation marks are either drawn from real contemporary dithyrambs or—just as likely—are merely intended to sound like what dithyrambic poets wrote; the τε's that link the phrases are not to be taken as part of the originals. Dithyrambic poetry is almost entirely lost, and we know it mostly through parodies such as these, which show that it was characterized by elaborate, circuitous, highly "poetic" language. Despite the ridicule comedy pours on it, it appears to have been extremely popular. Note the repeated use of "Doric *alpha*" throughout and the elevated compounds.   ὑγρᾶν νεφελᾶν στρεπτ-αίγλαν δάιον ὁρμάν "twisted-bright destructive rush of moist clouds" (an over-the-top way of saying "lightning bolt"). ὑγρᾶν and νεφελᾶν are Doric 1st-declension genitive plurals; cf. δροσερᾶν νεφελᾶν below and μεγαλᾶν ἀγαθᾶν and κιχηλᾶν in 339 with n. The *scholia* attribute the *hapax* στρέπτ-αιγλος specifically to the dithyrambic poet Philoxenus of Kythera (*PMG* 830).   πλοκάμους . . . ἑκατογ-κεφάλα Τυφῶ "tresses of hundred-headed Typho", a monster defeated by Zeus and said by Hesiod (*Theogony* 869) to be responsible for storm-winds. ἑκατογ-κεφάλα and Τυφῶ are Doric genitives.   πρημαινούσας . . . θυέλλας "hard-blowing whirlwinds".   ἀερίας διερᾶς "airy liquidities" (both properly adjectives).   γαμψούς τ᾽ οἰωνοὺς ἀερο-νηχεῖς "twisted-(taloned) birds that swim through the air". τ᾽ is found in only a few manuscripts and was accepted into the text by Dover; without it, these words must be in apposition to what precedes ("airy liquidities, (that is) twisted-(taloned) birds . . ."). ὄμβρους . . . ὑδάτων δροσερᾶν νεφελᾶν "storms of water produced by moist clouds".

338–9 κατ-έπινον literally "they drank down" (< κατα-πίνω); but the compound is used routinely of "gulping down" anything without bothering to chew. For the imperfect, 335n. Probably a reference to the post-performance feasts offered choruses and poets (thus the *scholia*; cf. *Acharnians* 1154– 5).   κεστρᾶν τεμάχη "barracuda steaks (< τέμνω, "cut")".   The Doric genitive plurals κεστρᾶν, μεγαλᾶν ἀγαθᾶν and κιχηλᾶν are a bit of silliness by Strepsiades, who is imitating the language of the poets he has been quoting (335–8n.).   κρέα . . . ὀρνίθεια κιχηλᾶν literally "avian bits of meat from thrushes" (a mock-dithyrambic periphrasis for "thrush-meat").

340–1 διὰ μέν-τοι τάσδ(ε) "(This is all) because of *them*" (126n.), meaning the Clouds.   τί παθοῦσαι / . . . εἴξασι; "what happened to them [antecedent action] that they resemble [perfect < ἔοικα = present action]?" + dative.

342 ἐκεῖναι i.e. the normal clouds Strepsiades is used to.   τοιαῦται < τ- (referring to something definite) + οἷος (155n.) + a feminine form of οὗτος; thus "of such a sort as these". Contrast interrogative **ποῖαι** in Socrates' response.   **γάρ** 191n.

343 δ(ὲ) οὖν "'anyway', implying 'although I don't *know*, I can tell you what they *look* like'" (Dover).   **ἐρίοισιν πεπταμένοισιν** "wool that's been spread out (perfect passive participle < πετάννυμι)".

344 ὁτιοῦν is an adverb < ὅστις, and **οὐδ(ὲ) ὁτιοῦν** is thus "not in any way at all".   **ῥῖνας ἔχουσιν** a puzzling remark: why does Strepsiades focus on the chorus' *noses*? And by extension, how are they dressed?

345–6 ἀπό-κριναι deponent aorist middle imperative < ἀποκρίνω ("answer"; also 1244–5); Socrates plays the teacher.   **ἅττ(α)** 250–1n.   **ἃν ἔρωμαι** Aorist subjunctive (< *ἔρομαι, "ask"), because the object is theoretical and vague ("whatever"); contrast indicative **βούλει** in Strepsiades' response, where the object is specific ("that which").   **λέγε . . . ταχέως** Colloquial English would say "hurry up and tell (me)!" (cf. 735, 775, etc.), just as for **ἀνα-βλέψας εἶδες** it would say "you looked up and saw".

347 εἶτα τί τοῦτο; literally "Then what's this?", i.e. "But so what?"

348–55 Aristophanic comedy is full of crude, blistering mockery of contemporary persons, especially politicians and poets. How "personally" or "seriously" these remarks were taken by the original audience is unclear, but they are probably best read in the first instance as evidence of the targets' general social prominence or notoriety. None of this advances the action, and the jokes must have been added because this sort of public abuse was regarded as amusing.

348–9 κα(ὶ ε)ἶτ(α) here ~ "so as a consequence".   **κομήτην / ἄγριόν τινα τῶν λασίων τούτων** Long hair was a mark of social pretensions (14n.), and the *scholia* claim that ἄγριος (literally "from the country"—i.e. "not from the city"—and thus "savage, crude") was a term for a man who was particularly interested in pederasty (it being taken for granted that everyone inclines somewhat in that direction; cf. Strepsiades at 196–7 and the Weaker Argument at 1072–3). What having heavy body hair, i.e. being "one of these shaggy (λάσιος) people", has to do with this is unclear. Perhaps **τὸν Ξενοφάντου** ("the son of Xenophantos")—according to the *scholia* the poet Hieronymus (*PAA* 533985) seemingly mentioned also at *Acharnians* 388–90—looked this way; or perhaps this was taken to be a general "tell" for identifying men with pronounced sexual tendencies in this direction.

350 σκώπτουσαι "as a way of mocking" + accusative. Cf. 334n. on the handling of the connection to the main verb; 352 is similar.   **κενταύροις** notoriously lust-filled creatures; picking up κενταύρῳ in 346.   Note the rough breathing on **αὐτάς** = ἑαυτάς; "themselves" (not "them").   **ἤκασαν** might be a gnomic aorist describing habitual behavior (see 399–400n.), or the point might be instead that "the son of Xenophantos" really was mocked by the Clouds recently, i.e. that this is a specific example of their behavior rather than a general account of their tendencies; cf. ἐγένοντο in 354 and 355.

351 τί γὰρ ἦν . . . , τί δρῶσιν; "(I'm puzzled,) what if . . . , what do they do?"   Simon "the snatcher" (ἅρπαξ < ἁρπάζω; see 333n.), i.e. embezzler, "of public funds (δημόσια < δῆμος)" (*PAA* 822065) is mentioned again at 399 as a perjurer and in Eupolis fr. 235 as filching money from Heracleia Pontica. That he was actually guilty of anything is unclear.

352 λύκοι Wolves were notorious plunderers of helpless lambs and kids; picking up λύκῳ in 347.   **ἐξ-αίφνης** (adv.) "suddenly, abruptly". In combination with the aorist verbs (also 350 ἤκασαν with n., 355 ἐγένοντο), this makes it clear that the clouds/Clouds are imagined as shifting abruptly from one impersonation to another as they drift over the city and look down, not as merely sometimes looking like one thing, sometimes another. Cf. 1303–20n.

353 Κλεώνυμον . . . τὸν ῥίψ-ασπιν "Cleonymus the shield-thrower (< ῥίπτω + ἀσπίς)", i.e. "the coward", was a prominent politician (*PAA* 579410) repeatedly attacked by Aristophanes, *inter alia* for his supposed sexual failings (cf. 673–6 with nn.), gluttony and duplicity (399–400). Hoplite shields were heavy (cf. 988–9 with n.), and desperate soldiers sometimes threw them away during retreats; perhaps Cleonymus was involved in such a situation, e.g. in the debacle at Delion in 424 BCE, and this was later held against him.   **χθές** 169n.

354 ὅτι "because" (LSJ *s.v.* V.B).   **ἔλαφοι** because deer notoriously run in the face of danger. A reference to bulls is expected (cf. 347 ταύρῳ, 352n.), making this a surprise and thus doubly amusing.

355 Κλεισθένη Cleisthenes (*PAA* 575540) was another prominent contemporary politician and is relentlessly attacked by Aristophanes for his failure to have a beard—supposedly because he wanted to look like a woman and thus be sexually attractive to other men, but more likely because he was unable to grow one.

356–7 χαίρετε (literally "rejoice!"; cf. singular χαῖρε in 358) is the normal way to say both "Hello" and "Goodbye"; cf. 609.   **τοί-νυν** 254n.   **εἴ-περ τινὶ κ(αὶ) ἄλλῳ** a polite request-formula (balanced by **κα(ὶ ἐ)μοί**), equivalent in function although not specific content to English "if you don't mind".   **οὐρανο-μήκη** (literally "heaven-wide"; also 460–1, in a song) and **παμ-βασίλειαι** ("queens of all") are both poetic.   **ῥήξατε … φωνήν** "break into speech!" (LSJ s.v. A.4), as also at 960.

358–9 The Clouds address first Strepsiades, then Socrates, who has summoned them and whom they regard at this point as their real interlocutor.   **πρεσβῦτα παλαιο-γενές, θηρατὰ λόγων φιλο-μούσων** "ancient-born old man, hunter of Muse-loving words", i.e. "of artistic language"; the compounds mark this as elevated style.   **λεπτοτάτων λήρων ἱερεῦ** "priest of most subtle blather".

360 ὑπ-ακούσαιμεν 263n.   **μετεωρο-σοφιστῶν** 227–8n., 331n.

361 πλὴν εἰ Προδίκῳ Here and at 734, the manuscripts offer πλὴν ἤ. But ἤ is superfluous after πλήν, and πλὴν εἰ seems to be the normal expression, which was occasionally corrupted into πλὴν ἤ after ει and η came to be pronounced alike.   Prodicus of Ceos, "the most distinguished and respected intellectual of the day" (Dover p. lv), had visited Athens around 430 BCE and probably repeatedly thereafter. The Clouds' comparison of their assessment of him with what they think of Socrates is very much to the disadvantage of the latter.

362 βρενθύει τ(ε) ἐν ταῖσιν ὁδοῖς καὶ τὼ (ὀ)φθαλμὼ παρα-βάλλεις "you both carry yourself haughtily in the streets and turn your eyes (dual) aside" amounts to saying the same thing twice (hendiadys): Socrates is too proud to make eye-contact with other people (= ugly behavior; cf. 425).

363 ἀν-υπό-δητος 103n.   **ἀν-έχει** is 2nd-person middle (not 3rd-person active); the context suggests that this is to be understood as ostentatiously self-denying behavior rather than as a mark of a genuine commitment to simplicity.   **ἐ(πὶ) ἡμῖν σεμνο-προσωπεῖς** "you make a haughty face in dependence on us", i.e. "you give people haughty looks because of your connection to us".

364 τοῦ φθέγ-ματος exclamatory genitive (153n.).   **ὡς** is also exclamatory, "how!" (also 646, 872, 1238, 1476); the adjectives that follow modify an implied φθέγμα.

365 τοι 327n.   **φλύαρος** "nonsense, babbling"; a badly attested but probably common word.

366 ὑμῖν The manuscripts almost universally have ἡμῖν ("as far as we're concerned"). But Strepsiades is not yet a student, and this is a common copyist's error (195n.).   **πρὸς τῆς Γῆς** 200n.

367 ποῖος Ζεύς; literally "What sort of Zeus?" But this is a common colloquial way (also 1337) of responding to a strange or stupid remark by quoting back what has just been said, ~ "What do you mean 'Zeus'?" Cf. 247n.   **οὐ μή ληρήσεις** 296n.

368 ἀπό-φηναι aorist middle imperative (here with the sense of the active) < ἀπο-φαίνω.

369 που ("somehow, I suppose") nominally reduces the emphatic force of δή in **δή-που,** but the combination is actually used routinely to mean "of course". Socrates moves again into school-master mode; cf. 345–6n.   **αὐτό** is the internal object of **διδάξω, σ(έ)** the external object.

370 Supply Δία as the subject of **ὕοντ(α);** referred to again as αὐτόν in 371.

371 καί-τοι "and yet", as again in 373: the speaker makes an addition (καί) that amounts to backing off from his previous point, and calls for attention to the move with τοι (327n.).   **χρῆν** (past tense of χρή; also 1359, 1463) refers to something that ought to have been the case, but is/was not; "it *would have been* necessary (if you were right about Zeus himself being the one who produces rain—as you aren't)". Although this is unreal action, ἄν is not required, because the subject is impersonal; cf. 1215n., 1359.   **αἰθρίας** is a one-word genitive absolute; supply οὔσης (as in some of the manuscripts, but against the meter), "when it's clear weather" (229–30n.).

372 τοῦτο . . . τῷ νυνὶ λόγῳ εὖ προσ-έφυσας "you grafted this on nicely to the argument you made just now" (= "a moment ago"; cf. 825), i.e. the claim that Zeus does not exist (367).

373 καί-τοι 371n.   **τὸν Δί(α) . . . διὰ κοσκίνου οὐρεῖν** "that Zeus was urinating through a sieve". An obviously idiotic remark: Aristophanes conspicuously skips the opportunity to offer a more compelling refutation of Socrates' atheistic arguments. Cf. 374n., and note the crude image saved for the end as a punchline.

374 Directly put, Strepsiades' question would be τίς ἐστιν ὁ βροντῶν; ("Who is it that makes thunder?").   **τοῦ(το) ὅ με ποιεῖ τετραμαίνειν** ("this thing that makes me tremble"; in rough apposition to **ὁ βροντῶν**) refers to the thunder, however it is produced. Strepsiades is again (cf. 373n.) characterized as not so much an intellectual conservative as a fool.

375 κυλινδόμεναι < κυλίνδω ("roll"; cognate with English "cylinder"); an obscure idea, setting up Strepsiades' question and the wild explanation in 376–8.   **τῷ;** 185n.   **τολμῶν** 457–8n.

376 ἐμ-πλησθῶσ(ι), ἀναγκασθῶσι aorist passive subjunctives < ἐμπίμπλημι, "fill" (+ genitive = "fill with"; also 386), and ἀναγκάζω, "compel", respectively. When Socrates has no real explanation for how something happens, he resorts to the quasi-scientific force of ἀνάγκη (also 377, 405).

377–8 κατα-κριμνάμεναι < κατα-κρίμναμαι, a by-form of κατα-κρέμναμαι ("hang down") omitted from LSJ because editors at that time generally wrote κατακρημνάμεναι here.   **βαρεῖαι / εἰς ἀλλήλας ἐμ-πίπτουσαι** English would specify "*because* they are heavy and bump into one another"; cf. 334n.

379 ὁ δ(ὲ) ἀναγκάζων ἐστὶ τίς αὐτάς; For the delayed interrogative, which makes the sense ~ "The one who compels them—who is he?", cf. 1286. Strepsiades thinks he has caught Socrates in a logical contradiction.

380–1 ἥκιστ(α) 316–18n.   Strepsiades mistakes Socrates' **αἰθέριος δῖνος** ("celestial vortex") for the proper name **Δῖνος** ("Vortex"), hence the uppercase *delta* in his question. Cf. 827–8 (where the old man repeats the idea as an example of the incredible learning he has picked up in the Thinkery), 1472–4. The original audience would hear δῖνος both times in 380, and would get the joke only at the end of 381; cf. 264–5n.   **τουτί** is in apposition to 381: "*this* . . . (the fact of) Zeus . . ."

382 The addition of the particle **πω** makes **οὐδέν** mean "nothing at all, nothing whatsoever"; cf. 530, 1188, 1228.

383 οὐκ ἤκουσάς μου . . . ὅτι φημί; literally "didn't you hear me, that I say . . . ?", i.e. "didn't you hear me say . . . ?"

384 ~ 378, with the idea behind the final prepositional clause drawn from 376.   **πυκνότητα** "density" (also 406, which is set up here).

385 τῷ; = τίνι;

386–7 ζωμοῦ "broth", in this case produced from the flesh of sacrificial animals (cf. below) and distributed to the crowds at the festival.   **Παν-αθηναίοις** "at the Panathenaic festival", celebrated annually in ~ June, with the "Great Panathenaia" (including athletic and musical contests, along with performances of other sorts; cf. 988–9 with n.) held every fourth year. For this bare use of the dative with a festival name, cf. 408 Διασίοισιν, 864, 988.   **ἐμ-πλησθείς** 376n.   **τὴν γαστέρα** is accusative of respect with **ἐταράχθης;**, "were you disturbed as regards your stomach?", i.e. "did you have an upset stomach?"   **ἐξ-αίφνης** 352n.   A κορκορυγή (onomatopoeic) is a rumbling noise, and **διε-κορκορύγησεν** seems to be a nonce-word, i.e. a one-time formation intended to express an unusual idea, here that a **κλόνος** ("agitation, turmoil") produced a rumble from one end of Strepsiades' guts to the other.

388 δεινά is an internal accusative with **ποεῖ**. The verb is present tense because it describes a common situation, of which Strepsiades' experience at the Panathenaia is only one example: "(in situations like that), it gets upset". The subject is Strepsiades' γαστήρ (not the κλόνος); Stepsiades himself is **μοι** ("dative of disadvantage", since he is affected in a negative way).   **εὐθύς** is adverbial ("straightaway, immediately"), as again in 785, 855, etc.

389 ζωμ-ίδιον The point of the diminutive is perhaps that even though only a little broth is involved, the noise is enormous—and clouds are much larger than Strepsiades' stomach (~ Socrates' point in 392, again using an diminutive)!   **δεινὰ κέκραγεν** "produces a terrible clamor" (internal accusative). κέκραγα is perfect (with present sense) < κράζω; also 1386.

390 ἀτρέμας (*alpha* privative + < τρέμω) is adverbial, literally "without trembling" and thus ~ "softly, gently".   **παππάξ παππάξ . . . παπαπαππάξ** Inarticulate sounds are often given -άξ-endings either because that is how they were pronounced or because they were conventionally represented thus. Dover suggests that Strepsiades actually sticks his tongue out and produces farting noises ("raspberries"; more likely in 391, as a sort of punchline, the less exuberant sound of intestinal rumblings being wanted here).

391 κομιδῇ is a colloquial adverbial intensifier ~ "absolutely".

392–3 See 389n.   **σκέψαι** aorist middle imperative < σκέπτομαι, "consider" (also 1071).   **τυνν-ουτου-ί** < τύννος ("so small") + οὗτος + -ί, thus "as small as this"; colloquial.   οἷα and μέγα are internal accusatives, the latter best regarded as adverbial ("the sort of farts you've produced" and "thunder loudly").   τὸν δ(ὲ) ἀέρα ("as for the air . . .") is a proleptic accusative, meaning that it lacks a construction until it is picked up in the second half of the verse as the subject of βροντᾶν.   πῶς οὐκ εἰκός; "how is it not likely/reasonable?", i.e. "wouldn't you expect?"   ἀ-πέραντον 3n.

394 The assignment of this verse is disputed; Dover gives it to Socrates as a bit of learned sophistic etymologizing.   βροντή and πορδή do not sound much alike to us with our reconstructed sense of Greek pronunciation. Dover suggests that 5th-century Athenians said the first word "βορ(ν)τή", which gets the two much closer.

395 αὖ "again", i.e. "furthermore, on top of (what we've already discussed)".   λάμπων πυρί ("shining with fire") is not needed for the sense and looks like a decorative "poetic" touch.

396 κατα-φρύγει "roasts away to nothing" (a common use of the pre-verb; cf. 407 κατα-καίων with n., 1488 κατά-σκαπτ(ε)); ~ English "fries to a crisp".   τοὺς δὲ ζῶντας περι-φλεύει "and scorches the edges of the living", i.e. "of those who survive being blasted".

397 ἐπί-ορκους < ἐπί (in the sense "against") + ὅρκος ("oath"), thus "perjurers" (also 400, picking up this remark, and cf. the cognate verb ἐπιορκέω in 402). Oaths were often sworn by Zeus, hence his supposed interest in protecting their sanctity.

398 μῶρος is literally "blunt", and thus figuratively "stupid, moronic" (a cognate).   Κρονίων ὄζων "smelling of Kronia" (cf. 50n. on the genitive), referring to a festival celebrated in honor of Zeus' father Kronos, and thus by extension "old-fashioned"; cf. 929 Κρόνος ὤν, 998 Ἰαπετόν with n., 1070 Κρόνιππος with n.   βεκκε-σέληνε is obscure, although the second element ought to mean "moon"; patently insulting in any case.

399–400 δῆτ(α) goes with πῶς in 398; the amount of space between the words is unusual.   οὐχὶ Σίμων(α) . . . / οὐδὲ Κλεώνυμον οὐδὲ Θέωρον for Simon and Cleonymus, 351n., 353n. Theoros (*PAA* 513680) is another Athenian politician mentioned repeatedly in Aristophanes' early plays (e.g. *Acharnians* 134–73, where he is introduced as an ἀλαζών (102n.)).   ἐν-έπρησεν aorist active < ἐμ-πίμπρημι, "set on fire". This is a "gnomic" aorist, i.e. it describes an action that has occurred (or in this case, has *not* occurred) in the past and, more important, is taken to be typical; cf. 350n., 836–7. English uses a present for these purposes: "he sets on fire".   **σφόδρα** 191n.   **ἐπίορκοι** 397n.

401 νεών is an Attic accusative singular form of ναός, "temple".   **Σούνιον** Cape Sounion (the southernmost tip of Attica, about 45 miles southwest of Athens) was the site of a temple of Poseidon still partially preserved today.   **ἄκρον Ἀθηνέων** looks like a reminiscence of *Odyssey* 3.278 ἀλλ᾽ ὅτε Σούνιον ἱρὸν ἀφικόμεθ᾽, ἄκρον Ἀθηνέων ("but when we came to sacred Sounion, Athens' cape"; from Nestor's account of his journey home from Troy), but is in any case another bit of elevated poetic color (cf. 395 with n.).

402 τί μαθών; a stock phrase ~ "what is he thinking?"; also 1506.

403 εὖ ... λέγειν "to be right"; cf. 1092 εὖ λέγεις, 1289 καλῶς λέγεις, and contrast 644 οὐδὲν λέγεις with n.   **γάρ** "(But I'm still not satisfied,) because ..."

404–7 Quasi-scientific babble, which no one except Socrates and the ever-credulous Strepsiades is supposed to take seriously.   **ταύτας** i.e. the clouds/ Clouds.   **κατα-κλησθῇ** aorist passive subjunctive < κατα-κλείω, "shut up, enclose", + ἄν (i.e. within ὅτ-αν) in a temporal clause (89n.).   **ὥσ-περ κύστιν** "just like a bladder". A modern author would have said "just like a balloon", but in any case this is all setting up Strepsiades' anecdote in 408–11. For -περ, 238n.   **ὑπ(ὸ) ἀνάγκης** 376n.   **ῥήξας** aorist active participle < ῥήγνυμι ("break").   **σοβαρὸς διὰ τὴν πυκνότητα** "in a sudden rush due to (their) density (384n.)".   **ὑπὸ τοῦ ῥοίβδου καὶ τῆς ῥύμης αὐτὸς ἑαυτὸν κατα-καίων** "itself burning itself up"—i.e. independently converting itself into flame—"due to its rush and momentum". For the pre-verb on κατα-καίω, 396n., cf. 411 κατ-έκαυσεν, 1505 κατα-καυθήσομαι.

408 γοῦν "for example" or "at any rate".   **ἀ-τεχνῶς** "with no τέχνη involved, simply", and thus "precisely, absolutely"; a colloquial intensifying adverb (also e.g. 425, 439, 453) here modifying τουτί.   **Διασίοισιν** "at the Diasia festival" (for the bare dative, 386–7n.; Δι- shows that it was celebrated in honor of Ζεύς, Διός), at which individual citizens apparently offered sacrifice. Mentioned again at 864; contrast the city-wide Panathenaia sacrifices referenced obliquely at 386.

409 ὀπτῶν γαστέρα literally "while roasting a stomach"; but Strepsiades means that he had stuffed the stomach of the sacrificial animal with fatty trimmings and was roasting it like a haggis.   **τοῖς συγ-γενέσιν** "for my relatives" (< σύν + γίγνομαι/γένος), suggesting a larger group than his immediate nuclear family.   **κα(ὶ εἶ)τα** 149n.   **οὐκ ἔσχων ἀ-μελήσας** "I carelessly failed to split (it) (< σχάζω)", puncturing the stomach being necessary to keep steam from building up inside, to avoid the disaster described in 410–11.

410 ἄρ(α) "as a consequence" (165n.), i.e. because of the thoughtlessness mentioned in 409.   The second *alpha* in **δια-λακήσασα** is long, and LSJ plausibly takes the participle to be < διά + ληκέω, "split apart" and thus "explode".

411 τίλος is "diarrhoea", and **προσ-ετίλησεν** is thus ~ "blew nasty goop into" (a deliberately disgusting image—but amusing since it supposedly happened to someone else).   **κατ-έκαυσεν** (aorist < κατα-καίω) ~ "thoroughly scorched"; cf. 407 with n.

412–19 The chorus acknowledge Strepsiades at length for the first time; contrast 358–63, where the focus is on Socrates.

412 ἄνθρωπε ("human being") implicitly distinguishes the addressee from the divine Clouds.

413 ὡς is exclamatory, "how . . . !"   **τοῖς Ἕλλησι** "the (other) Greeks".

414–19 The list of qualifications for fellowship with Socrates and the Clouds starts out benignly enough (414), but rapidly descends into a description of a harsh, pleasure-free existence (415–17) devoted to the unscrupulous use of rhetoric (418–19). The Clouds will later insist that they were here deliberately leading Strepsiades on, because they saw his bad intentions and wanted to teach him what is right (1303–20 with n., 1458–61 with 1456–7n.). Whatever one makes of that claim, the point is far from obvious here. Cf. 510–11n.

414 τὸ ταλαί-πωρον < τάλας ("suffering, wretched") + πωρέω (supposedly "to suffer"), thus "(the ability to put up with) living a hard life".

415 μὴ κάμνεις μή(τε) ἑστὼς μήτε βαδίζων "you don't get tired either standing (perfect active participle < ἵστημι) or walking".

416 ῥιγῶν ἄχθει "you're not upset when shivering", i.e. "you're not averse to shivering", since Socrates' students are required to do without outer garments (cf. 497–8).   **λίαν** 53–5n.   **μήτ(ε) ἀριστᾶν ἐπι-θυμεῖς** "and you don't desire to eat lunch" (ἄριστον with a long *alpha*; a different word from ἄριστος, "best", which has a short *alpha*)", since there is rarely food in the Thinkery (cf. 175).

417 ἀπ-έχει 2nd-person present middle < ἀπ-έχω, "you keep yourself away from, you avoid" + genitive.   **ἀ-νόητος** < privative *alpha* + νοέω, "thoughtless, foolish" (also 898, 919).

418–19 ὅ-περ εἰκὸς δεξιὸν ἄνδρα "precisely that which (it is) likely/ reasonable that a clever man (regards as best)", qualifying **τοῦτο**, which is then more precisely defined in the next verse. For -περ, 238n.   **πράττων καὶ βουλεύων** i.e. in both private and public affairs, with **τῇ γλώττῃ πολεμίζων** looking at both situations from a slightly different angle. πράττω here is "conduct business".

420–1 οὕνεκα + genitive "as far as . . . go, as for . . ."; picked up by οὕνεκα τούτων in 422. For οὕνεκα, 6n., 238n. Here and at 422, the manuscripts actually have ἕνεκα (unmetrical), εἵνεκα or ἕνεκεν, this being the sort of word that scribes unconsciously alter to fit the usage of their own times.   **στερρός** is "rugged, hard".   **δυσκολό-κοιτος . . . μέριμνα** is "thought that makes bed"—i.e. sleeping—"difficult"; cf. 12–14.   **φειδωλός** ("miserly"; cf. 65n.) is normally a three-termination adjective, which would mean that it goes here with **γαστρός** rather than **μερίμνης**, to which it seems better suited. LSJ *s.v.* suggests that the word is exceptionally two-termination in this verse. Alternatively, one might print φειδωλῆς for the manuscripts' φειδωλοῦ on the theory that this is a simple, early scribal error, the adjective having been drawn into the masculine by the long series of second-declension endings that surround it.   **τρυσί-βιος** is < τρύω ("wear out, distress") + βίος, thus ~ "that endures a difficult life".   **θυμβρ-επί-δειπνος** is "that dines on savory", i.e. on bitter herbs—and nothing else.

422 ἀ-μέλει "don't worry!" (also 488, 877, etc.); colloquial.   **θαρρῶν** 141n.   **ἐπι-χαλκεύειν παρέχοιμ(ι) ἄν** literally "I would supply (myself) to work bronze on", i.e. ~ "you can pound me like an anvil" and thus "you can do whatever you want with me". Cf. 439–42, 453–6.

423 ἄλλο τι is in colloquial apposition to everything that follows: "another point— . . ."   **οὐ νομιεῖς . . . θεὸν οὐδένα;** "you won't consider (future < νομίζω) anyone (to be) a god?", i.e. "you won't consider any god (to exist)?"; cf. 248–9n., and note the abrupt shift to the neuter plural **ἅ-περ** (not οὕσ-περ) in what follows.

424 τουτί The deictic *iota* suggests a gesture toward something visible onstage; cf. 1473–4n.

425 δια-λεχθείην deponent aorist passive optative < δια-λέγομαι, "have a conversation with" + dative (cognate with English "dialogue" and "dialect").   **ἀ-τεχνῶς** 408n.   **οὐδ(ὲ) . . . ἀπαντῶν** "not even if I came face to face with (< ἀπαντάω) them", i.e. "not even if I met them on the street" (362n., 452n.).   **ἄν** is often repeated for purely pragmatic reasons, to keep the unreal nature of the action fresh in the listener's mind (cf. 118, 840, 977, 1056–7, etc.); the sense is unaffected.

426 refers to three basic styles of Greek sacrifice: the slaughter of live animals; the pouring of liquids (most often wine); and the burning of frankincense (λιβανωτός), hence **οὐδ(ὲ) ἐπι-θείην** (aorist passive optative < ἐπι-τίθημι) "nor would I put . . . on (a brazier)". Cf. 578 with n.

427–8 A genitive must be supplied with **οὐκ ἀ-τυχήσεις**, "you won't fail to get (this)".   As present participles, **τιμῶν καὶ θαυμάζων καὶ ζητῶν** describe ongoing action contemporary with the main verb. Here the relationship is conditional: "if you . . ."

429 δέομαι here takes both a genitive (of the person from whom something is requested) and an accusative (of what is requested).   **τουτί** points verbally, as it were, to the content of 430.

430 λέγειν is an epexegetic infinitive (243n.) with **ἄριστον**, "best at speaking".   **ἑκατὸν σταδίοισιν** "by a hundred stades" (dative of degree of difference). A stade was the distance to one end of the local running track (whence English "stadium") and back, however long that might be, usually ~ 180 yards. Colloquial English would say "by a mile".

431 τὸ λοιπόν is adverbial, "as regards what remains", i.e. "in the future" (also 677, 850, 1423).   **ἀπὸ τουδί** sc. τοῦ χρόνου, "from *this* time on, from *this* very moment".

432 ἐν τῷ δήμῳ i.e. in the Assembly; the Clouds naively misunderstand what Strepsiades wants.   A γνώμη (< γιγνώσκω) is one's opinion on some matter, and **γνώμας νικήσει** is thus "you will be successful in regard to proposals", i.e. "you will carry motions"; cf. 419 βουλεύων. For this use of νικάω, cf. 1210–11 νικᾷς . . . τὰς δίκας.

433 μὴ (ἔ)μοιγε λέγειν γνώμας μεγάλας "don't (talk) to *me* about making major proposals!" (84n.). The implication is that other people may care about this sort of thing—but not Strepsiades.

434 ὅσ(α) ἐμαυτῷ στρεψο-δικῆσαι literally "to twist justice in regard to however many matters pertain to me", recalling Strepsiades' name (134 with n.; cf. 450 στρόφις, 776 ἀπο-στρέψαις). The verb is perhaps a nonce-word.   **τοὺς χρήστας δι-ολισθεῖν** (literally "to slip through my creditors") makes Strepsiades' intentions more explicit and thus amounts to a gloss on the more obscure first half of the line.

435 τεύξει deponent 2nd-person singular future middle < τυγχάνω.   **ὧν** = τούτων ὧν; a colloquial compression of a demonstrative and the relative pronoun dependent on it.

436 παρά-δος aorist active imperative < παρα-δίδωμι.   A πρό-πολος (< πρό + πέλομαι, "be, become") is a servant who "is before" his or her master (cf. ἀμφί-πολος, one who "is about", i.e. "attends"), and thus by extension a cult official for a god. Note the plural, referring not just to Socrates but to everyone in authority within the Thinkery.

437 δράσω . . . πιστεύσας The aorist participle conceives of the action in question as complete (rather than as ongoing, as with the present participle). With a future main verb, the action is almost automatically to be understood as antecedent; English would say "because I trust you, I'll . . ." or more colloquially "I'll put my trust in you and . . ."

438 κοππα-τίας 23n.   **ἐπ-έτριψεν** 243n.

439–56 Anapaestic dimeter (monometer at 451, 454); see Introduction §IV.A.2. The meter is often used in comedy for lists (441–2, 445–51).

439–41 "I supply my body here to them (to do) whatever they want (with it)". Some ancient copyist or editor found this too confusing and added χρήσθων (3rd-person plural deponent present middle imperative < χράομαι; "let them use!") to 439, matching 3rd-person plural present active imperative δρώντων in 453 (where the thought as a whole is repeated). The word produces metrical difficulties in what follows and was expelled from the text by the mid-19th-century Dutch classical scholar C. G. Cobet.

441–2 τύπτειν, πεινῆν, διψῆν, / αὐχμεῖν, ῥιγῶν, ἀσκὸν δείρειν is essentially another version of what the Clouds in 414–17 described as the treatment

Strepsiades would have to endure to acquire the ability to speak glibly and deceptively (418–19, echoed and expanded on here in 443–51).   **αὐχμεῖν** is literally "to be dry", but the real sense is "to go without oil", with which the Greeks routinely rubbed themselves after they bathed, and thus ~ "to be grubby". Cf. 44–5n., 836–7 with n., 920, 1002 with n.   **ἀσκόν** is an internal accusative with **δείρειν**, "to flay me into a wineskin" (an over-the-top image bringing this section of the list to an end).

445–51 All these terms are intended as abusive: Strepsiades *wants* to be called ugly names for successfully outmanuevering his opponents in court. But which of them were used on an everyday basis in Aristophanes' Athens and which are inventions or amusing one-off re-purposings of words generally employed in a more pedestrian fashion, is impossible to say.   **θρασύς** is "bold", but generally has the ugly sense "willing to do anything, shameless", as in 890, 915.   **τολμηρός** 457–8n.   **ἴτης** "reckless".   **ψευδῶν συγ-κολλητής** "a gluer-together" (< κολλάω; cf. English "collagen", the substance that holds bone, muscles and tendons together)—contemporary colloquial English would say "a cobbler-together"—"of lies".   **εὑρησι-επής** < εὑρίσκω + ἔπος, "a discoverer", i.e. a coiner, "of phrases".   **περί-τριμμα δικῶν** literally "something thoroughly (περι-) worn away (τρίβω + -μα (155n.)) via lawsuits", i.e. ~ "an experienced hand at lawsuits". Cf. οὐ τρίβων + genitive meaning "inexperienced in" at 869.   **κύρβις** one of the objects—shape and material not altogether clear—on which Solon's laws (cf. 1187n.) were inscribed and put on display in the Agora; thus ~ "a law book".   **κρόταλον** i.e. because his tongue will move so fast (26on.).   **κίναδος** "a fox", a conventional symbol of thievish cleverness.   **τρύμη** apparently "a drill" (thus the *scholia*, which also suggest the less convincing "a hole"; in any case < τρύω, "wear out"); perhaps comparable to figurative colloquial English "buzz saw", of an irresistible, destructive mechanical force.   A **μάσθλης** is literally "a piece of leather"; also used as a term of abuse for a fast-talking deceiver at *Knights* 269.   **γλοιός** ~ "grease, oil, scum".   **ἀλαζών** 102n.   A κέντρον is a "goad", which could be used for torture, and a **κέντρων** is apparently someone who has been thus handled, i.e. who deserves to be abused. Compare Strepsiades' treatment of one of his creditors at 1296–1302.   **μιαρός** is properly "polluted" with what we would call a religious or ritual stain (a μίασ-μα; cf. 995n.), but is used as a common form of abuse (1325 with n.).   **στρόφις** is < στρέφω; thus apparently a "twister, wriggler" (cf. 434 στρεψο-δικῆσαι).   **ματιο-λοιχός** is obscure—the *scholia* seem uncertain how to deal with the word—but the second element appears to be < λείχω, "lick". Since this is the final element in the list, it is easy to believe that it is an amusing, unexpected coinage.

452 (οἱ) ἀπαντῶντες "those who meet me" (note the rough breathing, which is all that remains of the definite article), i.e. in the street (cf. 425): Strepsiades wants his dirty reputation to precede him everywhere rather than being confined to the law courts.

453 δρώντων ἀ-τεχνῶς ὅ-τι χρήζουσιν cf. 439 with n.

455 ἔκ μου χορδήν "sausage made of me". A χορδή is literally a bit of intestine, and thus by extension the sausage made out of it when it is stuffed, or the string for a instrument produced by drying and twisting it (whence English "cord" and "chord", via Latin *chorda*).

456 παρα-θέντων 3rd-person aorist active "jussive" imperative ("let them . . . !") < παρα-τίθημι (literally "place beside"), the standard Greek verb for serving food or wine.

457–75 A song performed by the Clouds and Strepsiades, and mostly presented as a conversation between them confirming—or repeating—the preceding exchange. (Thus modern editors; the manuscripts give the Clouds' part to Socrates.) Like all choral songs, this one is doubtless accompanied by dance, hence in part the lack of new informational content, allowing the audience to concentrate on the spectacle alone. Dactylo-epitrite; see Appendix III.2. Note the scattering of high-style poetic vocabulary throughout.

457–8 Addressed to Socrates (or the world at large).   **λῆμα** < λῶ (rare in Attic) = θέλω + -μα (155n.), thus "desire, purpose" (also 1350); 5th-century poetic vocabulary.   **οὐκ ἄ-τολμον, ἀλλ(ὰ) ἔτοιμον** "not lacking in boldness, but ready (for anything)". τόλμα ("courage, boldness, daring") is an ambiguous word, however, that often shades over into "recklessness, overboldness, insolence" (as in 375, 445, 550).

459–62 Addressed to Strepsiades.   **ἴσθι** perfect active imperative < οἶδα.   For the chorus' occasional use of the first-person singular, cf. 463, 957.   **οὐρανό-μηκες** 356–7n.   βροτός ("mortal") is poetic vocabulary.

463–5 τί πείσομαι; like the parallel question in 466–7, "Hopeful, not apprehensive" (Dover).   **τὸν πάντα χρόνον** accusative of extent of time, "throughout all time, in perpetuity".   **ἀνθρώπων** might be taken with either βίον (~ "a human life that is most envied/enviable") or ζηλωτότατον (~ "a life that is most envied/enviable of (those led by) human beings").   **δι-άξεις** < δι-άγω.

466–7 See 463–5n.   ἆρα marks this as an question (note both the circumflex accent and the initial position of the particle; also e.g. 804, 1094), here impatient, while ἄρ(α) is inferential ("in that case": 121n.).

467–75 Supply ὄψει from ὄψομαι to govern the ὥστε-clause (~ "(You'll see) how . . ."). Alternatively, Strepsiades' remark in 466–7 can be treated as an interruption the Clouds ignore, with ὥστε . . . dependent on βίον . . . διάξεις in 464–5 and the full-stop at the end of 465 removed ("you'll lead a life—such that . . ."). σου is dependent on ἐπὶ ταῖσι θύραις. The practice described here is more often associated with Rome: individuals of lower status wait at an important man's door in the morning, hoping to get assistance in legal, political or financial matters.   εἰς λόγον ἐλθεῖν "to enter into conversation", with the accusatives of respect that follow defining the topics to be taken up.   A γραφή is an indictment (see 758–9n.), an ἀντι-γραφή the defendant's formal response: unsurprisingly, the Socratically educated Strepsiades is imagined as advising individuals who have been sued and need a creative way to beat the charges.   πολλῶν ταλάντων "worth many talents" (21n., 307n.).   ἄξια σῇ φρενί "worthwhile for your intelligence": Strepsiades will somehow profit from the consultation.   συμ-βουλευσομένους μετὰ σοῦ A colloquial mixture of two constructions: (1) συμ-βουλεύομαι + dative (as with most συν-compounds), and (2) βουλεύομαι μετά + genitive.

476–7 Addressed to Socrates. Anapaestic tetrameter catalectic; see Introduction §IV.A.2. Encouraging remarks of this sort are often called a *katakeleusmos* and tend to be found within formal debates (*agônes*), as at 959–60, 1034–5 in the confrontation between the two Arguments at 889–1112, and at 1351–2, 1397–8 in the final confrontation between Strepsiades and Pheidippides.   ἐγ-χείρει τὸν πρεσβύτην ὅτι-περ μέλλεις προ-διδάσκειν "put your hand to teaching the old man ahead of time whatever you intend to teach him!", i.e. "try to give the old man an advance taste of the education you have planned for him!" Although formally the infinitive goes with both the main and the dependent verb, the pre-verb really applies to the first.   δια-κίνει imperative (< uncontracted -κίνεε; contrast uncontracted indicative -κινέει, which would yield -κινεῖ). δια-κινέω is normally ~ "shake up"; here perhaps "rummage through, ransack".   ἀπο-πειρῶ deponent middle imperative (< uncontracted -πειράου) < ἀπο-πειράομαι, "make a test of" + genitive.

478–509 Iambic trimeter. See Introduction §IV.A.1.

478 ἄγε δή "alright" (also 636, 775); demanding an active response of some sort. Colloquial. ἄγε νυν (489) is used with the same sense where meter requires.   **τὸν σαυτοῦ τρόπον** 88n.

479–80 αὐτὸν εἰδὼς ὅστις ἐστί For the prolepsis, 250–1n.   **μηχανὰς / . . . πρός σε καινὰς προσφέρω** For the image, 481n.   **(ἐ)πὶ τούτοις** "after these things", i.e. "after I find out what I need to".

481 In his typically cloddish, literal-minded way (cf. 489–91), Strepsiades takes 479–80 ἵν(α) . . . μηχανὰς / . . . πρός σε . . . προσ-φέρω to mean ~ "so that I can apply siege-engines to you" and therefore asks **τειχο-μαχεῖν μοι δια-νοεῖ;** ("do you intend to engage in a wall-battle against me?").

482 βραχέα is an internal object with **πυθέσθαι** ("to learn a few things by asking questions"), with genitive **σου** referring to the person interrogated.

483 εἰ μνημονικὸς εἶ "(for example) if you have a good memory"; cf. 628–31, 785–90. For the form of the adjective (< μιμνήσκω), 27n.   **δύο τρόπω** a dual, here used adverbially; "(I'm μνημονικός) in two ways", i.e. "my memory functions in two different ways".

484 τι (accented in the text because it is one in a string of enclitics, only the last of which can be left accent-free) is the subject of **ὀφείληται**.

486–7 λέγειν ("(the ability) to speak (well)") is the subject of **ἔν-εστι**. Cf. **λέγειν** and **ἀπο-στερεῖν** ("(the ability) to cheat") in the next verse, the latter with the abbreviated **ἔν-ι** = ἔν-εστι.   φύσις is properly one's inborn (< φύω) nature and is thus more or less inflexible (e.g. 352, 515–16, 537), as opposed to one's τρόπος/τρόποι ("inclination/ manners"; cf. 478), which is/are at least theoretically more malleable. At other times, however, φύσις seems to mean ~ "appearance", i.e. what one *looks* like one is (276–7, 503).

488 ἀ-μέλει 422n.   **καλῶς** Supply the rest of the phrase from Socrates' **δυνήσει μανθάνειν;**.

489–90 ἄγε νυν 478n.   For **ὅπως** ("(see to it) that . . . !"), 257n.; here with future **ὑφ-αρπάσει** (< ὑφ-αρπάζω, "snatch away") at the end of the next line. The pre-verb suggests treacherous, secretive action, as if Socrates' words would scarcely be out of his mouth before Strepsiades would pounce on them, setting up 491.   For this use of προ-βάλλω ("pose" a problem or something similar), cf. 757. A puzzle of this sort is a πρό-βλη-μα (English "problem").

491 δαί (also 656, 1091, etc.) is a colloquial way of adding emphasis to the question: here *"What* (are you suggesting)?"   **κυνη-δόν** literally "dog-style", like e.g. ἱππη-δόν ("horse-style", i.e. "as if on horseback") at *Peace* 81 and κριη-δόν ("ram-style", i.e. "as if with a (battering) ram") at *Lysistrata* 309. Aristophanic dogs are notoriously devoted to stealing food (e.g. *Wasps* 835–8).   **σιτήσομαι** is a deponent future middle < σιτέω, "eat".

492 (ὁ) ἄνθρωπος Note the rough breathing (added by modern editors), which makes clear that this is to be taken with **οὑτοσί** rather than with **ἀμαθὴς . . . καὶ βάρβαρος.**   **ἀ-μαθής** 135n.; here the sense verges on "ineducable".   A **βάρβαρος** is someone who does not know Greek, and thus by definition an idiot.

493 δέδοικά σ(ε) . . . μὴ πληγῶν δέει literally "I am afraid as regards you, that you need blows", i.e. "I'm afraid you need a beating" (standard Greek educational practice to encourage faltering students; cf. 972n.). For the prolepsis, 250–1n.

494 φέρ(ε) ἴδω 21n.   **τί δρᾷς, ἤν τίς σε τύπτῃ;** The question follows logically on the comment in 493, and the culturally correct answer—not the one delivered—is "I hit him right back!" The point is not that Socrates is concerned about the consequences of carrying out his threat. Instead, the question exacts one final bit of evidence about Strepsiades' character (495–6): he is a typically litigious Athenian (208n.) and not much of a "traditional man".

495–6 ὀλίγον is an internal (adverbial) accusative with **ἐπ-ισχών** (aorist active participle < ἐπ-έχω), "after holding off a bit"; so too with **ἀ-καρῆ δια-λιπών**, "after allowing a little (time) to pass". Dover suggests that the first delay is intended to let Strepsiades lie about what has happened; or perhaps he merely wants to avoid being struck a second time and therefore backs off before reacting.   **ἐπι-μαρτύρομαι** "I call for witnesses" (< μάρτυς, cognate with English "martyr" = "witness (for one's faith)"), whom he could then take with him to court to swear to what had happened. Cf. 777 (the presence of witnesses crucial for winning a lawsuit), 1222–3 (Strepsiades calls for witnesses in support of the claim that the First Creditor has failed to follow proper legal procedure), 1297 (the Second Creditor calls for witnesses when Strepsiades assaults him).

497 κατά-θου (aorist middle imperative < κατα-τίθημι) "put down from yourself (onto the ground)!", i.e. "take off and set aside!" (also 500, 635).   **ἠδίκηκά τι;** "Have I done something wrong?"; τι is an internal accusative, cf. 1080 οὐδὲν ἠδίκηκας, "you did nothing wrong". This phrase nicely illustrates the fundamental character of a perfect and in particular why it is a primary rather than a secondary tense: Strepsiades' hypothetical misbehavior took place in the past, but its consequences and implications continue into the present (he appears to be due for a beating *now* because of what he did *then*).

498 γυμνός is "without a cloak" (i.e. wearing only a tunic), not "naked", as also in 965. Strepsiades never gets his *himation* back (856), and at the end of the play he notes that the residents of the Thinkery are in possession of it (1498; cf. 509n.). His shoes also disappear while he is inside the Thinkery (719, 858–9) and have presumably been sold by Socrates (cf. 175–9), since he and his students go barefoot (103n., 363). See also 856, 1103–4 with n.

499 φωράσων future active participle < φωράω ("search for a thief (φώρ)"), indicating purpose. If an Athenian thought another person had stolen something from him and concealed it, he was allowed to enter the accused man's house to search for the missing object (cf. *Frogs* 1362–3; Isaeus 6.42). This passage suggests that the law specified that he could not wear heavy clothing that might allow him to carry something inside and plant it there.

500 κατά-θου 497n.   **τί ληρεῖς;** ~ an order to stop doing this, as again in 829. The joke against Chairephon (104n.) that follows in 501–4 does not advance the action, hence the return to the idea after the interruption in 505 οὐ μὴ λαλήσεις.

501 ἐπι-μελής "careful", i.e. here "attentive, studious", as the more specific words that follow make clear.   **ὦ** present active subjunctive < εἰμί.   **προ-θύμ-ως** (adverb) literally "with a forward heart", i.e. "eagerly".

502 τῷ; = τίνι; **ἐμ-φερής** "similar to" + dative. Contrast δια-φέρω ("differ from" + genitive) in 503, 1428–9.

503 δι-οίσεις future active < δια-φέρω (502 n.); **οὐδέν** is an internal accusative.   **τὴν φύσιν** 486–7n.; accusative of respect.

504 ἡμι-θνής "half-dead". Aristophanes remarks elsewhere on Chairephon's pale, yellowish complexion (*Wasps* 1412–13); perhaps he had a liver condition.

505 οὐ μὴ λαλήσεις 296n. (on οὐ μή), 500n. This use of the future transforms ἀ-κολουθήσεις as well into ~ an imperative. λαλέω eventually comes to mean little more than "say, speak", but in Aristophanes routinely has an unfavorable sense ~ "chatter", as in 1053, 1394. The initial element of ἀ-κολουθέω is not a privative *alpha*, but is from a different pre-verb ~ σύν-, as also on ἅ-πας (e.g. 577). The second element is ~ κέλευθος ("road, path"), and the compound thus means "accompany"; cf. English "acolyte" (used e.g. of someone who assists a priest in a religious ceremony).

506 τι is an internal accusative with ἀνύσας ("hurry up a bit and . . ."; see 181n.), as again in 635, 1253.   θᾶττον (comparative < ταχύς) is used adverbially with 505 ἀ-κολουθήσεις to mean "quickly" (also 1253).

507–8 Trophonios was a Boeotian hero who gave oracles, and those who asked him for one were expected to offer a honey-cake (μελιτοῦττα < μέλι, "honey") to the snakes who shared his cave (hence **κατα-βαίνων**, "as I descend (into the Underworld)"). Strepsiades is being ridiculous, as usual. But he clearly sees entering the Thinkery as simultaneously awe-inspiring and frightening.   πρότερον is adverbial, "first".   εἰς Τροφωνίου "into (the residence) of Trophonios"; see 964–5n.

509 The accent on χώρει (contracted < χώρεε) shows that the word is imperative, not indicative; cf. 476–7n. on δια-κίνει.   κυπτάζω is ~ "skulk", as if Strepsiades were up to no good. For the combination of the indicative with ἔχων, 131n.   Strepsiades and Socrates exit the Thinkery, Socrates taking Strepsiades' cloak with him (cf. 498 with n.).

510–626 The parabasis, a standard, central element of Aristophanes' 5th-century comedies and seemingly those of his rivals as well. The precise significance of the name (< παρα-βαίνω, "step aside") is unclear. But the chorus commonly both address the audience directly, as if they represented the poet (518–62), and then speak for themselves as whatever they are costumed as in this particular play (575–94, 607–26). The standard formal elements of the parabasis are (1) the *kommation* (addressed to the departing characters; 510–17); (2) the parabasis proper (the poet's remarks to the audience; 518–62); (3) the ode (a song; 563–74); (4) the epirrhema (the chorus address the audience; 575–94); (5) the antode (a song corresponding metrically to the ode; 595–606); (6) the anteppirhema (matching the epirrhema in length, meter and character; 607–26).

510–17 The *kommation* (an ancient term meaning literally "little section"; < κόπτω, "cut" + -μα (155n.) + diminutive ending). Anapaests (510 monometer, 511 dimeter), followed by iambs; see Appendix III.3.

510–11 Addressed to the departing Strepsiades, whom the Clouds at this point appear again to be actively supporting and encouraging in his dubious undertaking; cf. 414–19n., and contrast 1303–20 with n., 1456–7n.   ἀλλ(ά) here introduces a command and urges action: "Come now!"   ἴθι χαίρων "go happily on your way!"

512 γένοιτο optative of wish, "might there be!"

513–17 προ-ήκων / εἰς βαθὺ τῆς ἡλικίας "having advanced into the depth of age", an elaborate ("poetic") way of saying "having grown old" that sets up the contrast with νεωτέροις . . . πράγμασιν ("matters appropriate to young people").   τὴν φύσιν αὐτοῦ is odd word order, τὴν αὐτοῦ φύσιν being expected. But cf. 905 τὸν πατέρ' αὐτοῦ.   χρωτίζω is an ill-attested verb cognate with χρώς ("skin") and apparently ~ "refinish".   σοφίαν ἐπ-ασκεῖ ("practices wisdom", as if this were a sport; the phrase recurs in 1024–5) expresses the preceding idea in a more straightforward way.

518–62 The parabasis proper: the poet speaks directly to the audience (518 ὦ θεώμενοι) through the Clouds, complaining about the reception of the original version of his play. Eupolideans; see Introduction §IV.A.4. Cf. the similar self-serving complaints at *Wasps* 1016–59 (422 BCE). Like all the spoken parts of the parabasis, these lines are probably pronounced by the chorus-leader (the coryphaeus) rather than by the entire chorus speaking in unison.

519 νὴ τὸν Διόνυσον τὸν ἐκ-θρέψαντά με "by Dionysus who brought me up" (aorist active participle < ἐκ-τρέφω; cf. 532 ἐξ-εθρέψατε), i.e. in his capacity as divine patron of poetry.

520–2 οὕτω (a short form of οὕτως also found at 535) is coordinated with ὡς: literally "thus might I be victorious (optative of wish), as I . . . !", i.e. "might my victories in dramatic contests now and in the future depend on the fact that . . . !"   σοφός . . . δεξιοὺς . . . σοφώτατ(α) The emphasis on the overriding importance of wisdom and cleverness—again at 526, 527, 535, 547–8, 562, 575—is striking in what might otherwise be taken to be an aggressively anti-intellectual comedy. Cf. 895n. (on cognate terms in the debate between the Arguments).   σοφώτατ(α) is adverbial with ἔχειν, "was the wisest"; the subject is ταύτην, "this (play)".

523 πρώτους . . . ἀνα-γεῦσ(αι) ὑμᾶς probably "that you first have a taste of it", although the compound is a *hapax* and its sense is not entirely certain. This is most easily read as an allusion to the fact that late 5th-century comedies and tragedies were sometimes reperformed in deme-theaters or similar settings after an initial staging at a major festival (cf. 556n.). The audience in the Theater of Dionysus—treated as if it were a single, unchanging entity—was thus privileged to see the premier of *Clouds I*, but then failed to hold up its end of the bargain (524–5).   ἠξίωσ(α) ("I thought it right") is echoed in 525 οὐκ ἄξιος ὤν ("although I didn't deserve (such treatment)"), the general point being that Aristophanes himself has done nothing wrong and has acted in complete good faith.

524 ἔργον πλεῖστον "the most work", *sc.* of any of Aristophanes' plays.   ὑπ(ὸ) ἀνδρῶν φορτικῶν refers to the other poets competing at the festival. φορτικός is "burdensome" (< φόρτος, "something one carries (φέρω), baggage" + the adjectival ending -ικος) and thus "something one has to put up with" and by extension "trashy, low-class".

525 ταῦτ(α) is the internal object of **μέμφομαι**, with the demonstrative pointing backward in the text, as properly and again in 526: "I have the preceding complaints".

526 τοῖς σοφοῖς (cf. 520–2n.) is here seemingly sarcastic.   **ταῦτ(α)** (cf. 525n.) is the internal object of **ἐπραγματευόμην**: "I engaged in the efforts just described".

527 οὐδ(ὲ) ὥς "not even so", i.e. despite the allegedly bad behavior on the audience's part just described.   **ὑμῶν . . . τοὺς δεξιούς** 520–2n. The implication is that not every member of the audience is clever, i.e. some will continue to applaud the plays of Aristophanes' rivals. But those who are clever—or would like to be thought clever—are, he claims, his real intended audience.

528–32 A riddling reference to Aristophanes' first play, staged in 427 BCE and normally referred to as *Daitalês* ("*Banqueters*"), although the poet himself here calls it ὁ σώ-φρων τε χὠ κατα-πύγων, ~ "The Modest/Chaste (Boy) and the Queer". κατα-πύγων (literally "down"—we would say "up"—"the butt") is an abusive term for someone who supposedly allows himself be used sexually by other men (also 909, cf. 1023 καταπυγοσύνης). Cf. the similarly abusive εὐρύ-πρωκτος (literally "with a wide asshole", *sc.* from being buggered so often and so hard) at 1084–98. For σώ-φρων, 537n. The handful of fragments of *Daitalês* that survive suggest that the play featured a father and two sons, one good and one bad, and at least touched on the theme of education. This is strikingly reminiscent of *Clouds*, although the suggestion in 529 is that the earlier play got a better reception.

528 ἐξ ὅ-του *sc.* χρόνου, "ever since the time (when)", as also at 1351. Coordinated with 533 ἐκ τούτου ("since that (time)").   **ἐνθάδ(ε)** i.e. apparently the Theater of Dionysus, in which case **ἀνδρῶν, οὓς ἡδὺ καὶ λέγειν** ("men whom it is pleasant even to mention") must be the portion of the original audience who regarded the play as a success, or the judges who sided with them.

529 ἄριστ(α) ἠκουσάτην literally "heard (3rd-person dual) best", i.e. "had nice remarks made about them". Cf. 1329 πολλ(ὰ) ἀκούων καὶ κακά, "hearing many bad things", i.e. "having many hostile remarks made about me".

530–1 Aristophanes unexpectedly casts himself as an unmarried girl (**παρθένος**; scarcely "virgin" in the strict sense of the word) who has gotten pregnant and is forced to dispose of the baby by exposing (**ἐξ-έθηκα** < ἐκ-τίθημι) it. The image appears to suggest that the poet was too young to stage *Daitalês* himself, and that another person—also apparently not very old (**παῖς δ(ὲ) ἑτέρα τις**)—"adopted" (**ἀν-είλετο** < ἀν-αιρέω) the play; perhaps a reference to a theatrical producer of a sort we know Aristophanes and other poets used routinely to facilitate the move from text to performance, and whose services might have been particularly important for a novice playwright.   **οὐκ ἐξῆν πω** "it wasn't possible at all", i.e. "it was completely impossible"; cf. 382n.

532 ἐξ-εθρέψατε 519n.   **γενναίως** "as a well-born person would", and thus "generously"; the reference is to the positive reception of *Daitalês* in the Theater.

533 ἐκ τούτου 528n.   **μοι** goes with ἐστί ("I have"; the accent on the verb as printed is a result of the elision). For the enclitic so far forward, 257n.   **πιστὰ παρ(ὰ) ὑμῶν γνώμης ... ὅρκια** "reliable pledges of judgment from you", i.e. "good reason to believe in your judgment".

534–6 Another unexpected—this time confused (or at least confusing)—image (cf. 530–1n.): *Clouds II* is like the famous (**ἐκείνην**: 180n.) Electra, the daughter of the murdered king Agamemnon, who found a lock of hair cut from the head of her brother (**τ(οῦ) ἀδελφοῦ τὸν βόστρυχον**) Orestes at Agamemnon's grave and thus realized that Orestes had returned to Mycenae. *Clouds II* is looking for similarly clever audience members (**θεαταῖς οὕτω**

σοφοῖς)—to recognize its relationship to *Clouds I*? (not difficult and not really the point); to help it take revenge for what was done to Aristophanes the first time around? (disturbingly dark, given the horrible character of the *Oresteia* killings); to be sure that it is treated as *Daitalês* was? (not an easy fit for the image). The reference would seem to be specifically to the beginning of Aeschylus' *Choephoroi*, which Aristophanes knew (cf. *Frogs* 1126–8), perhaps in part because Aeschylean tragedies were probably being revived already in this period (1366–7n.). Aeschylus' Electra does not go looking (ζητοῦσ(α) ἦλθ(ε)) for her brother, however, but simply discovers signs of his presence when she makes funerary offerings at Agamemnon's grave.   θεατής < θεάομαι, "view, gaze at" (cf. 518 θεώμενοι), a more focussed activity than ὁράω ("see"). The place where this is done is a θέατρον ("theater"), and the cognate adjective is θεατρικός ("theatrical").

537–48 Most of these remarks in praise of *Clouds* are untrue of the text we have. The reference might be to the original version, in which case the point is that the play is "naturally modest" (537 σώ-φρων ἐστὶ φύσει), even if the rewrite has been made coarser and cruder to suit the depraved tastes of the audience (cf. 524–5, 560). But the presence of presents (542, 543) and a perfect (544) suggests that the aorists in 538, 540, and 543 are timeless rather than historical. If so, the claims must be ironic—Aristophanes actually does everything he says he does not—which in turn makes it difficult to decide how much e.g. of the general attack on Socratic learning is to be taken seriously.

537 To call someone **σώ-φρων** (< σῶς, "safe" + φρήν, ~ "mind"; also 529) is to praise the basic decency and appropriateness of his or her moral and social character. The conservative Stronger Argument therefore uses the word and its cognates repeatedly (962, 1006, 1067; cf. 1027, and the Weaker Argument in response at 1060–2, 1071).

538 οὐδέν is adverbial, "not at all".   **ῥαψαμένη σκύτινον καθ-ειμένον** "after stitching together for herself"—aorist because it describes action antecedent to that of the main verb—"a dangling (perfect middle-passive participle < καθ-ίημι) thing of leather". This is a reference to the oversized theatrical phallus, which all adult male characters in comedy wore dangling outside their clothes. If this is more than a comically absurd misstatement of fact, perhaps the point is that the play is here represented as feminine and thus as lacking such equipment.

539 τοῖς παιδίοις ἵν(α) ᾖ γέλως i.e. "to make the boys laugh", this sort of thing being supposedly too unsophisticated to amuse adults.

540 οὐδ(ὲ) ἔσκωψεν τοὺς φαλακρούς "and it does not make fun (< σκώπτω) of bald men"; but repeated comparisons of Socrates to a Silen in Plato's *Symposium* (215a, 221d) make it clear that this one of his most distinctive physical features (and cf. 545n. on Aristophanes himself).   The κόρδαξ was an undignified dance typical of comedy; supposedly performed by an old woman in a comedy by a rival of Aristophanes at 555.   **εἵλκυσεν** aorist < ἕλκω ("drag, draw"; cf. 553 παρ-είλκυσεν with n.); used—presumably colloquially, and with obvious negative overtones—to refer to performing a dance also at *Peace* 328.

541–2 closely resembles what happens at 57–9.   **ὁ λέγων τὰ (ἔ)πη** "the one who speaks the verses".   **τὸν παρ-όντ(α)** "the one who is present" (<πάρ-ειμι; cf. 777), i.e. the other person onstage.   **ἀ-φανίζων** "as a way of covering up" (cognate with φαίνω); cf. 759, 972 (in each case with a slightly different sense).

543 Cf. Strepsiades' initial cry of woe (1), as well as 1490–3, where Strepsiades calls for a torch to burn the Thinkery down and one of the residents of the place emerges shouting precisely **ἰοὺ ἰού**.

544 ἐλήλυθεν picks up the idea in 538 ἦλθε before a new theme is taken up in 545–50.

545–50 The general good conduct of the poet himself (as opposed to the supposed virtues of *Clouds* in particular cataloged in 537–44).

545 τοιοῦτος ἀνὴρ ὢν ποιητής "despite being a poet of this sort", i.e. as wise, brilliant and accomplished as everything said in this section up to this point suggests. ἀνήρ is often used pleonastically (i.e. in excess of what is needed) with words describing occupations and the like; a "poet man" is simply a "poet". Cf. 749 γυναῖκα φαρμακίδ᾽ (literally "a witch woman"), 1219 ἀνδρὶ δημότῃ, 1437 ὦνδρες ἥλικες.   **οὐ κομῶ** i.e. as a sign of social pretensions (14n.). But long hair was not an option for the historical Aristophanes, who went bald very early (cf. *Peace* 767–74; Eupolis fr. 89).

546 With the pre-verb, one might expect ἐξ-απατάω to mean "thoroughly deceive". But this is simply the most common form of the verb in Attic, and there is little obvious difference in meaning from the simplex (i.e. the non-compound); cf. 1466.   **τ(ὰ) αὐτ(ὰ) εἰσ-άγων** "by introducing the same things (onstage)"; a curious (ironic?) claim in a rewrite of a play that itself probably reworked the main organizing idea of an earlier success (528–32n.).

547–8 recast 546 in a positive way.   οὐδέν is adverbial with ἀλλήλαισιν ὁμοίας: "not at all like one another", i.e. "completely different from one another".

549 A reference to Aristophanes' *Knights*, which took first prize at the Lenaea festival in 424 BCE and consists of a brutal attack (hence ἔπαισ(α) εἰς τὴν γαστέρα, "I punched him in the belly") on Athens' leading politician at the time, Cleon (*PAA* 579130), shortly after his huge military success at Pylos in 425 BCE (hence μέγιστον ὄντα, "when he was at his greatest"; cf. 186n.). Cf. 553–4n.

550 οὐκ ἐτόλμησ(α) not "I didn't dare", but ~ "I didn't go so far as" (457–8n.); i.e. with Cleon destroyed by means of *Knights*, the poet moved on to different targets (such as Socrates in the *Clouds*), while his theatrical opponents went on doing the same tired old thing. In fact, Aristophanes was back to attacking Cleon again in *Wasps* in 422 BCE.   ἐπ-εμ-πηδῆσ(αι) "to jump (πηδάω) on afterward" + dative; cf. 1375 ἐπ-ανα-πηδᾷ with n. Colloquial English would say "to kick him when he was down".

551–2 Hyperbolus (*PAA* 902050; mentioned also in 623–6, 876, 1065–6) was a wealthy potter—i.e. he or his family owned a pottery yard that generated enough income that he could devote himself to other matters—who seems to have emerged as a leading Athenian politician only after Cleon's death in 422 BCE. Hyperbolus was ostracized (exiled for political reasons by a popular vote) in 416 BCE or so, so the rewrite of *Clouds* must date before that.   οὗτοι i.e. the poet's rivals, already mentioned at 524–5 in the preface to this tirade and vigorously attacked both collectively and individually in what follows.   ὡς ἅπαξ "when once", i.e. "the moment".   λαβήν "a hold" (as if this were a wrestling contest; < λαμβάνω) and thus by extension "an opening".   κολετράω is attested only here and in *scholia* and lexicographic notes on this passage, which think it means ~ "trample" or "pummel".   καὶ τὴν μητέρα Attacks on the mothers of prominent figures are a common feature of late 5th/4th-century invective. At *Acharnians* 478, for example, Aristophanes abuses Euripides' (certainly well-born) mother as having supposedly sold vegetables in the marketplace. Cf. 555n.

553–4 Eupolis was Aristophanes' almost exact contemporary and seemingly his greatest rival. About 500 fragments of his comedies are preserved, including bits and pieces of Μαρικᾶς (421 BCE), the title character of which was a barbarian slave (standing in for Hyperbolus) who manipulated his master (representing the Athenian people). In this sense, the play certainly reworked the central idea of *Knights*, although how extensive any other borrowings were, is impossible to say. Eupolis (fr. 89) for his part claimed that *he* had actually helped "Baldy"—i.e. Aristophanes (545n.)—write *Knights*.   πρώτιστον is adverbial, designating this as the first item in a list; picked up by εἶ(τα) in 557.   παρ-είλκυσεν "brought on alongside (my own, pre-existing play)". But at 540 (n.), ἕλκω has negative overtones in reference to a performance, and there may be similar coloring here as well. The *scholia* claim that ἐκ-στρέφω was used of turning clothing inside out, i.e. to increase its life or to make it look new when it was not.   κακὸς κακῶς is a colloquial jingle that reflects Greek's fondness for juxtaposing words from the same root: Eupolis is a bad person (or at least a bad poet), and he thus inevitably made a mess of stealing the plot for his *Marikas*.

555 προσ-θείς aorist active participle < προσ-τίθημι ("add").   **αὐτῷ** i.e. *Knights*, now referred to in the singular (supply δράματι; contrast 554).   **γραῦν μεθύσην** "a drunken old woman"; generally taken as a reference to a character representing Hyperbolus' mother (cf. 551–2n.), who is also mentioned in Eupolis fr. 209 (from *Marikas*).   **τοῦ κόρδακος** 540n.

556 The comic poet Phrynichus was an older contemporary of Aristophanes. The *scholia* identify this as a reference to a parody of the story of Andromeda, who was threatened (note imperfect **ἤσθιεν**, "tried to eat") by a **κῆτος** ("sea-monster"), but was rescued by Perseus.   **ποιέω** here has the sense "represent in poetry" (also 557); the implication of the use of **πάλαι** with the perfect is that the play was written long ago, but that it continues either to circulate in written form or to be reperformed (523n.).

557 Hermippus was another older contemporary of Aristophanes. The *scholia* identify the play in question as *Artopôlides* ("*Female Bread-Vendors*"), fr. 8 of which is likely spoken by a character representing Hyperbolus' mother.   **ἐποίησεν** 556n.   **εἰς** here "against". Cf. 558, where English would say "on Hyperbolus"; but the repetition of the phrase is in any case intended to suggest the tedious nature of the attacks.

558 ἐρείδουσιν "they press hard", i.e. ~ "they pound".   **εἰς Ὑπέρβολον** 557n.

559 Despite plural **εἰκούς** ("images"; accusative plural <= εἰκών), the reference seems to be specifically to *Knights* 864–7, where Cleon is accused of stirring up trouble in Athens to advance his own agenda, in the same way that eel fishermen stir up riverbeds to flush out their quarry. Whether Aristophanes means that his rivals stole this image in particular (thus Dover), or the point is simply that they showed Hyperbolus disrupting the city in ways that benefitted no one but himself, is unclear.   μιμέομαι (also 1430) is "imitate" (cf. English "mime" and "meme", < μίμημα, "something imitated").

560 The relative clause ὅσ-τις . . . τούτοισι γελᾷ functions like a condition: "whoever laughs" ~ "if anyone laughs". Cf. the parallel ἢν δ(έ) in 561.   The parallel with τοῖς ἐμοῖς in the second clause shows that τούτοισι means not "these people" but "these plays".   μὴ χαιρέτω present active 3rd-person singular "jussive" imperative, "let him not rejoice!"

561 εὐ-φραίνομαι + dative is "take pleasure in"; the second element is < φρήν, thus literally ~ "have a happy mind".

562 εἰς τὰς ὥρας τὰς ἑτέρας "in other seasons", i.e. "in the future", in contrast to their disgraceful performance in 423 BCE (521–5). For this use of εἰς + accusative in reference to future time, cf. 1180.

563–74 ~ 595–606 The ode; sung by the entire chorus and accompanied by dance (note 564 εἰς χορόν). Iambic and dactylic, but closing with three Aeolic metra; see Appendix III.4. The language is elevated (i.e. "poetic") throughout; note the almost complete absence of definite articles. In contrast to Socrates' outspoken atheism (esp. 247–8, 365, 367), the Clouds invite Zeus (563–5) and Poseidon (566–8), as well as their father Aithêr (569–70) and the Sun-god (571–4), to join their dance. Cf. the antode, where Apollo (595–7), Artemis (598–600), Athena (601–2) and Dionysus (603–6) are similarly summoned.

563–5 ὑψι-μέδων (literally "high-ruling") is elevated poetic vocabulary, as are **Ζῆνα** as an accusative form of Ζεύς (normally Δία), τύραννος meaning "king" (normally ἄναξ), and **κικλήσκω** (equivalent to καλέω). Note also the elaborately interlaced word order.   πρῶτα is adverbial.

566–8 μεγα-σθενῆ τριαίνης ταμίαν "the very strong steward of the trident" = Poseidon, who decides how and when to deploy it.   μεγα-σθενῆ is elevated poetic style, as is the decorative, pleonastic use of ἁλμυρᾶς ("salty") to describe the sea.   A μοχλός is a "lever, pry-bar", and a μοχλ-ευ-τής (also 1397, in a figurative sense, of someone who does heavy work with ideas) is someone who wields one; the reference is to Poseidon's power to heave up the sea and the land (as god of earthquakes).

569–70 μεγαλ-ώνυμον "great-named (< ὄνομα)", i.e. "famous"; poetic vocabulary.   **βιο-θρέμμονα πάντων** "life-nourisher (< τρέφω) of all", i.e. "nourisher of all life"; the adjective is extremely rare, but is again obviously intended to sound "poetic".

571–4 ἱππο-νώμαν "horse-handler (< νωμάω)"; poetic vocabulary, referring to the chariot in which the Sun-god travels through the sky.   **ὑπερ-λάμπροις ἀκτῖσιν** "with exceedingly bright beams".   **κατ-έχει** "covers, fills"; 3rd-person rather than 2nd-person because the god is being described rather than addressed, although κατ-έχεις would also do (and cf. 598–9).

575–94 The epirrhema: the coryphaeus addresses the audience, speaking for the chorus as a whole and in character. Trochaic tetrameter catalectic (as typically in such sections); see Introduction §IV.A.3.

575 θεαταί 534–6n.   **τὸν νοῦν προσ-έχετε** "pay attention!" (colloquial; also 635, 1010, 1122, etc.).

576 -μεσθ(α) (also 1116, 1353, 1375) is a metrically convenient alternative form for -μεθα; there is no difference in meaning.   **ἐν-αντίον** "opposite", i.e. "face to face".

577 amounts to a concessive clause; "for although we . . ." The initial clause in 579 (making the same point) is similar: "we who . . ." = "although we . . ."   **πλεῖστα** is an adverbial internal accusative and is modified by **θεῶν ἀ-πάντων**. For ἅ-πας (a strengthened form of πᾶς), 505n.

578 οὐ θύετ(ε) οὐδὲ σπένδετε = the two most basic forms of Greek sacrifice, the slaughter of animals and the pouring of liquids (most often wine); cf. 426n., 620, 623.

579–80 αἵ-τινες τηροῦμεν ὑμᾶς 577n.   Weather-signs were taken seriously as expressions of divine will (cf. 582–3). But whether the point here is that the expedition (ἔξ-οδος) is already underway and is canceled at the last moment, or this is a short-hand reference to a debate ahead of time regarding such an expedition, is unclear.   **μηδενὶ ξὺν νῷ** "with no sense"; English would express this as an adjective ("senseless") modifying ἔξ-οδος.   A ψακάς is a drop of water, and ψακάζω is thus "drizzle".

581–2 θεοῖσιν ἐχθρόν (literally "enemy to the gods") is a set-phrase ~ "wretched, goddamned".   **βυρσο-δέψην Παφλαγόνα** i.e. Cleon, referred to as he was presented in *Knights*, as a Paphlagonian slave (punning on παφλάζω, "splutter, bluster") whose marketable skill was leather-tanning (because Cleon's family made its fortune in the leather industry; < βύρσα, "hide", + δέφω, "soften"). **ἡνί(κα)** "when" (also 607, 618, etc.). **ἡρεῖσθε** imperfect middle < αἱρέω, "you were in the process of choosing", i.e. "of electing". For this use of the verb, cf. 587.   Athens had twelve general military commanders (στρατηγοί; cognate with e.g. English "strategy"), with one coming from each tribe. The office was among the very few in the city that was not assigned by lot, above-average competence and the ability to inspire confidence in the troops being regarded as nonnegotiable job-requirements; cf. 623–5n. Cleon served continuously as a general from 425 BCE until his death.   **τὰς ὀφρῦς ξυν-ήγομεν** literally "we were bringing together our brows" (146–7n.) = "we were scowling".

583 δεινά is an internal accusative with **(ἐ)ποοῦμεν**, "we were kicking up a fuss"; what this means is specified in concrete terms in the second half of the verse.   **βροντὴ δ(ὲ) ἐρράγη δι(ὰ) ἀστραπῆς** ("and thunder burst forth in the midst of lightning") is identified by the *scholia* as borrowed from Sophocles' *Teukros* (fr. 578.2). That this disturbance actually occurred is extremely unlikely—the Assembly at which the election was taking place would have been canceled (cf. *Acharnians* 169–73)—but the Clouds see the choice of Cleon as general as disastrous and are willing to bend the facts to fit their convictions. Cf. 584–6n.

584-6 There were eclipses of the moon and the sun—events generically regarded as ominous—about five months apart in Greece in late 425 and early 424 BCE, respectively. The implication here is that they were simultaneous with the election of Cleon as general, which is untrue. Note the imperfect **ἐξ-έλειπε** (misleadingly suggesting a repeated event; for the sense, cf. English "eclipse") and **εὐθέως** (expressly coordinating the event with the election).   **σελήνη** and **ἥλιος** are both used as something approaching proper names here—the latter in particular—and a case could be made for capitalizing them; cf. 608. The problem is not with the Greek, but with the demands of modern typography; see 264–5n.   **τὴν θρυαλλίδ(α) εἰς ἑαυτὸν . . . ξυν-ελκύσας** "drawing together his wick into itself/himself", as if the sun were a lamp (cf. 59 with n.); a bit of elevated poetic blather.   What the sun/Sun said was that it/he would not shine εἰ στρατηγήσει Κλέων ("If Cleon is going to serve as general"). This is an indirect report of a speech made in the past (**ἔφασκεν**), and the future indicative verb is therefore converted into the future optative **στρατηγήσοι**.

587–9 εἵλεσθε aorist middle < αἱρέω in the sense "elect". Cf. 582 ἡρεῖσθε, and note the contrast of tenses: the election is no longer simply under consideration, but has been completed.   **φασὶ γὰρ** . . . refers to a common belief (attested also at *Ecclesiazusae* 743–5; Eupolis fr. 219) that Athens was under special divine protection that caused even her blunders to turn out well; cf. "American exceptionalism".   **προσ-εῖναι** "is attached to", i.e. "is endemic in" + dative.   **ταῦτα** (referring vaguely back to the consequences of the δυσ-βουλία mentioned above) is not altogether clear and is accordingly glossed with **ἅττ(α) ἂν ὑμεῖς ἐξ-αμάρτητ(ε)** ("whatever mistakes you might make"; ἅττ(α) is an internal accusative). This is not a reference to specific errors ("the mistakes you made") but vaguer and more general, hence the subjunctive (with ἄν, since this is a relative clause; cf. 1458–9).   **μέν-τοι** 329n.   **τοὺς θεούς** is the subject of **τρέπειν**.

590 καὶ τοῦτο ("also this") points backward in the text—as properly with forms of οὗτος—to the situation just described and in particular the election of Cleon as general.   **ξυν-οίσει** future active < συμ-φερω, used intransitively to mean "be advantageous" (also 594).   **ῥᾳδίως** is to be taken with **διδάξομεν**. The advice that follows would have made sense when *Clouds I* was written. But it is pointless after Cleon's death, showing that this section of the parabasis, at any rate, comes from the original version of the play.

591 τὸν λάρον δώρων καὶ κλοπῆς "the seagull of bribes and theft", i.e. "he who relentlessly seeks opportunities to be bribed and to steal", with reference to the bird's well-deserved reputation for greedy, shameless scavenging. J. W. Poultney, who produced the definitive study of the genitive in Aristophanes, takes these to be instead genitives of charge ("the seagull guilty of taking gifts and of theft"). This seems a clumsy combination of ideas, but there may be some influence from that construction.   **ἑλόντες** (here "convicting", as again in 845) is an ironic echo of the use of the verb in the sense "elect" in 582, 587.

592 φιμώσητε τούτου τῷ ξύλῳ τὸν αὐχένα "you muzzle his neck in the wood", referring to an imprisonment device similar to Early Modern stocks (also e.g. *Knights* 705, 1049; *Peace* 479).

593 εἰς τ(ὸ) ἀρχαῖον ὑμῖν "to your past situation", i.e. "to how things were for you before Cleon".   **εἰ . . . κα(ὶ)** The conjunction adds the sense "*even* if . . ."   **τι** is an internal accusative with (ἐ)ξ-ημάρτετε, "you made a mistake".

594 τὸ πρᾶγ-μα τῇ πόλει ξυν-οίσεται echoes 590 (n.), as the offer of advice comes to a close.

595–606 The antode, which matches the ode (563–74 with n.) in metrical form and content (various gods—here all unambiguously younger Olympians—are summoned to join the chorus in their dance; see 595n.), is again accompanied by dance.

595 According to the *scholia*, the phrase **ἀμφί μοι . . . ἄναξ** was used by the semi-legendary early poet Terpander (*PMG* 697) and was taken over enthusiastically by the dithyrambic poets (cf. 335–8n.). There is no main verb in the antode, and in contrast to the ode, the gods are all referred to in the nominative rather than the accusative. ἀμφί must accordingly suggest something like "come to join (us)!", and in any case represents a deliberate "poetic" flourish at the beginning of the chorus' song.   **μοι** 107n.

596–7 Κυνθίαν . . . ὑψι-κέρατα πέτραν "the high-horned Cynthian rock", i.e. "the Cynthian rock that sticks up like a horn"; a reference to a prominent spot on Delos (note **Δήλιε**), one of Apollo's cult centers. ὑψι-κέρατα πέτραν is borrowed from the lyric poet Pindar (fr. 325).   **ἔχων** 273n.; again in this sense in 598.

598–600 ἤ τ(ε) "and (you) who", as again in 601, 603.   **Ἐφέσου . . . πάγ-χρυσον . . . / οἶκον** A reference to Artemis' enormous temple at Ephesus, on what is today the Turkish Aegean coast. The point of the adjective is not that the temple is itself made of gold, but that it is full of gold dedications. The claim that the local non-Greek inhabitants of the area, and in particular their daughters (the **κόραι . . . Λυδῶν**), participate enthusiastically in Artemis' cult (**σε . . . / . . . μεγάλως σέβουσιν**) is repeated by the comic poet Autocrates, a rough contemporary of Aristophanes (fr. 1.1–2, 5–6 οἷα παίζουσιν φίλαι / παρθένοι Λυδῶν κόραι / . . . / Ἐφεσίαν παρ' Ἄρτεμιν / καλλίσταν, "the sort of dances the beloved maiden daughters of the Lydians perform in the presence of lovely Ephesian Artemis").   **ἔχεις** 596–7n.

601–2 ἐπι-χώριος "local".   **αἰγίδος ἡνί-οχος** literally "rein-holder (< ἡνία + ἔχω) of the aegis", i.e. "she who wields/controls the aegis". Dover suggests that the language implies that the goddess travels by flapping the aegis rather than merely wearing it and using it against her enemies.   With **ἡμετέρα**, the chorus momentarily slip into speaking as Athenians rather than "aetherial" Clouds.   **πολι-οῦχος** (< πόλις + ἔχω) is a generic epithet of a deity who "protects a city", as Athena protects Athens.   **Ἀθάνα** is the standard form of the goddess' name in drama.

603–6 Παρνασσίαν . . . / πέτραν A reference to Mount Parnassos, and thus to Delphi (note 605 **Δελφίσιν**), where Dionysus shared a cult with Apollo.   **κατ-έχων** "occupying, controlling"; seemingly a poetic usage (LSJ *s.v.* II).   **πεύκαις** "pine-torches", a common element in descriptions of Dionysus and maenads (e.g. Euripides *Ion* 716–17; *Bacchae* 146–7; fr. 752 = Ar. *Frogs* 1211–13).   **Βάκχαις Δελφίσιν ἐμ-πρέπων** "standing out among the Delphic Bacchants".   A **κῶμος** is a "revel", i.e. a crowd of κωμασ-ταί; cf. 1205 (ἐ)γ-κώμιον with n. The term can be used of Dionysiac bands (Euripides *Bacchae* 1167), but is most often applied in comedy to groups of drunken men who wandered Athens' streets at night armed with torches and looking for love, trouble or both, lending the final reference to Dionysus something of a double aspect.

607–26 The antepirrhema: the coryphaeus again addresses the audience, speaking for the chorus as a whole and in character. Trochaic tetrameter catalectic; see Introduction §IV.A.3.

607 ἡνί(κα) 581–2n.   **δεῦρ(ο)** i.e. to the Theater.   **ἀφ-ορμᾶσθαι** "to depart", *sc.* from the sky, where they happened to bump into the Moon/moon (608).

608 ἡ σελήνη 584–6n.   **ξυν-τυχοῦσ(α)** aorist active participle < συν-τυγχάνω, "encounter".   **ἡμῖν** is to be taken with both the participle and the main verb.   **ἐπ-έστειλεν** aorist active < ἐπι-στέλλω, "command, order".

609 χαίρειν 356–7n.   **τοῖς ξυμ-μάχοις** literally "those who fight with us" and thus "the allies", i.e. representatives of the subject-states of the empire, who were required to bring their annual tribute payments to Athens at City Dionysia time.

610 θυμαίνειν "that (she) is angry" (< θυμός, the seat of feelings and passions, ~ English "heart"); cf. 820n., 1478.   Supply ἔφασκε again with the long explanation that begins **δεινὰ γάρ**.   **δεινά** is an internal (adverbial) accusative with **πεπονθέναι**, "that she has suffered terribly".

611 ὠφελοῦσ(α) ὑμᾶς is concessive, "despite benefitting you".   **οὐ λόγοις** "not (merely) with words".

612–14 Athens' streets—like nearly all urban streets in antiquity—were dark, dirty and sometimes dangerous, and a torch was therefore standard equipment when venturing out at night.   **τοῦ μηνός** "per month" (genitive

of time within which, like ἑσπέρας, "in the evening", below).   εἰς δᾷδ(α)
English would say "on torches".   οὐκ ἔλαττον is an internal accusative
with 611 ὠφελοῦσ(α), and δραχμήν has been drawn into the accusative by
it; thus "no less than a drachma".   μὴ πρίῃ a prohibition (105n.), "Don't
buy!"; 2nd-person singular deponent aorist middle subjunctive < *πρίαμαι
(23n.).   φῶς is the contracted Attic form of φάος ("light").   Σεληναίης
is a grandiloquent, epicizing way of saying "the Moon-Goddess".

615 ἄλλα τ(ε) εὖ δρᾶν "she does you other favors as well". The Greeks used
a twelve-month lunar calendar, which rapidly drifted out of coordination
with the solar year, since each month had only twenty-nine or thirty days.
The problem was normally corrected via the occasional addition of whole
"intercalary" months. But the moon's complaint is that the specific days of
the month are not falling "where they should", suggesting that experiments
had recently been made in Athens to deal with the lunar-solar problem in
a different way, by adding a day or two to some individual months to get
the annual count right. 623–6 suggest that Hyperbolus was involved in the
attempted reform.   ἄγω has a much broader range of meanings than the
standard "lead, fetch, bring" (LSJ s.v. I) and here and in 626 clearly means ~
"reckon, count" (LSJ s.v. IV.2). For a similar sense, 621n.

616 οὐδέν is adverbial, "not at all".   ἄνω τε καὶ κάτω ~ colloquial English
"upside-down".   κυδοιδοπάω is attested elsewhere only at *Peace* 1142
and is apparently a colloquialism meaning ~ "throw into an uproar, disturb";
supply τὰς ἡμέρας from 615 as the object.

617 ἀπειλέω is both "promise" and—more commonly, as here—
"threaten".   ἑκάστ-οτε "on each occasion, every time".

618 ψευσθῶσι δείπνου "they are cheated (aorist passive subjunctive <
ψεύδομαι) of dinner", the idea being that the gods to whom sacrifice is made
share the food, by inhaling the smoke of whatever parts of the animal are
burned for them.

619 τῆς ἑορτῆς μὴ τυχόντες "after they miss the festival"; i.e. the gods show
up a day or two early because of the extra days that have been added to the
month (615n.).   κατὰ λόγον τῶν ἡμερῶν "in accord with the count of the
days", i.e. "because of how you count the days".

620–3 This is the same problem as the one referenced in 617–19, but viewed
from the divine perspective: there are proper days for certain sacrifices, and

the Athenians currently miss them, or even worse, they treat days properly devoted to mourning as an occasion for celebrations.

620 κᾆθ' = κα(ὶ ε)ἶτ(α).   **στρεβλοῦτε καὶ δικάζετε** "you apply torture and hold trials". Slaves could give testimony in Athenian courts only under torture, the theory being that they could not otherwise be trusted to tell the truth; free persons could not be tortured. It is impossible to tell how common torture was. But this line leaves no doubt that it was not just a theoretical legal possibility. For Athenian litigiousness, 208n.

621 πολλ-άκις "many times"; for the formation, 739n.   **ἡμῶν ἀγόντων τῶν θεῶν ἀ-παστ-ίαν** genitive absolute. ἄγω is here "celebrate (a festival or something similar)" (LSJ *s.v.* IV.1); cf. 615n. ἀ-παστ-ία is "fasting": < privative *alpha* + πατέομαι ("eat") + -ία (201n.).

622 πενθέω is "go into mourning for" + accusative.   **τὸν Μέμνον(α) ἢ Σαρπηδόνα** Memnon was a mortal son of the goddess Dawn, Sarpedon a mortal son of Zeus. Both died at Troy and are accordingly mourned by the gods as ~ members of their own family. For a single definite article with two coordinated nouns, 104n.

623–5 ἀν(τὶ) ὧν "in return for which (abuses)".   **λαχὼν Ὑπέρβολος** The Delphic Amphictyony (~ "League of States") protected Apollo's shrine at Delphi and set limited Greek "rules of war". Every member state was entitled to send a representative known as a ἱερο-μνήμων ("one who is mindful of sacred things"), whence ἱερο-μνημονέω, "serve as *hieromnêmôn*", to Amphicytony meetings. That a leading politician like Hyperbolus (551–2n.) held the office shows that these men were not chosen at random; cf. 581–2n. λαχών nonetheless makes it clear that there was more than one candidate, and that the decision among them was made by drawing names or through a similar process.   **τῆτες** adverb, "this year"; probably cognate with ἔτος ("year").   **κα(ὶ ἔ)πει(τα)** serves to explicitly coordinate the temporal relationship between the participle and the main verb. This is unusual and probably colloquial, given the parallel at *Knights* 391–2 τοιοῦτος ὢν ἅπαντα τὸν βίον, / κᾆτ' ἀνὴρ ἔδοξεν εἶναι (literally "being like this all his life, and then he came to be seen as a man"; compared by Dover).   **τὸν στέφανον ἀφ-ῃρέθη** "he was deprived (aorist passive < ἀφ-αιρέω) of his garland", which must have blown off his head at an embarrassing moment in a public ceremony (approximately thus Dover) or the like. Aggressive attacks on Hyperbolus are identified at 551–60 as typical of the plays of Aristophanes' uninventive rivals; but they obviously appealed to the audience, and Aristophanes is having it both ways.

625–6 μᾶλλον goes with **εἴσεται /** ... **ὡς** (~ "he'll be clearer about the fact that ..."), while **οὕτως** points back ("in the aforementioned way", i.e. "having been thus admonished").   **ἄγειν** 615n.   At the end of 626, the chorus return to their normal position in the orchestra, and the actors take over the action again.

627–803 Iambic trimeter. See Introduction §IV.A.1.

627 Socrates emerges from the Thinkery, swearing by his own style of divinities (e.g. 264–5, 423–4) and complaining about Strepsiades' incompetence as a student (628–31). 636–784 do not pick up from here, however, but seemingly move back in time, as if we were inside the Thinkery and this was the very beginning of Socrates' attempt to assess and educate his new pupil. After Strepsiades spectacularly fails again to learn or absorb anything, therefore, Socrates repeats his negative judgment on the old man's performance (785–90). Only then does the action move on to the logical next step in the action: Pheidippides will need to take his father's place (791–803). Ἀνα-πνοή "Respiration", a new addition to the Socratic pantheon, which is highly flexible because it has been invented by Aristophanes.   **Χάος** 171–2n.   For **μὰ τὸν Ἀέρα**, cf. 229–30n. and Strepsiades at 667.

628–9 οὐκ εἶδον ... **οὐδαμοῦ** literally "I never saw nowhere", i.e. "I never saw anywhere"; Greek happily piles on compound negatives, which do not cancel one another out quasi-mathematically, as English negatives do. Cf. 637 οὐκ ἐδιδάχθης πώποτ(ε) οὐδέν (literally "you were never taught nothing", i.e. "you were never taught *anything*"), 754 μηκέτ(ι) ... μηδαμοῦ (literally "no longer nowhere", i.e. "no longer *anywhere*"), and contrast the series of simple negatives at 802, which retain their force ("there's no way that I won't").   **οὕτως** (pointing backward, in this case to Socrates' recent experience of Strepsiades' stupidity inside the Thinkery) goes with **ἄγροικον** (here ~ "cloddish", as also in 646).   **ἄ-πορον** is < privative *alpha* + πόρος, "way, passage" and is thus "impossible" (also 703 ~ "a dead end", and cf. the cognate verb "be at a loss for" at 743).   **σκαιόν** literally "left-hand, left-handed", i.e. "clumsy, bumbling"; the opposite of δέξιος (literally "right-handed"); cf. 994.   **ἐπι-λήσμονα** "tending toward forgetfulness (< λανθάνω)", i.e. "forgetful"; cf. 630–1n.

630–1 ὅσ-τις is indefinite and thus not "who" but "the sort of person who".   **σκαλαθυρμάτι(α)** diminutive < σκαλάθυρμα; defined by the ancient lexica as σκαριφήματα, which is almost equally obscure but would seem to mean ~ "trivial points". Presumably colloquial.   **ἐπι-λέλησται** perfect middle < ἐπι-λανθάνω, which is here not obviously any different from the simplex form of the verb; cf. 629 ἐπι-λήσμονα, 785, 855.   **πρὶν μαθεῖν** "before he learns them"; cf. 780 πρὶν τὴν ἐμὴν καλεῖσθ(αι) ("before my case is called"), 1402 πρὶν ἐξ-αμαρτεῖν ("before making a mistake"), 1425 πρὶν τὸν νόμον τεθῆναι ("before the law was established").   **ὅμως γε μήν** (also 822) is strongly adversative; "but all the same".

632 καλῶ future (not present) active indicative.   **δευρί** Thus a 3rd-century papyrus. The manuscripts agree on δεῦρο, which is a more common form and thus more likely a late, pedestrian error.

633 ἔξ-ει < ἔξ-ειμι. The 2nd-person future is routinely used with a negative in a question as equivalent to an order ("won't you . . . ?": e.g. 735, 789, 1296). The same use without a negative ("will you . . . ?") is rarer; Dover suggests that it is confined to short phrases such as this, where the sense could be made clear via intonation (also 1299).   **ἀσκάντην** a light, low bed, perhaps nothing more than a rough, rustic sleeping cushion and probably identical to the bed in which Strepsiades and Pheidippides were sleeping when the play began.

634 Strepsiades emerges from the Thinkery, laboriously hauling his mattress and bedding with him. 718 (cf. 501–4) suggests that he has a new, noticeably paler mask, appropriate for one of Socrates' students (103n.). He is in case still wearing only his tunic, and is barefoot as well; cf. 497–8 with 498n., 719, 856–9.   **ἐῶσι** < ἐάω, "allow".   **οἱ κόρεις** "the bedbugs"; cf. 12, 699, 709–15 with 709 n., 725.

635 ἀνύσας τι 181n., 506n.   **πρόσ-εχε τὸν νοῦν** 575n.   **ἰδού** 82n.

636 ἄγε δή 478n.   **πρῶτα** is adverbial.

637 ὧν = τούτων ὧν, as at 435 (n.).   **οὐδέν** goes with the relative pronoun, "of which you were never taught anything" (628–9n.).   For the unexpected nature of this question and the attempt at instruction that follows, 627n.   **εἰπέ μοι** 82n.

638 There ought to be two alternatives with **πότερον;** (203n.), hence the combination of **ἐπῶν** and **ῥυθμῶν** both dependent on the second **περί** ("about *metra* or about *epê* or *rhythmoi*?"). This is arguably illogical—*epê* and *rhythmoi* do not go together well as a single set (below)—but the poet is preparing for Strepsiades picking *metra*.   As the discussion that follows makes clear, μέτρα are e.g. trimeters or tetrameters, i.e. lines produced by combining individual units of various *rhythmoi* (641–2, with no specification of whether e.g. iambs or trochees are in question); ῥυθμοί are e.g. dactyls or iambs, i.e. metrical units that can be combined into *metra* (650–1); and ἔπη are "words" (658–92).

639 ἔγωγ(ε) *sc.* βούλομαι διδαχθῆναι.   **ἔν-αγχος** "recently" (< ἄγχι, "near"); an Attic colloquialism.

640 ἀλφιτ-αμοιβός "a barley-meal dealer"; cf. 106n. That the grain has already been milled suggests (despite Dover) that Strepsiades is not selling barley he has grown on his farm, but is buying provisions in the market to make his meals.   **παρ-εκόπην** aorist passive < παρα-κόπτω, "false-strike", referring to forging coins, and thus by extension "cheat" and here specifically "short-change".   **δι-χοινίκῳ** "by a two-*choinix* measure" (dative of degree of difference), i.e. "by two *choinikes*" (for which, 643–5n.).

641–2 ὅ-τι κάλλιστον μέτρον / ἡγεῖ is an indirect question, and the original τί has accordingly been converted to ὅ-τι; cf. 157–8n. Because **ἐρωτῶ** is present (a primary tense), the original form of the verb in the question (**ἡγεῖ**) is retained.   **πότερον . . . ἤ;** 203n.   **τὸ τρί-μετρον . . . τὸ τετρά-μετρον** 638n.

643–5 ἐγὼ μέν Supply ἡγέομαι from 642 ἡγεῖ.   For **μέν** *solitarium* (with no answering δέ), 224n.   **πρότερον** "superior to" + genitive.   A ἑκτεύς (< ἕξ, "six") was 1/6 of a μέδιμνος (a standard dry measure ~ a bushel) and itself contained 8 χοίνικες (cf. 640). A ἡμι-έκτευς (genitive **ἡμι-έκτεω**) or "half-*hekteus*" thus contained 4 χοίνικες, allowing Strepsiades—who fails to see the point of any of this (648)—to mockingly confuse it with a **τετρά-μετρον** (literally "four-measure").   **οὐδὲν λέγεις** is a colloquial way of saying "you're making no sense" (also 781, 1095).   **ὦ (ἄ)νθρωπε** is more or less neutral in tone when used to address a stranger, but has a reserved and cutting edge when used for someone one knows, as here.   **περί-δου** aorist middle imperative < περι-δίδωμι, "make a bet", with the subject of the bet defined by **εἰ μὴ τετράμετρόν ἐστιν ἡμιέκτεων**, "whether or not . . ."

646 ἐς κόρακας 123n.   **ὡς** is exclamatory, "how . . . !"; cf. 364, 872.   **ἄγροικος** 628–9n.   **δυσ-μαθής** normally "difficult to learn (< μανθάνω)", but here "difficult (to cause) to learn", i.e. "hard to teach".

647 ταχύ is adverbial ("quickly")—and sarcastic.   **δύναιο** deponent present middle optative < δύναμαι.   **περὶ ῥυθμῶν** 638n.

648 ὠφελήσουσ(ι) future active < ὠφελέω, "benefit".   **πρὸς τ(ὰ) ἄλφιτα**
106n. Either Strepsiades is using the word very broadly, to mean "my everyday
life", or Socrates' response in 649–51 is not particularly responsive to the
question.

649 πρῶτον is adverbial, while **μέν** is *solitarium* (224n.; cf. 643).   **κομψόν**
"clever, accomplished"; cf. 1030–1 κομψο-πρεπῆ ("clever-seeming").   **ἐν
συν-ουσίᾳ** "in company (< σύν-ειμι + the abstract ending -ία)", by which
Socrates apparently means "at dinner parties and symposia", where music was
often performed (cf. 1354–72) and a refined knowledge of such matters could
create a good impression.

650 ἐπ-αΐω is "perceive".   **ὁ-ποῖός ἐστι . . . / . . . (καὶ ὁ)-ποῖος αὖ** indirect
questions, which in their original form would have been ποῖός ἐστι. . . ; καὶ
ποῖος αὖ. . . ;. For the interrogative itself, 155n.

651 κατ(ὰ) ἐν-όπλιον . . . κατὰ δάκτυλον literally "in accord with an
enoplion . . . in accord with a dactyl", i.e. "to be classified as an *enoplion . . .* to
be classified as a dactyl". Precisely what an ἐν-όπλιον was, is unclear, although
Xenophon (*Anabasis* 6.1.11) shows that men danced to it wearing armor
(ὅπλα), while δάκτυλον (literally "finger") may have had a broader sense
in Aristophanes' time than it does today (= the unit ‒◡◡ used to build e.g.
Homeric lines). Dover speculates that Socrates' "dactyls" refers to meters that
could be explained as neat combinations of units of dactyls, anapaests (◡◡‒
and variants) and spondees (‒‒), while his "*enoplia*" refers to those that used
the same basic *rhythmoi* but could not be so neatly divided.

652 νὴ τὸν Δί(α) affirms not Socrates' claim in 649–51 that Strepsiades is
ignorant about meter, but his insistence in what follows that he is not. He
therefore adds **ἀλλ(ὰ) οἶδ(α)**, "In fact, I know (about this)".   **εἰπὲ δή** "tell
me then!" (also 683, 748); the remark creates the illusion of back-and-forth
dialogue without actually contributing to the conversation (cf. 159n.).

654 The manuscripts offer what seem to be two separate responses to
Socrates' question, the other—the traditional line 653, expelled by Dover—
being τίς ἄλλος ἀντὶ τουτουὶ τοῦ δακτύλου;, "What other (finger) in place
of this one here?" Such intrusions are generally taken to represent either
early performance variants (which would suggest that *Clouds II* was not
only staged, but staged multiple times) or parallels that were noted in the
margin by ancient scholars and then brought into the text the next time it
was copied (since this was also how accidentally omitted lines were handled

by correctors). Cf. 723n. for what may be another example of the same problem.   **πρὸ τοῦ** 5n.   **μέν** is *solitarium*.   **ἔτ(ι) ἐμοῦ παιδὸς ὄντος** genitive absolute.   **οὑτοσί** Socrates' reaction in 655 shows that Strepsiades does something very rude here, apparently displaying the ancient equivalent of the modern middle finger—which some ancient sources suggest may have been the *little* finger.

655–6 ἀγρεῖος εἶ καὶ σκαιός amounts to an announcement that this phase of Socrates' attempt to educate Strepsiades is at an end; cf. 646 (concluding the discussion of μέτρα). ἀγρεῖος is not obviously different in sense from ἄγροικος (628 with n.). For σκαιός, 628–9n.   **γάρ** "(Yes), because" (191n.); Strepsiades' implication is that he would be a better student if the material interested him.   **ὦ (ὀ)ϊζυρε** literally "miserable creature"; a disparaging, colloquial way of addressing someone who makes the lives of *other* people miserable.   **τί δαί;** is here "*What* (do you want to learn)?" (491n.).

657 For the doubling of **ἐκεῖνο** as a sign of Strepsiades' desperation, 79n. Superlative **ἀ-δικώτατον** is probably to be understood the same way.

658 τούτου is dependent on adverbial **πρότερα**, "before this".

659–61 What Socrates is interested in is "which (names for) four-footed creatures (**τετρα-πόδων**) are properly masculine", i.e. how grammatical gender relates to the actual gender of the animal in question, as the discussion in 662–80 makes clear. Strepsiades takes him to mean instead ~ "which four-legged creatures are male", but manages to get even this wrong, first arguably with "dog" (see below) and then certainly by including a rooster. Socrates appears to be preparing to call him out for one or both of these blunders in 662, but goes off in another (even more absurd) direction.   Unlike the first three animal names Strepsiades offers ("ram, billy-goat, bull"), **κύων** (cognate with both "hound" and "Cynic" = someone who behaves like a dog) can be used of both male and female dogs, and in comedy—doubtless reflecting casual, everyday speech—is normally feminine.   **εἰ μὴ μαίνομαι** ("unless I've lost my mind") is also used at *Thesmophoriazusae* 470 and is probably a colloquial way of affirming an assertion.

662–4 At 847–53, Strepsiades attempts to make use of what he learns here to impress Pheidippides, but with less than spectacular results.

662–3 ἃ πάσχεις "what you're suffering", i.e. "what's happened to you".   **τήν τε θήλειαν καλεῖς / . . . κατὰ ταὐτὸ καὶ τὸν ἄρρενα** i.e. "you're referring to the male by a term also used for the female". κατὰ τ(ὸ) αὐτό is "in the same way".

664 πῶς δή, φέρ(ε); ~ "*How* (am I doing this), if you don't mind?"   ὅ-πως; repeats the implied question back; cf. 157–8n., 667. ὅ-πως is an emendation by the German classicist Gottfried Hermann, *inter alia* an expert on metrics, in his 1799 edition of *Clouds*, and is designed to eliminate the uncolloquial repetition of πῶς in the response in the manuscripts' πῶς δή, φέρε. πως;. Another solution is that of the early 19ᵗʰ-century English scholar Peter Elmsley (see also 1296n.), who assigned all four words to Strepsiades ("*How* (am I doing this), if you don't mind, *how?*"), which seems unnecessarily frantic.

666 ἀλέκτωρ ("rooster"; < ἀλέξω, "ward off, defend", with reference to the bird's combativeness) was already in use in this period (e.g. *Wasps* 1490; Aeschylus *Agamemnon* 1671) and may actually be an older word than ἀλεκτρυών. ἀλεκτρύαινα ("roosteress"), on the other hand, is an absurd coinage modeled on words like λέαινα ("lioness" < λέων) and κάπραινα ("sow" < κάπρος).

667 εὖ γε "well (done)!, well (said)!" (also 757, 866, etc.); a colloquial expression of praise and approval.   **νὴ τὸν Ἀέρα** The oath is appropriate as a response to a display of supposed Socratic brilliance; cf. 229–30n., 627.

668 δίδαγ-μα is < διδάσκω ("thing taught", i.e. "lesson, bit of learning").

669 δι-αλφιτώσω σου κύκλῳ τὴν κάρδοπον "I'll thoroughly barley your kneading-trough in a circle", i.e. "I'll fill your kneading-trough with barley", so that you can make as many barley-cakes as you like; by extension "I'll give you as much money as you can use". See 106n., 1248 (a trough of this sort actually brought onstage). But the more immediate point of putting the matter this way is to set up the discussion of the gender of κάρδοπος that follows. *omicron*-contracts are a productive way of creating verbs from nouns (in this case ἄλφιτα) and adjectives.

670–1 μάλ(α) intensifies **αὖθις,** "*again*".   **τοῦ(το) ἕτερον** "this (is) another (example)", *sc.* "of the errors you fall into".   **τὴν κάρδοπον / ἄρρενα καλεῖς θήλειαν οὖσαν** i.e the word is feminine but simultaneously second-declension. θήλειαν οὖσαν is concessive ("although it's feminine").   **τῷ τρόπῳ;** "In what way (am I doing this)?" The words could also be treated as the beginning of the question in 672 ("In what way am I referring to a kneading-trough as masculine?"). But this makes Socrates' response there ("Absolutely!") more difficult, since it must then be understood "(You are) absolutely (doing this)!"

672 μάλιστά γ(ε) 253n.

673–6 For Cleonymus, 353n. The joke here is obscure, but is generally taken to be sexual in character; Dover suggests that the "round mortar" is the two-handed grip Cleonymus took on his penis when he masturbated, and that Strepsiades adds gestures to make his point clear.

674 τ(ὸ) αὐτὸν δύναταί σοι κάρδοπος Κλεωνύμῳ "'Kneading trough' means the same for you as 'Cleonymus' (does)", because both sound masculine, but are actually feminine.

675–6 As Dover notes, the imperfects ἦν and ἀν-εμάττετο make it clear that the reference is to something Cleonymus actually did (or is supposed to have done).   ὦ (ἀ)γαθ(έ) ("my good sir"; also 726) is basically neutral in tone.   ἐν θυείᾳ στρογγύλῃ γ' ἀν-εμάττετο "he used to do his kneading in a mortar that was *round*". μάττω is cognate with μᾶζα ("barley-cake"; Yiddish *matzo* is < Hebrew *matzah*, which in turn came from Greek rather than the other way around).

677 τὸ λοιπόν is adverbial (431n.).   πῶς με χρὴ καλεῖν; "How should I refer (to it)?"; returning to the main point (cf. 670–1) after the joke about Cleonymus.   For πῶς . . . ; ὅπως;, 664n.

678 ὥσπερ καλεῖς τὴν Σωστράτην With the exception of a few legitimate public figures such as priestesses, "respectable" contemporary women are not named onstage in comedy. Knowing the name of a man's wife, sister or daughter implies familiarity of a sort that could easily be taken to imply sexual contact, and pronouncing such a name in public was apparently too insulting even for a genre that allows casual personal attacks of the sort that lie behind e.g. 675–6 (n.). Sostrate was thus probably a well-known courtesan (i.e. a high-class sex-worker; cf. 684n.), in which case the joke is again on Cleonymus, or else an otherwise unknown Sostratus is being attacked as allegedly effeminate.

679 θήλειαν We would say "first-declension". But technical grammatical vocabulary of this sort seems to have been unavailable in Aristophanes' time, and the point is that the noun rationalized in the way Socrates would like now ends in -η, as feminines routinely do.   ὀρθῶς γὰρ λέγεις literally "(Yes), for you're speaking correctly", i.e. "Yes, exactly".

680 Obscure and presumably corrupt (hence the obels in the text; for the term, see 1285–6n.). The manuscripts' ἐκεῖνο δ' ἦν ἂν must mean ~ "But it would be the following", which works neither as a response by Strepsiades (since δ' suggests resistance to the thesis to which he ought to be agreeing) nor as a conclusion by Socrates (who ought to be stating facts rather than drawing tentative conclusions). Nor is it clear whether one ought to print καρδόπη Κλεωνύμῃ ("a kneading-trough (fem.) for Cleonymê"; thus Wilson) or καρδόπη, Κλεωνύμη ("a kneading-trough (fem.), Cleonymê"; thus Dover), both of which pull the two jokes together, but in different ways. In either case, the conversion of Cleonymus' name into a feminine is clearly a final punchline before Socrates moves on to the next topic.

681 δέ γε 169n.   ὀνόματα here and at 685 means "proper names" (not "nouns", as often later on), as what follows makes clear.

682 Two indirect questions in primary sequence—i.e. imagined as being asked now, not in the past—hence the retention of indicative ἐστίν.

683 εἰπὲ δή 652n.

684 Λύσιλλα, Φίλιννα, Κλειταγόρα, Δημητρία are ordinary women's names. The *scholia* claim the reference is to four well-known contemporary courtesans—free, generally non-Athenian women, who lived outside the formal authority/protection of a male *kyrios* ("guardian") and supported themselves by attracting lovers or groups of lovers, who traded gifts of various sorts for the privilege of their company. But female Athenian sex-workers from the 5th and 4th centuries BCE were a subject of intense scholarly interest in the Hellenistic and Roman periods, and the *scholia*'s comment may represent a wild leap to unnecessary conclusions by an ancient academic authority. Cf. 686, where real persons seemingly *are* in question.

685 μυρία literally "tens of thousands, myriads"; but the word is used colloquially in the same way English "millions" is, to mean "too many to count". Cf. 738 μυρι-άκις with n., 1041 πλεῖν ἢ μυρίων . . . ἄξιον στατήρων.

686 An example of a relatively uncommon phenomenon, an iambic trimeter line that consists of only three words (also 1480).   Ἀ **Φιλόξενος** is mocked at *Wasps* 84 as a καταπύγων (528–32n.), while the way Ἀμεινίας is attacked in 689–92 suggests that he was in the public eye (cf. 693 on the supposed notoriety of the charges against him). Although **Μελησίας** is otherwise unknown, therefore, all three men were probably prominent in Athenian public life—which is all the claim that they are "not real men" can be taken to mean.

687 Dover characterizes **ὦ πόνηρε** (literally "miserable creature") as "not always abusive . . . , but . . . certainly brusque".

688 ὑμῖν "as far as you're concerned". The older manuscripts offer instead ἡμῖν, "as far as we're concerned" (a common error: 195n.), which would have Strepsiades buying explicitly into the Socratic view of things and asking for guidance as to what he is supposed to believe.

690 ὡδί "in this way" (< ὧδε + deictic *iota*).   **δεῦρο δεῦρ(ο)** "(Come) here, (come) here!", as also in 866, 1485 (both excited, urgent summonses).

691 γυναῖκα τὴν Ἀμεινίαν καλεῖς i.e. because Ἀμεινία in 690 looks feminine.

692–3 δικαί-ως "rightly, correctly" (a common sense of δίκαιος, which has a somewhat broader meaning than the conventional translation "just").   **ἥ-τις οὐ στρατ-εύ-εται** Athenian men of hoplite status—i.e. those who owned enough property to be able to afford hoplite armor (10% of the citizen population?), as opposed to poorer, more "average" individuals (including resident non-Athenians), who rowed in the fleet as paid volunteers—were subject to military draft on a constant basis, whenever their age group within their tribe was called up. There were legitimate ways to be excused from such service, but Ameinias is being accused of something more underhanded that shows that he is a coward, i.e. "a woman". In the next line, Strepsiades noticeably does not reject Socrates' argument as ridiculous (which it is) or as worthless for his purposes (contrast 648, 655–6), but as too obvious to be worth discussing: everyone already knows about Ameinias.   Some of the oldest manuscripts have ὅσ-τις, as properly in reference to a man, rather than ἥ-τις. But the incongruity of using the feminine for Ameinias is part of the joke, and the alternative reading must represent a misguided early attempt to correct what looked like a simple error in the text.

694–5 οὐδέν is seemingly an abbreviated, colloquial way of saying either ~ "(Indeed), there's no point (in doing this)", if this were a direct response to Strepsiades' complaint in 693, or "(It's) nothing", i.e. "Never mind!", if Socrates is instead giving up and moving on to the next step in Strepsiades' education.   **κατα-κλινεὶς δευρὶ … / ἐκ-φρόντισόν τι τῶν σεαυτοῦ πραγμάτων** brings the action of the play full circle to where it began, with Strepsiades lying miserably on his bed, trying to discover a way out of his troubles (cf. 12–40). This time he takes the path he did not the first time around, by requiring Pheidippides to enter the Thinkery as a student (794–803, 814–15; contrast 106–25).   **τί δρῶ;** another example (cf. 159n.) of an unnecessary remark that serves mostly to create the illusion of a real dialogue. δρῶ is a deliberative subjunctive (not indicative).   **κατα-κλινεὶς** masculine nominative singular aorist passive participle < κατα-κλίνω, which in the active is transitive ("lay something down"), but in the passive is intransitive ("lie down").

696 In addition to its use with questions (58n.), **δῆτα** also serves to add emphasis to negative responses to questions, orders and the like (also 733). Strepsiades uses **μή** because the verb to be supplied is a subjunctive ("Let me not … !") generated on the basis of Socrates' imperative ἐκ-φρόντισον in 695.

697 χαμαί adverbial, "on the ground" (cognate with χθών, "earth").   **αὐτὰ ταῦτ(α)** literally "these things themselves", i.e. "these things without interference" (from bedbugs, as 699 makes clear); not "these same things, these very things", which would be ταὐτὰ ταῦτ(α).

698 οὐκ ἔστι παρὰ ταῦτ(α) ἄλλα literally "There are not other things beside these", i.e. "There's no alternative".

699 οἵαν is exclamatory, "what a … !"; cf. 1303.   **δίκην δίδωμι** is "pay a penalty", here to the bedbugs (**τοῖς κόρεσι**) that Strepsiades knows infest his mattress (cf. 634) and that are accordingly awarded a definite article.   **τήμερον** ("today") is an adverb formed < an Indo-European deictic particle meaning "this" + ἡμέρα ("day").   Strepsiades lies down on his bed, pulls the sheepskins over himself (cf. 735, 740), and soon begins to toss about (cf. 707 with n.), just as at the beginning of the play (cf. 36). Socrates steps into the Thinkery and only returns at 723, to see if his pupil is making progress with his project.

700–6 A brief song, assigned to Socrates (along with 708 and 716) by the manuscripts—which have no authority in such matters, but merely record the judgments of ancient editors working in libraries in Alexandria, Pergamum or Rome hundreds of years after the original text was produced—but given to the chorus by modern editors. See 723n. Iambic; see Appendix III.5. The antistrophe at 804–13 (also sung by the chorus) ought to match the metrical pattern of this song, but in fact is longer. The ancient comments on the meter there do not suggest that any verses have fallen out of the text here, i.e. the problem existed already in antiquity and is not merely with our manuscripts. Dover suggests that Aristophanes struck something out after 706, but never went back to fill in the gap, which would make this another sign of incomplete revision.

700 δι-άθρει "look into (the matter) carefully!"

701–5 The chorus are using figurative language when they urge Strepsiades to **πάντα τρόπον ... σαυτὸν / στρόβει πυκνώσας** ("concentrate yourself and twirl in every way!") and **ταχὺς δ' ... ἐπ(ὶ) ἄλλο πήδα / νόημα φρενός** ("quickly leap upon another mental conception!"). But in the meantime he behaves this way in a literal fashion, curling up into a ball under the sheepskins, rolling about, and leaping in pain as the bedbugs bite.   **πάντα τρόπον** is treated as a single, unified idea, and **τε** thus links **δι-άθρει** and **πάντα τρόπον ... / στρόβει**.   For **εἰς ἄ-πορον**, 628–9n.   **πήδα** ("leap!"; cf. 1392) present active imperative < uncontracted πήδαε; the contraction of *alpha* and *epsilon* in the ultima lengthens that syllable, hence the acute accent on the long penult.

705–6 This command as well is perhaps to be understood as intended as figurative ("Stay (mentally) awake!").   **ἀπ-έστω** 3rd-person aorist active "jussive" imperative < ἄπ-ειμι ("be absent from" + genitive).   **γλυκύ-θυμος** "sweet-hearted", i.e. "pleasant"; an elevated poetic flourish at the end of the song.

707 ἀτταταῖ an inarticulate cry, most often expressing physical pain ("yi-yi-yi!"). Extrametrical, and perhaps produced while Strepsiades is still covered up. By 709, at any rate, he has his head out of the sheepskins.

708 Bacchiacs (see Introduction §IV.A.1), which serve to create an emotional atmosphere appropriate for paratragedy (709–21).

709–21 Anapaestic dimeter (717 and 721 monometer); see Introduction §IV.A.2. Strepsiades laments his situation in the style of a tragic hero.

709 ἀπ-όλλυμαι 16n.; picked up by 715 μ(ε) ἀπ-ολοῦσιν.   **δείλαιος** is used by Strepsiades at 12 to describe his misery in almost precisely the same situation in the initial version of this scene (cf. 694–5n.).   For the σκίμπους, 254n.

710 οἱ Κορίνθιοι The Corinthians were allies of Sparta and thus enemies of Athens. What are actually biting Strepsiades, however, are κόρεις (cf. 699, 725), and Dover suggests that the joke may be that Corinthians were sometimes punningly referred to as "bedbugs".

711 δαρδάπτω ("devour") is rare Homeric vocabulary, suiting the elevated tone.

712 Some of the oldest manuscripts have this verse between 713 and 714. Editors generally place it here to produce a contrast between the serious tone with which Strepsiades begins and the cruder language and ideas that follow.   ἐκ-πίνω is "drink dry, drain".

713 τοὺς ὄρχεις "my testicles" (cognate with English "orchid", apparently because of some perceived physical resemblance of the plant to human anatomy).   ἐξ-έλκω is "pull off, rip off".

714 δι-ορύττω is "dig through, excavate".

715 μ(ε) ἀπ-ολοῦσιν cf. 709 ἀπ-όλλυμαι with n. ὀλῶ is the Attic future of ὄλλυμι.

716 λίαν intensifies **βαρέως**.

717 καὶ πῶς; "And how (should I not be terribly upset)?", i.e. "Why (should I not be terribly upset)?" and thus ~ "What is this advice supposed to mean?" Cf. 1434 with n.   **ὅτε** 7n.

718–19 Aristophanes seemingly parodies Euripides' *Hecabe* at 1165–6 (n.), and Dover suggests that these verses echo another part of the same play, *Hecabe* 159–61 τίς ἀμύνει μοι; ποία γενεά, / ποία δὲ πόλις; φροῦδος πρέσβυς, / φροῦδοι παῖδες, "Who defends me? What family, what city? The old man is gone, my children are gone". But the parallel is not very close, and Strepsiades' language may just as well be intended to sound generically tragic.   **χροιά** "my complexion": Strepsiades has gone pale from his time inside the Thinkery, as promised (501–4); cf. 103n., 634n.   **φροῦδη ψυχή** cf. 712.   **φροῦδη δ(ὲ) ἐμ-βάς** cf. 498n., 634n., 858–9. ἐμ-βάδες (< ἐμ-βαίνω, "step into") are rough men's boots of a sort typically worn by working-class Aristophanic characters.

720 πρός "in addition to" + dative.

721 φρουρᾶς ᾄδων "while singing (a song) of guard-duty", i.e. "while patiently enduring a lonely vigil", referring to the time Strepsiades has spent onstage alone since 700, trying to discover a way out of his troubles. Presumably an otherwise unattested proverbial expression.   For ᾄδω = ἀείδω, 157–8n.

722 ὀλίγου adverbial, "almost".

723 If the song in 700–6 (n.) belongs to the chorus, Socrates emerges abruptly from the Thinkery at this point. 732 is similar, but is preceded in 731 by an explanation for *why* Socrates has come outside. If that verse is expected anywhere, it would be between 722 and 723, meaning that—contrary to the modern scholarly consensus and the text as printed here—700–6, 708 and 716 might perhaps instead be given to Socrates. Alternatively, 723–30 and 731–4 might be ancient variants, both of which have come down to us in our texts, although only one of the two is wanted; cf. 654n. for a more certain example of this sort of doubling.   **οὗτος** 220n.

724 νὴ τὸν Ποσειδῶ "Yes, by Poseidon, (I *am* thinking)!"

725 μού τι "a bit of me, any of me".

726 ἀπ-ολεῖ κάκιστ(α) literally "You will perish most unhappily" (κάκιστ(α) is adverbial), i.e. ~ "Damn you!" Socrates goes back into the Thinkery (but see 723n.).   **ὦ (ἀ)γαθ(έ)** 675–6n.   **ἀπ-όλωλ(α) ἀρτίως** "I've perished just now", i.e. "I've *already* perished (by being eaten by the bedbugs)". ἀρτίως (also 1149) is < ἄρτιος; simple ἄρτι is older and more common, particularly in prose.

727–8 For the verbal adjectives **μαλθακισ-τέ(α), περι-καλυπ-τέα** and **ἐξ-ευρε-τέος** (indicating necessity), 131n.   **ἀπο-στερητικός** "typical of cheating, fraudulent"; for the formation, 27n.   **ἀπ-αιόλη-μ(α)** is < ἀπό + αἰόλος ("nimble, wriggling, varying") + the noun-making suffix -μα (155n.), and thus means ~ "cheating".

729–30 τίς ἄν . . . ἐπιβάλοι; is not really a question but a hopeless wish ~ "if only someone would . . . !"   **ἐπι-βάλοι** "throw on top of (me)".   **ἐξ ἀρνακίδων** "outside of sheepskins (< ἀρήν, "sheep"), aside from sheepskins", of which Strepsiades already has plenty.   **ἀπο-στερητρίς** is an otherwise unattested feminine form of the similarly rare adjective ἀπο-στερητής, which is equivalent in sense to ἀπο-στερητικός (728 with n.).   Strepsiades wraps himself up in the sheepskins again (cf. 707n., 727). This time, however, he must not leap miserably about (contrast 701–5 with n.), since Socrates initially suspects he is asleep (732). At any rate, a bit of time—unnoted in our text (cf. 11n.)—probably elapses between 730 and 731.

731 Socrates emerges (again?; cf. 723n.) from the Thinkery.   ἀθρήσω πρῶτον, ὅ τι δρᾷ, τουτονί is another example of prolepsis (250–1n.), despite the insertion of the ὅ τι-clause between the main verb and its object (making the word order closer to the normal ὅ τι δρᾷ οὑτοσί). ὅ τι is printed thus to avoid confusion with the conjunction ὅτι, as again at e.g. 737, 753.   ἀθρήσω is hortatory aorist active subjunctive (not future) < ἀθρέω, "observe, inspect".   πρῶτον is adverbial. But what Socrates wants to do this before, is unclear; before offering Strepsiades—up to this point, working entirely on his own—further guidance in his efforts to discover a way out of his troubles? (Cf. the old man's baffled question in 736.)

732 οὗτος 723n.

733 οὐ δῆτ(α) 696n.   οὐδὲν πάνυ; "Nothing whatsoever?"

734 πλήν εἰ 361n.   πέος is a crude colloquial word for a penis ("dick, pecker"), suggesting that this is intended as a punchline that brings this subsection of the dialogue to an end.   ἐν τῇ δεξιᾷ *sc.* χειρί; i.e. Strepsiades claims to have been masturbating, this being on comic logic the obvious thing for a man to do when an easy opportunity presents itself.

735 οὐκ . . . φροντιεῖς; For the 2nd-person future used with a negative in a question as equivalent to an order, 633n.   τι is an internal accusative.   ταχέως 345n.

736 τοῦ; = τίνος;, as also at 1223. Cf. 185n.   γάρ indicates the omission of a prefatory clause—perhaps better thought of as logically following rather than preceding what Strepsiades actually says— ~ "I'm at a loss, so . . .", i.e. ". . . because I'm at a loss".

737 ὅ τι βούλει is dependent on ἐξ-ευρὼν λέγε. English would take the subordinate clause expressly with the participle, and would then tacitly supply it with the main verb ("after you figure out what you want, tell (me) (this)"). Greek does not mark the relationship so clearly and simply allows the subordinate clause to be understood *apo koinou* ("in common") with both verbal elements in the main clause.

738-9 μυρι-άκις "countless times, a million times", < μυρία (685n.) + the adverbial suffix -άκις, as also in e.g. 621 πολλ-άκις ("many times"); *Peace* 242 πεντ-άκις ("five times"), 1079 τουτ-άκις ("this many times"); *Lysistrata* 698 ἑπτ-άκις ("seven times").   There is a colloquial anacolouthon—a "failure to follow", i.e. a break in the syntax—between 738 and 739. What Strepsiades means is "(I want to know) about my debts, how I could . . ." **ὅ-πως ἂν ἀπο-δῶ μηδενί** is an indirect question, which in its original form was πῶς ἀπο-δῶ μηδενί; (deliberative subjunctive). ἄν has been added with the subjunctive because this is now a subordinate clause.

740-2 Similar—also not very specific—advice about how to think in a creatively "airy" fashion is offered at 743–5, 761–3.   σχάζω is here "let go, release".   **λεπτήν** is predicative of **τὴν φροντίδα**, "so that it is subtle" and thus appropriate for a Socratically trained thinker (cf. 230, 320, 359).   **κατὰ μικρόν** "little by little". περι-φρονέω (here in the present imperative) is used by Socrates at 225 (n.) in his initial description of his own intellectual activities, in that case regarding the sun.   δι-αιρέω is "split up", i.e. "analyze, parse".   After he says **οἴμοι τάλας** (23n.), Strepsiades must go down under the sheepskins again to think, with 743–5 serving to cover his absence from the audience's view.

743 ἔχ(ε) ἀτρέμα "Stay still!" ἀτρέμα/ἀτρέμας is an adverb (< privative *alpha* + τρέμω, "tremble" (a cognate)) and thus combines with ἔχω to yield a sense equivalent to εἰμί + adjective.   **κ(αὶ ἐ)ὰν ἀ-πορῇς τι τῶν νοημάτων** For the verb (which takes the genitive of what one is at a loss for), 628–9n. τι is an internal ("adverbial") accusative, "at all".

744 ἀφ-εὶς ἄπ-ελθε "let (the question) go (aorist active participle < ἀφίημι) and go off!", i.e. "think about something else for a while!"

745 ζυγωθρίζω (attested nowhere else) is explained by the *scholia* as being < ζυγόν ("beam of a scale"), and thus apparently means "weigh up, assess".

746 Strepsiades emerges once more from the sheepskins, but when he actually leaves the bed is unclear. Socrates never tells him to cover himself up again (contrast 735, 740), and Dover suggests that this is as good a point as any for the old man to stand up. On the other hand, e.g. 760–4 could be amusingly staged with Strepsiades ducking down under the covers to think and then emerging Jack-in-the-box fashion with his latest, nominally brilliant idea. By 771 (n.), he seems to be on his feet.   **ὦ Σωκρατίδιον φίλτατον** is a flattering, coaxing form of address (cf. 80, 110): Strepsiades wants Socrates to approve of the suggestion he is about to offer (749–56) and is trying to smooth the way for it. Cf. 747–8n.

747–8 γνώμην ἀπο-στερητικήν cf. 728–30 with 727–8n.   **τόκου** is dependent on the pre-verb of **ἀπο-στερητικήν** ("capable of cheating someone out of interest").   **ἐπί-δειξον** aorist active imperative < ἐπι-δείκνυμι.   **τὸ τί;** "What in particular?"; cf. 765 ποίαν τινά;, 775. The question seems unnecessary, and if it is not being used merely to break up Strepsiades' remarks (like Socrates' **τί, ὦ γέρον;**), it perhaps suggests that the old man—still uncertain of himself (cf. 746n.)—hesitates before explaining what he has come up with, and Socrates intervenes to push him forward.

749–52 is a long, multipart protasis of a "future less vivid condition", hence εἰ plus the string of optatives; cf. 754–5n. An apodosis along the lines of "wouldn't that be brilliant?", "wouldn't that solve my problem?" (cf. 753) is expected, but Socrates interrupts.

749 γυναῖκα φαρμακίδ(α) . . . Θετταλήν "a Thessalian witch", the power described in 750 being one of their specialties (also Plato *Gorgias* 513a). φάρμακα are not just "drugs" but magical devices of all sorts; cf. 766–8. -ίς is routinely used as an ending for the female version of masculine words for occupations and the like; a sorcerer is a φαρμακεύς. For the pleonastic use of γυνή, 545n.   **πριάμενος** i.e. as a slave. For the verb, 23n.

750 καθ-έλοιμι aorist active optative < καθ-αιρέω ("bring down").   **νύκτωρ** 173n.

751 καθ-είρξαιμ(ι) aorist active optative < καθ-είργνυμι, "shut up, confine".   **λοφεῖον στρογγύλον** "a round crest-case (< λόφος, "crest")", properly used for the crests hoplite soldiers wore on their helmets to make themselves appear taller and more intimidating (*Acharnians* 1109).

752 ὥσ-περ κάτροπτον "just like a mirror", the point probably being not that mirrors were commonly stored in crest-cases, but—by a somewhat messier logic—that the moon is like a mirror in being round and bright. Inscriptions show that this is the proper spelling of the word, which routinely appears as κάτοπτρον in manuscripts, as if it were connected to καθ-οράω, κατ-όψομαι (which it is not).   **τηροίην** present active optative < τηρέω, "guard, retain". For the combination with **ἔχων**, 131n.

753 τοῦτ(ο) is the internal object of ὠφελήσειεν, σ(ε) the external object.   ὅ τι; echoes τί; in the direct question that makes up the rest of the line.

754–5 A vaguely imagined, entirely theoretical situation, for which optatives are therefore appropriate (a "future less vivid" or "should-would" condition, in which only the apodosis takes ἄν); so too 758–9, 769–72 with 769n.; cf. 749–52n.   μηκέτ(ι) . . . μηδαμοῦ 628–9n.

755 ἀπο-δοίην 118n.   ὁτιὴ τί δή; "Because why, in fact?", i.e. "And why would that be, exactly"?; cf. 784 (without δή). For ὁτιή, 331n.

756 κατὰ μῆνα "in accord with a month", i.e. "by the month": if the moon can no longer be seen, the reckoning of time for such purposes is suspended (cf. 615n.) and interest will never be due (cf. 17–18 with 18n.).

757 εὖ γε 667n.   σοι προ-βαλῶ τι δεξιόν recalls the language with which Socrates describes his teaching style at 489–90, as does 775.   δεξιόν i.e. that requires a clever answer.

758–9 This starts out as "future less vivid" condition (754–5n.), but the apodosis is replaced by an imperative (εἰπέ) governing an indirect question (ὅ-πως ἄν αὐτὴν ἀ-φανίσειας;), which directly put would have been πῶς ἄν αὐτὴν ἀφανίσειας; σοι indicates that the imaginary lawsuit (δίκη) will involve Strepsiades. Because we know this will not be good for him, this can be described as a "dative of disadvantage", although the Greek is not so direct. English would say more specifically "against you". Cf. 774, which echoes 758.   γράφοιτο literally "should be written"; English concentrates on a different part of the legal process and says "would be filed". Cf. 467–75n. on γραφή ("indictment"), 1481–2 γραφὴν / . . . γραψάμενος.   πεντε-τάλαντος i.e. for an enormous sum of money; see 21n.   ἀ-φανίζω is here "cause to disappear"; cf. 764 ἀ-φάνισιν.

760 The repetition of ὅ-πως; marks Strepsiades' agitation as he reacts to a difficult question (79n.); cf. the repeated τί πρῶτον ἦν; in 787. On the staging (details obscure), 746n.

761–3 See 740–2n.   εἵλλω is "shut in, shut up, confine".   ἀπο-χάλα present active imperative < ἀπο-χαλάω, "let loose" (before contraction, ἀπο-χάλαε).   λινό-δετον ὥσ-περ μηλολόνθην τοῦ ποδός "tied by a string, like a cockchafer"—a large European beetle—"by its foot", i.e. allowed to buzz freely about, but not to escape. A reference to a children's game (probably not enjoyed as wholeheartedly by the beetle) and thus an example of bathos (a sudden, amusing lowering of tone, in this case from abstract advice about intellectual matters to bugs). λίνον (cognate with English "linen" and "line") is flax thread, used e.g. for making fishing lines and fishing nets, as well as for clothing. Genitives are used not only to modify other nouns or adjectives (307n.), but also to indicate that an action affects not the entire object (for which an accusative would be used), but only a part of it, here the beetle's leg.

764 ἀ-φάνισιν τῆς δίκης "a way of making the case disappear"; cf. 155n. (on nouns in -σις), 759 (on ἀ-φανίζω).

765 ὥστ(ε) αὐτὸν ὁμο-λογεῖν σέ μοι literally "so that you yourself would agree with me", i.e. "(so clever) that you too would have to acknowledge its brilliance". The use of the infinitive rather than the indicative with ὥστε indicates that this is a potential result, not a real one; contrast 833.   **ποίαν τινά;** "What sort (of ἀφάνισις) in particular (have you discovered)?"

766–8 Whether ὕαλος here refers to glass or to a polished rock crystal is unclear. But the fact that φαρμακο-πῶλαι are selling the object—a primitive lens of some sort—leaves no doubt that it is rare and understood to have magical properties (749n.) because it produces fire. This passage and Herodotus 3.24 are the earliest attestations of ὕαλος in Greek, although glass itself is much older. Strepsiades' elaborate, circuitous way of describing the lens, before Socrates in 768 finally realizes what he means, suggests that the word was uncommon, even if the idea of a burning lens must have been sufficiently well-known for the jokes in this section of the text to work.

769 τί δῆτ(α) ἄν; "what would (happen)?" or "what would (you say)?" This is the apodosis of another "future less vivid" construction (754–5n.), the εἰ-clause of which extends through the end of 772.

770 The **γραμματεύς** is the secretary of the court, who is supervising the work of an undersecretary (ὑπο-γραμματεύς), hence middle **γράφοιτο** ("cause to be written") rather than active γράφοι.

771 ἀπω-τέρω στὰς ὧδε "standing quite a distance back, like this"; most easily understood as said as Strepsiades backs away from Socrates, meaning that he has left his bed by now (cf. 746n.). ἀπω-τέρω is a comparative adverb < ἄπω-θεν.   **πρὸς τὸν ἥλιον** "facing the sun", i.e. "in the sunlight".

772 ἐκ-τήξαιμι aorist active optative < ἐκ-τήκω, "melt out". For writing on wax, 19n.

773 σοφῶς γε "Cleverly (conceived)!"   **νὴ τὰς Χάριτας** ("by the Graces!") is a unique oath in comedy, and—unlike most Aristophanic oaths (83n.)— has apparently been chosen to match the situation: Strepsiades' idea is not just clever but elegant. The *scholia* connect the oath instead with a tradition (Pausanias 1.22.8; 9.35.7; Diogenes Laertius 2.19) that Socrates was trained as a sculptor and had produced statues of the Graces that were located in the entrance hall to the Acropolis (the Propylaea).   **οἴμ(οι)** is almost always used to express grief and pain (23n.), but is here associated with pleasure (~ an ecstatic "*Oh!*"), as what follows makes clear.

774 echoes 758 (n.), except that here the verb is δια-γράφω ("draw through", i.e. "scratch out") and the dative is one of "advantage" rather than of "disadvantage" (since this is supposedly good news for Strepsiades).

775 ταχέως τουτὶ ξυν-άρπασον cf. 490 εὐθέως ὑφ-αρπάσει, 757n.   **τὸ τί;** 748n.

776–7 The indirect question (thus **ὅ-πως** for πῶς;) is in apposition to τουτί in 775 ("this, how you would . . ."). **ἀπο-στρέψαις** is an alternative form of the aorist active optative of ἀποστρέφω ("twist away", i.e. "rebut", recalling Strepsiades' name; cf. 134n., 434n.), ἀπο-στρέψειας being expected (cf. 689 καλέσειας, 759 ἀ-φανίσειας).   **ἀντι-δικῶν** "when you were presenting (present active participle) a contrary case". Thus most of the early manuscripts—although they have no authority in matters of accentuation, meaning that one might alternatively read ἀντι-δίκων δίκην ("a suit filed by your legal adversaries (genitive plural)").   μέλλω + future infinitive means "be on the verge of" doing something, in this case losing a lawsuit and owing money (ὀφλισκάνω; see 34n.).   **μὴ παρ-όντων μαρτύρων** genitive absolute; for witnesses, 495–6n. Because the situation is purely theoretical, μή rather than οὐ is used as the negative. παρ-όντων is < πάρ-ειμι (541–2n.).

778 φαυλότατα καὶ ῥᾷστ(α) adverbial, "as simply and easily (< ῥᾴδιος) as possible".   **καὶ δή** is often used in responses to commands (also 1097), with the imperative or equivalent (here **εἰπέ**) echoed in the reply (here **λέγω**).

779–80 εἰ . . . ἀπ-αγξαίμην τρέχων is the protasis of another "future less vivid" condition (754–5n.); supply ἀπο-στρέψαιμι ἄν τὴν δίκην from 776 as the apodosis. ἀπ-άγχω is "strangle, choke" (cf. 1385) and thus in the middle

"hang oneself" (cf. 988 with n.). **πρόσθεν ἔτι μιᾶς ἐν-εστώσης δίκης**
genitive absolute. ἐν-εστώσης is perfect active participle < ἐν-ίστημι (here
used as a technical term ~ "be on the docket, be pending"). πρίν +
infinitive following an affirmative clause (in logical terms; here the actual
order of the words is inverted) means "before", as also at 631. Contrast 267
(following a negative clause, in the sense "until") with n. **πρὶν τὴν ἐμὴν**
καλεῖσθ(αι) is thus "before my own (case) is called" (another technical
use of a common verb). **ἀπ-αγξαίμην** aorist middle optative < ἀπ-
άγχω. **τρέχων** "running"; English would say "run off"—i.e. to some more
convenient spot—"and . . ."

781–2 οὐδὲν λέγεις 643–5n. **ἔγωγ(ε)** *sc.* λέγω τι. **εἰσ-άξει** "will
introduce (into the court)".

783 ὑθλέω ("talk nonsense") is colloquial vocabulary attested only in
comedy. **ἄπ-ερρ(ε)** is literally "wander off!", i.e. "to destruction"; a
brusque, colloquial way of saying ~ "go to hell!" Potential optative **οὐκ**
ἂν διδαξαίμην σ(ε) is more polite, but also stronger than a future indicative
would be: "I decline to teach you". The middle (in place of the active) is
surprising, but enough other scattered examples survive (e.g. *Wealth* 687)
to make it clear that this was regarded as legitimate usage, as least in this
period. Contrast 1338, where ἐδιδαξάμην . . . σε means the expected "I got you
educated (for my own purposes)".

784 ὁτιὴ τί; 755n. **ναί** "Yes"—colloquial English would say "No", rejecting
the idea put forward by the other party—"(*do* teach me)!" Cf. 1468, where the
word is doubled to add emphasis.

785 This is more or less exactly what Socrates said at 630–1, at the beginning
of this scene; see 627n., and cf. 854–5. **εὐθύς** 388n. **ἐπι-λήθει** 630–
1n. **ἅττ(α) ἂν καὶ μάθῃς** "whatever you learn", not "what you learned"
(587–9n.).

787 φέρ(ε) ἴδω 21n. For the repetition of **τί πρῶτον ἦν;**, cf. 760 with
n. For **μέντοι** adding emphasis to a question ("What *was* it?"), cf. 788.

788 Cf. 668–80, where the name of the object—first supplied by Strepsiades
himself—is not really the point in any case. **τίς** (rather than neuter τί)
implicitly acknowledges that the joke had to do with gender, while **ἐν ᾗ**
suggests feminine κάρδοπος.

789 οὐκ ἐς κόρακας ἀπο-φθερεῖ; literally "Perish (< ἀπο-φθείρω) to the ravens!", a slightly expanded version of the normal curse (123n.) that explicitly adds the idea "die!" (also *Knights* 892; Eupolis fr. 359; cf. 871). For the question as equivalent to an order, 633n.

790 ἐπι-λησμότατον καὶ σκαιότατον an even more emphatic echo of 629 σκαιὸν . . . ἐπι-λήσμονα (where see n.); cf. 627n. ἐπι-λησμονέστατος is expected as the superlative of ἐπι-λήσμων, but ἐπι-λησμότατος is metrically guaranteed here.   This sounds like an exit line, especially given Strepsiades' resort to the Clouds for help in 793. But Socrates is still onstage at 803 (n.), and perhaps for a few verses after that, since 804–13 are addressed to him. Perhaps he stalks momentarily away.

792 ἀπὸ . . . ὀλοῦμαι = ἀπ-ολοῦμαι (also 1440). "Tmesis" (literally "cutting", < τέμνω), i.e. separation of pre-verb and verb, is attested occasionally in both tragedy (e.g. Euripides *Hippolytus* 257) and comedy (also e.g. *Birds* 1506). In this period, at least, it may be not a poeticism but a colloquial means of adding emphasis ("I'll be *ruined*").   **γλωττο-στροφεῖν** (literally "to tongue-turn", i.e. to talk in an evasive and misleading manner; cf. 776 with n. on στρέφω) is a *hapax* that captures a basic element of what Strepsiades wishes he could do (speak in an elaborately innovative style).

793 χρηστόν τι is an internal accusative with **συμ-βουλεύσατε**, "give me some helpful advice!"

795 ἐκ-τεθραμμένος perfect passive participle < ἐκ-τρέφω ("raise, bring up"), here ~ "full-grown".

796 μανθάνειν "to be a student", which is a continuing process, hence the present infinitive; not "to learn", for which aorist μαθεῖν would be appropriate.

797 ἀλλ(ὰ) ἔστ(ι) ἔμοιγ(ε) υἱός "Why yes, I *do* have a son!" As Dover observes, if the sense were supposed to be ~ "I have a son", emphatic ἔμοιγ(ε) ("*I* have a son") would be wrong, and the word must instead be standing in for nominative ἔγωγ(ε), which often means ~ "I do indeed!" (e.g. 769).   **καλός τε κἀγαθός** 101n.

798 ἀλλ(ὰ) . . . γάρ "but since . . ."   **τί ἐγὼ πάθω;** "what's to happen to me?" (deliberative subjunctive), i.e. "what can I do?"

799 ἐπι-τρέπεις *sc.* αὐτῷ, "do you give in (to him)?", i.e. "do you let him get away with this?" For the moment, at least, the Clouds sound like representatives of a very traditional view of proper social relations. Contrast 804–13.   **εὐ-σωματεῖ γὰρ καὶ σφριγᾷ** "(Yes), because he's well-built and vigorous". This is a new idea, which sets up what is to come in 1321–1451: Strepsiades is not just a foolishly indulgent father but actually afraid of Pheidippides, and in particular of how relatively big and strong he is.

800 κα(ὶ ἐ)στ(ὶ) ἐκ γυναικῶν εὐ-πτέρων καὶ Κοισύρας "and he's descended from well-feathered"—i.e. prosperous and thus socially powerful—"women, and in particular from Koisyra" (for whom, 48n.).

801–2 μέτ-ειμι (< εἶμι, *ibo*) is "will go after" and thus "will fetch".   In contrast to a "should–would/future less vivid" condition (754–5n.), which features optatives and imagines the events in question in only a very tentative fashion, this is a "future more vivid" condition, which uses a subjunctive in the protasis and the equivalent of a future in the apodosis ("there's no way that I won't") and presents the events it describes as solid possibilities. For the series of simple negatives, both of which retain their force, 628–9n.   **οὐκ ἔσ(τι) ὅπως** is used thus also in 1275, 1307.   **ἐξ-ελῶ** future active < ἐξ-ελαύνω.

803 Addressed to Socrates. Remarks like this generally seem to conform closely to what goes on onstage. In this case, however, Socrates does not leave until 813 or so; another sign of incomplete revision? 843 is almost identical.   **ἐπ-ανά-μεινον** aorist active imperative < ἐπ-ανα-μένω (seemingly a short-lived alternative for ἀνα-μένω, which has the same sense).   **ὀλίγον . . . χρόνον** is accusative of extent of time, "for a little while".   Strepsiades exits into his house.

804–13 The first six verses of this song are a metrical match for 700–6 (n.), but it then unexpectedly continues. See Appendix III.5. Addressed to Socrates. The advice is strikingly different in tone from 799 (n.): Strepsiades is a fool, and Socrates should take advantage of the opportunity his patron goddesses have furnished him with.

804–5 αἰσθάνει . . . / . . . ἕξων; "Do you realize that you're going to have?"

806 ὡς "since".

808–9 ἀνδρὸς ἐκ-πεπληγμένου / καὶ φανερῶς ἐπ-ηρμένου "when a man has been knocked out of his senses (< ἐκ-πλήττω) and manifestly excited (< ἐπ-αἴρω)"; genitive absolute, which then supplies a genitive object for ἀπο-λάψεις in 810–11.

810–11 γνούς aorist active participle < γιγνώσκω, "recognizing (that this is the situation)". **ἀπο-λάψεις** "you will lick (< λάπτω) off of (him; see 808–9n.)"; probably an uglier image in English than it is in Greek. "The future here is not quite equivalent to an imperative, but rather to 'You will, I hope (I am sure, I have no doubt) . . .'" (Dover). **ὅτι πλεῖστον δύνασαι** "as much as you are capable of", the point being that Socrates' skill in this sort of activity is well established.

812–13 ταχέως goes with ἀπο-λάψεις in 810–11, and putting it at the end of the phrase makes the sense ~ "and be quick about it!" **φιλεῖ γάρ πως τὰ τοιαῦ(τα) ἑτέρᾳ τρέπεσθαι** ("because matters of this sort somehow have a tendency to turn in a different direction") is not obviously ominous at this point, but certainly looks so in retrospect at the end of the play.   Socrates enters the Thinkery.

814 Strepsiades and Pheidippides enter from their house. That Strepsiades must call his son over to him at 822 suggests that there is some distance between them at that point; perhaps Pheidippides comes out first, with the staging making it clear that his father is actually throwing him out.   **μὰ τὴν Ὁμίχλην** "by Mist" (cf. 330). Seemingly intended as a typically Socratic oath (cf. 627) and in any case setting the stage for Pheidippides' much more conventional "by Olympian Zeus" in 817 and Strepsiades' rejection of the idea behind this (818–19).   **ἐνταυθοῖ** "here", i.e. Strepsiades' house.

815 ἔσθι(ε) ἐλθὼν τοὺς Μεγακλέους κίονας literally "Go and eat Megakles' columns!", i.e. "Go live off your Uncle Megakles!" (cf. 46, 69–70); rare evidence for the architecture of wealthy private dwellings in this period.

816 ὦ δαιμόνιε 38n.   **τί χρῆμα** is an internal accusative with **πάσχεις**, "what's the matter with you?"

817 οὐκ εὖ φρονεῖς i.e. "you're crazy"; cf. 844 παραφρονοῦντος with n.

818 ἰδού ("look!") calls the addressee's attention to something allegedly ridiculous he has just said, as also in 1469.   **τῆς μωρ-ίας** an exclamatory genitive (153n.), literally "the bluntness!", i.e. "the stupidity!" (< μῶρος + the abstract ending -ία; cognate with English "moron").

819 is an exclamatory infinitive (268n.): Δία is the object of νομίζειν ("to believe in Zeus!"), ὄντα τηλικ-ουτον-ί ("being this age"; referring to Pheidippides) the subject. 821 shows that Strepsiades means "being as *young* as you are", not "as old as you are".   The manuscripts have τὸν Δία, an early copyist having been confused by the construction; corrected by the 18th-century Dutch scholar Ludovicus Valckenaer.

820 τοῦτ(ο) i.e. the behavior described in 819.   ἐν-θυμέομαι is "consider" (< ἐν + θῦμος, ~ "heart" (610n.); thus literally ~ "take to heart").

821 ἀρχαϊκά is an internal accusative with φρονεῖς, "you think old-fashioned thoughts", i.e. "you think like an old man". Cf. the Weaker Argument's hostile characterization of the Stronger Argument and what he represents as ἀρχαῖος at 915, 984, and Pheidippides' denunciations of Strepsiades at 1357, 1469.

822 ὅμως γε μήν 630–1n.   πρόσ-ελθ(ε) "come over here!"; see 814n.

824 For ὅπως meaning "(See to it) that . . . !", 258n. Strepsiades is enforcing the commitment to secrecy imposed on him for his part by Socrates' slave at 140–3.   διδάσκω here takes a double accusative, one of the thing taught (τοῦτο), the other of the person instructed (μηδένα). This is a prohibition, and it therefore takes μή rather than οὐ.

825 ἰδού Pheidippides does what Strepsiades has asked (82n.).   ὄμνυμι + accusative is "swear by" someone/something.

826 The definite article has the power to turn any other word into a noun; thus τὸ μανθάνειν is "being a student, learning" (a so-called "articular infinitive", since it is preceded by an article).

827 ἀλλὰ τίς; is literally "Well, who (is)?"; but Strepsiades' response in the next line shows that what the question really means is "Well, who occupies Zeus' position, if Zeus isn't in charge?"

828 For this bit of misguided learning, see 379–81.   τὸν Δί(α) ἐξεληλακώς nicely illustrates the character of a perfect participle: Vortex drove Zeus out of power (< ἐξελαύνω) at some point in the past relative to the main verb βασιλεύει. But this is not merely a report of something that happened previously (for which an aorist participle would be appropriate), but has implications that matter *now*: having got Zeus out of the way, Vortex can occupy his position.

829 αἰβοῖ 102n.   **τί ληρεῖς;** 500n.   **ἴσθι τοῦ(το) οὕτως ἔχον** is literally "know that this is thus!" (οὕτως ἔχον = τοιοῦτο ὄν), i.e. "be aware that this is so!"

830 Σωκράτης ὁ Μήλιος ("Socrates of Melos") represents an attempt— on Aristophanes' part, although not necessarily Strepsiades'—to associate Socrates with the notoriously impious Diagoras of Melos, who was banished from Athens and threatened with death sometime before 414 BCE (*Birds* 1073–4).

831 ὃς οἶδε τὰ ψυλλῶν ἴχνη cf. 144–52.

832 σὺ δ(ὲ) εἰς τοσ-οῦτον τῶν μανιῶν ἐλήλυθας; literally "have you come to so great a point of your madness . . . ?", i.e. "have you gone so crazy . . . ?" τοσ-οῦτον is picked up by ὥστ(ε) in the next verse.

833 πείθει is 2nd-person singular passive (not 3rd-person singular active). This is a real result, and **ὥστ(ε)** accordingly takes an indicative; contrast 765 with n.   χολάω is to suffer from an excess of bile (χολή) and in particular black (μέλας) bile, which was supposed to make a person melan-cholic, i.e. crazy.   **εὐ-στόμει** "speak well!", i.e. "watch your mouth!" (~ 297 εὐ-φήμει with 263n.).

834 μηδὲν εἴπῃς 105n. Here the verb has both an internal and an external object; "don't say anything . . . about men . . . !"   **φλαῦρον** "bad, nasty" (also 1157, 1303).

835–7 A gratuitous dig at the supposed poverty and filthiness of the Thinkery's inhabitants; cf. 144–79, where the same criticisms underlie a series of nominally admiring anecdotes.   φειδωλ-ία (a rare Attic variant for φειδώ) is "thrift" (note the abstract ending), a seemingly positive term undercut both by what follows and by the audience's awareness that Socrates is not just thrifty but poor.   **ἀπ-εκείρατ(ο), ἠλείψατο** and **ἦλθε** are "gnomic" aorists (399–400n.). English uses the present in such cases ("gets his hair cut", "anoints himself with oil", "goes").   **οὐδ(ὲ) ἠλείψατο, / οὐδ(ὲ) εἰς βαλανεῖον ἦλθε λουσόμενος** For bathing (here at a commercial establishment) and covering oneself with oil afterward, 44–5n., 441–2n., 991 (disapproved of by the Stronger Argument, at least to the extent that warm water is involved). Here the ideas are arranged *hysteron-proteron* (81n.). The future participle indicates purpose, "in order to . . ."; cf. 301 with n.

837–8 σὺ δὲ / ὥσπερ τεθνεῶτος κατα-λόει μου τὸν βίον seemingly means "but you are washing my livelihood off of yourself as if I were dead", i.e. ~ "you're pouring my money down the drain as if you had already inherited it". μου modifies τὸν βίον. The awkwardness of the image is due to Strepsiades' attempt to rework **λουσόμενος**; cf. the similarly feeble 29, 33. For the pre-verb κατα-, 849n.

840 καί adds a sneering emphasis to **μάθοι . . . ἄν;**, "could one *learn?*"   For the repetition of **ἄν**, which reinforces the sense rather than altering it, 425n.

841 ἄληθες; The normal neuter form of the adjective is ἀληθές. With this accent, it is adverbial and means "*Really?, Seriously?*"   **ὅσα-πέρ ἐστιν . . . σοφά** "whatever wise things there are"; English would say "everything that's wise". The early manuscripts are divided between ὅσα πάρεστιν, ὅσα πάρεστ', ὅσαπέρ ἐστ' ἐν, and ὅσαπερ. But this looks like the best way to arrange the letters, given that Aristophanes does not use πάρ-εστι ("exist") elsewhere to mean "belongs to".

842 γνώσει δὲ σαυτὸν ὡς "you'll recognize yourself, that . . .", i.e. "you'll recognize that you are" (prolepsis: 250–1n.). Perhaps an allusion to the famous Delphic (and Socratic) dictum γνῶθι σαυτόν ("Know yourself!").   **παχύς** literally "thick", i.e. "dense, stupid", as opposed to ἀ-μαθής, "uneducated".

843 ~ 803 (n.). Strepsiades exits again into his house.

844 δράσω is a deliberative aorist active subjunctive (not future indicative); so too 845 ἕλω, 846 φράσω.   **παρα-φρονοῦντος τοῦ πατρός** genitive absolute. παρα-φρονέω is "think differently", *sc.* than one should, i.e. "be insane". Cf. 817 οὐκ εὖ φρονεῖς with n., 845 παρα-νο-ίας with n., 1475.

845–6 πότερον . . . / ἤ . . . ; 203n.   παρα-νο-ία (whence English "paranoia") is "different thinking" (note the abstract ending), i.e. "insanity, dementia"; cf. 844 παρα-φρονοῦντος with n., 1476, 1480 παρα-νοήσαντος, and on old men losing their ability to think clearly, 1417 with n.   **εἰσ-αγαγών** i.e. inside their house, so that the old man ceases to be an embarrassment (or a danger) to others or himself.   **ἕλω** (for the form, 844n.) is < αἱρέω in the sense "convict" (cf. 591 with n.) + genitive of the charge.   **τοῖς σορο-πηγοῖς** literally "to the coffin-peggers (< πήγνυμι)", i.e. the coffin-makers, who are to be given a heads-up that one of their products will be needed shortly.

847 Strepsiades re-emerges from his house, carrying a rooster and a hen (in cages?). The discussion of words for roosters and chickens that follows echoes the one he had with Socrates at 662–6 (nn.). When the birds are cleared from the stage and by whom is unclear; but perhaps they are still onstage at 1427–31, when Pheidippides uses the behavior of chickens as part of his argument from nature.

848 καλῶς γε sc. λέγεις (cf. 1289) or something similar; ~ "Correct!"

849 ἄμφω τ(ὸ) αὐτό; "(You call) them both the same (name)?" ἄμφω is accusative dual of all genders.   When κατα- is used as a pre-verb, it frequently has the sense ~ "unto destruction", an extension of the common sense "down"; cf. 838 κατα-λόει, 857 κατα-πεφρόντικα, 871 κατ-αρᾷ, 944 κατα-τοξεύσω. κατα-γελάω (< γελάω, "laugh") is thus ~ "mock" (1238), and the cognate adjective **κατα-γέλαστος** is "laughable, ridiculous, absurd".

850 Supply e.g. ποίει with **μή** ("don't do this!").   **τὸ λοιπόν** 431n.   **καλεῖν** The infinitive can be used as an imperative in solemn—i.e. here absurdly over-serious—requests, as also at e.g. Wasps 937.

852–3 ταῦτ(α) . . . τὰ δεξιά; "are these the clever lessons?" (internal accusative with **ἔμαθες**).   **ἄρτι** 144n.   **τοὺς γη-γενεῖς** "The earth-born" are properly the Giants, who fought against the Olympian gods and were destroyed by them (cf. Birds 824–5). This is thus both a characterization of Socrates and his students and a suggestion as to what should happen to them; perhaps there is also a hint that they are physically dirty.

854–5 echoes Socrates' accusation at 785, with the addition of the idea that the specific source of the problem is Strepsiades' advanced age (cf. 790).   Imperfect **ἐπ-ελανθανόμην** describes repeated action in the past, with **ἄν** adding a sense of potentiality; "I would always forget it"; cf. 977 (+ aorist) with n., 979–80.

856 (τ)ὸ ἱμάτιον ἀπ-ώλεσας cf. 497–500, 634n. ἀπ-όλλυμι is both "ruin, destroy" (LSJ s.v. I), as at e.g. 26, and "lose" (LSJ s.v. II), as also in 857, 859.

857 κατα-πεφρόντικα "I've thought it away" (849n.). This is a one-time ("nonce") use of the compound, which normally means "think little of, despise".

858 τὰς ... ἐμβάδας 718–19n.   **ποῖ τέτροφας;** literally "whither have you turned (< τρέπω)?", i.e. "what have you done with?"   **(ἀ)-νόητε** 417n.

859 is an allusion to a story known from Plutarch *Pericles* 23.1. After Pericles put down the Euboean revolt (211–13n.), he submitted a list of expenses that included 10 talents **εἰς τὸ δέον** ("for what was necessary"). The money had in fact been used to bribe one of the Spartan kings to withdraw an army from Attica, and the Assembly knew better than to ask any further questions about where it had gone.   **ἀπ-ώλεσα** 856n.

860–1 ἴωμεν hortatory subjunctive < εἶμι *ibo*; "let's go!"   **εἶτα** ("furthermore") introduces a new argument, **τῷ πατρὶ / πιθόμενος ἐξ-άμαρτε**, literally "obey your father and make a mistake (< ἐξ-αμαρτάνω)!", i.e. "do it because your father says to, whether it seems like a good idea or not!" (presumably proverbial).

862 Supply ἐξ-άμαρτον (from 861 ἐξ-άμαρτε) with **ἐξ-έτει σοι τραυλίσαντι πιθόμενος.**   ἐξ-έτης is "six years old".   τραυλίζω is ~ "lisp", i.e. "talk baby-talk" (also 1381, as part of a series of very similar anecdotes).

863–4 ἡλιαία—or ἡλιαία; whether the word ought to have a rough or a smooth breathing is disputed—may originally have been a term for a particular court, but in this period refers to law courts and legal service generally. ἡλιαστικός is thus "for jury service", which in this period actually paid three obols (i.e. half a drachma) rather than one.   **τούτου** is a genitive of price (cf. 876, 1396) and refers back to the obol mentioned in 863: "the first obol I made—for this amount of money I bought ..."   **Διασίοις** "at the Diasia festival" (386–7n., 408n.).   A ἁμαξίς is probably "a little cart" (diminutive < ἅμαξα), i.e. a pull-toy, as again in 880 (n.).

865 ἦ is a strong affirmative that generally begins its clause and is here emphasized by **μήν**, as again in 1242; ~ "have no doubt that ... !, you can be sure that ... !"   **τῷ χρόνῳ ποτ(ε)** dative of time when: "eventually".   ἄχθομαι + dative is "be grieved by" and thus here "come to regret".

866 δεῦρο δεῦρ(ο) 690n.

868 ἄκων "unwilling" (< private *alpha* + ἑκών, "willing"). The participle is concessive, "although he didn't want (to come)".   Socrates emerges from the Thinkery and takes a moment or two—unnoted in the text—to look

Pheidippides over.   **νη-πύτιος** is a diminutive of νή-πιος (105n.) and is attested elsewhere only in Homer; the *scholia* suggest that Socrates picks the word to impress his future student.

869 κρεμαστά (< κρεμάννυμι) are the "hanging gear" on a ship, i.e. its sails and ropes, and **τῶν κρεμαστῶν οὐ τρίβων τῶν ἐνθάδε** is thus apparently ~ "inexperienced in (cf. 445–51n.) the ropes here", i.e. "unacquainted with our way of doing business". Socrates is even more dismissive of Pheidippides in 872–5, but is also not put off by the boy's hostile response in 870, suggesting that a potentially nasty, insolent temperament is exactly what he is testing for.

870 A **τρίβων** is a thin, inexpensive cloak, and Pheidippides picks up on Socrates' use of the homonym meaning "experienced" in 869 to produce an ugly response via a "future less vivid" condition: "You'd be a *tribôn* yourself, if you were to be hung up (*sc.* as a robe is hung on a peg, but also as a slave is suspended for a beating)!"   **κρέμαιο** is 2nd-person singular aorist passive optative < κρεμάννυμι and recalls κρεμαστῶν in 869 (n.).

871 Supply ἀπο-φθερεῖ (as in 789) or a verb with a similar sense with **οὐκ ἐς κόρακας;** (123n., 633n.).   κατ-αράω is "curse, damn" (+ dative); for the pre-verb, 849n.

872–3 As again in 1469, **ἰδού** (~ "look at this!") here introduces a contemptuous quotation of something another character has just said; colloquial.   **ὡς** is exclamatory, **ἠλίθιον** adverbial; "how foolishly!", i.e. "in what a silly, juvenile fashion!" (cf. 868 with 869n.). Whether there is actually something odd in Pheidippides' pronunciation of κρέμαιο is impossible to say. Perhaps from the very beginning of the play he has used a recognizable sociolect—a nonstandard style of speech typical of a distinct group of people within a larger language community—appropriate to the smart set of young horsemen to which he at least aspires to belong (esp. 119–20). Or perhaps this remark was set up in the original version of the play (e.g. via a verbal misunderstanding between Strepsiades and Pheidippides, or in one of the lessons Socrates offered Strepsiades about language), and this is another mark of incomplete revision.   **τοῖσι χείλεσιν δι-ερρυηκόσιν** "with his lips spread apart (perfect active participle < δια-ρρέω)", referring to how Pheidippides has articulated—or more likely failed to articulate—the word in question.

874–5 πο(τε) goes with **πῶς;** "how in the world?" (187n.).   ἀπό-φευξις (< ἀπο-φεύγω), κλῆσις (< καλέω) and χαύνωσις (< χαυνόω) are all gerunds

(155n.) and mean "escaping conviction" (cf. 167 with n.), "summoning" (also 1189), and "inflating", i.e. using grand language, respectively.   ἀνα-πειστήριος is "that serves to convince (< ἀνα-πείθω)"; a *hapax*.

876 is a bit of teasing salesmanship: having just suggested that training Pheidippides to be an effective law-court speaker is probably impossible, Socrates concedes that this might nonetheless (**καί-τοι**) be done—for a sufficient fee.   **ταλάντου** is a genitive of price ("for a talent"); Socrates confirms again that he teaches for money (cf. 98n.), while simultaneously dirtying the reputation of Hyperbolus (551–2n.), who apparently relies on the weaker argument and has paid enough to learn it to make clear that he is getting extremely rich out of public life.

877 ἀμέλει 422n.   **θυμό-σοφος** "wise by heart", i.e. "naturally clever". The word is not attested elsewhere in the classical period, but Strepsiades uses it so offhandedly that it may be an ill-attested colloquialism rather than a coinage.

878 τυνν-ουτον-ί "as little as this" (accompanied by a gesture showing just how tiny Pheidippides was when he put on the displays of precocious brilliance mentioned in 879–81); a colloquial Attic combination of < τύννος ("so small") + demonstrative οὗτος + the deictic suffix -ί.

879–81 are interesting evidence for children's play in classical Athens: dollhouses (although no mention of dolls), toy boats, pull toys (as also in 864), and animal figurines. Cf. 763 (a captive beetle) with n.   Dover suggests that **ἔνδον** means "before he was old enough to leave the house and join other boys in the street or field", i.e. when he was still a toddler. But Pheidippides is already using a knife in these anecdotes, to carve wood and cut up leather and pomegranates; so perhaps the point is instead that he was the sort of industrious boy-genius who preferred quietly building things at home to running around wildly outside.   The imperfects (**ἔπλαττεν, ἔγλυφεν, ἠργάζετο, ἐποίει**) mark all this as a habitual action, "he used to . . ."   γλύφω "carve" (as in English "hiero-glyphs", literally "sacred carvings").   **συκίνας** ("made of fig-wood") is a conjecture by the late 19th-century Dutch scholar Samuel Naber for the manuscripts' σκυτίνας ("made of leather"), which seems impossible as a description of material for a miniature cart.   **(ἐ)κ τῶν σιδίων βατράχους ἐποίει** "he used to produce frogs from our pomegranates" (i.e. from the skins of the fruit).   **πῶς δοκεῖς;** is not really a question, but a colloquial exclamation ~ "can you imagine!"; cf. 1368 πῶς οἴεσθε;

882–5 Cf. 1107–10, where Strepsiades says something very similar to the Weaker Argument, with nn.

883 ὅσ-τις ἐστί 113n.

884 is echoed by the Weaker Argument himself in 901.   ἀνα-τρέπω is literally "overturn, upset", and thus in this context "defeat".

885 ἐὰν δὲ μή *sc.* τὼ λόγω μαθήσηται, "but if he doesn't (learn both arguments)".   **πάσῃ τέχνῃ**—literally "by every device"—is a colloquial means of adding urgency to an imperative (here an implied "see to it that he learns!"); also 1323.

887–8 τοῦτο . . . μέμνησο(ο), ὅπως literally "remember (perfect = present middle imperative < μιμνήσκομαι) this, how . . . !" + future, i.e. "be sure that . . . !" Cf. 1107–10 (a slightly more colorful version of the same request).

888–9 The entry of the two Arguments represents the most significant staging problem in the text of *Clouds* as we have it. Socrates (= Actor #2) has announced in 887 that he will be absent when Pheidippides receives his intellectual training and thus during the debate between the two Arguments that follows, and he apparently exits at 888. Strepsiades (= Actor #1) and Pheidippides (= Actor #3) remain onstage to listen, although they do not speak until 1107–12, when Pheidippides is finally turned over to the Weaker Argument for training. The Arguments must be represented by two additional actors, meaning that a total of four actors are onstage throughout the scene that follows, and the problem is complicated further by the fact that there is insufficient time between 888 (when Socrates exits) and 891 (when the Weaker Argument appears) for Actor #2 to put on a new mask and costume. The scene thus requires five actors, which is impossible on the standard understanding of the staging of both comedy and tragedy in this period, which allows only three actors (with comedy occasionally using an extra for minor bit parts). Already in antiquity, it was believed that a choral song had been lost between 888 and 889 (thus the *scholia*), giving Actor #2 time to reappear as one of the Arguments. But this still leaves us needing four actors, and it seems likely that the problem has once again to do with the unfinished nature of Aristophanes' revision of the play, and that in the original Strepsiades went into his house at this point, Socrates went into the Thinkery, and Pheidippides either went in with him or (after a song) met one or both of the Arguments onstage.

889–948 Anapaestic dimeter; see Introduction §IV.A.2.

889 The Stronger Argument emerges from the Thinkery, trailed by the Weaker Argument. The Stronger Argument is an old man (908 with n., 929, 961–2, etc.) who looks poor and uncared for (920). The Weaker Argument, by contrast, is richly dressed (920), and the deliberate visual contrast with the Stronger Argument suggests that he is also represented as much younger. The two Arguments are thus in many ways onstage mirror-figures of Strepsiades and Pheidippides in the play's opening scene in particular.

890 καί-περ θρασὺς ὤν "although you're bold (cf. 445–51n.)", *sc.* "and can be expected to do this anyway". The Stronger Argument seems to imagine that what the Weaker Argument represents is so shameful that he will be—or ought to be—embarrassed to show his face in public. This is emphatically not the case (891–2).

891 ἴθ(ι) ὅποι χρῄζεις ("go whither you like!") is borrowed from Euripides' now-lost *Telephos* (fr. 722), the name-character of which was a sophistically gifted king disguised as a beggar; cf. 921–4 with 922n.

892 ἐν τοῖς πολλοῖσι i.e. "in public, before a mass audience".

893–4 ἀπ-ολεῖς σύ; *sc.* με. The main function of the next two lines or so is to identify these characters for anyone in the Theater who has not yet worked out precisely who the Arguments are, after which they are assigned basic intellectual programs as well (895–902).   **ἥττων γ(ε) ὤν** "Yes, but being a weaker one!"

895 σοφός and σοφία are among the key terms in this initial back-and-forth between the two Arguments (899, 925), along with the opposing terms "fools" (898, 919) and "madness" (925, 932). Cf. 520–2n. on the importance of σοφός and cognates in the characterization of the poet and his comedies in the parabasis.

896 γνώμας καινὰς ἐξ-ευρίσκων Cf. the chorus' reference to the Weaker Argument's "new education" in 937a–b; his own description of his argumentative procedure in 943–4; and the chorus' advice at 1032.

897–8 ταῦτα refers back vaguely to 896 and is thus ~ "interest in such novelties".   ἀνθέω is "bloom" (< ἄνθος, "blossom, flower", used metaphorically in 1027) and thus "flourish", as also in 962, 1174 ἐπανθεῖ.   **τουτουσὶ / τοὺς ἀ-νοήτους** i.e. the audience (indicated with a gesture).

899 ἀπ-ολῶ σε κακῶς In expressions of this sort, the adverb refers not to the action itself but to its consequence; "I'll destroy you and make you miserable" (not "I'll do a bad job of destroying you"). Cf. 920 αὐχμεῖς αἰσχρῶς ("you're scruffy and thus disgraceful", not "you're doing a disgraceful job of being scruffy"); English "he was badly beaten".

900–1 ἀνα-τρέψω 884n.   **αὐτ(ὰ) ἀντι-λέγων** "by contradicting these things" (echoing and reversing the Stronger Argument's **λέγων**).

902 "Because I deny (**οὐ- . . . φημί**) that Justice even"—thus **οὐδέ** rather than simply οὐ—"exists at all (**πάνυ**)".   As Dover notes, "justice" in the abstract sense in Attic is not δίκη but δικαιοσύνη, and **Δίκην** ought accordingly to be capitalized as a reference to the Hesiodic goddess who sits beside Zeus (cf. 904b) to inform him when mortals misbehave (*Works and Days* 256–62); but see 264–5n. on the ambiguity of the Greek in such cases.

904b–6 Δίκης οὔσης genitive absolute.   **τὸν πατέρ(α) αὐτοῦ / δήσας** is a reference to the story of how, after Zeus and the Olympians defeated Kronos (their father) and the Titans, Zeus confined Kronos to Tartarus. The same issue is raised at Aeschylus *Eumenides* 640–2 Ζεὺς . . . ἔδησε πατέρα πρεσβύτην Κρόνον ("Zeus bound his old father Kronos"), and the Stronger Argument's reaction in 906–7 suggests that it was a rhetorical commonplace used to argue against the reality of any sort of abstract, universal justice. Although the reference to Zeus and Kronos seems like a throwaway remark here, the idea of physical abuse of one's father as evidence of moral depravity surfaces again later in the play, when the Socratically educated Pheidippides beats Strepsiades (1321–1451). For τὸν πατέρ' αὐτοῦ in place of the expected τὸν αὐτοῦ πατέρ', 513–17n.

906–7 αἰβοῖ 102n.   **καὶ δή** here merely signals that something—i.e. **τουτὶ . . . / . . . τὸ κακόν** ("this nasty (argument)")—is abruptly apparent; thus ~ "oh look!"   **δότε** aorist active imperative < δίδωμι; addressed to the audience.   **λεκάνην** "a basin", i.e. to throw up into (as at Cratinus fr. 271; Theopompus Comicus fr. 41).

908 τῦφος is "nonsense, raving", and a **τυφο-γέρων** is thus an old man who talks crazy; cf. 844–6. The word is attested elsewhere only at *Lysistrata* 335 and must be a colloquial insult.   **ἀν-άρμοστος** (< privative *alpha* + ἁρμόζω, "fit, join") ~ "unhinged".

909 κατα-πύγων 528–32n.

910 ῥόδα is the internal object of **εἴρηκας, μ(ε)** the external object; "you've said roses about me", i.e. "you've said lovely things about me". Cf. 911, as well as Pheidippides' response to a very similar insult by Strepsiades at 1330: "Sprinkle me with many roses!"   A **βωμο-λόχος** is properly someone who lingers discretely (λοχάω) around an altar (βωμός) to cadge some of the offerings. But the word is routinely used as a rough insult meaning ~ "cheap buffoon"; cf. 969 (of horsing around musically).

911 κρίνεσι στεφανοῖς "You're garlanding (< στεφανόω) me with lilies".   A **πατρ-αλοίας** is literally someone who threshes (ἀλοάω), i.e. beats, his father (πατήρ), although the word is sometimes simply used as an insult (1327—where Pheidippides *has*, however, just beaten Strepsiades).

912 χρυσῷ πάττων μ(ε) literally "sprinkling me with gold"; but Dover suggests that the intended sense is actually "spangling me with gold", i.e. "putting gold ornaments all over me". Cf. the Socratically educated Pheidippides' use of πάττε at 1330, in response to a similar insult.

913 οὐ δῆτα πρὸ τοῦ γ(ε) "not before *this* (time)!", i.e. "in the past", when the world was less depraved, "you certainly wouldn't (have said it was *gold* I was spangling you with)!"   μόλυβδος is "lead" (a loan word from Anatolia), which was a by-product of smelting silver (cf. 98n.) and almost valueless.

914 κόσμος "ornamentation, decoration".   As again in 915, 920, **δέ γε** marks this as a lively response to what another speaker has just said; contrast 169 (used to pick up the conversational thread after an interruption) with n.

915 θρασὺς εἶ πολλοῦ literally "you're bold of much" (for the adjective, 445–51n.), i.e. "there's not much you wouldn't try".   **ἀρχαῖος** 821n.

916 φοιτάω is "go (to school)", as also in 938. For a description of the traditional education, 963–76.

917 μειράκιον (also 928) is a colloquial Attic term for someone who is older than a παῖς ("boy, child"), but not yet an ἀνήρ ("man"); ~ "teenager" (although not applied to girls), "young man".

918–19 γνωσθήσει . . . Ἀθηναίοις / οἶα διδάσκεις "you'll be known (2nd-person singular future passive < γιγνώσκω) to the Athenians for the sort of things you teach", i.e. "the Athenians will figure out the sort of things you teach". οἶα is the internal object of διδάσκεις, **τοὺς ἀ-νοήτους** the external object.   **ποτ(ε)** "eventually".

920 αὐχμεῖς αἰσχρῶς 441–2n., 899n.   As in English, **εὖ πράττεις** (literally "you're doing well") ~ "you're prospering".

921 πρότερον is adverbial, "previously".   **ἐπτώχ-ευες** "you were a beggar (πτωχός)".

922 Τήλεφος εἶναι Μυσὸς φάσκων The Mysian king Telephos was wounded by Achilleus in the events leading up to the Trojan War and came, disguised as a beggar, to ask to be healed by him. The reference here is almost certainly to the Euripidean tragedy of 438 BCE, in which Telephos was the central figure (cf. 891n.), which Aristophanes parodies at length in both *Acharnians* (414–56) and *Thesmophorizusae* (466–519).

923–4 A πηρ-ίδιον (diminutive < πήρα) is a beggar's pouch used for carrying food, and the point is that in the old days the Weaker Argument had nothing to eat but his γνῶμαι ("arguments"), whereas now he has grown rich and sassy.   **Πανδελετείους** Nothing is known of Pandeletos (whose name yields this adjective) except that the *scholia*—most likely guessing—claim that he was a sycophant and a politician, and say that he was also mentioned by the comic poet Cratinus (fr. 26). The name is not otherwise attested in Athens, increasing the possibility that this is in fact a proverbial character or something similar, particularly given that the literal meaning of the name is ~ "All-enticer, Ensnarer of All" (< δέλετρον).

925 ὤμοι is an elevated, literary equivalent of colloquial **οἴμοι**; here the words are paired with the genitives of cause σοφίας and μανίας ("alas for . . . !"). The manuscripts have the form with *omega* twice, and it makes sense as a sign of the Weaker Argument's intellectual pretensions picking up the characterization of him as a tragic character in 921–4. The Stronger Argument presumably replies with the common form.

926–7 τῆς σῆς πόλεώς (τε) / ἥτις "yours—and that of the city which . . ."

928 λυμαινόμενον τοῖς μειρακίοις cf. 917n. As Dover notes, the accusation is strikingly reminiscent of the charge of corrupting Athens' youth brought against Socrates in 399 BCE (Plato *Apology* 24b; Xenophon *Memorabilia* 1.1.1).

929 Κρόνος ὤν 398n.

930 εἴπερ γ(ε) "(I *will* teach him), if at any rate . . ."   **σωθῆναι** "to be kept safe".

931 ἀσκέω is "practice" (cognate with English "ascetic"). **λαλιάν** is the internal object of the verb, while **μόνον** is adverbial.

932 Addressed to Pheidippides; **τοῦτον** is the Stronger Argument.   **ἔα** present active imperative < ἐάω, "allow, let".

933 κλαύσει literally "you'll weep" (deponent future middle < κλαίω), i.e. "you'll be sorry!"; a colloquialism.   **τὴν χεῖρ(α) ἢν ἐπι-βάλλῃς** "if you try to lay your hand on (him)".   The reference to μάχη ("fighting") in 934 suggest that the Arguments come close to trading blows here before the chorus demand that they cool down and argue the issue out.

934 The middle of παύω is used to mean "cease (doing something)", with a genitive of the activity the subject stops engaging in.   **λοιδορίας** 62n.

935–7b ἐπί-δειξαι (2nd-person singular aorist active imperative < ἐπι-δείκνυμι) is taken separately with **σύ τε** in each of its two occurrences.   **τοὺς προτέρους** is the external object of **ἐδίδασκες**, **ἅττ(α)** the internal object: "what you taught the men of previous generations".   **ἅττ(α)** stands for the interrogative τίνα; in direct speech.   **παίδευσιν** "method of education" (also 986; see 155n. on -σις-nouns), not "learning" in reference to the content of the education, which would be παίδευμα.

937b–8 ὅπως ἄν . . . / . . . φοιτᾷ is a purpose clause in primary sequence; φοιτᾷ must accordingly be present active subjunctive rather than indicative. Aristophanes often includes ἄν in such clauses with no effect on the meaning.   **ἀκούσας . . . / . . . κρίνας φοιτᾷ** English would say "after he hears . . . he can decide and go (to school)"; for φοιτάω in this sense, 916n.   **σφῷν** is gen. dual of the 2nd-person pronoun, "the two of you" (dependent on ἀκούσας).

939–1104 The first *agôn*, or debate, in which one character tries to prove the other wrong about some central point in the action. There is a second *agôn* at 1345–1451.

942 ἐκ τούτων ὧν ἂν λέξῃ An accusative is wanted as the direct (internal) object of λέξῃ, meaning that what is meant is ἐκ τούτων ἅ ("from these things which . . ."). But the relative has been attracted into the case of its antecedent, as often happens, producing ἐκ τούτων ὧν.

943 ῥη-μάτ-ιον is a diminutive < ῥῆ-μα ("word, saying"), which in turn is formed < εἴρω/ἔρομαι ("speak, ask").   For the Weaker Argument's reliance on novelty—which he sees as a good thing—cf. 896 with n., 1032.

944 κατα-τοξ-εύω is literally "shoot down", i.e. "destroy" (849n.). Aristophanes uses the image (arguments as arrows) also at *Acharnians* 707, as does Plato at *Theatetus* 180a, so it may have been a commonplace.

945 τὸ τελευταῖον is adverbial, "ultimately".   γρῦ is a colloquial word for the smallest unit of articulate speech ("a peep"), and ἀνα-γρύζω is thus ~ "say anything at all"; cf. 217n., 963 γρύξαντος. The manuscripts are divided between present subjunctive **ἀνα-γρύζῃ** (printed by all recent editors), which must mean "tries to say anything" or "starts to say anything", and aorist subjunctive ἀνα-γρύξῃ, which would mean simply "says anything"; either might be right.

946–7 A different image, but cognate with the one in 943–4: words not as arrows but as stingers.   **τὸ πρόσωπον ἅπαν καὶ τ(ὼ) ὠφθαλμώ** accusatives of respect with **κεντούμενος** (< κεντέω, "stab, sting"). τ(ὼ) ὠφθαλμώ is a dual.   **ὑπ(ὸ) ἀνθρηνῶν** "by hornets".

949–57 ~ 1024–33 A brief iambic song; see Appendix III.6. The metrical match with the antistrophe is less exact than expected.

949 δείξετον is a 3rd-person dual verb (future active indicative < δείκνυμι), τὼ πισύνω a nominative dual. πίσυνος is < πείθω, "trusting in, relying on" + dative. Cf. the dual αὐτοῖν again in 953.

950 περι-δέξιος is "extremely clever".

952 γνωμο-τύποις "maxim-minting". The image (used by Aristophanes also at *Knights* 1379; *Thesmophoriazusae* 55; *Frogs* 877) is borrowed from the production of coins, which were "struck" against a die to impress an image onto the flan.

953–4 The obels reflect metrical difficulties with the text rather than a problem with the sense, which is clear enough (probably because it has been rewritten to make it easier).   **λέγων ἀμείνων … / φανήσεται** "will appear better by means of his speaking", i.e. "will show himself superior through the arguments he makes", as also in 962; not "will appear better at speaking", which would require λέγειν (suggested as an emendation by Frederick Henry

Marvell Blaydes, a 19th-century British clergyman and classical scholar whose interventions in the text of Aristophanes often tend toward recklessness; cf. 998–9n., 1128–9n., 1285–6n., 1360n.).

955–6 ἅπας κίνδυνος . . . σοφίας literally "an entire risk of wisdom", i.e. a game of chance and skill, in which the players' claims to wisdom are 100% at risk.   **ἀν-εῖται** imperfect passive indicative < ἀν-ίημι, "toss up", as if dice or knucklebones were being thrown.

957 Note the accent on **πέρι**, showing that it governs the relative pronoun that precedes it.   **τοῖς ἐμοῖς φίλοις** "for my"—that is "our"—"friends", i.e. the two Arguments: the chorus leave no doubt that they themselves are entirely on the side of Socrates and the Thinkery, even if they show no preference for one Argument or the other.

959–1008 Anapaestic tetrameter catalectic; see Introduction §IV.A.2.

959–60 A *katakeleusmos* addressed to the Stronger Argument; cf. 476–7 n., 1034–5 (the balancing *antikatakeleusmos*).   **ῥῆξον φωνὴν ᾗ-τινι χαίρεις** literally "break (aorist active imperative < ῥήγνυμι) the voice in which you rejoice!", i.e. "begin to speak in the way you prefer!"

961–1023 The Stronger Argument's description of his own style of education stresses order, a sense of decency, conformity, deference to elders and ascetic self-control. The Weaker Argument interrupts occasionally to denounce this as old-fashioned nonsense (984–5, 1000–1).

961 τὴν ἀρχαίαν παιδείαν ὡς δι-έκειτο is a proleptic (lilies-of-the-field) construction (250–1n.). διά-κειμαι is "be in a condition, be laid out, be set up".

962 λέγων 953–4n.   **ἤνθουν** 897–8n.   **σωφροσύνη** 537n. **(ἐ)νενόμιστο** pluperfect passive (with imperfect sense) < νομίζω, "take seriously, believe in".

963 πρῶτον is adverbial, "first of all".   **μηδέν(α)** is the subject of **ἀκοῦσαι**; **παιδὸς . . . γρύξαντος** is the object of **ἀκοῦσαι**; and **φωνήν** is the internal object of **γρύξαντος**. For γρύζω, 945n.

964–5 The subject of **βαδίζειν** is **τοὺς κωμήτας**, "the boys from the village" (κώμη—one of the candidates for the origin of the term κωμῳδια, "comedy"): the Stronger Argument's "good old days" are fundamentally pre-urban.   **εὐ-τάκτ-ως** "in good order" (< τάσσω/τάττω, whence e.g. English "tactics" and "taxonomy").   **εἰς κιθαριστοῦ** "to the lyre-player's (house)", i.e. "the lyre-teacher's house", musical training being a basic part of a "good" Greek education. Cf. 1355–6, where Strepsiades asks the now-educated Pheidippides to offer a performance on the lyre, there called a λύρα rather than a κιθάρα (cognate with English "guitar"). This is a common use of the genitive with a gapped accusative; thus e.g. ἐν παιδοτρίβου (973) is "in the gymnastic master's (house)" and εἰς ὀρχηστρίδος (996) is "into a dancing-girl's residence".   **γυμνούς** "wearing only a tunic" (498n.).   **ἀθρόους** "in a group".   **κριμνώδη** "like barley meal (κρίμνον)", i.e. in large, white flakes; an internal (adverbial) accusative with **κατα-νείφοι** ("it should snow").

966 προ-μαθεῖν "to learn by rote, to memorize".   The subject of ἐδίδασκεν is the κιθαριστής (964).   **τὼ μηρὼ μὴ ξυν-έχοντας** "not holding their thighs (dual) together". The Stronger Argument is extremely concerned with boys' genitals (973–8 with nn.), and here he seems to be imagining dissolute modern youth squeezing their legs together to push their penises out so as to put them on display.

967 Παλλάδα περσέ-πολιν δεινάν ("terrible Pallas, sacker of cities") and **τηλέ-πορόν τι βόαμα** ("a far-traveling cry") are apparently quotations drawn from well-known traditional poems, according to the *scholia* (citing the Alexandrian scholar Eratosthenes of Cyrene) by Lamprokles of Midon and Kydidas (better Kydias?) of Hermion, respectively (= *PMG* 735b; 948). The content of both passage is notably martial, this being part of the Stronger Argument's view of good traditional values.

968 ἐν-τειναμένους τὴν ἁρμονίαν literally ~ "stretching tight the scale"; the Stronger Argument is referring to the process of converting words (966–7) into music, and he wants this done the old-fashioned way.

969 βωμο-λοχεύσαιτ(ο) 910n.   **κάμψειέν τινα καμπήν** literally "bend a bend", referring to musical modulations of some sort typical of the so-called "New Music" of the second half of the fifth century (attacked in similar terms at e.g. Pherecrates fr. 155.9); cf. 971 δυσκολο-κάμπτους. καμπήν is a cognate internal accusative, which is awkward in English but not in Greek; cf. 1049 πόνους πονῆσαι, 1069n.   Between this verse and the next one, Brunck (276–7n.) added a line in the same meter created by Jonathan Toup, one of the greatest English classical scholars of the mid-18th-century, from an entry in the *Suda* (215n.) αὐτὸς δείξας ἐν θ᾽ ἁρμονίαις Χιάζων ἢ Σιφνιάζων ("himself putting on a show and performing in Chian or Siphnian style in the harmonies"). The addition of the line (~ Ar. fr. 930) to the text of *Clouds* has been rejected by subsequent editors, but an echo of it remains in Brunck's numbering.

971 οἵας οἱ νῦν "the sort (of 'bends') that modern (musicians produce)".   **κατὰ Φρῦνιν** "in the style of Phrynis", a mid-5th-century lyre-singer from Mytilene treated by the Stronger Argument as an example of musical depravity.   **δυσκολο-κάμπτους** literally "bent with difficulty" (969n.), i.e. ~ "complex to perform" or more likely "hard to listen to". A two-termination adjective.

972 πολλάς is an internal accusative with **τυπτόμενος**, "by being beaten many blows", i.e. "by getting a thorough thrashing". Physical punishment was common in Greek educational settings; cf. 493, 1107 (where Strepsiades turns Pheidippides over to the Weaker Argument for training in rhetoric with the words "Teach and punish (him)!"), 1410–12 with n.   **ὡς** "on the grounds of".   **ἀ-φανίζω** is here "disfigure, obliterate, obscure".

973–4 ἐν παιδοτρίβου "in the gymnastic master's (house)" (964–5n.). Training in sports—practiced in the nude—was another basic part of an aristocratic Greek boy's education.   **τὸν μηρὸν ἔδει προ-βαλέσθαι / τοὺς παῖδας, ὅπως τοῖς ἔξωθεν μηδὲν δείξειαν ἀπηνές** i.e. the boys were supposed to arrange their legs in such a way that their penises were tucked between them out of sight (contrast 966 with n.).   **τοῖς ἔξωθεν** "to the men outside", who are imagined hanging about on the street, trying to get a glimpse of the deliciously firm young bodies on display inside.   **δείξειαν** is 3rd-person plural aorist active optative < δείκνυμι.   **ἀπηνές** "cruel", due to the torture of the lust the sight inspires.

975–6 ἀν-ισταμένους "when they stand up". Some early manuscripts have instead ἀν-ιστάμενον, in which case there is a colloquial shift to the singular from the plural. But this is more difficult with **τοῖσιν ἐρασταῖσιν**, since it would imply that the particular boy referred to has multiple lovers, and the move to the singular is better at 977, where it is explicit (οὐδεὶς παῖς).   **συμ-ψῆσαι** aorist active infinitive < συμ-ψάω, "sweep together", i.e. "sweep smooth (the sand)". The boys' rear ends have left an impression on the ground or in the sand—an **εἴδωλον . . . τῆς ἥβης** ("likeness of their youth")— where they have been sitting. They are accordingly expected to erase this to avoid driving the adult men who are in love with them (their ἐρασταί) frantic with desire.

977 ἄν + aorist describes something that might potentially have taken place in the past—or in this case, with οὐδεὶς παῖς, something that could *not* possibly have occurred: "no boy would have . . .". Cf. 855 ἐπελανθανόμην ἄν with n.   **τοῦ (ὀ)μφαλοῦ . . . ὑπένερθεν** "below his navel", a nominally circumspect way of referring to the crotch.

978 τοῖς αἰδοίοισι δρόσος καὶ χνοῦς . . . ἐπ-ήνθει "dew and fuzz flowered on his/their genitals". For αἰδοῖα, 995n. The tone of righteous moralizing characteristic of the Stronger Argument's speech up to this point veers momentarily off into dreamy fantasy. It is unclear whether this is supposed to undercut everything he says, by making him appear ridiculous, or if the point is that the average member of the audience—almost if not entirely male—is expected to be in sympathy with the notion that teenage boys are generically attractive.   A μῆλον is most often an apple, but the sense of the word is broader than that, and the reference to χνοῦς ("fuzz") suggests something more like an apricot or a peach, although neither fruit is known to have been cultivated in Greece before the time of Alexander "the Great" (late 4th century BCE).

979–80 The presence of ἄν in second position signals from the first that the situation being described is unreal, even if the main verb (ἐβάδιζεν) comes only at the very end.   φυράω is "knead" (here used metaphorically of something being self-consciously prepared to please another person).   **πρὸς τὸν ἐραστήν** is to be taken with ἐβάδιζεν.   **ἑαυτὸν προ-αγωγεύων τοῖν ὀφθαλμοῖν** "prostituting himself with his eyes", i.e. "casting sexy glances".

981 ἑλέσθαι . . . κεφάλαιον τῆς ῥαφανῖδος "to take for himself (aorist middle infinitive < αἱρέω) a radish-head", the idea apparently being that this is the nicest part of the vegetable and that boys in the old days would never have presumed to claim it for themselves.   **οὐδ' ἄν** goes with ἐξῆν ("it would not have been possible"). The letters might be divided οὐδ' ἀνελέσθαι (thus most modern editors) instead, in which case this is a simple statement of fact ("it was impossible"); but cf. 982n. In any case, ἐξῆν also governs the infinitives in 982–3.

982 ἄνηθον is "dill", while **σέλινον** is "celery".   ἄνηθον is sometimes written ἄννηθον, and Karl Wilhelm Dindorf, a 19th-century German scholar who produced editions of all the Greek dramatic poets, accordingly conjectured οὐδ' ἄννηθον here in place of the manuscripts' **οὐδ' ἄν ἄνηθον** or οὐδ' ἄνηθον (unmetrical). The change (adopted by most modern editors) converts all of this into a reference to real action, consonant with reading οὐδ᾽ ἀνελέσθαι in 981 (n.). But οὐδ᾽ ἂν ἄνηθον scans, and it is easier to believe that ἂν was lost before ἄν- in certain parts of the textual tradition than that the particle was added in some copies *and* that ἄνηθον was universally corrupted to ἄννηθον.   **τῶν πρεσβυτέρων** is "belonging to their elders", i.e. the older men with whom the boys are now imagined dining.

983 ὄψον is anything eaten in addition to the barley-cakes or bread that were the major portion of a normal Greek meal, to make the latter more interesting. ὀψο-φαγέω is thus ~ "be a glutton" or "have elegant tastes". Cf. 1073, where the Weaker Argument warns Pheidippides that devoting himself to sober living will mean missing out on ὄψα.   **κιχλίζειν** "to giggle" (onomatopoeic, like καχάζω, "go *cha-cha*", i.e. "laugh").   **ἴσχειν τὼ πόδ(ε) ἐν-αλλάξ** "to keep his feet crossed"; apparently body language signaling a casual attitude.

984–5 Δι-πολιώδη is a neuter nominative plural adjective < Δι-πολίεια, the name of a festival celebrated in honor of Zeus of the πόλις; cf. below on the Βου-φόνια. The implication is that the festival was dull and old-fashioned, at least by the standards of someone as fashionably up-to-date as the Weaker Argument.   **τεττίγων ἀνά-μεστα** ("full of cicadas") refers to the Athenian fashion—obsolete by the late 5th century—of men wearing a cicada-shaped brooch in their hair (*Knights* 1331; Thucydides 1.6.3).   Kekeides is identified by the *scholia* (citing Cratinus fr. 168) as "a very early dithyrambic poet", about whom nothing else, however, is known. A man named Kedeides is attested in a mid-5th-century inscription as a trainer (διδάσκαλος) of tragic choruses (*IG* I³ 965.3), and Johann August Nauck (a German scholar of the second half of the 19th century remembered especially for his work on the tragic poets) therefore emended to Κηδείδου.   The Βου-φόνια (literally "Cattle-murder") was part of the Διπολίεια festival (above): a bull was sacrificed to Zeus of the πόλις; the priest who carried out the sacrifice fled; and the ax was then tried for the killing (Pausanias 1.28.10).   **ἀλλ(ὰ) οὖν** "but nonetheless, but all the same".

986 Μαραθωνο-μάχας A reference to the extraordinary Athenian defeat of a Persian expeditionary force on the Athenian coast at Marathon in 490 BCE. The "Marathon fighters" are evoked repeatedly by Aristophanes as Athens' "Greatest Generation" (also *Acharnians* 181, 697–8; *Knights* 781, 1334; *Wasps* 711).   **ἡμή** = ἡ (ἐ)μή.   **παίδευσις** 935–7bn.

987 εὐθύς i.e. "as their first item of business".   **ἐν ἱματίοισι . . . ἐν-τετυλίχθαι** "to be rolled up (perfect middle-passive infinitive <

ἐν-τυλίσσω) in cloaks", i.e. to wear multiple heavy outer garments, which in the Stronger Argument's view of things makes people physically feeble (988–9); cf. Pheidippides in bed at the beginning of the play (10), and contrast the good, underdressed boys in a snowstorm at 964–5.

988–9 μ(ε) ἀπ-άγχεσθ(αι) "I'm choked (with anger)", or perhaps "I could hang myself out of anger"; cf. 779–80n., 1036 πάλαι 'γὼ 'πνιγόμην. Use of the infinitive (rather than the indicative) in the ὥστε-clause signals that this is not something that actually happened, but instead the sort of thing that could be expected to happen in the situation described in what follows.   **ὀρχεῖσθαι Παν-αθηναίοις δέον αὐτούς** is an accusative absolute, which is used in place of the far more common genitive absolute when its main verb—here δέον, "it being necessary"—is impersonal. The dance in question is the πυρρίχη, which was performed holding a hoplite shield, which weighed 15–20 pounds; cf. 353n. The Stronger Argument's disgust stems from the fact that the dancers—spoiled by wearing too much clothing (987) and presumably other physical indulgences as well (cf. 991 with n.)—are too weak to keep the shield up before their bodies, and instead are able only to hold it in front of their thigh (**τῆς κωλῆς προ-έχων**).   **ἀ-μελῆ . . . Τριτο-γενείας** "shows no care for"—i.e. neglects, fails to honor—"Athena", in whose honor the Παν-αθήναια (386–7n.) was celebrated. The epithet is traditional, and what it meant ("Thrice-Born"? "Born from Triton"?) was obscure already in antiquity.

990 πρὸς ταῦτ(α) "in response to these things", i.e. "taking into account the points just made", as also in 1433.   **αἱροῦ** present middle imperative < αἱρέω.

991 ἐπιστήσει μισεῖν ἀγοράν "you'll know"—i.e. you'll learn—"to hate the marketplace", which was not only a place to do business (something of which the Stronger Argument does not obviously disapprove) but also a notorious spot for lounging around, gossiping and the like (the kind of loose, aimless undemanding behavior the Stronger Argument hates), as in 1003. The Weaker Argument picks up these points to launch a devastating attack on the Stronger Argument at 1043–57.   **βαλανείων ἀπ-έχεσθαι** "to stay away from bathhouses" (835–7n.), here apparently simply because this is another way of wasting time, although the Stronger Argument eventually ends up arguing that warm water weakens a man (1045–6).

992 τοῖς αἰσχροῖς αἰσχύνεσθαι amounts to "to know what is shameful and accordingly avoid it", with **κἂν σκώπτῃ τίς σε, φλέγεσθαι** being the flip side of this behavior, to know when you have been insulted and get angry.

993 A θᾶκος is a "chair, seat". ὑπ-αν-ίστασθαι "to rise up from" + genitive, accompanied here by a dative of the other individuals involved, to whose advantage (i.e. "for whom") one does this (τοῖς πρεσβυτέροις . . . προσ-ιοῦσιν).

994 μὴ περὶ τοὺς σαυτοῦ γονέας σκαι-ουργέω literally "to do nothing left-handed (cf. 628–9n.) involving your ancestors", i.e. to avoid embarrassing your family. A γονεύς (< γίγνομαι) can be simply a "parent", but the sense need not be so restricted.

995 τῆς Αἰδοῦς . . . τ(ὸ) ἄγαλμ(α) ἀνα-πλήσειν "to infect (< ἀνα-πίμπλαμαι) the statue of Decency (with pollution)". For the verb, cf. 1023; the expression is odd enough that Dover took the text to be corrupt. For bad behavior as infectious in the sense that the ritual foulness it brings can be transmitted to anyone who gets too close, 445–51n. on μιαρός, 1325n. αἰδώς is an inhibitive emotion that prevents one from engaging in behavior other people will probably disapprove of; often translated "shame", which is however a concern about one's own internal feelings. Cf. 1236, where Strepsiades' bald-faced willingness to perjure himself so as to avoid repaying his debts is termed ἀν-αιδεία. Genitals are thus αἰδοῖα (978), "objects of αἰδώς", because any well-socialized person knows not to flash them about in public.

996–7 εἰς ὀρχηστρίδος 964–5n. Dancing-girls were slave-entertainers hired for symposia and the like. The assumption is that they are sexually available—this one is accordingly described in the next line with the more straightforward πορν-ίδιον ("little whore", < πέρνημι, "sell"; cf. English "porno-graphy")—and by extension ready to get their claws into young men who fail to recognize their mercenary motives and the fact that they are not "decent people". **εἰσ-ᾴττειν** "to rush into", suggesting no substantial advance consideration of the likely consequences of the action. **ἵνα μὴ . . . τῆς εὐ-κλείας ἀπο-θραυσθῇς** literally "so that you're not broken off of", i.e. so that you don't lose, "your good reputation". **ταῦτα** i.e. the physical attractions of the girl. **κεχηνώς** 172n. **μήλῳ βληθείς** (aorist passive participle < βάλλω) makes clear that tossing a piece of fruit (978n.) at another person could be taken as a nonverbal expression of sexual interest.

998–9 ἀντ-ειπεῖν "to talk back to" + dative; **μηδέν** is an internal (adverbial) accusative, "at all". Iapetos was the brother of Kronos (398n.). **μνησι-κακῆσαι** is normally "to bring up past injuries" and takes the genitive (to which Blaydes wanted to emend the noun that follows; cf. 953–4n.). Here it seems to mean "to mention maliciously" and takes the accusative. **ἐξ ἧς**

ἐνεοττο-τροφήθης literally "since which you were raised like a nestling", a complicated way of saying that Pheidippides' father—who is now old—has devoted his entire life to bringing up his son.

1000–1 A "future most vivid" condition, which uses future indicatives in both protasis and apodosis to describe a frightening prospect as vividly as possible. Cf. 1393–6 with n.   **ὦ μειράκιον** an ironic echo of 990.   **πείθω** in the middle-passive takes a dative of the person the subject obeys/is convinced by (here **τούτῳ**, referring to the Stronger Argument).   **νὴ τὸν Διόνυσον** see 91n.; but Dionysus is doubtless invoked in part because he stands for some of the pleasures Pheidippides can be assumed to crave.   **τοῖς Ἱπποκράτους υἱέσιν** Precisely who the Hippocrates in question is, is uncertain. But his sons Telesippos, Demophon and Pericles are ridiculed as idiots also at Eupolis fr. 112 and as having oddly shaped heads at Aristophanes frr. 116; 568.   **εἴξεις** < εἴκω "resemble".   **καλοῦσι** is future (not present).   According to the 2ⁿᵈ-century CE grammarian Phrynichus, who was interested in Attic vocabulary, βλιτο-μάμμας (clearly a colloquial insult) is < βλίτον (an edible weed) + μάμμα (baby-talk for "mother"; see 1382–4n.) and means something like "mama's boy".

1002 λιπαρός is literally "shiny with oil, sleek", but here it has an extended sense ~ "happy and comfortable". Cf. 441–2n. (on αὐχμεῖν), 1012 (λιπαρός ~ "healthy-looking").   **εὐ-ανθής** literally "covered with flowers", i.e. "flourishing" or perhaps "garlanded (as a victor)" (cf. 911).   **δια-τρίψεις** 199n.

1003 στωμύλλων "chattering" (more often middle).   **κατὰ τὴν ἀγοράν** 991n.   τρίβολος is a generic terms for prickly plants; ἐκ-τράπελος is "turned (< τρέπω) away from (the ordinary way of things)", i.e. "perverse"; and **τριβολ-εκ-τράπελ(α)** (internal accusative with στωμύλλων; a nonce-word) are thus nasty, hostile things.

1004 ἑλκόμενος "being hauled (into court)", be it as defendant or witness (as in 1218).   γλίσχρος is literally "sticky" and by extension "insistent"; ἀντί-λογος is "contradictory"; ἐξ-επί-τριπτος is an intensified form of ἐπί-τριπτος, "ruinous, damned"; and a case that is **γλισχρ-αντι-λογ-εξ-επιτρίπτου** (another nonce-word; cf. 1003 with n.) is thus one that demands a man's attention, is full of problems, and makes him miserable.

1005 εἰς Ἀκαδήμειαν The Academy was a park with a *gymnasion* (a public athletic-training facility) located just outside Athens' city walls. In the 4ᵗʰ century, the place became the site of Plato's school, hence the contemporary English sense of the word.   μορίαι were sacred olive trees, which were scattered throughout Attica and belonged to Athena. They were inspected once a month by city officials to be sure they had not e.g. been uprooted by the individuals whose land they were on, the penalty for doing so being banishment and confiscation of one's property (Lysias 7.29, 41).   **ἀπο-θρέξει** deponent future middle < ἀπο-τρέχω.

1006 κάλαμος "sweet flag", a fragrant, iris-like plant.   ἡλικιώτης "age mate" (< ἡλικία, "age", as in 999), i.e. "friend of your own age".

1007 σμῖλαξ is probably *Smilax aspera* (rough bindweed or sarsaparille), a species of flowering vine with fragrant yellow/green flowers and bright red (eventually black) fruit.   For ὄζω + genitive, 5n.   ἀ-πραγμοσύνη is a policy or attitude that attempts to avoid becoming involved in πράγματα, i.e. "troubles" or "business" of any sort, especially political and legal problems (often lending it a quietly antidemocratic character). Cf. 1215–16 with 1216n.   **λεύκης φυλλο-βολούσης** "leave-dropping white poplar". (Note the accent on λεύκη; the adjective meaning "white", by contrast, is λευκός.) The point of the adjective—taken by Dover to be corrupt—is unclear, except that the Stronger Argument is now waxing poetic, as even more emphatically in 1008.

1008 ὁπόταν πλάτανος πτελέᾳ ψιθυρίζῃ "whenever the plane tree whispers to the elm", i.e. as the wind blows through its branches; elevated, alliterative blather (1007n.).

1009–23 Anapaestic dimeter (1023 catalectic), with monometers mixed in at 1011, 1016. See Introduction §IV.A.2.

1012–14 στῆθος λιπαρόν 1002n. R and V (the two oldest manuscripts of the play) have not λιπαρόν but λευκήν, which is metrical but will not do, since white skin is inappropriate for a real man (103n.); cf. 1017 (someone who sides with the Weaker Argument will have χροιὰν ὠχράν).   **γλῶτταν βαιάν** "a small tongue", its size being increased by exercise (i.e. by talking) and the Stronger Argument's expectation being that anyone who subscribes to his program will mostly keep silent.   **πυγὴν μεγάλην, πόσθην μικράν** "a big butt, a little penis"; vase-painting evidence suggests that these were contemporary ideals of male beauty. πυγή and πόσθη are both inoffensive, innocent terms rather than obscenities.

1015 ἐπιτηδεύω is "practice, make one's business"; ἅ-περ οἱ νῦν ("the things that people today (make their business)") is the internal object of the verb.

1017–19 repeat most of the items in the matching list in 1012–14 (n.), but this time with unfavorable adjectives and with ψήφισ-μα μακρόν ("a large vote") at the end as a surprise. The noun is a typical -μα compound (155n.) < ψηφίζω, which means to vote by means of a ψῆφος ("pebble"), as in Athens' courts. Cf. 1429 ψηφίσματ(α) with n.   For ὠχρός (also 1112), 103n.   In 1019, the manuscripts offer πυγὴν μικράν, κωλῆν μεγάλην ("a little butt, a big thigh"). If this is a six-item list (as in 1012–14), πυγήν and κωλῆν on the one hand, and μικράν and μεγάλην on the other, are probably variant readings that have all been passed on, and μεγάλην is clearly wrong, since a big thigh would be a sign of athleticism. The choice is thus between printing **πυγὴν μικράν** and κωλῆν μικράν; since the former sets up the joke that follows by pointedly recalling πυγὴν μεγάλην in 1014, it is to be preferred.

1022–3 πρὸς τούτοις "in addition to these things".   **τῆς Ἀντιμάχου /** **κατα-πυγοσύνης** "the up-the-assedness (528–32n.) of Antimachus", who is perhaps the lyric poet attacked at *Acharnians* 1150, but is otherwise unknown.   **ἀνα-πλήσει** is future < ἀνα-πίμπλαμαι (995n.); + a genitive of that with which one is infected.

1024–33 An iambic antistrophe roughly balancing the strophe at 949–58; see Appendix III.6.

1024–5 καλλί-πυργον "fair-towered"; a showy, high-style adjective (attested elsewhere only in Euripides) that imagines the Stronger Argument's wisdom as an imposing city.   **σοφίαν / . . . ἐπ-ασκῶν** cf. 517 with n.

1026–7 ὡς ἡδύ is exclamatory, "how pleasant!, how nice!"   **σου** modifies **τοῖσι λόγοις**.   **σῶφρον . . . ἄνθος** 537n., 897–8n.

1028 ἄρ(α) ("then") adds emphasis to the emotional **εὐ-δαίμονες**, ~ "they were *lucky*, then!"

1029 τότ(ε) ἐπὶ τῶν προτέρων "in those days in the time of our predecessors" is overfull (pleonastic) and arguably illogical: those who lived "in those days" *were* the chorus' predecessors (thus Dover, who expels ἐπὶ τῶν προτέρων from the text). But this is bland, gushing praise, and the sense is clear enough.

1030–5 Addressed to the Weaker Argument.

1030–1 κομψο-πρεπῆ μοῦσαν ἔχων "having a clever-seeming muse", i.e. "speaking in an inspired, seemingly clever way". Cf. 649 κομψόν (how someone who can identify poetic meters will look to other people).

1032 δεῖ σε λέγειν τι καινόν For novelty as essential to the Weaker Argument's style, 896n.

1034–84 Iambic tetrameter catalectic; see Introduction §IV.A.1.

1034–5 The *antikatakeleusmos*, balancing the *katakeleusmos* at 959–60.   **σοι … ἔοικε δεῖν** "it appears that you need" + genitive of what is wanted.   ὑπερβάλλω is here "outdo, overcome".   γέλωτ(α) ὀφλισκάνω is literally "owe laughter", i.e. "bring laughter upon oneself, make a fool of oneself".

1036 An imperfect with πάλαι has a sense equivalent to a combination of a pluperfect and an imperfect. **πάλαι … (ἐ)πνιγόμην** is thus "I've been being choked for a long time" + accusative of respect **τὰ σπλάγχνα** ("my guts"), ~ "I've been very upset". Cf. 988–9n.

1037–40 ἅπαντα ταῦτ(α) i.e. the points the Stronger Argument has been making.   **συν-ταράξαι** aorist active infinitive < συν-ταράττω, "throw into confusion". The Weaker Argument is not interested in making a positive case, since he is by definition in the wrong. Instead, he wants to push back against what the Stronger Argument has said (ἀντι-λέξαι), confuse the situation, score points with the audience for cleverness, and ultimately force the Stronger Argument to throw up his hands in defeat (as he does at 1102–4). ἐπι-νοέω is "figure out how" + infinitive.

1041 στατήρ (< ἵστημι in the sense "weigh") is a generic term for a large coin, often of gold (in contrast to Athenian coins, which were made exclusively from silver or bronze).

1042 ἔπειτα literally "then, thereafter"; but here the sense is "nevertheless".

1043–4 Addressed to Pheidippides.   **σκέψαι δὲ τὴν παίδευσιν ᾗ πέποιθεν, ὡς ἐλέγξω** "consider the style of education in which he has put his confidence, how I will interrogate it!", i.e. "watch how I'll interrogate . . . !" Prolepsis (250–1n.).   **ὅσ-τις σε θερμῷ . . . φησὶ λοῦσθαι . . . οὐκ ἐάσειν** "who says he won't allow (< ἐάω) you to bathe (< λούω) with hot water". The Stronger Argument did not in fact say this, although he did condemn hanging about in bathhouses (991, cf. 1053–4) and although he does get drawn into defending the position (1045–6).   **πρῶτον** is adverbial, "first of all".

1045 ψέγω is "find fault with, censure" + accusative (also 1055).   **τὰ θερμὰ λουτρά** takes a definite article because the topic is already under discussion, thus ~ "the hot baths we have been discussing".

1046 κάκιστον "the worst thing possible", although Dover suggests that the word is colored by κακία (the cognate abstract noun) in the sense "cowardice".   **τὸν ἄνδρα** "the man (who indulges in them)".

1047 ἐπί-σχες (aorist active imperative < ἐπ-έχω) used absolutely is "wait!, hold on!"   **σε μέσον ἔχω λαβὴν ἄ-φυκτον** "I have you around the middle in a hold that can't be escaped (internal accusative)"; another image borrowed from wrestling (cf. 126 with n., 551)—somewhat ironically, given the Stronger Argument's claim in 1054 that people who talk this way are almost by definition non-athletes.   **ἄ-φυκτος** (two-terminations) is < privative *alpha* + φεύγω.

1048–9 The Weaker Argument wants the Stronger Argument to address everyone present, not just himself. **μοι** is thus better taken as marking this as a nominally polite request ("if you don't mind") than as an indirect object with **φράσον**; cf. 1088 with n.   **ψυχήν** is accusative of respect with **ἄριστον**.   **εἰπέ** is unnecessary for the syntax and instead serves to suggest impatience.   **πόνους πονῆσαι** For the cognate internal accusative, 969n.

1050 A very conventional answer, and apparently the one the Weaker Argument was expecting, given the alacrity with which he jumps on the claim in what follows.

1051 The implication of the Weaker Argument's question is that hot springs were regularly referred to as "baths of Heracles". This passage appears to be the only substantial evidence for that, although there was an altar to Heracles near the hot springs at Thermopylae.

1052–4 The Stronger Argument has walked into the Weaker Argument's trap. More significant, he proves unable to find his way out of it, when what he takes to be obvious, undeniable truths are rejected and his own points are twisted and turned back against him.   **ταῦτ(α) ἐστὶ ταῦτ(α) ἐκεῖνα, ἅ** "These (arguments you have just made) are those (I was discussing earlier), which . . .", with the repetition of ταῦτ(α) reflecting the Stronger Argument's agitation.   **τῶν νεανίσκων . . . λαλούντων** is a genitive absolute, with ἅ serving not only as the subject of **ποεῖ** but also as the internal object of the participle ("when young men make them", although λαλέω is more judgmental than this: 505n.).   **δι(ὰ) ἡμέρας** literally "though a day", i.e. "all day long"; colloquial Attic.   **πλῆρες τὸ βαλανεῖον ποεῖ** For the idea, cf. 991. In 1055, the Weaker Argument picks up the Stronger Argument's second point there, which is that a decent young man will also know that he should hate the marketplace.

1055 ἐν ἀγορᾷ τὴν διατριβήν = τὴν ἐν ἀγορᾷ διατριβήν. For διατριβή, 199n.   **ψέγεις** 1045n.

1056–7 is most easily understood as an unreal present condition, with an imperfect in the protasis and imperfect + ἄν in the apodosis, as if Homer were a contemporary of the speaker.   Nestor, the king of Pylos, was a wise old man, and Homer refers to him as an ἀγορητής at *Iliad* 1.248; 4.293. But the Weaker Argument is playing word-games, because what Homer means is "a speaker in the assembly" not "someone who hangs about the marketplace".   **οὐδὲ τοὺς σοφοὺς ἅπαντας** is wild exaggeration, although Homer does use ἀγορητής of the Trojan elders at *Iliad* 3.150 and of Peleus at *Iliad* 7.126.

1058–9 ἄν-ειμι . . . ἐντεῦθεν "I move on from there". The Weaker Argument argues methodically (cf. 1075), but he also—wisely—declines to linger on a point where more inspection would show that he is being misleading (1056–7n.).   **ἣν ὁδὶ μὲν / οὔ φησι χρῆναι τοὺς νέους ἀσκεῖν** refers (somewhat over-broadly) to remarks by the Stronger Argument such as those at 963, 994, 998–9, 1003 and 1013 with n. The Weaker Argument is now momentarily addressing Pheidippides rather than the Stronger Argument (to whom he returns his attention with σύ in 1061).   **ἐγὼ δέ φημι** "whereas *I* say (that it *is* necessary)".

1060 καὶ . . . αὖ "and on top of that".   **σωφρονεῖν . . . χρῆναι** For the Stronger Argument's emphasis on the need for self-control, 537n.   **δύο κακὼ μεγίστω** i.e. not learning to speak convincingly (1058–9) and living a modest life.

1061–2 Addressed to the Stronger Argument.   **μ(ε) ἐξ-έλεγξον** "prove me wrong!" (aorist active imperative < ἐξ-ελέγχω), something the Weaker Argument is confident the Stronger Argument is incapable of doing.

1063 ὁ γοῦν Πηλεὺς ἔλαβε διὰ τοῦτο τὴν μάχαιραν In a standard ancient story-pattern, Hippolyte, the wife of Peleus' host Akastos, attempted to seduce him. When Peleus refused to sleep with her (thus displaying his σωφροσύνη), Hippolyte accused *him* of having approached *her*, and Akastos responded by having Peleus sent off to a region full of wild animals. Hephaestus, however, saved the hero by giving him a dagger. The definite article ("the dagger, his dagger", not "a dagger") shows that the audience is supposed to know the story, perhaps from having watched Sophocles' or Euripides' *Peleus*.   γοῦν "for example".

1064 ἀστεῖόν γε κέρδος is sarcastic. For the adjective, 204n.

1065 Ὑπέρβολος ... ὁ (ἐ)κ τῶν λύχνων literally "Hyperbolus (551–2n.) from the lamps", i.e. "from the lamp-market, from the place in the market where lamps are sold". Characterizations of this sort are a standard way of denigrating a man who was not a member of Athens' traditional social and political elite, but who nonetheless involved himself in politics. Cleon (whose family had been very rich for at least a generation), for example, is constantly referred to by Aristophanes as a leather-maker because his fortune came from a tannery.   **πλεῖν ἢ ... πολλά** "more than many" is "an enormous number of".

1067 The Nereid Thetis was in fact given to Peleus not because of Peleus' σωφροσύνη, but because Zeus had learned that any son she bore would be greater than his father, which meant that she needed to be married off to a mortal. The marriage lasted long enough to produce the hero Achilleus, but not much longer.

1068 ἀπο-λείπω is the proper Athenian legal term for a woman leaving her husband's house (equivalent to divorce, since "marriage" was defined by socially recognized cohabitation and nothing more; cf. 1128–9n.).   **ὑβριστής** normally has a negative valence ("violent, overbearing, abusive"), and 1069–70 make it clear that the Weaker Argument believes that women like being slapped around a bit and that aggressiveness of this sort is sexually appealing. For ὕβρις, see also 1077n., 1299n., 1506.

1069 ἐν τοῖς στρώμασιν For στρῶμα, 37n., and cf. colloquial English "between the sheets".   **τὴν νύκτα παν-νυχίζειν** "to spend the whole night (with)". English treats repetitions of the same stem in close proximity as inelegant, but Greek finds them attractive; cf. 969n. (on cognate internal accusatives).

1070 σιναμωρέω (< σίνος, "injury") is very rare, but is used by Herodotus of ravaging cities; for the idea, 1068n.   The first element in **Κρόν-ιππος** certainly means "old, old-fashioned" (398n.), but the point of the second is unclear. Dover compares words like ἱππόπορνος (literally a "horse-whore", i.e. "a big whore"; cf. English "horse-fly", "horse-chestnut", etc.), but there ἱππο- always comes first. Perhaps the Stronger Argument means ~ "typical of the upper class" (cf. 63–4 with 63n.), for whose traditional values he has no use; or perhaps -ιππος is simply a conventional element used to make something "sound like" a name.

1071–2 σκέψαι 392–3n.   **ἐν τῷ σωφρονεῖν ἅπαντα / ἃ (ἔ)ν-εστιν** i.e. "everything that being σώφρων involves".

1073 παίδων, γυναικῶν = "sex" (a theme taken up in more detail in 1075–82). Cf. 996–7, where the Stronger Argument claims that in his day young men avoided getting involved with cheap women. For pederasty as unsurprising behavior, 348–9n.   *Kottabos* was a drinking game that involved throwing wine lees at a target, and **κοττάβων, ὄψων** (983n.), **πότων, καχασ-μῶν** thus ~ "parties". Cf. the Stronger Argument's restrictions on events of this sort—or at least on having fun at them—at 981–3.   **καχασ-μῶν** (< καχάζω, "laugh"; see 983n.) is the reading in R, the oldest manuscript of the play. The other manuscripts have κιχλισμῶν ("giggles"), which would also do; the problem must go back to confusion between majuscule Λ and Λ.

1074 τούτων ἐὰν στερηθῇς picks up 1072 ἡδονῶν θ' ὅσων μέλλεις ἀπο- στερεῖσθαι before the Weaker Argument moves on to his next point.

1075 εἶέν 176n.   **πάρ-ειμ(ι) ἐντεῦθεν** cf. 1058 ἄν-ειμι . . . ἐντεῦθεν with n.   **τὰς τῆς φύσεως ἀνάγκας** literally "the necessities of nature", by which the Weaker Argument means sex, which he presents as an appetite that must be satisfied.

1076 ἥμαρτες sums up the situation described in more detail in the rest of the verse: "you messed up: you . . ."   **ἡράσθης** deponent aorist passive < ἔραμαι ("experience desire, feel lust").   **τι** is an internal accusative with **ἐμοίχευσας** and serves to render the idea more casual: "you had a bit of illicit sex". μοιχός (whence μοιχ-εύω, "be a μοιχός") is often translated "adulterer", but actually refers to a man who has sex with a free woman who is out of bounds for him, and has nothing to do with the man's own marital status. Thus a married man who sleeps with a slave prostitute is not a μοιχός, whereas the term is properly applied to an unmarried man who sleeps with the unmarried daughter or sister of an Athenian citizen, or with another citizen's wife.   **ἐλήφθης** aorist passive < λαμβάνω.

1077 ἀπ-όλωλας "you've had it, you're doomed". Attic law allowed an adulterer caught in the act to be killed on the spot. But this was a dangerous way of proceeding, since the victim's family might e.g. claim entrapment (see Lysias 1, which turns on precisely this issue), while if the case was pursued in the courts (as an act of *hybris*, "outrageous behavior"; cf. 1299n.), the woman's reputation would be destroyed and the legitimacy of all her children cast into doubt. Many cases of μοιχεία were thus probably resolved either through marriage (when an unmarried woman and her lover were caught by their family, and the match could be made to look plausible) or through informal payments allowing the man to buy his way out of trouble and humiliations like those described in 1083–4.

1078 χρῶ τῇ φύσει "make use (deponent present middle-passive imperative < χράομαι) of your nature!" (cf. 1075), i.e. "do whatever you feel like doing!"   **σκίρτα** "skip about!" (again suggesting a lack of concern for what anyone else thinks of one's behavior).   **νόμιζε μηδὲν αἰσχρόν** cf. 909–10 (the Stronger Argument calls the Weaker Argument "shameless" and the Weaker Argument claims to be honored), 1020–1 (the Stronger Argument warns that confusing τὸ καλόν and τὸ αἰσχρόν will be one of the consequences of signing up with his rival).

1079 ἢν τύχῃς ἁλούς "if you happen to be caught (aorist active participle— passive in sense— < defective ἁλίσκομαι)". This takes the situation back to the one imagined in 1076, but now with the man in question having the advantage of advanced rhetorical training (contrast 1077).   **τάδ(ε)** is "the following", as properly with forms of ὅδε (vs. οὗτος, which properly points backwards, although the distinction tends to break down in practice).   **ἀντ-ερεῖς** "you'll say in response". The present tense of the compound is not attested (which is different from saying that it did not exist).   **αὐτόν** i.e. the man who has caught you having sex with one of his female relatives.

1080 οὐδὲν ἠδίκηκας 497n.   λέγε or a similar verb is to be supplied with **ἐπ-αν-ενεγκεῖν** (aorist active infinitive < ἐπ-ανα-φέρω), as well as with the ὡς-clause that follows: "(say) you refer the matter to Zeus, and how he . . ."   **ἥττων** + genitive is "inferior to", i.e. "unable to resist". Cf. 1082 θεοῦ . . . μεῖζον with n., 1087n.

1082 μεῖζον is adverbial with **δύναιο**, "be more powerful than" + genitive.

1083 Supply subjunctive ᾖ or the like with τί δ(έ), "what would happen . . . ?"   ἢν ῥαφανιδωθῇ . . . τέφρᾳ τε τιλθῇ literally "if he were radished and plucked with ash", referring to two potential forms of private humiliation: having a root vegetable jammed up one's anus and having one's pubic hair burned off with hot ash.

1084 ἕξει τινὰ γνώμην λέγειν τὸ μὴ . . . εἶναι; "will he have any argument to make to the effect that he's not . . . ?"; the articular infinitive is an internal object of λέγειν.   For the abusive εὐρύ-πρωκτος, 164n., 528–32n., and cf. 1330 λακκό-πρωκτε with n. μὴ εὐ- is to be scanned as a single long syllable (synizesis).

1085–8 Iambic trimeter.

1085 πείσεται deponent future < πάσχω.

1086 μὲν οὖν "to the contrary" (rejecting the Weaker Argument's implicit claim in 1085 that being εὐρύ-πρωκτος is nothing bad).   τί . . . μεῖζον is an internal accusative with ἂν . . . πάθοι, "what greater suffering could he endure" + genitive ("than . . ."). ποτέ intensifies the question (187n.).

1087 ἢν τοῦτο νικηθῇς ἐμοῦ "if you are defeated by me in regard to this". This is not a standard use of νικάω and instead represents a colloquial assimilation to constructions such as ἥττων + genitive (1080 with n.).

1088 τί δ(έ) ἄλλο; "what else (could I do)?"   μοι ("please, if you don't mind") goes with φέρε rather than with φράσον.

1089–1104 Mostly iambic dimeter (monometer in 1101, trimeter in 1103, an abbreviated final foot ⏑−−, i.e. a bacchiac, in 1104).

1089 A συν-ήγορος ("fellow-speaker", i.e. "advocate") spoke in court on behalf of another person or the state in certain official proceedings; "lawyer" is perhaps the closest modern equivalent.   ἐκ τίνων; "from what group?", i.e. "what group of people are the συνήγοροι drawn from?"

1090 πείθομαι ~ "I think you're right", i.e. "Precisely!"

1091 τί δαί; "What about *this*?" (491n.).   τραγῳδέω is probably "perform a tragedy" (i.e. "be a tragic actor") rather than "write a tragedy" (i.e. "be a tragic poet"). Actors' contests at the two Athenian dramatic festivals began in the mid-440s BCE or so, and the profession grew increasingly visible and important over the course of the next few centuries, to some extent eclipsing authors, especially in the case of reperformances (523n.) of what came to be standard pieces.

1092 εὖ λέγεις 403n.

1093 δημ-ηγορέω is "address the people", i.e. "involve oneself in politics".

1095 ἔγνωκας; "have you come to recognize?", i.e. "do you realize now?"

1096 Imperative σκόπει (1097n.) is the main verb, τῶν θεατῶν ὁ-πότεροι πλείους an indirect question dependent on it.   ὁ-πότεροι "which of the two", i.e. εὐρύπρωκτοι or non-εὐρύπρωκτοι.   πλείους (comparative of πολύς) is nominative plural.

1097 The Weaker Argument's σκόπει in 1096, picked up in the Stronger Argument's σκοπῶ here, does not obviously mean anything more than "consider". But the Stronger Argument's "consideration" involves actually looking out at the audience in the Theater, hence the Weaker Argument's τί ... ὁρᾷς; ("What do you see?") and the mocking remarks in 1098–1100.

1098–1100 Supply ὁρῶ.   πολὺ πλείονας ... τοὺς εὐρυπρώκτους "the εὐρύπρωκτοι are the great majority", although the structure of the Greek allows the punchline to be saved for the end.   τουτονὶ ... κα(ὶ ἐ)κεινονὶ / καὶ ... τουτονί The deictics make it clear that the Stronger Argument nominally points at particular persons in the Theater, including one elegant man with long hair (τὸν κομήτην; see 14n.).

1101 τί δῆτ(α) ἐρεῖς; returns to the challenge at 1087: the Stronger Argument has lost the argument—or at least decides he has—and now has no choice but to surrender and keep quiet in the future (cf. 1088 σιγήσομαι. τί δ' ἄλλο;).

1102–4 Dover suggests that the Stronger Argument throws his robe to the other characters onstage, meaning that the Weaker Argument, Strepsiades and Pheidippides are the "you" addressed in ὦ βινούμενοι / ... δέξασθε, while the "you" referred to in πρὸς ὑμᾶς are the audience. But this sits oddly with everything said up to this point—1097–1100 show that the Stronger Argument takes the audience to consist almost entirely of εὐρύπρωκτοι, whereas no one has leveled a similar charge against Strepsiades and Pheidippides in particular—and on a practical level, such a shift would require explicit marking in the text ("*you* on the one hand . . . , whereas *you* on the other") to be comprehensible. In any case, the Stronger Argument apparently leaps off the stage, across the orchestra and into the audience (or out of the Theater?), which is very odd staging and perhaps another mark of the unfinished or essentially nontheatrical character of the text as it has come down to us. Throwing off his *himation* as he does so must be a way to make his escape easier. But it simultaneously assimilates him to Strepsiades, who is also dressed now only in a tunic (498 with n.).   In 1102, the manuscripts offer ὦ κινούμενοι < κινέω (literally "move"), a relatively mild verb when used to mean "have sex with" (1371). But κ and β are virtually identical in minuscule, to the extent that substituting one letter for the other scarcely counts as an emendation. I accordingly print instead **ὦ βινούμενοι** < βινέω, a cruder and more aggressive verb ~ "fuck" that seems more appropriate as the Stronger Argument's final summary characterization of the audience as almost entirely composed of εὐρύ-πρωκτοι.   **ἐξ-αυτο-μολέω** is "desert from a place/group", here implicitly the Stronger Argument's "decent" allies and followers. The final element in the compound is < βλώσκω ("go, come"), the aorist of which is ἔμολον.

1105–6 Addressed to Strepsiades.   **τοῦτον ἀπ-άγεσθαι λαβὼν / . . . τὸν υἱόν** "to take your son here and leave", i.e. to give up on the idea of a Thinkery education, now that the Stronger Argument is out of the picture.   **διδάσκω;** is a deliberative subjunctive, "should I teach (him)?"

1107 κόλαζε 972n.   For **μέμνησ(αι) ὅπως** + future, 887–8n.   **στομώσεις αὐτόν** "you'll give him an edge" (literally a στόμα, "mouth"), as if Pheidippides were a knife that needed differential sharpening for a variety of purposes.

1108–10 Despite the formal **μέν-δέ** balance, the construction shifts in a colloquial fashion between the two clauses from "see to it that you sharpen him on the one side of his face!" to "sharpen his other jaw (γνάθος, feminine)!"   **οἷον δικιδίοις . . . οἵαν εἰς τὰ μείζω πράγματα** literally "such as for minor legal matters . . . such as for the larger concerns", i.e. "so that he's fit for minor legal matters . . . so that it's fit for bigger business". Contrast 431–4: Strepsiades is apparently willing for Pheidippides to go into politics, provided his own personal concerns are dealt with as well.

1111 Deponent κομιοῦμαι is the future < κομίζω, "receive, carry off" (i.e. later on, when the training is complete).

1112 ὠχρόν 103n.   Pheidippides reluctantly allows himself to be led into the Thinkery by the Weaker Argument, while Strespiades exits into his house.

1113–14 Iambic; see Introduction §IV.A.1.   χωρεῖτέ νυν is addressed to all three characters as they exit, but σοί refers to one of them alone, presumably Strepsiades—who will in fact in the end deeply regret getting Pheidippides educated in the Thinkery. This is the first substantial hint that the Clouds are not simple, straightforward advocates of Socratic rhetorical depravity; cf. 563–74, 595–606 (an unexpected invitation to the supposedly nonexistent Olympian gods to join the chorus' dance), on the one hand, and the much more explicit 1303–20 with n., 1452–61, on the other.   μετα-μέλει (generally deponent, but active here) + dative is "give someone cause for concern afterward", i.e. "for regret"; ταῦτα is the subject of the infinitive.

1115–30 The second parabasis, initially directed to the audience generally (1115–16), but after that specifically to the judges at the competition. Trochaic tetrameter catalectic; see Introduction §IV.A.3.

1115–16 τοὺς κριτὰς ἃ κερδανοῦσιν . . . / . . . βουλόμεσθ(α) ἡμεῖς φράσαι "we want to discuss the judges, what benefits they will get", i.e. "we want to discuss the benefits the judges will get" (prolepsis: 250–1n.). The dramatic competitions in Athens were not decided by popular vote but by ten men, one per tribe; they must have been lobbied heavily by their peers in ways not altogether dissimilar to what follows. Cf. 1128–9n. For -μεσθα, 576n.   τι is an internal accusative with ὠφελῶσ(ι).   ἐκ τῶν δικαίων literally "from the things that are right", i.e. "on a just basis": the chorus are not requesting favoritism, because they know they *deserve* to win.   R and V (the two earliest manuscripts of the play) have ἡμεῖς, while the others have ὑμῖν ("to you", i.e. the audience in the Theater). The latter reading seems at first glance better, since there is no obvious need for the emphatic personal pronoun with βουλόμεσθ(α). But it is also very awkward with ὑμῖν referring to someone else (the judges) in 1118, hence the text as printed here and in e.g. Dover's edition of the play.

1117–25 The original audience for the play (and the judges as their representatives) must inevitably have included some deeply urbanized individuals. They are nonetheless imagined here as farmers, this being an important aspect of Athenian self-identity, especially as it is presented in comedy.

1117–18 νεᾶν "to plow".   ἐν ὥρᾳ "in season" and thus in Attica—despite LSJ *s.v.* ὥρα, whose implicit perspective is Northern European—"in fall", when barley and wheat were sown after the fall rains began (thus ὕσομεν < ὕω, as again in 1126, 1129), and when the man who got his crops in the ground first had an advantage over his neighbors.

1120 ὥστε μήτ(ε) "to prevent" + accusative-infinitive construction, describing something that does not occur.   **ἄγαν** (199n.) is here adjectival with **ἐπ-ομβρίαν**, "excessive precipitation" (< ὄμβρος, "thunderstorm, rainstorm").

1121 ἢν δ(ὲ) ἀ-τιμάσῃ τις ἡμᾶς i.e. by voting to give the prize to a different comedy.

1122–3 προσ-εχέτω 3rd-person singular present "jussive" imperative < προσέχω. The clause that follows is balanced colloquially against this order: "let him pay attention, the evils he will endure (internal accusative)!", i.e. "let him note the evils . . . !"   **λαμβάνων οὔτ(ε) οἶνον οὔτ(ε) ἄλλ(ο) οὐδὲν ἐκ τοῦ χωρ-ίου** is the opposite of the promises in 1117–19, with olive trees now thrown into the mix.   **τοῦ χωρ-ίου** "his bit of land (diminutive < χῶρος), his field".

1124 βλαστάνωσ(ι) is here "set fruit".

1125 ἀπο-κεκόψονται future perfect passive—at the point when the olives and vines are evaluated, the damage will have been done—< ἀπο-κόπτω, "knock off"; thus "they will have been knocked off". The subject is the new fruit (to be supplied from 1124 βλαστάνωσ(ι)).   **τοιαύταις σφενδόναις** is exclamatory, "with such sling-balls!" (perhaps referring figuratively to hailstones—mentioned explicitly in 1127—or simply to overwhelming, damaging rain).   **παιήσομεν** is an unusual (also *Lysistrata* 459), metrically convenient alternative future form of παίω, the future of which is normally παίσω.

1126–7 A πλίνθος is a "brick", and **πλινθ-εύω** is thus "work as a brickmaker, make bricks"; the subject of the participle is a vague "someone", i.e. "one of you judges". Sun-baked bricks laid on a stone socle were the basic Greek construction material; cf. 1327n. Roofs, by contrast, were generally made of wooden beams (cf. 1494–6 with 1495–6n.) supporting terracotta tiles (**τοῦ τέγους / τὸν κέραμον**; cf. English "ceramic"), which were actually fired in a pottery kiln and could be broken (cf. 1486–8).   **ὕσομεν** 1117–18n.   **χαλάζαις στρογγύλαις** "with round hailstones"; the adjective is unnecessary for the sense and is a poetic flourish.

1128–9 The central event at a Greek wedding was a procession from the family house of the bride to that of the groom, which represented a way of publishing the fact that the two of them were now living together (cf. 1068n.).

Rain was thus even more of a disaster then than it is generally conceived to be today.   ἢ τῶν ξυγ-γενῶν ἢ τῶν φίλων "or (one) of his relatives or (one) of his friends", a rare use of the genitive probably to be explained as an example of casual, colloquial language. Blaydes (953–4n.) suggested emending to ἢ τῶν ξυγγενῶν τις ἢ φίλων to eliminate the problem. That the threat is not limited to the judges means that anyone who might be in a position to help them make the right decision (1115–16n.) is well-advised to do so.   τὴν νύκτα πᾶσαν accusative of extent of time; cf. 75 ὅλην τὴν νύκτα with n.

1129–30 βουλήσεται / κα(ὶ ἄ)ν ἐν Αἰγύπτῳ τυχεῖν ὤν "he will wish that he could actually happen to be in Egypt", because whatever else one may say about Egypt, it almost never rains there. ἄν makes the action described by the infinitive merely potential.   κρῖναι κακῶς i.e. from the chorus' perspective, to vote for one of Aristophanes' rivals.

1131 Strepsiades emerges from his house, talking to himself (or the world at large). After the 20th, days were counted down backward toward the end of the month, with the final day of the month being ἕνη καὶ νέα (ἡμέρα) ("old and new day", 1134 with n.). The first day of the next month was νου-μηνία, "new month day" (1191). The implication of Strepsiades' opening πέμπτη is that it is now what we would call the 25th or the 26th, and thus (cf. 17n.) that about a week has passed since Pheidippides entered the Thinkery.   τετράς is a noun rather than an adjective, and means "the fourth day" (normally reckoning from the beginning of the month rather than the end, as here).

1133 δέδοικα καὶ πέφρικα καὶ βδελύττομαι "I fear and I shudder at (< φρίσσω; perfect = present) and I loathe". The over-the-top repetition of the same basic idea by means of three different verbs suggests Strepsiades' extreme agitation.

1134 ἕνη τε καὶ νέα 1131n. τε has been added for metrical reasons and is not a normal part of the expression. ἕνος is properly "belonging to the former of two periods", in this case the previous month.

1135–6 ὀμνύς present active participle < ὄμνυμι, "with an oath" (= the circumstances under which θείς μοι πρυτανεῖ᾽ ἀπολεῖν μέ φησι κἀξολεῖν takes place).   The relative clause οἷς ὀφείλων τυγχάνω modifies πᾶς ... τις, "every one (of those) to whom ..."   θείς μοι πρυτανεῖ(α) "by depositing (aorist active participle < τίθημι) prytaneia against me", a reference to money (in the 4th century, 30 drachmas—a substantial sum) a man filing a lawsuit turned over to state authorities to guarantee that he was serious about his case, and which he forfeited if he lost. Cf. 1178–80, 1189–1200.   **με** is the object (not the subject) of **ἀπ-ολεῖν . . . κα(ὶ ἐ)ξολεῖν.**

1137 and the quote that follows in 1138–9 are all a single genitive absolute. The "moderate and fair" terms Strepsiades requests, as a way to stay out of court, amount to his creditors giving up their money (1138–9), as they recognize (1139–41), leaving them with no alternative but to sue him (1141).   **ἐμοῦ τε μέτρια** The manuscripts have ἐμοῦ μέτρια τε, an early scribe having altered the order of the words out of a conviction that what was being coordinated was **μέτρια** and **δίκαι(α)**, not this clause and the preceding one; corrected by the mid-19th century German philologist Theodor Bergk in his edition of Aristophanes. The alternative is to print κα(ὶ ἐ)μοῦ μέτρια τε (a conjecture by an anonymous early scholar preserved in some of the later manuscripts).

1138–9 There is not much difference among Strepsiades' various requests— "Don't take this part now, put that part off, let this part go!"—and Dover suggests that these are best thought of as three separate encounters with individual creditors all rolled into one.   **ὦ δαιμόνιε** 38n.   **μὴ λάβῃς** a prohibition, i.e. a negative command (105n.).   **ἀνα-βαλοῦ** aorist middle imperative < ἀναβάλλω ("put off").   **ἄφ-ες** aorist active imperative < ἀφ-ίημι ("let go, abandon").

1140 λοιδοροῦσί με 62n.

1141 ὡς ἄ-δικός εἰμι represents the content of the "abuse" (62n.) referenced in 1140, "(alleging) that . . ."   The middle of δικάζω (again in 1142) is "go to court (against), sue".

1142 δικαζέσθων 3rd-person plural "jussive" imperative, "let them sue!" (1141n.).   **ὀλίγον . . . μοι μέλει** "it's of little concern (internal accusative) to me", i.e. "I couldn't care less"; colloquial. Cf. 1282 οὐδέ μοι μέλει, "and I don't care".

1144 τάχα (cognate with ταχύς, "fast") is an adverb, "quickly".   **εἴσομαι** deponent future middle < οἶδα.   **κόψας τὸ φροντιστήριον** "by knocking (< κόπτω) on the (the door of) the Thinkery".

1145–6 ἠμί "I say!" This is the verb that supplies the imperfect ἦν in the Platonic ἦν δ' ἐγώ ("and I said").   Strepsiades goes over to the Thinkery door and pounds on it. Although he calls for a slave (cf. 132), someone else

answers. Most editors take this to be Socrates, but 1148–9 τὸν υἱὸν . . . / . . . ,
ὃν ἀρτίως εἰσήγαγες ("my son whom you led in (to the Thinkery) just now")
requires that it be the Weaker Argument instead.   ἀσπάζομαι (literally "I
greet") + accusative appears to be a standard politeness formula; Strepsiades
echoes it in abbreviated form in κα(ὶ ἔ)γωγέ σ(ε) (ἀσπάζομαι).   What
Strepsiades offers the Weaker Argument as he says ἀλλὰ τουτονὶ . . .
λαβέ, is unclear. But whatever this is, it must represent something that
Strepsiades, at least, regards as an appropriate fee for Pheidippides' education
(98n.).   πρῶτον is adverbial.

1147 ἐπι-θαυμάζειν τι "to show some respect/honor to" + accusative of the
person honored. τι is an internal accusative.

1148–9 τὸν υἱὸν εἰ μεμάθηκε . . . , εἰ(πε) prolepsis (250–1n.).   ὅν refers
back to τὸν υἱόν rather than to τὸν λόγον / ἐκεῖνον.   ἀρτίως 726n.

1150 εὖ γ(ε) "well (done)!"   παμ-βασίλει(α) Ἀπ-αιόλη "Fraud, queen of
all". No such deity is attested elsewhere, but she fits comfortably in the Socratic
universe; cf. 331–4 (the Clouds as goddesses of fast talk), 424 (the Tongue as
a Socratic divinity). Ἀπ-αιόλη is < αἰόλος "variable" and thus "deceptive"; the
prefix adds the idea of taking something away from someone.

1151 The first ἄν goes with ἀπο-φύγοις (potential optative), the second with
βούλῃ (a subjunctive in a relative clause). For ἀπο-φύγοις . . . δίκην, 167n.

1152 Active δανείζω is "loan money out at interest", while the middle (as
here) is "borrow". Note the imperfect, "while I was securing the loan".

1153 μᾶλλον modifies an implied ἀποφύγοις ἄν (to be supplied from 1151),
while πολλῷ γε is a dative of degree of difference: "(you'd be acquitted) by
much more", i.e. it would actually be an advantage for witnesses to have been
present, given the Weaker Argument's ability to turn seeming truth on its
head.

1154–70 A song of triumph, followed by a bit of lyric—i.e. sung—dialogue. A
mix of meters (see Appendix III.7); much of the language is paratragic.

1154–5 βοάσομαι . . . τὰν ὑπέρ-τονον / βοάν Various scholia—obviously
working at second hand from the original source, whatever it may have
been—attribute these words to Sophocles' Peleus, Euripides' Peleus and
Phrynichus' Satyrs; note "Doric alpha" (278n.).   ὑπέρ-τονος (two-

terminations) is "stretched (τείνω) to the utmost" and thus here "extremely loud". **τἄρα** = τ(οι) ἄρα, ~ "then, you can be sure!"   **ἰώ** is used in combination with a vocative (also 1170) to mean "ho!, yo!"   **κλάετ(ε)** is imperative.   An (ὀ)βολο-στάτης is properly someone who "weighs" (< LSJ *s.v.* ἵστημι A.4) obols, i.e. a money-changer. But the profession—widely despised, then as now, by those not engaged in it (who presumably saw themselves as facilitating the free flow of commerce for a modest fee)—overlaps with "moneylender" and "banker", both of whom needed to know exactly how much the various coins they took in and gave out were worth.

1156 αὐτοί τε καὶ τ(ὰ) ἀρχαῖα χοἰ τόκοι τόκων "you yourselves and your principle and the interest on your interest", but playing on the idea that actual families are in question (~ "you yourself and your ancestors and the children of your children").   **χοἰ** = κ(αὶ) οἱ; the breathing mark is turned around because it is already represented in the χ. Cf. 34n.

1157 οὐδὲν . . . φλαῦρον (834n.) is the internal object of **ἄν . . . ἐργάσαισθ(ε)**, while **με** is the external object.

1158–9 οἷος ἐμοὶ τρέφεται / . . . παῖς is exclamatory ("such a child . . . !") and amounts to an explanation of the happy state of affairs described in 1157 (thus ~ ὅτι τοιοῦτος "given that such a child . . ."). **τοῖσδ(ε) ἐνὶ δώμασι** The use of poetic ἐνί (= ἐν) and its position between the adjective and the noun it modifies are marks of elevated style.

1160 ἀμφ-ήκει γλώττῃ λάμπων "shining with a two-edged tongue", i.e. "conspicuous for his two-edged tongue" (an over-the-top way of referring to Strepsiades' request at 1108–10, which he expects has now been fulfilled).

1161 A **πρό-βολος** is anything or anyone thrown out in front (< προ-βάλλω) of one, i.e. a "protector, bulwark".

1162 λυσ-ανίας literally a "grief-looser" (< λύω + ἀνία); an obscure "poetic" word, which a *scholium* identifies as "Sophoclean in character".

1163–4 τρέχων appears to be a standard way of adding emphasis to requests of this sort (also *Wealth* 1103; Plato Comicus fr. 71.2). Whether the Weaker Argument actually runs to fetch Pheidippides is unclear, but 1165–6 serve to cover his exit into the house and return onstage in any case.   **ὡς ἐμέ** 237n.

1165–6 appears to be modeled on Euripides *Hecabe* 172–4 (the captive Trojan queen Hecabe summons her doomed daughter Polyxena onstage) ὦ τέκνον, ὦ παῖ / † δυστανοτάτας ματέρος, ἔξελθ᾽ / ἔξελθ᾽ οἴκων, ἄιε ματέρος αὐδάν. Cf. 718–19 n.   ἄιω is a high-style word meaning "hear, heed" (+ genitive).

1167 The Weaker Argument opens the door of the Thinkery again and presents Strepsiades with Pheidippides, who is now wearing a paler version of his mask (1171b).

1169 ἄπ-ιθι λαβών apparently struck some early readers as too abbreviated to be comprehensible, since R and V (the two earliest witnesses to the text) add a direct object: ἄπιθι λαβὼν τὸν υἱόν σου. The other early manuscripts have ἄπιθι σὺ λαβών, which would make this a paratragic dochmiac (×––×–, here ⏑⏑––⏑–; emotionally colorful) and require that the line be sung. This is not impossible, although the emotion seems all to belong to Strepsiades rather than to the Weaker Argument, who merely hands Pheidippides over, tells his visitor to go away, and closes the door.

1170 ἰὼ ἰώ, τέκνον 1154–5n.

1171a ἰοὺ ἰού 1n.

1171b πρῶτα adverbial, "first of all"; so too πρῶτον in 1172.

1172–3 ἰδεῖν is an epexegetic infinitive (243n.) with **ἐξ-αρνητικός** ("full of denials", < ἐξ-αρνέομαι, "deny completely"; cf. 1230 ἔξ-αρνος) and **ἀντι-λογικός** (~ "full of objections"), both of which are stylish adjectives of a sort typical of contemporary intellectuals (27n.) and thus perfect for describing the Socratically educated Pheidippides.   **(ἐ)πι-χώριον** "indigenous, local" (< χώρα, "place").

1174–5 ἐπ-ανθεῖ 897–8n.; supply σοί as the object of the pre-verb.   **"τί λέγεις σύ;"** is to be understood as obnoxiously aggressive ("What are you talking about?" ~ "You're full of it").   **δοκεῖν / ἀ-δικοῦντ(α) ἀ-δικεῖσθαι** "to pretend that one is being wronged when one is actually doing wrong".   **καὶ κακο-εργοῦντ(α)** "even as one is accomplishing evil"; the second element in the verb is < ἔργον (cognate with English "work").   **οἶδ(α) ὅτι** "I know that (this is so)"; a colloquialism ~ "that's for sure!"

1176 Ἀττικὸν βλέπος "an Attic look", i.e. a hostile scowl of the sort that would suit a man who spoke as in 1172–5.

1178 That Strepsiades responds to Pheidippides' question with an accusative (τὴν ἕνην τε καὶ νέαν; see 1131n.) shows that φοβεῖ ... τί; means "What are you afraid of?" (2nd-person middle + accusative) not "What is frightening you?" (nominative + 3rd-person active).

1179 τις ἡμέρα "a particular day".

1180 εἰς ἥν "(It's the one) on which ..."; for the use of εἰς, 562n.   θήσειν τὰ πρυτανεῖα 1135–6n. θήσειν is future active infinitive < τίθημι.

1181 οὐ ... ἐσ(τὶ) ὅπως "there's no way that, it's impossible that".

1182 οὐκ ἂν γένοιτο; is not so much a question with its own content as a baffled echo of what Pheidippides has just said.

1183 εἰ μή "(That would be impossible,) unless (it were also true that) ...".

1185–6 νενόμισται "this is the established legal procedure", i.e. what both custom and the law require, νόμος covering both.   οὐ ... τὸν νόμον / ἴσασιν ὀρθῶς, ὅ τι νοεῖ literally "they do not correctly know the law, what it intends"; prolepsis. The "they" in question is whoever is in charge of administering the lawsuit-deposit process, and by extension whoever blindly takes their understanding of matters seriously.

1187 Solon was Athens' great early-6th-century legislator and political and social reformer, to whom traditional laws and procedures of all sorts were routinely attributed even if he did not necessarily invent them; cf. 445–51n. on κύρβις. Substantial excerpts of his poetry survive (collected in M. L. West (ed.), *Iambi et Elegi Graeci* ii.139–65).

1188 οὐδέν πω πρός "(is) nothing at all regarding (+ accusative)", i.e. "has nothing whatsoever to do with".

1189–95 The point of Pheidippides'—preposterously amusing—analysis is that ἕνη καὶ νέα in the allegedly Solonic legislation actually refers not to one day but to two, the second being the 1st of the new month. Any legal processes dependent on a contrary analysis, allowing lawsuit deposits to be made on the last day of the previous month, are thus invalid (cf. 1181–2).

1189 κλῆσιν 874–5n.

1191 θέσις "depositing"; a -σις-noun (155n.) < τίθημι (cf. 1180 θήσειν, 1181 οἱ θέντες).   τῇ νου-μηνίᾳ is a dative of time when, "on the 1ˢᵗ" (literally "on new-month day"; cf. 1131n.).

1192 ἵνα . . . τί; "in order that what?", i.e. "for what purpose?"; picked up by Pheidippides in his response.   ὦ μέλε 33n.

1193–4 ἡμέρᾳ μιᾷ / πρότερον literally "by one day earlier," i.e. "one day in advance".   ἀπ-αλλάττοιν(το) ἑκόντες "might escape from (the suit) voluntarily", i.e. might avoid actually being dragged into court by coming to an agreement about their debts; cf. Strepsiades' own nominal attempts to negotiate at 1138–9.

1195 ἕωθεν literally "from dawn", when official Athens opened for business.   ὑπ-ανιάομαι is "suffer a bit of distress (ἀνία; cf. 1162 λυσ-ανίας)".

1196 πῶς; "how (is it that)?, why?"

1197 α(ἱ ἀ)ρχαί "the magistrates, the officials"; referred to generically, since the detail of which court officer takes the deposits (τὰ πρυτανεῖ(α)) is irrelevant to the point at hand.

1198 The main construction is δοκοῦσί μοι παθεῖν, with α(ἱ ἀ)ρχαί from 1197 as the subject.   παθεῖν governs the relative clause ὅ-περ (πάθουσι), the subject of which is οἱ προ-τένθαι.   προ-τένθαι were officials charged with eating (τένθω), i.e. sampling, food served at public events ahead of time. (Thus the learned Athenaeus in the 2ⁿᵈ century CE, citing also Phillylius fr. 7 and a 4ᵗʰ-century BCE inscription, making it clear that he had access to good antiquarian sources, but also that the term was not a common one.)   παθεῖν suggests that the bad behavior being described is essentially out of the subjects' control: they do what their impulses—here greed—make them do.

1199 ὅπως τάχιστα = ὅπως ὡς τάχιστα. Some manuscripts have ἵν(α) ὡς τάχιστα, which looks like an attempt by an early editor to make the text easier.   ὑφ-ελοίατο 3ʳᵈ-person plural aorist middle optative < ὑφ-αιρέω, "filch, steal discreetly". (Under certain phonemic conditions, the *nu* in the expected 3ʳᵈ-person endings -ντο and -νται becomes an *alpha*; cf. the accusative singular of 3ʳᵈ-declension consonant-stem nouns in -α). This is a typical Aristophanic characterization: anyone who has the opportunity to cheat or steal, will do so.

1200 προ-ετένθευσαν ἡμέρᾳ μιᾷ literally "they acted like προ-τένθαι by one day", i.e. they moved the deposit date forward one day, so as to get earlier access to the money they intended to embezzle.

1201 εὖ γ(ε) "Well (argued)!"   **ὦ κακοδαίμονες** Addressed to the audience sitting (note **κάθησθ(ε)**) in the Theater, whom Strepsiades casts not just as empty-headed idiots but (esp. 1202) as the future victims of himself and anyone else with access to formal rhetorical training.   **ἀ-βέλτεροι** literally "not better" and thus "inferiors, fools"; colloquial Attic.

1202–3 ἡμέτερα κέρδη τῶν σοφῶν literally "our profits of the *sophoi*", i.e. "a source of money for us who are *sophoi*". The colorful images that follow are both obvious and mostly ill-attested.   **ἀριθμός** "a number", i.e. something that stands in for a person, but nothing more.   **πρόβατ(α) ἄλλως** "randomly sheep/goats, aimlessly sheep/goats", i.e. "as aimless as sheep/goats".   **ἀμφορῆς νενημένοι** "stacked-up (< νέω C) amphorae"—meaning "as indistinguishable as amphorae"? or "as empty(-headed) as amphorae"?

1205 ἐπ(ὶ) εὐ-τυχίαισιν "in response to our good fortunes", i.e. "in celebration of our good luck".   **ᾀσ-τέον** "it must be sung" (< ἀείδω/ᾄδω; for the impersonal verbal adjective in -τέον, 131n.), i.e. by those who see and appreciate the situation (cf. 1209–11); **(ἐ)γ-κώμιον**—a song sung "in a κῶμος" (603–6n.) in celebration of a victory—is an internal accusative rather than the subject.   The sense of **μο(ι)** is slightly different from that of **εἰς ἐμαυτὸν καὶ τὸν υἱὸν τουτονί**: the song will be "about, in celebration of" Strepsiades and Pheidippides, but it will be directed to or intended to satisfy Strepsiades alone (cf. 1206–8).

1206–13 Iambic. See Appendix III.8.

1206–8 μάκαρ . . . / αὐτός τ(ε) ἔφυς, ὡς σοφός, / χοῖον τὸν υἱὸν τρέφεις literally "blessed you are both yourself, how wise, and your son, the sort you are raising!", i.e. "you are blessed both on account of your own wisdom and on account of the sort of son you are raising".   **μάκαρ** or μακάριος (the latter form somewhat less elevated) is a standard, conventional term of praise (e.g. *Wasps* 1275 ὦ μακάρι' Αὐτόμενες, ὥς σε μακαρίζομεν, 1512 ὦ Καρκίν', ὦ μακάριε τῆς εὐπαιδίας).   For **χοῖον** = καὶ οἷον, 34n., 1156n.

1209 μ(ε) accusative of respect with **φήσουσι**.   **χοὶ δημόται** 37n., 210n. In fact, his fellow demesmen are some of the people Strepsiades is most likely to be cheating (1219 with n.), making this an overly rosy vision of future events. For χοὶ = καὶ οἱ, 34n., 1156n.

1210–11 νικᾷς is subjunctive (not indicative), as the presence of ἄν makes clear: this is imaginary rather than real action.   τὰς δίκας is the internal object of νικᾷς (432n.); λέγων explains how this will be done ("by arguing").

1213 πρῶτον is adverbial: "before (we get involved in legal matters)".   ἑστιᾶσαι + accusative is properly "have to one's hearth (ἑστία)" and thus by extension "entertain, invite to dinner"; the passive is "to feast" (as in 1354). Strepsiades tells the story of the dinner—which nominally goes on offstage for the next 140 lines, although it is twice briefly interrupted by visitors—at 1354–76.   Strepsiades and Pheidippides exit into their house.

1214 Two men enter from a wing. The first is fat (1237–8), which serves as a visual signal that he is rich, this being a world in which calories were perpetually in short supply. 1217–19, 1224–5 further identify him as one of Strepiades' demesmen, who has foolishly loaned him money for a horse. For the manuscripts' identification of the First Creditor as Pasias, 21n. The second man—about whose appearance nothing can be said—is present only as a witness to what is being done (1218 with n.). He is accordingly played by a mute rather than by one of the actors, there having been no time backstage to re-costume the man who plays Pheidippides to take the part.   εἶτ(α) suggests that the Creditor has been caught in mid-complaint, grumbling to his companion.   προ-ἰέναι present active infinitive < προ-ίημι, here "let go, abandon".   τῶν αὐτοῦ τι "a bit of his own property", referring to a loan made to Strepsiades that has not been repaid. Cf. 1217 τῶν ἐμαυτοῦ . . . χρημάτων.

1215 κρεῖττον εὐθὺς ἦν τότε "it would have been better immediately at that point", i.e. when he was being asked for money. ἄν is omitted in expressions of unfulfilled obligation with the imperfect when the subject is impersonal; cf. 371 with n., 1359. This is the reading in the oldest manuscripts. Others have the easier word order κρεῖττον ἦν εὐθὺς τότε, which is also metrical; but one basic guiding principle of textual criticism is, all other things being equal, to prefer the *lectio difficilior* ("more difficult reading") on the ground that scribes and editors are routinely concerned to make texts simpler to read.

1216 ἀπ-ερυθριάω is "give up turning red (ἐρυθρός)", i.e. feeling shame.   πράγματα is here ~ "business" and thus by extension "trouble": the Creditor momentarily adopts the posture of an ἀ-πράγμων, a man who tries to avoid political and legal entanglements of all sorts (1007n.), but he then reverses course in 1220–1.

1217 ὅτε 6–7 n.

1218 ἕλκω ("I'm hauling") suggests that the second man's presence is, if not precisely involuntary, at least a duty imposed on him by the obligations of friendship, kinship or the like.   κλητ-εύω is "be a κλητός", i.e. a person called (καλέω) into court to witness that something took place, in this case that Strepsiades was told expressly in advance that he was going to be sued on a particular day (1221–2) in regard to a particular matter (1224–5), after which he nonetheless failed to deal with the situation.

1219 ἔτι πρὸς τούτοισιν "furthermore in addition to these considerations".   **ἀνδρὶ δημότῃ** i.e. Strepsiades. For the pleonastic use of ἀνήρ, 545n.

1220–1 κατ-αισχυνῶ future < κατ-αισχύνω, "bring shame upon (+ accusative)". The joke—not obviously intended as such by the Creditor, who is merely appealing pompously to the trope that one must not act in ways that disgrace one's family/ancestors/city—is that Athenians are addicted to litigation (208n.), so that no decent person from there would pass up the opportunity to sue someone.   **καλοῦμαι** deponent future middle < καλέω in the technical sense "summon to court". This is not the announcement of a suit, but the announcement of an intention to sue in a few days' time. The Creditor does not knock, and the implication of the passage is that making such an announcement in a loud voice before a man's house in the presence of at least one witness was enough to support a claim that he had been given adequate warning that he was in arrears and that further action was going to be taken against him. Strepsiades nonetheless emerges abruptly from the door, interrupting the Creditor (1221) and then trying to lay the groundwork for undermining his case in court (1222–3).

1222–3 μαρτύρομαι 495n.   **ὅτι εἰς δύ(ο) εἶπεν ἡμέρας** i.e. and that the entire procedure is thus flawed; cf. Pheidippides at 1178–1200.   **τοῦ χρήματος;** is a genitive of charge, "(You're going to sue me) about what matter?" So too in 1224 "(I'm going to sue you) about the twelve minas".

1224 τῶν δώδεκα μνῶν 21n., 1222–3n.

1225–6 ψαρόν "dappled" (used by Aristotle of a starling).   **οὐκ ἀκούετε;** Strepsiades appeals again to the world at large, this time to witness (cf. 1222–3) that the accusations being made against him are—supposedly—patently absurd.   **ὅν** "(he's saying this about me), whom . . ."

1227 ἐπ-ώμνυς imperfect active < ἐπ-όμνυμι, "swear by" + accusative. Imperfects are often used with verbs of speaking (also e.g. 1456 ἠγορεύετε) where we would expect an aorist (which would leave us no choice but to take this as a reference specifically to the ceremony that accompanied the original loan). But perhaps the idea is "you repeatedly swore", i.e. when confronted less aggressively on other occasions for failing to pay the debt.

1228 μὰ τὸν Δί' The manuscripts have τὸ χρέος (supplying an object for ἀποδώσειν in 1227), followed in the oldest copies of the play by μὰ Δί', which is unmetrical. Somewhat later copies of the text also feature various attempts to expand **οὐ γάρ** that seem designed to mend the meter. The easiest solution to the problem is to expel τὸ χρέος as a marginal note that made its way into the text, and to print μὰ τὸν Δί', a simple change suggested by Demetrius Triclinius, a 14ᵗʰ-century Byzantine scholar responsible for numerous metrically driven corrections in the text not just of Aristophanes (also 1349), but of the three great tragedians as well.

1229 μοι "for my benefit, to my advantage".   **ἀ-κατά-βλητον** "un-knock-downable (< κατα-βάλλω)", i.e. "invincible"; the word is attested nowhere else and may be a nonce-formation.

1230 ἔξ-αρνος 1172–3n.

1231 τί ... ἄλλ(ο) is an internal accusative with **ἀπο-λαύσαιμι**, while **τοῦ μαθήματος** is dependent on the pre-verb: "What other pleasure would I get from the instruction?", i.e. "Why else would I have had him educated?"

1232 ἀπ-ομόσαι is aorist active infinitive < ἀπ-όμνυμι, "deny under oath", and here takes two accusatives, one of what is denied (**ταῦτ(α)**, "these (allegations)"), the other of the figure sworn by (**τοὺς θεούς**).

1233 ἵν(α) ἂν κελεύσω (ἐ)γώ σε "wherever I might order (aorist subjunctive) you (to do so)", e.g. before an altar, where the consequences of perjury would be more obvious and more threatening, since the god would be more likely to be listening.   **τοὺς ποίους θεούς;** literally "By the what-sort-of gods?", i.e. "By which gods in particular?"; cf. 1270 τὰ ποῖα ταῦτα χρήμα(τα);, "What money is this in particular?"

1235 ἂν προσ-κατα-θείην γ(ε) ... τρι-ώβολον "I would put three obols down in addition (aorist active optative < προσ-κατα-τίθημι)", i.e. "I'd pay three obols *more*".   **ὥστ(ε) ὀμόσαι** "so as to swear", i.e. "for the privilege of swearing".

1236 ἀπ-όλοιο 6–7n.   ἀν-αιδεία is "shamelessness" (201n., 995n.).   ἔτι might either intensify ἀν-αιδείας ("this shamelessness in addition to (your other fault)") or mean "someday".

1237 Like Strepsiades' follow-up remark in 1238, addressed to the world at large (or to the second man?), in reference to the size of the Creditor's belly.   **ἁλσὶν δια-σμηχθείς** "smeared (aorist passive participle < δια-σμήχω) with salt (ἅλς)", i.e. as one of the initial steps in converting a skin into leather, in this case into a leather wineskin in particular.   **ὄναιτ(ο)** literally "would profit" (aorist middle optative < ὀνίνημι), i.e. "would be nice, would be useful".

1238 ὡς κατα-γελᾷς is exclamatory (364n.); supply με as the object. For the verb, 849n.   **ἒξ χοᾶς χωρήσεται** "he'll have room for" (< χωρέω, "have space (χῶρος)"), i.e. "he'll hold six *choes*" (roughly five gallons).

1240 κατα-προίξω (always future) is "escape punishment"; + genitive of the person whose punishment one avoids.   **ἥσθην θεοῖς** ~ "I love (your reference to) 'gods'", with the Creditor's θεούς in 1239 converted to dative to fit the syntax here. For this use of the aorist, 174n. A *scholion* suggests that Strepsiades laughs before this and is thus essentially explaining his unexpected nonverbal reaction to the Creditor's threat.

1241 ὀμνύμενος goes with **Ζεύς**, to which **γέλοιος** is in apposition; literally "Zeus when sworn by is laughable".   **τοῖς εἰδόσιν** literally "for those who know (< οἶδα)", i.e. for educated people.

1242 ἦ μήν 865n.   **τούτων** is dependent on **δίκην**, "a penalty for these (actions/attitudes)".   **τῷ χρόνῳ** "in time" (dative of time when), i.e. "eventually".

1243–4 εἴτ(ε) ἀπο-δώσεις μοι τὰ χρήματ(α) εἴτε μή is an indirect question dependent on **ἀπο-κρινάμενος**. The second half of it can accordingly use either οὐ (metrically impossible here) or μή. For ἀπο-κρίνομαι, 345–6n. ἀπο-κρινοῦμαι in 1245 is the future form of the verb.   **ἔχε . . . ἥσυχος** "keep still!", i.e. "don't move!" (an intransitive use of ἔχω more often associated with an adverb, as in 261 ἔχ(ε) ἀτρεμεί).

1245 ἀπο-κρινοῦμαί 1243–4n.   Strepsiades ducks back into his house.

1246 Addressed to the second man, in regard to Strepsiades. Alternatively, the second half of the line (punctuated as an assertion rather than a question) could be given to the second man, since nominal "mutes" are occasionally entrusted with a tiny bit of dialogue when the poet needs a fourth actor. The line serves in any case mostly to cover Strepsiades' brief absence from the stage.

1247 Strepsiades re-emerges from his house, carrying a kneading-trough (κάρδοπος), and attempts to put what he learned at 670–1 to use.   **(ὁ) ἀπ-αιτῶν** The verb here takes two accusatives, one of the person asked, the other of the object whose return is demanded.

1248 is a particularly clear example of how a direct question (**τουτὶ τί ἐστι;**) is converted into an indirect question (**τοῦθ' ὅ τι ἐστί;**) with an implied "You're asking me . . . ?" (157–8n.).

1249 τ(ὸ) ἀργύριον A number of manuscripts have simply ἀργύριον, "money" (rather than "the money" or "your money"), but the parallels at 1247, 1283 seem to require the definite article. Alternatively, one could argue that Strepsiades is broadening his claim: the Creditor, as an ignoramus, is not the sort of person who deserves to be repaid by *anyone*; cf. the generalizing 1250–1.

1250 οὐδ(έ) goes with **ὀβολόν**, "not even an obol" (although the "not" cannot be taken over into the English translation, where only one negation is possible).

1251 ὅσ-τις καλέσειε κάρδοπον τὴν καρδόπην is a generalizing relative clause, with the main verb (in 1250) in the optative. The use of ὅσ-τις rather than ὅς makes it clear that this is not a specific judgment (not ~ "you who . . ." but ~ "the sort of person who . . .").

1252 οὐχ ὅσον γ(ε) ἔμ(ε) εἰδέναι "Not as far as *I* know!" The same expression is used once by one of Plato's characters (*Theatetus* 145a) and sounds like a snide colloquialism.

1253 For ἀνύσας τι θᾶττον + future, cf. 505–6 with 506n.   **ἀπο-λιταργιεῖς** future < ἀπο-λιταργίζω, "hurry off" (rare Attic vocabulary).

1254 καὶ τοῦτ(ο) ἴσθ(ι) is threatening, as also at *Birds* 1408.

1255 ἢ μηκέτι ζῴην ἐγώ (1st-person singular present active optative of wish < ζῶ, "be alive"); a colloquial equivalent of ~ "or I'll be damned!", i.e. "I'll be damned if I'm not going to . . ." The First Creditor and his companion exit into the wing from which they came. 1256–8 are probably spoken to their retreating backs.

1256 προσ-απο-βαλεῖς future < προσ-απο-βάλλω "throw away in addition to" + accusative.   **ἄρα** marks this as a conclusion from what has just been said, "in that case".   **ταῖς δώδεκα** "your twelve (minas)" (for which, cf. 1224–5).

1257 σε is the subject of **παθεῖν**, **τοῦτο** the object.

1258 (ἐ)κάλεσας . . . τὴν κάρδοπον "you used the word *kardopos*".   **εὐ-ηθικῶς** < εὐ-ήθης, literally "good-natured" (< ἦθος) and thus "simple-minded".

1259a A man—identified in 1267–8 as another of Strepsiades' creditors—enters from a wing, probably limping or stumbling (cf. 1272). It rapidly emerges that he has had two chariot-related accidents: one an actual wreck, the other the fact that he loaned Strepsiades money for Pheidippides' hobby and has not got it back. A late *scholion* gives the Second Creditor the name Amynias, i.e. Ameinias, after the man said at 31 to have loaned Strepsiades three minas for a light chariot and wheels.

1259b ἔα "Whoa!, Yikes!" (expressing surprise, displeasure, or a combination of the two).

1260 R and V (the two oldest manuscripts of the play) have not **τίς οὑτοσί ποτ' ἔσθ' ὁ θρηνῶν;** but τίς ἔσθ' ὁ θρηνῶν οὗτος;, which looks like the product of an unsuccessful attempt to squeeze the extrametrical ἔα in 1259b into the beginning of this line.   θρηνέω is "sing a dirge, sing a song of lament", as characters in tragedy often do.

1261 Carcinus was a contemporary tragic poet known to us mostly through references to him and his sons (who were tragic playwrights, actors and dancers) in Aristophanes. A note in the 1515 Juntine edition of Aristophanes—the second printed edition of the plays, after the Aldine of 1498—suggests that a deity actually issued cries of lament in one of Carcinus' tragedies. As gods normally feel no pain, Dover argues that this is instead an elaborate joke, in which **δαιμόνων** appears in place of παιδῶν or something similar.   **ἐφθέγξατο** deponent aorist middle < φθέγγομαι, "speak".

1263 κατὰ σεαυτὸν . . . τρέπου literally "turn yourself in your own direction!", the idea being that bad luck is catching and that Strepsiades—being utterly unsympathetic to his visitor's troubles—does not want any.

1264–5 An ancient *scholion* claims that these lines are borrowed from the *Tlempolemos* or *Likymnios* of Xenocles, one of Carcinus' sons (cf. 1261n.), although with **θραυσ-άντυγες** ("chariot-rail-breaking") replacing Xenocles' **χρυσ-άντυγες** ("with chariot-rails of gold"). Cf. 1266n., 1272n.   **ἵππων ἐμῶν** i.e. "caused by my horses".

1266 In Xenocles' play (1264–5n.), Alkmene, a female relative of Likymnios, supposedly spoke the original version of these words after Likymnios was killed by Tlempolemos (by means of a booby-trapped chariot?).   **σε** is the external accusative of **εἴργασται**, **κακόν** the internal accusative.

1267 ὦ τᾶν (also 1432; colloquial Attic) is polite, "my good sir": the Creditor is playing for sympathy and trying to be as inoffensive as possible—not that it does him any good.

1268, 1270 This is the first hint in the play that Pheidippides, rather than Strepsiades, has borrowed money for his horse-racing. Perhaps this is the Creditor's attempt to be oblique and thus polite (cf. 1267n.), with the blame for the current situation being nominally put on the old man's son. But the debt is associated with the household, so Strepsiades (as the master there) is responsible in any case. Cf. 1285–6 (where corruption conceals what may have been a similar point).

1268 ἅλαβεν = ἃ (ἔ)λαβεν.

1269 ἄλλως τε μέντοι καί "both on other accounts and especially", i.e. "for various reasons but above all else".   **κακῶς πεπραγότι** goes with μοι in 1267.

1270 τὰ ποῖα ταῦτα χρήμα(τα); 1233n.   **ἀδανείσατο** = ἃ ἐδανείσατο, as also in 1306.

1271 The Creditor's response in 1272 suggests that he believes Strepsiades is changing the subject by commenting on his injuries. More likely the old man is merely being crudely unsympathetic once again (cf. 1263) by saying ~ "You're in trouble, then, (if you think you're going to get that money back)!"   **ὄντως** "really".   **ὥς γ(ε) ἐμοὶ δοκεῖς** literally "as you seem to *me*", i.e. "on *my* understanding of your situation".

1272 ἐξ-έπεσον "I fell out (of my chariot)", *sc.* because the rail broke; cf. 1264–5n.

1273 ὥσ-περ ἀπ' ὄνου κατα-πεσών is a word-division pun: Strepsiades says that the Creditor is talking as if he fell down "off of a donkey (ὄνος)" rather than out of his chariot. But what he means is "out of your mind" (ἀπὸ νοῦ, < νόος/νοῦς). Plato *Laws* 701c uses a similar expression, suggesting that this is an established joke or proverb.

1275 οὐκ ἔσ(τι) ὅπως "there's no way that" (801–2n.).   **σὺ γ(ε) αὐτός** must mean "you yourself (in contrast to your money)" (thus Dover) or perhaps "(in contrast to your horses)", but is in any case a bit obscure. Hermann (664n.) conjectured αὖθις ("again"), which is not much clearer, but is nonetheless printed by Wilson in the OCT.

1276 "You seem to me like someone who's been shaken (< σείω) in respect to his brain", i.e. "whose brain has been shaken, who's had a concussion".   **ἐγ-κέφαλον** literally "what's in one's head (κεφαλή)".

1277–8 is a future "more vivid" condition, and thus a threat.   **σὺ δέ** supply ἴσθι, "But you (be aware that) . . . !"   **νὴ τὸν Ἑρμῆν** Aristophanic oaths are often chosen on purely metrical grounds. But Hermes was *inter alia* the god of commerce and cheating—not entirely unrelated phenomena—so there might be a point here.   **προσ-κεκλήσεσθαι** future perfect passive infinitive < προσκαλέω, "summon"; the subject is again "you".   Dative **ἐμοί**, as routinely, indicates that the person in question (here the speaker) is involved in the action but not the direct object; with a perfect passive, it designates the agent (here the person issuing the summons).   **εἰ μἀπο-δώσεις** = εἰ μὴ ἀπο-δώσεις, "unless you give back (< ἀπο-δίδωμι)".

1279–84 This is Socratic knowledge, as *Clouds* imagines it, but not something Strepsiades has been taught onstage. Hippocrates (an early "scientific thinker" roughly contemporary with Aristophanes) appears to have understood the connection between evaporation and rainfall (*On Airs, Waters, Places* 8), so such ideas would have been part of the intellectual climate of the late 5th century, at least among educated people. (Contrast the bumpkin Strepsiades on rain as Zeus urinating through a sieve at 373.) See 1290–4n.

1279–80 καινόν goes with **ὕδωρ**, which is the object of **ὕειν**, while **τὸν Δία** is the subject.

1282 ὁ-πότερον "which of the two" (an indirect question), *sc.* "is right". **οὐδέ μοι μέλει** 1142n.

1283–4 Cf. the very similar sentiment at 1249–51 with 1249n. on **τ(ὸ) ἀργύριον.**   **δίκαιος εἶ** "are you right", i.e. "do you deserve".

1285–6 The obels—so-called because of their resemblance to spits (118n.) on which bits of meat were roasted—indicate that the text is sufficiently corrupt that no attempt at correction can be anything more than a dubious guess. The basic problems are (1) the mismatch between singular **σπανίζεις** and plural **ἀπό-δοτε** and (2) **μοι** at the beginning of the apodosis. A number of manuscripts have attempted to get around the first difficulty by writing singular **ἀπό-δος.** Blaydes (953–4n.) suggested σπανίζετ' ἀργυρίου, which is good as far as it goes, but then proposed τὸν γοῦν τόκον for the end of the line, which is not so much an emendation as an arbitrary rewriting of the text; it is nonetheless printed by Wilson in the OCT.   σπανίζω is "be short of, be in need of (+ genitive)".   **τοῦτο δ' ἔσ(τι), ὁ τόκος, τί θηρίον;** "This creature (184n.), interest—what is it?" For the delayed interrogative, 379n.

1288 πλέον πλέον "more (and) more"; a colloquialism.

1289 ὑπο-ρρέοντος τοῦ χρόνου genitive absolute. ὑπο-ρρέω is literally "flow gradually", i.e. ~ "slip by, pass". This is an unusual use of the word that serves to set up Strepsiades' sophistic argument in what follows: if the "flowing" of time creates more interest, then the flowing (1294) of rivers must create more sea, but if one sort of flowing does not create more of that substance, then no sort of flowing creates more of any substance.   **καλῶς λέγεις** 403n.

1290–4 Although the text does not make the point explicit, this is the proof that rainfall must be the result of evaporation, i.e. that the second, atheistic explanation offered in 1279–81 is correct: if rain always represented new water, the level of the sea would gradually rise, as it does not. Aristophanes was thus patently familiar with this sort of argument. Whether he expected his audience to be as well—i.e. to see the connection between 1279–81 and 1290–4—is unclear. But this certainly represents a nod to at least some of them, signaling that the poet is not merely an uninformed anti-intellectual.

1290–1 ἐσ(τὶ) ὅτι . . . / . . . νομίζεις; "is it the case that you consider?" (+ accusative and an implied εἶναι).

1292 οὐ . . . δίκαιον "it (is) not right that" (+ accusative, referring to the sea, and infinitive). What the Creditor means is ~ "it's not the case". But Aristophanes' point in having him use this—somewhat unexpected—adjective in particular, is that the Creditor thus implicitly concedes that his claim to get his money back is also ἄδικος, at least as Strepsiades would have it (1292–5).

1293 οὐδέν is an internal (adverbial) accusative with **γίγνεται**, "not at all".

1294 ἐπι-ρρεόντων τῶν ποταμῶν genitive absolute.   **πλείων** is nominative singular (a predicate adjective with 1293 αὕτη), not genitive plural (which would be πλειόνων).

1296 ἀπο-διώξει σαυτόν literally "drive yourself away", as if the Creditor were himself a chariot or a horse (cf. 1298–1300), but with word-play on διώκω in the sense "prosecute". The verb is deponent in the future in Attic, but the manuscripts have the active -διώξεις (corrected by Elmsley, for whom, see 664n.).   **ἀπὸ τῆς οἰκίας** The oldest manuscripts agree on ἐκ τῆς οἰκίας. But Aristophanes elsewhere uses that expression only to mean "out of the house" (e.g. 123, 802), not "away from the house".

1297 φέρε μοι τὸ κέντρον For orders of this sort directed to the slaves within the house, one of whom immediately does what his master has requested, 18n.   A **κέντρον** is a "goad" (< κεντέω, "prick, poke, stab"; see 1300).   **ταῦτ(α) ἐγὼ μαρτύρομαι** What the Creditor is calling for witnesses regarding (495–6n.)—at this point, perhaps merely Strepsiades' defiant refusal to pay his debt—is unclear. But Strepsiades certainly has his horse-goad by the beginning of 1298 at the latest and is jabbing it at the Creditor, who in 1299 (n.) complains of ὕβρις.

1298 ὕπ-αγε "Move forward!, Get a move on!" "Giddyup!"—i.e. "Get yourself up!"—would be very funny and appropriate to the image in English, but is too specific for the Greek.   **ἐλᾷς** future < ἐλαύνω ("drive", i.e. "pull", with "your chariot" to be supplied as the object; cf. 1299 ἄξεις; with n.).   **σαμ-φόρα** 122n.

1299 ταῦτ(α) οὐχ ὕβρις δῆτ(α) ἐστίν; is a rhetorical question equivalent to an assertion ~ "This is obviously . . . !" and is intended for the benefit of whoever is watching and thus potentially available to serve as a witness (1297).   **ὕβρις** (~ "outrage") is behavior that may not be illegal in and of itself, but that adds the element of insult to another matter and makes the situation far more serious: to threaten someone with a goad is merely assault, whereas to do so while addressing him as if he were a horse converts this into *hybris*.   ἄξεις; "Will you pull (your chariot)?" (cf. 1298), i.e. "Pull (your chariot)!" For this rare use of the future without οὐκ (contrast 1298) as equivalent to a command, 633n.   ἐπ-ιαλῶ future < ἐπ-ιάλλω ("to send upon"); supply τὸ κέντρον as the direct object and "you" as the indirect object. The verb is attested nowhere else in this specific sense, but this may nonetheless have been a standard expression.

1300 ὑπὸ τὸν πρωκτόν i.e. "between your legs (from behind)", suggesting that the Creditor has now turned to run (cf. 1301) and Strepsiades is pursuing him with the goad.   A σειρα-φόρος is a horse that is not fastened to the yoke but merely runs alongside the horses that pull the chariot, being attached to it and them by a rope (σειρά).

1301 A form of μέλλω + future infinitive describes a possibility in the future relative to the time referred to in the main verb; thus **ἔμελλόν σ(ε) . . . κινήσειν** is "I was likely to set you in motion". Cf. 1340 (future action relative to the present).   ἄρα (which normally introduces a question, as in 466, and goes first) stands in here for metrical reasons for ἄρα ("then, apparently"; post-positive).

1302 αὐτοῖς τροχοῖς τοῖσι σοῖσι καὶ ξυνωρίσιν is an idiomatic way of saying "your wheels and racing chariots (15n.) and all", i.e. "along with all your chariot stuff".   The Second Creditor flees into the wing from which he came, and Strepsiades re-enters his house, seemingly triumphant.

1303-20 An iambic song, divided into strophe and antistrophe; see Appendix III.9. The chorus abruptly and unexpectedly offer a conventional, moralizing interpretation of the action, as if they were innocent spectators to Strepsiades' bad behavior rather than divine patrons of deceptive sophistic blather of all sorts who have deliberately sent him down this path (esp. 412–19, 429–36). Perhaps this is another mark of the unfinished state of the text, or perhaps the Clouds are now mocking the audience, imitating their supposed reaction to Strepsiades, as they routinely do with other ridiculous human beings they catch sight of (340–55 with nn.). Cf. the arguably even more out of character 1454–5, 1458–61, where the Clouds claim that their goal is always get the "lover of wicked things" into trouble, so as to teach him to fear the traditional gods.

1303-4 οἷον is exclamatory, "what a (bad) thing (is) . . . !"   τὸ . . . ἐρᾶν is an articular infinitive.   ἐρασθείς picks up πραγμάτων ἐρᾶν φλαύρων and thus means "after falling in love (with such things)".

1305–6 ἀπο-στερέω here takes an accusative of what the subject wants to defraud another person of.   **ἀδανείσατο** 1270n.

1307 οὐκ ἔσ(τι) ὅπως 801–2n.

1308–10b The text transmitted in the manuscripts (and printed here with obels) means ~ "he (i.e. Strepsiades) will get something that will make this sophist (i.e. Strepsiades again), from the villainous deeds he began, abruptly to get a bit of trouble". The basic sense is clear, but the words are very awkward and 1310b does not respond metrically to 1320. Bergk (1137n.) proposed κακόν λαβεῖν τι in place of † τι κακόν λαβεῖν † to solve the metrical difficulty. But Dover suggests that the real problem is that some recherché way of saying "get trouble" has been driven out of the text by a note that used simpler, clearer language.

1313–15 δεινὸν . . . / . . . λέγειν 243n.   **οἱ** "to his (i.e. Strepsiades') advantage, for him".   **τοῖσιν δικαίοις** is dependent on **ἐν-αντίας**, "opposed to what is right".

1318 παμ-πόνηρ(α) = παν-πόνηρ(α), "utterly bad".   **ἴσως δ' ἴσως** The repetition seems to be very much like that in colloquial English "perhaps perhaps".

1320 κ(αί) modifies the entire clause, "that he actually be . . ."   **ἄ-φωνον** "without a voice (φωνή), mute".

1321 Strepsiades bursts out of the house, crying out in distress and pain (**ἰοὺ ἰού**; see 1n.). Perhaps he is wearing a new mask with e.g. blood streaming from his mouth and nose. Pheidippides saunters out after him (onstage by 1325 at the latest). The confrontation that follows is in many ways formally parallel to that between the Stronger Argument and the Weaker Argument at 889–1104, with the older man and the traditional morality he represents once again being soundly defeated by a depraved but rhetorically flashy younger man.

1322 Strepsiades is not contemplating legal action, and he therefore does not call for witnesses (contrast the Second Creditor at 1297). Instead, he wants to be rescued by the sort of people most likely to lend one aid in a true emergency: "neighbors, relatives"—the assumption is that the extended family lives in the same general area—"and fellow demesmen". Cf. 1326 with n.

1323 ἀμυνάθω is a lengthened form of ἀμύνω ("defend, protect") attested elsewhere only in tragedy and in late lexicographic sources and the like. Cf. the almost equally rare διωκάθω for διώκω at 1482.   **πάσῃ τέχνῃ** 885n.

1324 **τῆς κεφαλῆς καὶ τῆς γνάθου** genitives of cause with **κακοδαίμων**, "unfortunate (me) due to . . .", in reference to the places where Strepsiades has been struck.

1325 For **μιαρέ** as a general term of abuse, 445–51n. That Strepsiades uses it so insistently of Pheidippides here (also 1327, 1332; cf. 1388), however, suggests that he is appealing at least in part to the word's root sense: to beat one's father is not just socially unacceptable behavior, but violates basic norms and thus makes it impossible for other people to associate with one due to the risk of being infected with one's impurity. Cf. 995 with n.   **φημί** "I say (that I do)".   **ὦ πάτερ** sounds like an insolent touch ("Do you beat your father?" "I do, *father*.").

1326 is addressed to the world at large; cf. 1322n.   **καὶ μάλα** "And very much so!", a colloquial, emphatic formula of consent or agreement ~ "Absolutely right!"

1327 **πατρ-αλοῖα** 911n.   A τοιχ-ωρύχος is literally "someone who digs through (ὀρύσσω) a wall (τοῖχος)", and thus in a society in which most buildings were made of mud brick (1126–7n.), a "burglar". But the word is also used as a general form of abuse, as here.

1328 **πλείω** is accusative plural (going with **τ(ὰ) αὐτὰ ταῦτα**).

1329 **ἆρ(α) οἶσθα;** Colloquial English would say "Are*n't* you aware?"   **πολλ(ὰ) ἀκούων καὶ κακά** 529n.

1330 **λακκό-πρωκτε** literally "cistern-asshole", meaning "buggered hard and repeatedly enough that your asshole is the size and depth of a cistern". The word is attested also at Cephisodorus fr. 3.4 and Pollux 6.127, while the cognate λακκο-πρωκτία appears at Eupolis fr. 385.4, which is enough to show that this was a common, colorful expression.   **πάττε πολλοῖς τοῖς ῥόδοις** Cf. the Weaker Argument at 910–12 with 912n.

1331 **κ(αί)** "(Yes,) and . . ."

1332 ἐν δίκῃ σ(ε) ἔτυπτον ~ "I was right to beat you", as also in 1333, 1379.   **μιαρώτατε** 1325n.

1333 πῶς γένοιτ(ο) ἄν . . . ἐν δίκῃ; "how would it be right?" (cf. 1332 with n.) + infinitive.

1335 Supply λέγων from 1334 to govern **τουτί** (a colloquial omission).   **πολύ** is adverbial with an implied νικήσω σε, ~ "(I'll defeat you) soundly".

1336–7 ἑλοῦ 2nd-person singular aorist middle imperative < αἱρέω.   Strepsiades never actually chooses between the weaker argument and the stronger argument. But his response in 1338–41 makes it clear not just that he will opt for the stronger argument, but that he does so because it seems obvious to him that it will prevail.

1338 ἐδιδαξάμην μέντοι σε "The sense is plainly 'I *have* had you taught . . .', spoken bitterly", although there is no exact parallel for the use of the particle (Dover).   **ὦ μέλε** 33n.

1339–41 For μέλλω + future infinitive, 1301n.   **ἀνα-πείσειν** takes **ταῦτα** as an internal object, "to be convincing about this", i.e. "to make this case"— defined in **ὡς δίκαιον καὶ καλὸν / τὸν πατέρα τύπτεσθ' ἐστὶν ὑπὸ τῶν υἱέων**—"convincing". Some later manuscripts write μ' ἀναπείσειν, giving the infinitive an external object as well ("to convince me about this"; cf. 1342, where the pronoun σ(ε) is a matter of metrical necessity).   **τὸν πατέρα τύπτεσθ(αι) . . . ὑπὸ τῶν υἱέων** is an awkward combination of "that a father be beaten by his son" and "that fathers be beaten by their sons".

1343 οὐδ(ὲ) αὐτός is emphatic, "not even you yourself".

1344 καὶ μήν "alright then".   **ὅ τι καὶ λέξεις** ("what in fact you will say") is an indirect question standing in for the direct question τί καὶ λέξεις;

1345–1451 The second *agôn*. Cf. 939–1104.

1345–50 A brief choral song, balanced by 1391–6 (introducing Pheidippides' response to Strepsiades). Iambic; see Appendix III.10.

1345–8 ὅπῃ / . . . κρατήσεις is an indirect question standing in for direct πῇ κρατήσω;   **ὡς** "since".   **εἰ μή τῳ (ἐ)πεποίθειν, οὐκ ἂν ἦν / οὕτως**

ἀ-κόλαστος is a past unreal (contrary to fact) condition, "if he hadn't . . .
he wouldn't have . . .". τῳ = τινι. Use of pluperfect (ἐ)πεποίθειν—a variant
form of the 3rd-person singular active indicative—signals that Pheidippides
acquired his confidence at some point before the main action took place, and
then maintained it.   ἀ-κόλαστος "unchecked, unchastised" (< κολάζω),
i.e. willing to speak and act in what would otherwise seem to be a recklessly
outrageous fashion.   ἔσ(τι) ὅ-τῳ θρασύνεται "there's (something) in
which he takes confidence", i.e. "there's some basis for his confidence". Since
the antecedent is indefinite, the compound relative ὅσ-τις is used.

1349–50 The end of 1349 is metrically deficient. Triclinius (1228n.) inserted
γε, one of his standard space-fillers. This is not enough to fill the gap here,
however, hence the further addition of τοι by Hermann (664n.).   τὸ λῆ-μα
τ(ὸ) ἀνθρώπου The manuscripts have τὸ λῆμ' ἐστὶ τἀνθρώπου, and Dover
expelled ἐστί—easily explained as a pedestrian gloss accidentally brought into
the text—to make the line match 1396. Hermann (664n.) suggested instead
τὸ λῆμα τὸ τἀνδρός (printed by Wilson in the OCT), which is much further
from the paradosis and ignores that fact that Pheidippides is not an ἀνήρ but a
μειράκιον (e.g. 990).   λῆ-μα 457–8n.

1351–85 Iambic tetrameter catalectic; see Introduction §IV.A.1.

1351–2 A *katakeleusmos* (476–7n.).   ἐξ ὅτου . . . ἤρξα(το) ἡ μάχη
γενέσθαι is an indirect question standing in for direct ἐκ τίνος ἤρξαθ' ἡ μάχη
γενέσθαι;   ἤδη λέγειν χρὴ πρὸς χορόν· πάντως δὲ τοῦτο δράσεις "You
must speak now to (the) chorus; but you will do this in any case". The chorus'
reference to itself as a third party and the absence of the definite article with
χορόν are unexpected, and the second clause is odd almost to the point of
meaninglessness. The Dutch classical scholar Henrik van Herwerden (a
professor at Utrecht from 1864–1902) conjectured ἤδη λέγειν χρή· πρὸς χάριν
πάντων δὲ τοῦτο δράσεις ("You must speak now; but you will do this to the
pleasure of everyone"; printed by Wilson in the OCT), which keeps δέ in
second position if πρὸς χάριν πάντων is regarded as a single sense-unit.

1353 πρῶτον is adverbial.   λοιδορεῖσθαι 62n.

1354 εἰστιώμεθ(α) 1213n.   ὥσ-περ ἴστε represents an authorial nudge
reminding the audience of the invitation issued at 1212–13, which they might
reasonably have forgotten about after the intervening scenes with the two
Creditors.

1355-6 An educated person was supposed to be able to play the lyre and to know numerous traditional songs by heart (cf. 964–8), and taking turns at singing was standard symposium behavior (esp. *Wasps* 1219–49). Strepsiades accordingly asks Pheidippides—who has just completed his education, this being a graduation party of sorts—to sing something by the late 6ᵗʰ/early 5ᵗʰ-century lyric poet Simonides, and in particular "Krios, how he was shorn (< πέκω)", i.e. "how Krios was shorn" (*PMG* 507). ("Krios" is literally "Ram", and the poem apparently described how Krios, whoever he may have been, met his come-uppance.) Pheidippides, however, will have none of this (1357–8).   ᾆσαι aorist active infinitive < ἀείδω; cf. 1371 ᾖσ(ε).

1357-8 ἀρχαῖον 821n.   πίνον(τα) is present tense, thus "while drinking".   ὡσ-περ-εὶ κάχρυς γυναῖκ(α) ἀλοῦσαν "just as if (one were)", i.e. "just like a woman grinding (< ἀλέω) parched barley (κάχρυς; accusative plural)" to reduce it to meal. The reference is to a work song that serves to make hard manual labor less tedious. Whether the woman is supposed to be a slave or a housewife too poor to own one, is unclear; but this is in any case the sort of labor a well-to-do man would never dirty his hands with.

1359 τότ(ε) εὐθύς "immediately at that point", i.e. without waiting for further supposed outrages to be committed.   οὐ . . . χρῆν σ(ε) ἀράττεσθαί τε καὶ πατεῖσθαι; "wasn't it necessary that you be both beaten and stomped?", i.e. "shouldn't you have been . . . (although you weren't)?"; cf. 371n., 1215n.

1360 ὡσ-περ-εὶ τέττιγας ἐστιῶντα "as if you were entertaining cicadas" (famous in Greek literature for their singing). The plural is somewhat unexpected—only Strepsiades and Pheidippides are obviously at the party— and Blaydes (953–4n.) accordingly conjectured τέττιγα μ' ("entertaining me as if I were a cicada"; printed by Wilson in the OCT). But this is a generalizing hypothetical rather than a description of the specific situation at the party.

1363 μόλις 326n.   ἠν-εσχόμην aorist middle < ἀνέχω (in the middle "hold out, bear up, be patient"; cf. 1373 ἐξ-ην-εσχόμην) with double augmentation.   τὸ πρῶτον is adverbial ("initially") and serves to signal in advance that Strepsiades' patience eventually gave out (1373).

1364-5 ἀλλά can be used with an imperative to mean "at any rate" (as in 1369) and is here retained from the original order that Strepsiades reports in indirect form.   μυρρίνην λαβόντα By the late 5ᵗʰ century, holding a laurel branch as one sang was traditional symposium behavior. The original significance of this practice is unclear, but here it is extended to the quotation of other sorts of poetry.   τῶν Αἰσχύλου λέξαι τι "to recite (< λέγω) one of the (speeches) of Aeschylus", the greatest Athenian tragic playwright of the first half of the 5ᵗʰ century and already established by this time as a classic and a voice of traditional bravery, nobility, etc. (i.e. the sort of values the Stronger Argument nominally represents). Cf. 1366–7n., 1370 (for the construction), 1371–2n.

1366–7 Pheidippides' seeming initial praise of Aeschylus is sarcastic, as what follows makes clear. Aeschylean tragedies were probably being revived already by the mid-420s BCE (cf. 534–6n.)—the pseudo-Aeschylean *Prometheus Bound* may have been produced for this market—and the criticisms in 1367 are echoed in *Frogs* (924–41) by "Euripides" and Dionysus, who make it clear that many average theater-goers found the language of Aeschylus' plays impressive but difficult to understand.   **νομίζω** is a deliberative present active subjunctive (~ "am I supposed to consider?"), not indicative.   **ψόφου πλέων** "full of noise".   **ἀ-ξύ-στατον** "incoherent" (< privative *alpha* + συ-στατέω ~ συν-ίστημι).   **στόμφακα** "a big-mouth"; for the formation, 333n.   **κρημνο-ποιόν** "a cliff-maker", i.e. someone who piles words up to the sky.

1368 πῶς οἴεσθε; 879–81n.   ὀρεχθέω is "swell" (here with emotion).

1369–70 τὸν θυμὸν δακών literally "biting (< δάκνω) my anger", i.e. "biting back my anger, repressing my anger" at one of his favorite poets being disrespected.   **ἀλλά** 1364–5n.   **λέξον** For this use of λέγω, 1365 with n.   **ἅττ(α) ἐστὶ τὰ σοφὰ ταῦτα** is, if not exactly sarcastic, at least dubious ("whatever these 'wise things' are").

1371–2 ᾖσ(ε) . . . ῥῆσίν τιν(α) "he sang a speech" is strange, especially after λέγω apparently meaning "recite" in 1365, 1370. Dover prints ἦγ(ε) (~ "perform"?), but is hard put to identify a convincing parallel.   **ὡς ἐκίνει (ὁ) ἀδελφὸς . . . τὴν ὁμομητρίαν ἀδελφήν** The reference is to Euripides' *Aiolos*, in which Makareus married his sister Kanake (thus a *scholion*). The point of the specification **ὁμο-μητρίαν** ("from the same mother") is that in Athens a man's son and daughter could marry, provided they had different mothers, so that *that* would not have been shocking in Strepsiades' eyes.   **ἐκίνει** 1102–4n.   **ὦ (ἀ)λεξί-κακε** "O warder-off of evil!", a generic call to a protector god to intervene; colloquial English would say "God help us!"

1373 κἀγὼ οὐκέτ' is to be scanned ——◡ (synizesis, i.e. combination into a single syllable, of -ὼ οὐ-).   **ἐξ-ην-εσχόμην** "I held out (1363n.) from (saying anything)".   **ἀράττω** is here metaphorical ("assault"); contrast 1359.

1374 οἷον εἰκός "as (is) likely/reasonable", i.e. "as you would expect".

1375 ἔπος πρὸς ἔπος ἠρειδόμεσθ(α) "we pounded (< ἐρείδω) word against word for ourselves", i.e. "we went back and forth with insults".   **ἐπ-ανα-πηδᾷ** ("he leaps on top of") is a historical present, meaning that the present tense is used to describe past events in a particularly vivid way. In 1376, Strepsiades shifts to the more normal imperfect ("he began to . . .").

1376 φλάω and **σποδέω** are both "crush, pound, beat", while **πνίγω** is "choke" (cf. 1036, 1389). Note the imperfects ("he began to . . .").   **(ἐ)π-έθλιβεν** (< θλίβω, "press, squeeze") is the reading in R and V, the two oldest manuscripts of the play; the others have (ἐ)π-έτριβεν (for which, cf. 972 ἐπ-ετρίβετο τυπτόμενος πολλάς with n.). The precise sense of the prefix is no clearer in either case, and the verb in RV is much rarer and thus the *lectio difficilior* (1215n.).

1377 The subject of **οὔκουν δικαίως** ("didn't (I do this) rightly?", i.e. "wasn't I right to do this?") is different from that of **ὅστις οὐκ . . . ἐπαινεῖς** ("(you) who don't praise"), and σε must be supplied as the object of the first verb and thus the antecedent of ὅστις in order to bridge the gap. A colloquial ellipse.

1378 σοφώτατον[1] is a predicate of Εὐριπίδην in 1377, "as supremely wise".   **γ(ε)** is sometimes used when one character echoes a word or phrase spoken by another (here σοφώτατον). It is unclear whether Strepsiades' response is intended as incredulous or as sarcastic.

1379 αὖθις αὖ ("yet again") is a common pleonasm in Attic.   τυπτήσω (also 1443) is the Attic future of τύπτω; in the middle, "I'm going to get myself beaten".

1381–5 ὅσ-τις . . . σ(ε) ἐξ-έθρεψα This is the same argument Strepsiades relied on at 861–4 to convince Pheidippides to enroll in the Thinkery. At that point, it was successful—before Pheidippides had learned to look at the world from a Socratic perspective.

1381 αἰσθάνομαι here takes a genitive of the person understood (σου, accompanied by a concessive participle **τραυλίζοντος**) and an accusative of what is understood (**ὅ τι νοοίης**, an indirect question); thus ~ "understanding what you had in mind, even though you were using baby-talk".   For τραυλίζω, 862n.

1382–4 βρῦν, μαμμᾶν, κακκᾶν are all accusative singular; cf. 1390 "I made κακκᾶν" with n. This is some of our best evidence for Greek baby-talk (see also 1000–1n.); the only obvious "adult" cognate is κάκκη ("poop") at *Peace* 162. μαμμία seems to be "Mommy" at *Lysistrata* 878–9 and must be connected to μαμμᾶν ("breast-milk!" ~ "I want to nurse", and thus by extension "food!" ~ "I'm hungry").

1382 A past general condition. Instead of the more usual imperfect indicative alone, Aristophanes uses **ἄν** + aorist in the apodosis to indicate that Strepsiades' reaction was habitual; cf. ἄν + imperfect to the same effect in 1383, 1385.   **ἐπ-έσχον** is < ἐπ-έχω "hold out", i.e. "offer".

1383 μαμμᾶν δ' . . . αἰτήσαντος genitive absolute, here equivalent to the protasis of a past general condition with an aorist verb (as in 1382).   Despite its position, the first **ἄν** does not go with the genitive absolute, but with imperfect **ἧκον**. Repetition of the particle, as again in 1384–5, does not alter the sense (425n.).

1384–5 ἄν οὐκ ἔφθης φράσας i.e. "the words would not have been out of your mouth". ἔφθης is 2nd-person singular aorist active < φθάνω. ἄν marks the action as unreal.   Greek houses sometimes had the equivalent of an outhouse, and chamber pots were also used. But it was probably easier to take a small child out into the street, which is where filth of all sorts was dumped in any case (and then eaten by dogs or pigs).

1386–90 A "pnigos"—i.e. a long series of short verses spoken in a single breath, thus "strangling" (πνίγω) the speaker—bringing Strepsiades' remarks to an end. Cf. 1445–51 at the end of Pheidippides' speech (but there divided between two speakers). Iambic dimeter (1390 catalectic); see Introduction §IV.A.1.

1386 κεκραγό(τα) 389n.

1387 χεζητιῴην present active optative < χεζητιάω ("need to shit"; cf. 183n.), i.e. as a consequence of the beating. This is an indirect report of something said in the past, and the original present indicative ("I need to shit!") has accordingly been converted into an optative.

1388–90 ἔξω (ἐ)ξ-ενεγκεῖν . . . / θύραζε . . . / . . . κακκᾶν is an echo of 1384–5 κακκᾶν . . . θύραζε / ἐξ-έφερον.   **αὐτοῦ** is properly genitive < αὐτός, but functions as an adverb meaning "there, in that place"; cf. ποῦ "where", πολλαχοῦ "in many places", etc.　(ἐ)πόησα κακκᾶν (literally "I made poo-poo") must be another example of slightly more advanced baby talk (1382–4n.).

1391–6 Another brief choral song, balancing 1345–50. Iambic; see Appendix III.10.

1392 πηδᾶν ὅ τι λέξει "are leaping (701–5n.), whatever he will say", i.e. "are leaping (in anticipation of) his speech".

1393–6 Best understood as a "future most vivid" condition (of something feared and thus conceived of with particular clarity by means of a future indicative; cf. 1000–1 with n.), although with potential optative + ἄν (referring to the future) in the apodosis.　**τοιαῦτα** is in the first instance the internal object of ἐξ-ειργασμένος, but can simultaneously be understood as accusative of respect with ἀνα-πείσει ("will be convincing about them").　**λάβοιμεν ἄν** i.e. "we could buy".　**ἀλλ(ά)** is to be taken closely together with οὐδ(ὲ) ἐρεβίνθου: "why, not even for a chickpea" (genitive of price), i.e. "for next to nothing".

1397–1444 Iambic tetrameter catalectic (with the exception of 1415, which is iambic trimeter); see Introduction §IV.A.1.

1397–8 An *antikatakeleusmos* (476–7n.), balancing 1351–2.　**σὸν ἔργον** "(It's) your task".　**κινητὰ καὶ μοχλ-ευ-τά** "mover (< κινέω) and leverer (566–8n.)". Dover suggests the latter may have been a common term for a man who specialized "in constructional problems", i.e. in getting heavy blocks to fit properly with one another, although there is no positive evidence to that effect.　**πειθώ** (note the accent on the ultima, in contrast to that on the cognate verb πείθω; accusative singular) is "persuasion, means of persuading".　**ὅ-πως δόξεις λέγειν δίκαια** is an object clause, i.e. it describes what the verb of effort (here ζητεῖν) aims to accomplish, and stands in rough apposition to πειθώ τινα. English would say ~ "to seek to make yourself seem convincingly in the right".

1399–1400 The idea is repeated in 1404, as Pheidippides finally gets to his point (in 1405).　**ὡς ἡδύ** is exclamatory, "how pleasant it is . . . !"　ὁμιλέω is "associate with" + dative.　**καθ-εστώτων** intransitive perfect active participle < καθ-ίστημι ("be established, be settled").　**ὑπερ-φρονεῖν** 225–6n. (but here with the genitive rather than the accusative).

1401 τὸν νοῦν μόνῃ is Bentley's (215n.) emendation of the manuscripts' τὸν νοῦν μόνον (R), τὸν νοῦν μόυ (V) and μόνῃ τὸν νοῦν (others), all of which seem to represent crude—and in the latter two cases, unmetrical—attempts to simplify the text. μόνον might be retained and regarded as adverbial ("when I only focussed my attention on horsemanship"). But Bentley's text makes better sense of μόνῃ in the non-RV manuscripts (transposed to put it next to ἱππικῇ, with which it belongs).

1402 οὐδ(ὲ) ἄν . . . οἷός τ(ε) ἦν "I wouldn't even have been able" + infinitive.   **πρὶν ἐξ-αμαρτεῖν** 630–1n. The pre-verb seemingly adds the idea that there is a specific target from which one deviates (here speaking clearly and sensibly), as also in 1419.

1403 οὑτοσὶ . . . αὐτός i.e. Strepsiades, who forced Pheidippides to go to school. Only at 1408 does Pheidippides begin to address Strepsiades directly.   **μ(ε) . . . τούτων ἔπαυσεν** One stops someone (accusative) from something (genitive), here the stupid behaviors described in 1401–2.

1404 λεπταῖς is to be taken with all three nouns, but agrees in gender with the one to which it is closest.   **ξύν-ειμι** literally "I associate with", i.e. "I'm involved with, I'm immersed in".

1405 κολάζειν The word is carefully chosen and sets up the next argument: Pheidippides will show not that it is right to *beat* one's father, but that it is right to *punish* him (sc. since he is in the wrong; cf. 7, 972n., 1377–9, 1434).

1406–7 ἵππ-ευε 15n.   **ὡς** "since".   **ἵππων . . . τέθρ-ιππον** literally "a four-horse team (< τέτταρες + ἵππος) of horses".   **ἐπι-τριβῆναι** is perhaps a deliberate echo of 243, where Strepsiades complains that νόσος μ' ἐπ-έτριψεν ἱππική.

1408 ἐκεῖσε δ(ὲ) ὅ-θεν ἀπ-έσχισάς με τοῦ λόγου μέτ-ειμι "I will pursue (the question) from that point whence you split me off from my speech", i.e. "from where you interrupted me"; a strikingly haughty formulation. In what follows, Pheidippides poses questions to Strepsiades and then turns his answers back on him, much as the Weaker Argument did with the Stronger Argument at 1036–1104.

1410–12 εὐ-νοῶν τε καὶ κηδόμενος is not intended to sound self-serving or ironic, nor is Pheidippides' response supposed to be anything but brilliantly perverse: the Greeks clearly believed that physical discipline was good for children, even if the absurdity of the idea that hitting someone (τύπτειν) can be a sign of loving concern (εὐ-νοεῖν) is effectively pointed out here. Cf. 972n.   τοῦτ(ο) is in apposition to τὸ τύπτειν, "this, meaning to beat (someone)".

1413–19 This is a different argument (or jumble of arguments) than 1409–12: Pheidippides insists that he is a free person and therefore ought not to be subject to physical violence (1413–15; cf. 494–6), and that if anyone ought to be punished, it is in any case his father, who as an adult is more culpable for his bad behavior (1416–19).

1413 ἀ-θῷον "exempt from" (< privative *alpha* + θωή, "penalty") + genitive.

1414 ἔφυν is here probably specifically "I was born".

1415 is iambic trimeter and appears to be an adaptation of Euripides *Alcestis* 691 (Pheres explains why he is unwilling to die in place of his son Admetos) χαίρεις ὁρῶν φῶς· πατέρα δ᾽ οὐ χαίρειν δοκεῖς;, "You enjoy seeing the light; don't you think your father enjoys (the same thing)?" (quoted by Aristophanes at *Thesmophoriazusae* 194, leaving no doubt that he knew the verse). The point is not the common self-justifying claim that parents suffer when their children are punished ("This hurts me as much as it does you"), but something more like "Children cry, so don't you think their fathers ought to cry as well?", with the sense obscured by the need to match the structure of the tragic model.

1416 νομίζεσθαι . . . τοῦτο . . . εἶναι "that this is considered to be".   τὸ (ἔ)ργον properly "the work", but here ~ "the job, the proper role" (also 1494).

1417 δὶς παῖδες οἱ γέροντες ("old men are twice children", i.e. "are children a second time", with reference to what we would call Alzheimer's disease; cf. 844–6 with nn.) or some variant thereof appears to have been proverbial (also Sophocles fr. 447; Cratinus fr. 28; Theopompus Comicus fr. 70).

1418 μᾶλλον . . . τι ("somewhat more") is an internal (adverbial) accusative with κλάειν. The sentiment is echoed in 1439, as Strepsiades surrenders to Pheidippides' reasoning.   ἢ νέους Thus Bentley (215n.) for the manuscripts' ἢ τοὺς νέους (R and others) or ἢ τοὺς νεωτέρους (V and others), neither of which scans. A second definite article is not needed (104n.), but must have seemed to be to an overly conscientious early scribe, who added it to the text.

1419 ὅσῳ-περ "by precisely as much as" (dative of degree of difference), i.e. "to the exact extent that". **ἧττον δίκαιον** (supply ἐστί) is the main construction, with **ἐξ-αμαρτάνειν . . . αὐτούς** dependent on it. For the sense of ἐξ-αμαρτάνειν, 1402n.

1420–2 νόμος is both "custom" and "law"; cf. 1427–9n. Strepsiades' **νομίζεται** refers to customary practice. But Pheidippides acts as if actual legislation were in question, and is therefore able to argue that since such regulations are deliberately proposed and approved at some particular point in time, they can be just as arbitrarily altered. Put another way, there is no justice (902–7), only legal convention, which is itself the product of one man's ability to impose his own—inevitably self-serving, and not necessarily definitive—views of right and wrong on other people through the use of rhetoric. **τὸ πρῶτον** is adverbial and goes with **ὁ . . . θείς** ("who initially established") rather than with **ἦν**.

1423 ἧττόν τι δῆτ(α) ἔξεστι κα(ὶ ἐ)μοί; "is it somehow less possible also for me?", i.e. "do I not have an equal right?" **τὸ λοιπόν** is adverbial, "for the future".

1425–6 εἴχομεν is here "we received, we took". **ἀφ-ίεμεν** (< ἀφ-ίημι) "we let go", i.e. "we agree to ignore". A nominally magnanimous gesture; the idea is repeated in what follows. **δίδομεν αὐτοῖς προῖκα συγ-κεκόφθαι** Literally "we give to them to have been soundly thrashed (< συγ-κόπτω) for free", i.e. "we ask no recompense" for wrongs done us by our fathers in the past. A προίξ (attested already in Homer) is a gift or present; this adverbial use of the accusative is an Attic colloquialism.

1427–9 This is another new argument (cf. 1413–19n.), from nature (~ the "law of the jungle"): human beings are a species of animal and ought to be judged as such. The same idea surfaces at *Birds* 755–9, 1344–50, and reflects a genuine strand of late 5th-century "sophistic" thought. 1430–1 is a devastating response, to which Pheidippides has no effective reply (1432 with n.). **βοτά** (< βόσκω, "feed, tend") are domesticated animals, as opposed to θηρία (184n.). **ταυτί** does not obviously point to something visible onstage and must instead mean ~ "that we are all familiar with" or "that are always cited in such arguments". But see 847n. **ἀμύνεται** agrees with neuter plural τ(ὰ) ἄλλα τὰ βοτὰ ταυτί, as the subject closest to it. **τί;** is an internal accusative with **διαφέρουσιν;** English would say "how?" **διαφέρουσιν / ἡμῶν** 502n. **ψηφίσματ(α)** are "decrees (of the Assembly)" (< ψῆφος, "pebble" and thus "voting token"—cf. 1017–19n.—

although most if not all Assembly voting seems actually to have been by show of hands), which were regarded as having less permanent significance than νόμοι ("laws"). The remark thus ties into Pheidippides' proposal at 1420–2 (n.), but at the same time represents a passing dig at alleged general Athenian over-enthusiasm for legal matters generally and legislative fickleness (208n.).   **γράφουσιν** "draft".

1430–1 ἅπαντα is an internal (adverbial) accusative with **μιμεῖ** (for which, 559n.).   **τὴν κόπρον** "dung" (an inoffensive term). The point of the definite article is unclear ("your own dung"? "the dung we know is always found in barnyards"?).   **ξύλου** "a piece of wood", i.e. "a roost".

1432 ὦ τᾶν 1267n.   **οὐδ(ὲ) ἂν Σωκράτει δοκοίη** A strikingly weak response. Dover in 1968, in a remark rooted as much in his own time as in Aristophanes', comments: "Ar(istophanes) reveals in these four words his awareness that what passes as rational criticism of irrational authority is sometimes no more than transfer of allegiance to another authority".

1433 πρὸς ταῦτα 990n.   **εἰ δὲ μή** "otherwise", i.e. "if you fail to take my advice".   αἰτιάομαι is "accuse, blame".

1434 καὶ πῶς; "And how (should I not beat you)?", i.e. "And why (should I not beat you)?"; cf. 717 with n.

1435 ἢν γένηταί σοι "if one should be born to you", with the subject to be supplied from **τὸν υἱόν** ("your *own* son").

1436 κεκλαύσεται impersonal future perfect passive < κλαίω + dative of agent; literally "it will have been wailed by me".   **ἐγ-χανών** aorist active participle < ἐγ-χάσκω (literally "gape toward", i.e. "grin at" and thus "mock"); supply μοι as the object of the pre-verb.   **τεθνήξεις** future perfect active < θνήσκω. All the action described in this verse is imagined from the perspective of Pheidippides many years in the future, when Strepsiades is dead and Pheidippides realizes that his childhood beatings have been for nothing, since he has no one to abuse in turn.

1437–9 Like the Stronger Argument (1102–4), Strepsiades surrenders to his rhetorically more gifted opponent. But then Pheidippides goes one step too far, moving into a realm where his father's reaction is emotional rather than rational (1440–51).   **ὦ (ἄ)νδρες ἥλικες** "men of my age, age-mates". For the pleonastic use of ἀνήρ, 545n.   **τὰ (ἐ)πι-εικῆ** is the subject of **δοκεῖ**, on which **συγ-χωρεῖν** is in turn dependent (~ "the reasonable course seems to me", i.e. "I think the reasonable course is" + infinitive).   συγ-χωρέω is literally "congregate with, combine with", i.e. "yield to, agree with".

1440 κα(ὶ ἑ)τέραν ἔτι "yet another". For χἀτέραν rather than χάτέραν, cf. 34 χἄτεροι with n., 1156 χοἰ with n.   **ἀπὸ γὰρ ὀλοῦμαι** "(No,) for this will be the *death* of me!" (792n.).

1441 οὐκ ἀχθέσει supply "if you hear me out". The participial clause that follows is concessive ("although you . . .").

1442 τί is the internal object of **ἐπ-ωφελήσεις**, **μ(ε)** the external object: "What further benefit will you bestow on me?"

1443 τυπτήσω 1379n.

1444 τί δ' ἦν ἔχων "What (would you do/say) if, having . . ." The manuscripts are badly confused, offering τί δῆτ' ἂν ἔχων (thus R and V, the earliest witnesses), τί δῆτ' ἦν ἔχω, τί δῆτ' ἦν ἔχων and τί δ' ἦν ἔχων (others). Only the last of these both makes sense and scans, but the reading appears to be the product of ancient emendation—i.e. the other variants are all attempts to correct what is offered in RV—and Hermann's (664n.) τί δῆτ' ἄν, ἤν might be right instead.

1445–51 Another "pnigos" (1386–90n.).

1448–51 τὸ βάραθρον "the Pit", a rock cleft near the city into which persons convicted of particularly awful crimes against the Athenian people were thrown. Despite Dover, this was a means of execution, not merely a way of disposing of bodies; see Xenophon *History of Greece* 1.7.20.   **τὸν λόγον τὸν ἥττω** is coordinated with **σεαυτόν** in 1448 as a second object of **ἐμ-βαλεῖν**; thus "yourself and the Weaker Argument", not—as the use of the accusative case makes clear, and despite the word order—"along with Socrates and the Weaker Argument".

1453 ἀνα-θείς aorist active participle < ἀνα-τίθημι, here "entrust".

1454–5, 1458–61 The Clouds complete their pivot to presenting themselves as aggressive advocates of conventional piety (cf. 1303–20 with n.). This takes a considerable amount of fun out of the story. But more disturbing is the fact that the Clouds' supposed unswerving dedication to all that is good and right here leads direct to a form of nasty vigilante justice (esp. 1481–5) that they indirectly endorse.

1454–5 αὐτὸς . . . σαυτῷ σὺ τούτων αἴτιος "you yourself are responsible to yourself for these things", i.e. "you have only yourself to blame for what has happened". Note the drumbeat **αὐτός, σαυτῷ σύ, σεαυτόν**, that helps bring this point home.   **στρέψας** is an ironic echo of Strepsiades' name.

1456–7 is a reasonable question that the Clouds fail to answer directly. Strepsiades is not a sophisticated or perhaps even a fundamentally "good" person, but proper moral guidance might have made him better. The Clouds have instead opted to let him ruin himself and hurt others as well, as a brutal form of "learning through suffering" (on the implicit theory that this is the *only* way to learn to tell good from bad?).   **ἠγορεύετε** 1227n.   **ἐπήρατε** aorist < ἐπ-αίρω, "stir up, encourage"; cf. 42n. Better imperfect ἐπ-ήρετε, since this was an ongoing project?

1458–9 ταῦ(τα) is the internal object of **ποοῦμεν, ὅν-τιν(α)** the external object: "we do these things to anyone whom . . ."   At the end of 1458, the manuscripts are divided between ὅταν τινά ("whenever we recognize someone . . .") and ἄν τιν' οὖν (apparently intended to mean "if we recognize someone . . ."). ἑκάστοθ' ὅταν τινά would be metrically unusual—an oddly split anapaest—particularly because 1452–64 otherwise contain no resolution, apparently as part of an attempt to make the lines sound more solemn and grand. Editors therefore universally print **ὅντιν' ἄν**, an emendation by the brilliant late 18th-/early 19th-century classical scholar (and rival of Gottfried Hermann; see 664n.) Richard Porson, who produced the first systematic explanation of the intricacies of the iambic trimeter.   **γνῶμεν** aorist active subjunctive < γιγνώσκω; with **ἄν**—nestled neatly in second position in its clause, as in 1458 and again in 1460 and 1461—since this is a relative clause (cf. 589).

1460–1 ἕως ἄν αὐτὸν ἐμ-βάλωμεν εἰς κακόν is a temporal clause ("until . . ." + subjunctive + ἄν, with the main verb in 1458 referring to a customary action and this one defining its anticipated end), **ὅπως ἄν εἰδῇ τοὺς θεοὺς δεδοικέναι** a purpose clause ("in order that . . ." + subjunctive, since the main verb in 1458 is a primary tense; ἄν is possible but not obligatory in such clauses).   **τοὺς θεούς** is the object of **δεδοικέναι**.

1462 πονηρά γ(ε) 102n.

1463–4 με is the subject of ἀπο-στερεῖν, τὰ χρήμα(τα) the object (with ἃ (ἐ)δανεισάμην offering clarification as to exactly what money is in question). ἀπο-στερέω is here "filch, withhold" + accusative. The present infinitive is imperfective, "to try to filch".

1464 νῦν–1466 Addressed to Pheidippides.   ἐξ-ηπάτων 546n.   The reference to Chairephon, who has taken no part in the action up to this point, is unexpected; see 1493–1505n.

1468 ναὶ ναί 784n.   κατ-αιδέσθητι πατρῷον Δία is most likely a phrase borrowed from a now-lost tragedy (= adesp. tr. fr. 59), for the following reasons: (1) τρ in πατρῷον would in comedy not normally lengthen the *alpha* before it, but does so here, as routinely in tragedy; (2) κατ-αιδέομαι is otherwise confined in the 5th century to tragedy and Herodotus (i.e. Ionic prose); (3) Athens had no cults of "paternal Zeus" (Plato *Euthydemus* 302c–d), but the god is repeatedly mentioned in tragedy (e.g. Aeschylus fr. 162.4; Sophocles *Trachiniae* 288; Euripides *Electra* 671).   κατ-αιδέσθητι deponent aorist passive imperative < κατ-αιδέομαι, "show αἰδώς (995n.) toward" + accusative.

1469 ἰδού γε Δία πατρῷον 818n.   ὡς ἀρχαῖος εἶ cf. 915 (the Weaker Argument to the Stronger Argument).

1470–1 Pheidippides repeats what Strepsiades taught him at 827–8—indeed, 1471 echoes 828 word for word—although he is putting the point to unexpected use. There Pheidippides responded by calling his father a babbling lunatic (829, 832–3). He ends up saying something very similar here (1475), the difference being that in the meantime he has been convinced—clearly by Socrates and Chairephon (cf. 1464–7)—that Zeus does *not* in fact exist, or at least is no longer in power, and that Dinos *is* the new king of the gods.   Only R and V (the two oldest manuscripts of the play) repeat οὐκ, the second appearance of the word being unnecessary for the sense and thus easily omitted, but also being wanted for the sake of the meter.

1473–4 διὰ τουτονὶ τὸν δῖνον leaves little doubt that a drinking cup is visible onstage and has, as far as one can tell from the text, been visible there all along. A *scholion* suggests that something resembling one (or a statue of Vortex himself) stands in front of the Thinkery, representing Socrates' favorite personal deity, and thus what is taught in his school. Cf. 424 τὸ Χάος τουτί with n., 1478–85n. (a previously unmentioned statue of Hermes onstage as well; perhaps it holds the cup).   ὤμοι δείλαιος, ὅτε καὶ σὲ χυτρεοῦν ὄντα θεὸν ἡγησάμην is addressed to the cup/statue.   For ὅτε καί, see 6–7n., 34 with n.   χυτρεοῦν ὄντα is concessive, "although you're (only) made of clay, although you're (only) pottery".

1475 σαυτῷ "for your own benefit", i.e. "to yourself".   παρα-φρόνει present active imperative < παρα-φρονέω (844n.).   φληνάφα present active imperative < φληναφάω, "chatter, babble".   Pheidippides exits, but whether he goes into Strepsiades' house or the Thinkery is unclear. If he enters the house, he has chosen to maintain some basic allegiance to his family, despite his ugly quarrel with his father. If he enters the Thinkery, he must now think of himself as belonging to Socrates and Chairephon (cf. 1464–9, esp. 1467). In the latter case, he is in the Thinkery when Strepsiades sets fire to it in what follows. Either he is one of the otherwise anonymous Students who emerge from the building in 1493ff., therefore, or—even more disturbing, if perhaps less likely—he is not, and we must assume that he remains trapped inside and dies.

1476 οἴμοι παρα-νο-ίας see 153n. (on the exclamatory genitive), 845–6n. (on the noun), and cf. 1480 παρα-νοήσαντος.   ὡς ἐμαινόμην is exclamatory (364n.).

1477 ἐξ-έβαλον "I repudiated, I rejected". R (after correction) and V have ἐξ-έβαλλον ("I tried to repudiate"), which would require expelling either καί (adverbial, "actually") or τούς from the text.

1478–85 Strepsiades speaks to a statue of Hermes that has seemingly been onstage all along (cf. 1473), and then reacts as if he has got an answer from it. Cf. *Peace* 661–3, where Hermes himself does something very similar with a statue of the goddess Peace.

1478 θύμαινε 610n.

1479 συγ-γνώμην "forgiveness" (< συγ-γιγνώσκω; see 138n.) + genitive of the person for whom one feels this (1480).

1480 A three-word trimeter; cf. 686.   ἐμοῦ παρα-νοήσαντος ἀδολεσχ-ία genitive absolute. ἀδολεσχία (etymology uncertain; the *alpha* is long and is thus not a privative) is implicitly useless talking, "chatter". Note the ending in -ία, marking this as an abstract noun (201n.), and cf. 1485 ἀδολεσχής (someone who engages in such chatter).

1481–2 γενοῦ 107n.   **γραφὴν / . . . γραψάμενος** "after filing a suit"; see 467–75n., 758–9n.   **διωκάθω** (subjunctive) is a lengthened form of διώκω. Cf. 1323n.   **εἴ(τε) ὅ τι σοι δοκεῖ** "or (advise me as to) what seems good to you"; a colloquial ellipse introducing an indirect question.   There is a brief pause in the stage action, as Strepsiades holds his ear up to Hermes' mouth and Hermes supposedly offers him an answer to his question.

1483–4 The syntax is tangled in a fashion typical of ordinary speech; literally "you advise me correctly, not allowing me to . . . , but to . . .", i.e. "you rightly do not allow me to . . . but instead you advise me to . . ."   **ἐῶν** present active participle < ἐάω.   **δικο-ρραφεῖν** "to stitch together a lawsuit". The verb is used later by another comic poet (Apollodorus Comicus fr. 13.12), while Phrynichus in the 2ⁿᵈ century CE identifies the cognate nouns δικο-ρράπτης and δικο-ρράφος as good Attic vocabulary (*Praeparatio Sophistica* p. 62.15). This must accordingly be an ill-attested colloquialism rather than a word Aristophanes has invented as a one-off joke.   **ἐμ-πιμπράναι** present active infinitive < ἐμ-πίμπρημι ("set fire to" + accusative).

1485 τῶν ἀδολεσχῶν 1480n.   **Ξανθία** is literally "Blondie", a generic slave-name suggesting that the person in question had been brought to Athens from Scythia (where blond hair was common, as it was not among the Greeks). Mute slaves in Aristophanic comedy are routinely given names (as here), while slaves with speaking parts just as often are not (as at 56–9).

1486 κλίμακα "a ladder" (cognate with English "climax, climactic"). **σμινύην** "a mattock", a chopping tool similar to a pickax, but with a broad horizontal blade, used e.g. to break hard earth or here roof tiles (1488).   At some point in the lines that follow, Xanthias emerges from the house. carrying the items Strepsiades has requested (cf. 18n.). He leans the ladder up against the front of the stage-house and climbs up onto the roof and begins destroying it. The staging of the end of the play is chaotic and difficult to reconstruct—perhaps more evidence of incomplete revision—but Strepsiades seemingly follows him up (1500–3) and then down again (1508–10).

1487 ἐπ-ανα-βάς "after going up onto", with the first pre-verb picked up by ἐπί in what follows.

1488 κατά-σκαπτ(ε) literally "keep digging down!", i.e. "go on destroying (396n.) by using the mattock (1486n.)!" or "try to destroy . . . !"   **εἰ φιλεῖς τὸν δεσπότην** seems like an odd way of putting things: why would any slave feel affection for his master (cf. 57–8 with 5n. and 6–7n.)? But the fact is that some perhaps did; that masters were happy to believe that this was the situation, and also happy to see onstage masters and slaves getting along well; and that Strepsiades' words really amount to little more than "Please!" in any case (cf. 82).

1489 ἕως is "until", with an anticipated future action (ἂν . . . ἐμ-βάλῃς).

1490 δᾷδ(α) . . . ἡμ-μένην literally "a lit (perfect passive participle< ἅπτω) torch".   ἐνεγκάτω 3ʳᵈ-person singular "jussive" aorist active imperative < φέρω.   Somewhere in the course of the next line or two, another slave emerges from Strepsiades' house, carrying the requested item. Presumably the slave stays onstage to assist in the assault on the Thinkery.

1491–2 τιν(ὰ) αὐτῶν is the subject of δοῦναι, δίκην its internal object.   κ(αὶ) εἰ σφόδρ(α) εἰσ(ὶ) ἀλαζόνες The idea is apparently that people like this might ordinarily be expected to be able to talk their way out of trouble—but not today. σφόδρ(α) adds emphasis to ἀλαζόνες (102n.).

1493–1505 Who the characters are who cry out in alarm and protest in the course of the lines, is unclear. One is certainly Socrates (generally given 1502, 1504, because these seem like the climax of the scene). The otherwise gratuitous reference to Chairephon at 1465–6 suggests that he might be another (thus some manuscripts for what in the text presented here is simply an anonymous Μαθητής); in that case he likely wears a sickly pale mask (cf. 504 with n.) to make his identity apparent to the audience. The third (here treated as another anonymous Μαθητής) might be the Weaker Argument, the slave who shows Strepsiades around the Thinkery at 133–221, or perhaps Pheidippides (1475n.). 1493 and the first half of 1495 in particular could easily be shouted from a window. But by 1508–9 the Thinkery residents are out of the house and being chased offstage (1510–11). As only a line or two are spoken by any of these extra characters, they might be played by extras, so that there is no violation of the three-actor rule. But we know in any case from the second hypothesis that this scene appeared only in the revised version of the play, meaning that the playwright may not have systematically thought through some issues of performability.

1494 σὸν ἔργον "it's your job" (1416n.).

1495–6 The second and third questions might conceivably be spoken by Xanthias (thus R and V), as might also 1499 τοῦτ᾽ αὐτό–1501, 1503. This makes the staging easier, by eliminating the need to get two actors up onto the roof and then down again. The obvious objection is that assigning the lines to Xanthias takes the audience's attention off of Strepsiades at the climactic moment of the action.   **δια-λεπτο-λογοῦμαι ταῖς δοκοῖς τῆς οἰκίας** "I'm having a subtle conversation with the roof-beams of the house", i.e. as he tries to set them on fire. The compound is a one-off intensification of λεπτο-λογέομαι (320n.) that plays on the image of the subtle logic-chopping of the Thinkery (153 with n.), while **δοκός** puns on δόξα and cognates.

1497 πυρ-πολεῖ is properly "tend a fire", but then by extension "set on fire, burn".

1498 For Strepsiades' vanished *himation*, 497–8 with 498n. Note the plural verb: Strepsiades is not claiming that someone is wearing his robe, only that it has been appropriated from him by the group he is attacking.

1499 ἀπολεῖς, ἀπολεῖς supply με or ἡμᾶς.

1500 μοι . . . τὰς ἐλπίδας English would say "my hopes", whereas Greek uses the dative separately to indicate who will be affected if the mattock fails to do its job.   **προ-δῷ** 3rd-person singular aorist active subjunctive < προ-δίδωμι, "betray".

1501 πρότερον is adverbial, "before (that)".   **ἐκ-τραχηλισθῶ** aorist passive subjunctive < ἐκ-τραχηλίζω, "throw from one's neck (τράχηλος)", as an unruly horse might do, and thus by extension "dump off, toss down" or the like.

1502 οὗτος 220n.   **ἐτεόν** is adverbial, "precisely, in fact".

1503 ἀερο-βατῶ καὶ περι-φρονῶ τὸν ἥλιον is a mocking echo of Socrates at 226.

1504–5 These lines do not advance the action, so perhaps they cover the time it takes Strepsiades and Xanthias to climb back down off the roof.   **οἴμοι τάλας** 23n.   **ἀπο-πνιγήσομαι** future passive < ἀπο-πνιγέω, "suffocate" (cf. 95–6n.).   **κατα-καυθήσομαι** future passive indicative < κατα-καίω (396n., 404–7n.).

1506–7 The two charges are closely connected, as at 225–6: astronomical inquiry is sacrilege. Cf. 1509, where the charge of abusing the gods is repeated. One or two of the early manuscripts have dual forms (metrical) in place of ὑβρίζετε and ἐσκοπεῖσθε, as if the reference were specifically to Socrates and Chairephon.   The manuscripts are divided between middle ἐσκοπεῖσθε and active ἐσκοπεῖτε; the meaning is identical in any case.   τί … μαθόντες; 402n.   τὴν ἕδραν "the location". But Dover suggests that the word has a second sense, "rear end" (LSJ *s.v.* III), as if the moon were a woman and Socrates and his students were playing Peeping Tom with her.

1508–9 Addressed to Xanthias by Strepsiades, as the two of them chase Socrates and his students off the stage and down the *eisodos*, ahead of the chorus (1510–11). Some manuscripts give the words to Hermes—who is, however, only a statue (1478–85n.).

1510–11 Anapaestic tetrameter catalectic; see Introduction §IV.A.2.   Most Aristophanic comedies end with a triumphal procession of some sort. Here there is no place for one, and the play instead closes with a pair of colorless, generic lines that do little more than announce that the action is complete.   ἡγεῖσθ(ε) ἔξω "lead (us) out (of the Theater)!"; addressed to Strepsiades and Xanthias.   κεχόρευται … μετρίως … ἡμῖν literally "it has been danced within due limits", i.e. enough, "by us".   τό γε τήμερον "as regards today, at any rate": the poet and his chorus will be back at the next festival.

Appendix I

Fragments of the original *Clouds*

fr. 392 (referring to Socrates); iambic trimeter
Εὐριπίδῃ δ᾽ ὁ τὰς τραγῳδίας ποῶν
τὰς περιλαλούσας οὗτός ἐστι, τὰς σοφάς
This is the man who writes the chattering
tragedies for Euripides, the wise ones

fr. 393 Iambic trimeter
κείσεσθον ὥσπερ πηνίω βινουμένω
the two of you/them are going to lie there like a pair of bugs fucking

fr. 394 (apparently referring to the Clouds; Lykabettos is a large limestone
hill in Athens northeast of the Acropolis more or less in the line of
sight from the Acropolis to Parnes); anapaestic tetrameter catalectic
ἐς τὴν Πάρνηθ᾽ ὀργισθεῖσαι φροῦδαι κατὰ τὸν Λυκαβηττόν
they've gone off in anger to Parnes in the direction of Lykabettos

fr. 395 Probably the end of an anapaestic tetrameter catalectic
μηδὲ στέψω κοτυλίσκον
and that I not garland a little cup

In addition, frr. 396, 398–*401 cite the following words or phrases—not in
Clouds II—from the play: οὐ μετὸν αὐτῷ (in place of the more common οὐ
ἐξὸν αὐτῷ, "it being impossible for him"), ζυμήσασθαι ("to be leavened" or
the like), ἠπίαλος ("chill" preceding a fever), κόλασμα ("punishment"), and
μετεωρολέσχας ("mid-air gossips" or the like; in reference to Socrates and
his colleagues), while fr. 397 reports that the Athenian general Phormio was
mentioned in it.

Appendix II

A. Additional passages from comedy referencing Socrates; note also *Clouds I* frr. 392; *401 (in Appendix I):

1. Aristophanes *Birds* 1280–2 (414 BCE)
   πρὶν μὲν γὰρ οἰκίσαι σε τήνδε τὴν πόλιν,
   ἐλακωνομάνουν ἅπαντες ἄνθρωποι τότε,
   ἐκόμων, ἐπείνων, ἐρρύπων, ἐσωκράτων
   Because before you founded this city,
   everyone used to go crazy for the Spartan lifestyle:
   they grew their hair long, went hungry, didn't bathe, acted like Socrates

2. Aristophanes *Birds* 1554–5 (414 BCE)
   πρὸς δὲ τοῖς Σκιάποσιν λί-
   μνη τις ἔστ᾿, ἄλουτος οὗ
   ψυχαγωγεῖ Σωκράτης
   In the land of the Shadowfeet
   there is a lake, where the unwashed
   Socrates summons up souls

3. Aristophanes *Frogs* 1491–9 (405 BCE)
   χαρίεν οὖν μὴ Σωκράτει
   παρακαθήμενον λαλεῖν,
   ἀποβαλόντα μουσικὴν
   τά τε μέγιστα παραλιπόντα
   τῆς τραγῳδικῆς τέχνης.   1495
   τὸ δ᾿ ἐπὶ σεμνοῖσιν λόγοισι
   καὶ σκαριφησμοῖσι λήρων
   διατριβὴν ἀργὸν ποιεῖσθαι,
   παραφρονοῦντος ἀνδρός
   It's gracious behavior not to sit
   beside Socrates and chatter,
   discarding culture

and abandoning the most important aspects
of the tragic art.   1495
To lazily waste one's time
on haughty words
and nonsensical nitpicking
is the mark of a lunatic

4. Eupolis fr. 386 (from an unidentified play; before 412 BCE or so)
   μισῶ δὲ καὶ † Σωκράτην
       τὸν πτωχὸν ἀδολέσχην,
   ὃς τἄλλα μὲν πεφρόντικεν,
   ὁπόθεν δὲ καταφαγεῖν † ἔχοι,
       τούτου κατημέληκεν
   I also hate † Socrates
       the impoverished chatterer,
   who has considered other matters,
   but whence he † could eat,
       this he has utterly ignored

5. Eupolis fr. 395 (from an unidentified play; before 412 BCE or so)
   δεξάμενος δὲ Σωκράτης τὴν ἐπιδέξι᾽ ⟨ᾄδων⟩
   Στησιχόρου πρὸς τὴν λύραν οἰνοχόην ἔκλεψεν
   And Socrates received the branch of bay (?) being passed from left to right,
       <and as he sang>
   a bit of Stesichorus to the lyre—he stole the wine pitcher

6. Callias Comicus fr. 15 (from *Men in Fetters*; Callias was already active in
   the 440s and 430s BCE, but his career may well have continued after that)
   (A.) τί δὴ σὺ σεμνοῖ καὶ φρονεῖς οὕτω μέγα;
   (B.) ἔξεστι γάρ μοι· Σωκράτης γὰρ αἴτιος
   (A.) Why are you so haughty and so proud?
   (B.) Because I can be! For Socrates is responsible

7. Amipsias fr. 9 (perhaps from *Konnos*, City Dionysia 423 BCE)
   Σώκρατες ἀνδρῶν βέλτιστ᾽ ὀλίγων, πολλῶν δὲ ματαιόταθ᾽, ἥκεις
   καὶ σὺ πρὸς ἡμᾶς; καρτερικός γ᾽ εἶ. πόθεν ἄν σοι χλαῖνα γένοιτο;
       * * *
   τουτὶ τὸ κακὸν τῶν σκυτοτόμων κατ᾽ ἐπήρειαν γεγένηται
       * * *
   οὗτος μέντοι πεινῶν οὕτως οὐπώποτ᾽ ἔτλη κολακεῦσαι
   Socrates, best of a few men and most foolish of many, have you too
   come to us? You're tough! Where would you get yourself a heavy wool
       cloak from?
       * * *
   This problem originated as an insult to the shoemakers
       * * *
   Although he's hungry, this fellow never ventured to be a flatterer

8. Teleclides fr. 41 (from an unidentified play; Teleclides was active already in the 430s BCE)

Μνησίλοχος ἐστ' ἐκεῖνος ⟨ὃς⟩ φρύγει τι δρᾶμα καινὸν
Εὐριπίδῃ, καὶ Σωκράτης τὰ φρύγαν' ὑποτίθησιν

Mnesilochus is the one who's roasting a new play for Euripides,
and Socrates is feeding wood to the fire

9. adespota comica fr. 490 (tragic parody, seemingly referring to one of Socrates' accusers)

κεῖται δ' ὁ τλήμων τὸ στόμα παρεστραμμένος,
ὃ τὸν δίμορφον Σωκράτην ἀπώλετο

The wretch lies there with his mouth twisted to one side
(the mouth) that destroyed the two-formed Socrates

B. Additional passages from comedy referencing Chairephon:

1. Aristophanes *Wasps* 1406–8, 1412–14 (422 BCE)

(Αρ.) προσκαλοῦμαί σ', ὅστις εἶ,
πρὸς τοὺς ἀγορανόμους βλάβης τῶν φορτίων,
κλητῆρ' ἔχουσα Χαιρεφῶντα τουτονί.
. . .
(Φι.) καὶ σὺ δή μοι, Χαιρεφῶν,
γυναικὶ κλητεύεις ἐοικὼς θαψίνῃ
Ἰνοῖ κρεμαμένῃ πρὸς ποδῶν Εὐριπίδου;

(Bread-seller woman) I'm going to summon you, whoever you are,
to the market-commissioners on a charge of damage to merchandise,
with Chairephon here as my summons-witness.
. . .
(Philocleon) Are you in fact, please, Chairephon,
acting as summons-witness for a woman, acting as a sallow
Ino clinging to the feet of Euripides?

2. Aristophanes *Birds* 1296 (414 BCE)

Χαιρεφῶντι Νυκτερίς
for Chairephon (the nickname is) "Bat"

3. Aristophanes *Birds* 1562–4 (from the same song as A.2 above; Peisander has just sacrificed a camel in a way reminiscent of Odysseus' underworld sacrifice in *Odyssey* 11) (414 BCE)

κᾆτ' ἀνῆλθ' αὐτῷ κάτωθεν
πρὸς τὸ † λαῖτμα τῆς καμήλου
Χαιρεφῶν ἡ νυκτερίς

And then there arose from him from below
toward the † gulf of the camel
Chairephon the bat

4.-9. Eupolis fr. 253 (before 412 or so BCE); Aristophanes fr. 554 (undated); Cratinus fr. 215 (423 BCE); Eupolis fr. 180 (421 BCE); Aristophanes frr. 295 (undated); 584 (late 420s/early 410s BCE?)

Εὔπολις μὲν οὖν ἐν Πόλεσι διὰ τὴν χροιὰν πύξινον αὐτὸν καλεῖ, Ἀριστοφάνης . . . ἐν δὲ Τελμισσεῦσιν εἰς συκοφάντην ἀποσκώπτει· Κρατῖνος Πυτίνῃ εἰς αὐχμηρὸν καὶ πένητα· Εὔπολις δ᾿ ἐν Κόλαξιν Καλλίου κόλακα λέγει, Ἀριστοφάνης δ᾿ ἐν β´ Δράμασι κλέπτην, ἐν δ᾿ Ὥραις νυκτὸς αὐτὸν παῖδα καλεῖ

Eupolis in *Cities* calls him "box-wood" because of his color, Aristophanes . . . in *Telmisseis* mocks him as an abuser of the legal system; Cratinus in *Pytinê* (mocks) him as a grubby pauper; and Eupolis in *Flatterers* calls him a flatter of Callias, while Aristophanes in *Dramas II* calls him a thief and in *Seasons* a child of night

Appendix III
The Songs

The songs in *Clouds*—performed by the chorus and/or the characters, to musical accompaniment provided by a pipe—are mostly dactylic or iambic, and are constructed out of the following units, represented here in their ideal form (with − representing a long syllable; ◡ a short syllable; × an anceps syllable, which can be either long or short; and ○○ a pair of anceps syllables, one of which must be long). In practice, long syllables can occasionally be resolved into two shorts (with such situations represented here as ◡◡), and two shorts can sometimes be replaced with a long (with such situations represented here as ⏖):

DACTYLIC METRICAL UNITS

da(ctyl)	−⏖
D	−◡◡−◡◡−
D³	−◡◡−◡◡−◡◡−◡◡−
e	−◡−
E	−◡−×−◡−

IAMBIC METRICAL UNITS

ba(cchiac)	◡−−
ch(oriamb)	−◡◡−
cr(etic)	−◡−
iamb	×−◡−
io(nic)	◡◡−−
ithyphallic	−◡−◡−−
lek(ythion)	−◡−×−◡−
paroem(iac)	−−◡◡−◡◡−−

OTHER METRICAL UNITS

aeol(ic) da(ctyl)	××–◡◡–◡◡–
an(apest)	◡◡ ◡◡ ◡◡ ◡◡
dochm(iac)	×––×–
gly(conic)	○○–◡◡–◡–
pherecr(atean)	○○–◡◡––
pol(yschematist)	○○–×–◡◡–
reiz(ianum)	×–◡◡–×

When songs are divided into a matching strophe and antistrophe (e.g. 275–90 ~ 298–313), a symbol such as ≌ indicates that the syllable in question scans differently in the two sections, with the upper scansion found in the strophe, the lower scansion found in the antistrophe. ◠◠ indicates a long or anceps syllable that has been resolved into two shorts. A number before the abbreviation for a metron indicates that the metron is repeated that many times in succession in the line in question; thus for example 2ia = ia ia. ‸ indicates that the metron in question is syncopated (i.e. abbreviated). Note that, in distinction from the ideal descriptions of individual metrical units offered above, the analyses offered here are of the actual lines of verse in the text. In some cases, alternative analyses are possible. For detailed discussion, see L. P. E. Parker, *The Songs of Aristophanes* (Oxford, 1997) 184–213.

1. 275–90 ~ 298–313 Primarily dactylic.

275 ~ 298	–◡◡–◡◡–	D
276–7 ~ 299–300	–– –◡◡ –◡◡ –◡◡ –– ––	dactylic hexameter (a *spondeiazôn*)
278–86 ~ 301–9	–◠◠ × 31	31da
287 ~ 310	–◡◡– ◡––	ch ba (= Aristophanean)
288–90 ~ 311–13	–◠◠ × 8 ––◡◡–◡◡––	8da paroem

2. 457–75 Dactylo-epitrite; note that individual metrical units are generally connected by a single long or short syllable.

457	–◡–◡–◡– ◡ –◡–◡–◡– ◡	E ◡ E ◡
459–61	–◡–	e
	–◡◡–◡◡–◡◡–◡◡– ◡	D³ ◡
462	–◡–◡––	ithyphallic
463	◡ –◡– – –◡◡–◡◡	◡ e – D
464–5	– –◡◡–◡◡–	– D
	– –◡– –	– e –
466–7	–◡◡–◡◡– ◡	D ◡
	–◡◡–◡◡–	D
468–9	– –◡◡–◡◡–	– D
	× –◡– –	× e –

470–1	−∪∪−∪∪− −	D −
	−∪∪−∪∪− −	D −
472–3	−∪∪−∪∪−	D
	− −∪− −	− e −
474–5	−∪∪−∪∪−	D
	− −∪∪−∪∪−	− D

3. 512–17 Iambic.

512–13	−∪∪− ∪−∪−	ch ia
	−∪ω ∪−−	cr ba
514	−∪∪− −∪∪−	2ch
515–16	∪−∪− −∪∪−	ia ch
	−−∪− −−∪−	2ia
517	−∪∪− ∪−−	ch ba (= Aristophanean)

4. 563–74 ~ 595–606 Iambic and dactylic, closing with three Aeolic metra.

563 ~ 595	−∪∪− ∪−∪−	ch ia
564 ~ 596	−∪∪− ∪−∪−	ch ia
565 ~ 597	−∪∪− ∪−−	ch ba (= Aristophanean)
566–8 ~ 598–600	−∪∪− ∪−∪−	ch ia
	−∪∪− −∪∪− ∪−∪−	2ch ia
	−∪∪− ∪−−	ch ba (= Aristophanean)
569–70 ~ 601–2	−∪∪ × 9	9da
571–2 ~ 603–4	−−∪− −∪∪−	ia ch
	ᴗ−−−−∪∪−	pol
573 ~ 605	−×−∪∪−∪−	gly
574 ~ 606	−−−∪∪−−	pherecr

5. 700–6 ~ 804–9 Iambic.

700–1 ~ 804–5	−−∪− −∪∪−	ia ch
	−∪∪− ∪−−	ch ba (= Aristophanean)
702–4 ~ 806–7	∪−∪− −∪−∪∪−∪∪−	ia aeol da
	∪−∪− ∪−−	ch ba (= Aristophanean)
705–6 ~ 808–9	∪−∪ᵕ ∪−∪−	2ia
	−∪∪− ∪−∪−	ch ia

The antistrophe continues:

810–11	−∪∪− −∪∪− −∪∪−	3ch
812–13	ω−∪− −−∪−	2ia
	−∪∪− ∪−−	ch ba (= Aristophanean)

6. 949–58 ~ 1024–33 Iambic.

949 ~ 1024	⏤⏤◡⏤ ⏤◡◡⏤	ia ch
950 ~ 1025	⏤◡◡⏤ ◡⏤⏤	ch ba (= Aristophanean)
951–2 ~ 1026–7	⏑⏤◡⏤ ⏤◡◡⏤	ia ch
	⏤◡◡⏤ ◡⏤⏤	ch ba (= Aristophanean)
†953–4† ~ 1028–9	⏤⏤◡⏤ ⏤◡◡⏤	ia ch
	⏤⏤◡⏑⏑ ⏤◡◡⏤	ia ch
955 ~ 1030	⏤◡◡⏤ ⏤◡◡⏤ ⏤◡◡⏤	3ch
956 ~ 1031	⏤◡◡⏤ ⏤◡◡⏤ ⏤◡◡⏤	3ch
957–8 ~ 1032–3	⏤◡◡⏤ ◡⏤◡⏤	ch ia
	⏤◡◡⏤ ◡⏤⏤	ch ba (= Aristophanean)

7. 1154–70 Mixed (paratragic).

1154	◡⏤◡⏤ ⏤◡⏤◡⏤	ia lek
1155	◡⏤◡⏤ ⏤◡⏤◡⏤	ia lek
1156	⏤⏤◡⏤ ⏤⏤◡⏤ ◡⏤◡⏤	3ia
1157	⏤⏤◡⏤ ◡⏤◡⏤ ◡⏤◡⏤	3ia
1158	⏤◡◡⏤◡◡⏤	D
1159	⏤◡◡⏤◡◡⏤	D
1160	⏤⏤⏤⏤ ⏤⏤⏤	an anp
1161	◡⏑⏑◡⏤ ⏤⏤◡⏤ ⏤⏤◡⏤	3ia
1162	⏤⏑⏤◡⏤ ⏤⏑⏤◡⏤	2dochm
1163–4	⏤⏑⏤◡⏤ ⏤⏑⏤◡⏤	2dochm
1165	⏤⏑⏤⏤ ⏤⏤⏤⏤	2an
1166	✕⏑⏤◡⏤	dochm
1167	⏑⏤⏑⏤	an
1168	⏤⏑⏤◡⏤	dochm
1169	◡⏑⏑◡⏤	ia
1170	◡⏑⏤◡⏤	dochm

8. 1206–13 Iambic.

1206	◡◡⏤⏤ ◡◡⏤	io iop
1207	⏤⏤◡⏤ ⏤◡⏤	ia cr
1208	⏤⏤◡⏤ ⏤◡⏤	ia cr
1209	⏤⏤◡⏤ ⏤◡⏤⏤⏤◡⏤	ia lek
1210–11	⏤⏤◡⏤ ◡⏤◡⏤ ⏤◡⏤ ⏤◡⏤	2ia 2cr
1212–13	⏤⏤◡⏤ ◡⏤◡⏤	2ia
1213	⏤◡⏤◡⏤⏤	ith

9. 1303–10 ~ 1311–20 Iambic.

1303–4 ~ 1311–12	⏤⏤◡⏤ ◡⏤◡⏤ ⏤⏤◡⏤	3ia
	◡⏤◡◡⏤⏤	reiz
1305 ~ 1313	⏑⏤◡⏤ ⏤⏤◡⏤	2ia

1306 ~ 1314	⏓–⏑– ⏓–⏑–	2ia
1307–10b ~ 1315–20	––⏑– ––⏑–	2ia
	–⏑–⏑–⏑–	lek
	–⏑–––⏑–	lek
	––⏑– ––⏑–	2ia (lacunose?)
	–⏑–⏑–⏑– ––⏑–	lek ia
	––†⏑⏑–⏑–†	(corrupt)
	––⏑– ⏑––	ia ba

10. 1345–50 ~ 1391–6 Iambic.

1345 ~ 1391	⏓–⏑– ⏓–⏑– ––⏑–	3ia
1346 ~ 1392	⏓–⏑⏑––	reiz
1347 ~ 1393	––⏑– ⏓–⏑– ––⏑–	3ia
1348 ~ 1394	⏔–⏑⏑––	reiz
1349 ~ 1395	⏔–⏑– ⏑–⏑– ⏔–⏑–	3ia
1350	⏑–⏑–––	reiz
~ 1396	––⏑⏑––	

Index of People, Places, and Objects

References in italics are to line-number notes rather than to pages.

1261, 1275, 1308–10b, 1338, 1349–50, 1371–2, 1397–8, 1432, 1448–51, 1506–7

dual, 31

eclipse, 584–6

education, role of athletics in, 973–4
   role of music in, 964–5, 1355–6
   traditional, 961–1023
   use of physical punishment in, 493, 972

ekkyklêma, 8; 183

Electra, 534–6

Eleusinian Mysteries, 302–4

Elmsley, Peter, 664, 1296

enclitics in second position, 257

epexegetic infinitive, 243, 260

Ephesus, 598–600

Euboea, 211–13, 859

Eupolis, 2, 3, 5; 553–4, 1330
   Marikas, 553–4, 555

Euripides, 243, 247; 30, 41b, 551–2, 1024–5, 1366–7
   Aiolos, 1371–2
   Alcestis, 1415
   Hecabe, 718–19, 1165–6
   Helen, 280
   Peleus, 1063, 1154–5
   Telephos, 891, 922

farming as basic to Athenian identity, 1117–25

farting, 9

first-person singular used by chorus, 459–62

forgiveness, 138

future without οὐκ as equivalent to imperative, 1299

garland, 255–6

gender, grammatical, 659–61

general, 581–2

genitive, ablatival, 153, 166
   absolute, 171–2
   exclamatory, 153
   functions of, 307
   indicating that an action affects only part of an object, 761–3
   with gapped accusative, 964–5

geometry, 202

Giants, 852–3

"giving the finger," 654

gnomic aorist, 399–400, 835–7

Graces, 773

grammatical vocabulary, 679

head, as place where troubles settle, 40

hendiadys, 362

Heracles, 257, 1051

Hermann, Gottfried, 664, 1275, 1349–50, 1444, 1458–9

Hermes, 1277–8, 1475–85, 1481–2, 1508–9

Hermippus, Artopôlides 557

Herwerden, Henrik van, 1351–2

Hieronymus son of Xenophantos, 348–9, 350

Hippocrates (contemporary Athenian) and sons, 1000–1

Hippocrates (physician), 1279–84

Hippolyte, 1063

Homer, 868, 1056–7, 1425–6

hoplite and hoplite equipment, 353, 692–3, 751, 988–9

horse, 14, 23, 32, 122, 571–4, 1070, 1296, 1299, 1300, 1406–7

hypallage, 311–13

Hyperbolus, 5; 551–2, 553–4, 555, 557, 615, 623–5, 876, 1065

hysteron-proteron, 81, 835–7

iambic trimeter, three-word, 686

Iapetus, 998–9

imperfect, of verb of speaking, 1227
   with ἄν, 53–5, 854–5
   with πάλαι, 1036

imperialism, Athenian, 298–313

indirect question, 20, 145, 157–8, 214, 1248

infinitive as imperative, 850

interjections intended for audience, 263–74

internal accusative, 99

judges, of dramatic competitions, 1115–16

Juntine edition of Aristophanes, 1261

Kanake, 1371–2

katakeleusmos, 476–7, 959–60, 1351–2

Kekeides (Kedeides?), 984–5

Kekrops, 299–301

Kikynna, 134

kiss as greeting, 81

kneading-trough, 669

knights, Athenian, 120

Knights, 549, 555, 559, 581–2, 987

Koisyra, 48

kommation, 510–626, 510–17

koppa, 23

kottabos, 1073

Krios, 1355–6

Index of Greek Words

References are to line-number notes.

ἄγε δή vs. ἄγε νυν, *478*
ἄγω καὶ φέρω, *241*
ἀέναος, *275*
ἀήρ vs. αἰθήρ, *229–30*
αἰβοῖ, *102*
αἰδώς, *995*
-άκις, *738–9*
ἀκολουθέω, *505*
ἀλαζών, *102*
ἄλφιτα, *106*
ἄν, repeated, *425*
　　standard positions of, *118*
　　+ imperfect, *53–5*
　　+ subjunctive, *89*
ἀνήρ used pleonastically, *545*
ἀνύσας, *181*
-αξ, formations in, *333*
　　for inarticulate sounds, *390*
ἀπραγμοσύνη and ἀπράγμων, *1007*
ἄρα vs. ἆρα, *121, 466–7, 1301*
ἄριστον, *416*
ἀτάρ, *30*
αὐτός, *219*

βαδίζω, *128*
βολβοί, *188*
βόσκω, *331*

γάρ implying a previous remark left
　　unexpressed, *191*
γνῶθι σαυτόν, *842*
γραφή, *467–75, 758–9*
γυμνός, *498*

δαί, *491*

δαίμων, *76*
δάκτυλον, *651*
δέ γε, *169, 914*
δεῦρο, *91*
δή, *90*
δήπου, *369*
δῆτα, *58*
-δόν as adverbial ending, *491*

εἰ . . . γέ in protasis following negative, *108*
εἰέν, *176*
εἰς vs. ἐς, *123*
εἶτα, repeated use o,f *149*
ἐκεῖνος with personal name, *180*
ἐκτεύς, *643–5*
ἐμβάδες, *718–19*
ἐν, absence of as poeticism, *310*
ἐνόπλιον, *651*
ἐπακούω, *263*
ἔπη, *638*
ἐς κόρακας, *123, 789*
εὐ-, adjectives in, *299–301*
εὐθύ or εὐθύς + genitive, *160–2*
εὐφημέω, *263*
-εύω/-εύομαι, *15*
ἔχω, use of participle of, *131*

ζα, *283*
-ζω, for verbs describing production of an
　　inarticulate sound, *217*

ἤ, *865*
ἢ ἤ, *105*
ἤδη, *293–5*
ἡλιαία/ἡλιαία, *863–4*

261

ὑμῖν/ἡμῖν, confusion of, *195*
ὑπακούω, *263*

φάρμακα, *749*
φελλεύς, *71*
φεῦ, *41a*
φροντιστήριον, φροντιστής and cognates, *94, 266*
φύσις, *486–7*

χορδή, *455*
χρῆμα + gen., *2*
χρῆν, *371*

ψήφισμα vs. νόμος, *1427–9*

ὤμοι vs. οἴμοι, *925*
ὡς = εἰς, *237*
ὥστε, *765, 833, 988–9*

Printed and bound by CPI Group (UK) Ltd, Croydon, CR0 4YY

09/06/2025

14685646-0004